" borrowed
scenery" p. 209
(later in
book)

Insi
gate
a

Un.

the

what has been
left out + how
selected? criteria?

yacht
boat
sled over ice
carriage
horseback

60,000 acres?
Ten miles appox p. 215

" see.
wRb

Ideas of Chinese Gardens

PENN STUDIES IN LANDSCAPE ARCHITECTURE

John Dixon Hunt, Series Editor

This series is dedicated to the study and promotion of a wide variety of approaches to landscape architecture, with special emphasis on connections between theory and practice. It includes monographs on key topics in history and theory, descriptions of projects by both established and rising designers, translations of major foreign-language texts, anthologies of theoretical and historical writings on classic issues, and critical writing by members of the profession of landscape architecture.

The series was the recipient of the Award of Honor in Communications from the American Society of Landscape Architects, 2006.

Ideas of Chinese Gardens

Western Accounts, 1300–1860

EDITED BY

Bianca Maria Rinaldi

PENN

University of Pennsylvania Press

Philadelphia

Copyright © 2016 University of Pennsylvania Press

Published by
University of Pennsylvania Press
Philadelphia, Pennsylvania 19104-4112
www.upenn.edu/pennpress

Printed in the United States of America
on acid-free paper
10 9 8 7 6 5 4 3 2 1

Library of Congress Cataloging-in-Publication Data
Ideas of Chinese gardens : Western accounts, 1300–1860 / edited by Bianca Maria Rinaldi.
    pages cm— (Penn studies in landscape architecture)
  Includes bibliographical references and index.
  ISBN 978-0-8122-4763-3 (alk. paper)
1. Gardens, Chinese—China—History—Sources. 2. Gardens—China—History—Sources.
3. Landscape architecture—China—History—Sources. 4. China—Description and
travel—History—Sources. 5. Aesthetics, Oriental. 6. Voyages and travels—History.
7. Travelers writings—History. I. Rinaldi, Bianca Maria, editor. II. Series: Penn studies in
landscape architecture.
SB457.55.I43   2016
712'.60951—dc23
                                                                      2015017211

CONTENTS

Introduction

For seventeenth- and eighteenth-century Europeans, China represented both an irresistible model of reference and an exotic mode of sophistication. Its culture, celebrated through widely read publications, and its refined products imported to Europe held an intense fascination for Westerners and exerted significant influence on Western culture and taste.[1] An emblematic case of that influence was the constant reference to the Chinese garden in the scholarly debate accompanying the evolution of Western garden aesthetics from compositions inspired by geometry to those inspired by nature.[2] References to the apparent naturalness of Chinese gardens were first cited in England, beginning in the last decade of the seventeenth century, to support the reaction against the geometries of the French garden style, as well as the development of the English landscape garden. The importance of the Chinese garden as a model for Western gardens was made explicit by the name given to the English landscape garden when it was transposed onto French soil during the second half of the eighteenth century: the *jardin anglo-chinois*.

In the diverse phases of the European landscape garden, knowledge of the Chinese garden, or rather the *idea* of that garden, took its inspiration from the accounts of Western travelers visiting China. Jesuits and other missionaries, merchants, diplomats, casual tourists, and plant hunters provided Europe with their understanding of Chinese gardens through journals, letters, travel accounts, missionaries' reports, and general descriptions of China and its culture. These writings unveiled gardens characterized by irregularity and a diffused naturalness. Over time, they included an increasing wealth of details about the variety and surprising sequences of scenes of Chinese gardens.[3] Based on the travelers' personal experiences of China, these accounts were considered authoritative sources on Chinese garden design and offered literary support to the theoretical debate on the evolution of Western garden art.

This book discusses the ways in which Chinese gardens were perceived and communicated by Western observers. With this aim, it reconstructs the framework of the texts through which European intellectuals developed the idea that the Chinese garden was characterized by that naturalness, irregularity, variety, and proximity to the rural landscape that the Occident was seeking. The chronology of the descriptions included in this anthology bears witness to the evolution of Western travelers' perceptions: from the curiosity of the thirteenth century, when the first fragmentary information on Chinese gardens reached Europe; to the general fascination for their apparent naturalness of the seventeenth century; to the increasingly methodical approach of the eighteenth century, when Western eyewitnesses tried to codify their distinctive design principles; and, finally, the progressively declining appeal of China and its gardens in the nineteenth century, following the frustrated commercial ambitions of the western European powers in China.

Western knowledge of Chinese gardens was the result of a double interpretative effort: the literary accounts through which Western eyewitnesses tried to convey their experience of Chinese gardens, and the reception of those narratives by European intellectuals who had never traveled to China.[4] The knowledge that resulted from this process inevitably made the Chinese garden in Europe an indistinct concept, which was never fully grasped in its sophisticated aesthetic and complex design. Nevertheless, for European intellectuals the Chinese garden represented a surprisingly versatile model of reference that was used to question or support Western garden styles, those already established or newly developed ones. For late seventeenth- and early eighteenth-century British intellectuals, the Chinese garden was the image of a garden designed as a fragment of a natural landscape, as opposed to the constrained geometry of Baroque gardens. In late eighteenth-century France, it became a model of the many and diverse possibilities in garden design, in contrast with both the lack of variety of French formal gardens and the tranquil simplicity of the English landscape garden. Eventually, in England, from the last decades of the eighteenth century, the Chinese garden came to be seen as a negative model and was increasingly rejected as a possible stylistic source for the development of Western garden art. The apparent naturalness of Chinese garden design came to be considered as too extravagant, as well as having a forced and elaborated artificiality, as opposed to the more composed and subtle reconstruction of nature in the English landscape garden.[5]

The discussion of the Chinese garden that animated Europe between the late seventeenth and the mid-nineteenth centuries was not only a question of design related to changes of style and taste in the evolution of the Western garden aesthetic, and to the cultural translation of distant models. It was linked as well to symbolic meanings of gardens as expressions of social, political, and economic values, and to their role in supporting discourses on national identity. Western travelers were well aware of the role of gardens in supporting a political ideology, both in Europe and in China. In the second half of the eighteenth century, Jesuit missionaries often referred to the imperial park of Yuanming yuan, the "Garden of Perfect Brightness," as the "Versailles of China" or the "Versailles of Peking [Beijing]," suggesting the role of the parks of the Chinese emperor as expressions of status and power.[6] Thus, the Chinese garden was more than a context: it was a pretext, used to discuss ethical and political questions and the complex and contradictory relationship between West and China. The Chinese garden became a metaphor for all of China and a touchstone for interpreting and judging the entire country. Western views of Chinese gardens changed over time, shifting from curiosity to admiration and then to rejection, echoing the changes in Western attitudes toward China.

IMAGES OF CHINA

The image that Europe had of China was influenced for a long time, even after the beginning of the modern period, by the narratives of Marco Polo about his travels through the Mongol Empire and his years at the court of Kublai Khan (r. 1260–94), the founder of the Mongol-led Yuan dynasty (1271–1368). Polo's stories were a combination of reality, hearsay, and fantasy bound together in the literary form of a travelogue, which nourished European perception of China as a fabulous, but generic, Orient. The notion of China as a fabled Oriental country was to remain rooted in European culture for centuries, increased by the isolationist policy adopted by the Ming dynasty (1368–1644) in 1441 and the subsequent closure of China to foreign penetration.

Only in the second half of the sixteenth century did a form of permanent interaction between Europe and China begin. With the establishment of the Portuguese settlement in Macao, on the southeastern coast of China, in 1557, the rapid commercial and geographical expansions of the western European nations in the Far East that followed, the founding of the Jesuit mission in the late sixteenth century, and the growing importance of the port city of Guangzhou (Canton) as a trading base for Westerners, Europe received an increasing quantity of information about China from a wide variety of sources. In addition to tea, other imported goods, such as decorated porcelain, lacquerware, and silk, created a flourishing market in exotic objects, while accounts of Western travelers' experiences in the country satisfied the demand of intellectuals by describing the historical, geographical, and cultural context of Chinese objects helping to shape a growing familiarity with China in Europe.

Firsthand accounts exploring a wide range of topics and presenting an impressive body of information on China and its culture made a substantial contribution to European knowledge of China.[7] The image of China that Western observers gave in their narratives was based on their direct experience and their own perceptions, but it was nonetheless conditioned by a series of factors: by the roles they were playing, their aims, the strategies they adopted to establish relationships with the Chinese, the length of their stays, their expectations, and, finally, by their opinions formed inevitably through the accounts they had read before undertaking their voyages to China.

In the seventeenth and eighteenth centuries, Jesuit missionaries played the major role in shaping European knowledge of China. They represented the main group of Westerners, and of missionaries, to reside in China throughout the time of their mission, from the late sixteenth century until the late eighteenth century, and to write about it widely (see Fig. 1). Their prolonged stay in China and their privileged position at the imperial court, particularly during the Qing dynasty (1644–1911), where they performed various tasks for the emperors, provided the Jesuits a unique perspective on China. To solicit support for their missionary enterprise, Jesuits presented the knowledge they gained to the European public in a series of detailed and successful writings that generated a great enthusiasm for the country. In their comprehensive and sympathetic accounts, Jesuits praised China's stability, prosperity, and its rich and refined culture. They helped create a generally positive image of China in Europe as a wealthy country with an ancient civilization, governed under an enlightened political system based on meritocracy in line with the principles of Confucianism, and managed by highly educated scholars. China, as described by Jesuits, became a critical mirror for European customs; it was a nation that philosophers such as Leibniz and Voltaire indicated as a model for Europe.

The Jesuit narratives were followed by those written by other Western visitors: ambassadors and diplomats, mainly Dutch and British, seeking advantageous trade agreements with the Chinese empire, merchants, and occasional travelers (see Fig. 14). Motivated by practical interests, and by the intention to gain access to China's commodities and markets, they offered a less laudatory but also a more limited picture of China. Their observations were linked to the contingencies of their diplomatic or commercial missions and to the difficulty of the language, which, unlike the Jesuits, only a very few of them learned. They tended to underline all that was incongruous: the red tape, the limitations imposed by etiquette, and the restrictions and conditions of their movement within the country.[8]

That diversity of judgment, born of different contextual perceptions, was described well by Lord George Macartney (1737–1806), who led the first British diplomatic embassy to the Qianlong emperor (r. 1735–96) in 1793, in relation to an exchange with the French Jesuit Jean Joseph Marie Amiot (1718–93), after the embassy was dismissed by the emperor. Amiot, employed at the imperial court at the time, offered the ambassador his view on the events that occurred during and after the reception of the diplomatic mission at Chengde. Reflecting on Amiot's words, Macartney noted in his journal that the Jesuit, "from living half a century in this country, possibly from well-grounded knowledge and experience . . . has taken much pains and, in some instances, not without success, to remove several false ideas entertained in Europe of their [the Chinese] character, customs, and policy." But empathy for Chinese culture like that expressed by Amiot could lead to indulgence. Macartney wrote that Amiot "is besides a man of such probity and universal charity, that his opinion is entitled to considerable respect from me; nevertheless, from the great deference and veneration which the Chinese have long paid to his acknowledged virtue and abilities, he may have insensibly contracted too great a partiality for them, and may view their government through a flattering medium."[9]

Belief that the reading of Chinese culture proposed by the Jesuits was distorted by an idealized perception had insinuated itself into the West by the end of the eighteenth century, when European fascination with China had begun to decline. The gradual alteration of the view of China was due to a series of factors, including the weakening of the Society of Jesus, which was eventually suppressed in 1773. It was mainly the result, however, of highly prosaic motivations: the restrictive trade policy conducted by the Chinese empire, which had limited Western trade activities to the southern port of Guangzhou, and the failure of diplomatic missions, especially British ones, sent to the Qing court in the hope of obtaining increased trading rights. The economic imbalance between a Europe that imported a vast quantity of goods from China without being able to export almost anything at all, and the Chinese limitation of Western trade, considered an indispensable vehicle of modern civilization, transformed the Chinese empire in Western eyes into a weak and decadent country, the prototype of despotism and stagnation. Yet again, China represented the other face of Europe, but now it had been transformed from a positive model into an antagonist hostile to progress.[10]

Criticism of Chinese civilization and of the Chinese social and political system, "Oriental" and therefore despotic by definition, constituted the justification of two conflicts that England and its allies used to impose expansion of their trading privileges: the Opium War (1840–42) and the Arrow War (1856–60). This second military campaign was capped by a cultural crime against one of the symbols of imperial power: the looting and burning of the imperial park of Yuanming yuan, near Beijing, in 1860 by the joint Anglo-French military expedition led by Lord Elgin and Jean-Baptiste-Louis Gros (see Fig. 22).[11] The destruction of Yuanming yuan represented a radical change in Western attitude to China. Admiration, widespread until the second half of the eighteenth century, had definitely been replaced by rejection, establishing an inclination that was destined to mark the following two centuries and that was intensified by the fears provoked first by the political developments in China, and then by its economic growth.

IMAGES OF CHINESE GARDENS

In his daily life, a wealthy European of the seventeenth or eighteenth century was able to get information about how a Chinese garden might appear through a variety of contacts and channels, each of which, regarding specific characteristics and the content delivered, played a role in the general Western perception of Chinese garden design.

The most widespread message came in a form that was only indirectly conceived as a medium of communication but had an intriguing visual allure: porcelains, textiles, and lacquerware imported from China. The decorations of these heterogeneous objects transmitted stylized images of fragments of rural landscapes or courtly scenes that evoked exotic gardens. These graceful scenes sometimes suggested more about ambience than actuality; however, they seem to validate the emerging idea of continuity between garden and landscape that, from the very early eighteenth century, was informing new models for garden design in England and, later, in western Europe. If the information relayed by those images was of little importance in shaping Western knowledge of Chinese garden design, due to the vagueness of the scenes depicted, of greater importance was their contribution in transforming Western taste in the decorative arts, encouraging the development of an aesthetic imaginary nurtured by the idea of the exotic. They prompted the appearance of chinoiserie, inventive European interpretations of Chinese-inspired motifs as applied to the decorative arts and architecture, which spread through England and continental Europe in the eighteenth century.[12] Chinoiserie reduced the image of China and its gardens to fantastic lush landscapes, dotted with fanciful pavilions and pagodas and populated by figures in "Chinese" robes (see Fig. 19). Chinese artifacts, however, posed a problem of authenticity or verisimilitude of some significance in Enlightenment Europe. Produced in China specifically for export to Europe, those objects had been adapted to the canons of Western taste. In time, their imitation by European designers and craftsmen engendered the paradox whereby objects of "Chinese" taste or style, declared to be Chinese or perceived as such, not only did not come from China at all, but were entirely European creations.[13]

The fortune of those refined scenes depicted on porcelain, fabrics, and lacquerware as ideal images of the gardens of China was also due to the lack of visual material offering plausible images in Europe of specific Chinese gardens. The first reliable graphic representation of a Chinese garden to reach Europe was the collection of views that the Neapolitan missionary Matteo Ripa (1682–1746) brought back from China in 1724. In 1713, Ripa, who had arrived in Beijing in 1711, had been entrusted by the Kangxi emperor (r. 1661–1722) with the task of executing a series of copper engravings, the first ever done in China, depicting thirty-six views of the vast imperial summer residence of Bishu shanzhuang (Mountain Estate for Escaping the Summer Heat), built not long before in modern Chengde, in northern China. During his return voyage to Italy Ripa stopped in London, bringing with him some copies of his album of views of Kangxi's park in Chengde (see Figs. 4–5). On that occasion, those images were seen and some perhaps sold, giving Ripa's engravings some visibility among local artists and intellectuals. Among them was Joseph Spence, a poet, historian, and garden designer himself, who confirmed that the images brought to

London by Ripa offered some visual hints of the natural appearance of the gardens of China. They also offered a term of comparison for the first gardens designed in the English landscape style.[14] In 1751, Spence reported that in the "thirty-six prints of a vast garden belonging to the present Emperor of China: there is not one regular walk of trees in the whole round, they seem to exceed our late best designers in the natural taste."[15] Yet those views, even if relatively accurate, gave only a partial image of the great imperial park. They depicted the main architectural complexes in the gardens, and these were shown as emerging from singularly natural settings: the buildings were surrounded by hills overlooking irregular lakes, placed amidst valleys, or raised at the top of high mountains. Ripa's views framed only segments of landscape, without any general panoramas or plans able to offer an overall unitary sense of the different scenes. Nonetheless, these images awakened great curiosity, to the point that eighteen of the views were reengraved and published in London in 1753.[16] The new images considerably altered the views produced by Ripa in order to adapt them to European taste. Fantastic animals were inserted into the scenes along with human figures and shadows that extended the space represented in the drawings, which, conceived in accord with the Chinese canon, lacked spatial depth to Western eyes. The views of the imperial park in Chengde, executed in China under Ripa's direction, remained for several decades the sole concrete images (in their various versions) of a great Chinese garden in circulation within Europe.

The principal source for Western understanding of the Chinese garden was thus generated from other media: verbal accounts recounting the experiences of the few direct observers of gardens. Their descriptions, widely published and read in Europe, compensated for the absence of visual records drawn directly from real Chinese gardens. The channels of a purely verbal culture were widespread and acceptable in eighteenth-century Europe, where discussion about the evolution of Western garden art took place through treatises, pamphlets, and literary descriptions with very little use of graphic material.[17] Accounts by Western travelers therefore became the main medium for Western reception of the Chinese garden. It was through the descriptions by missionaries, diplomats, and travelers who spoke from direct experience of the sites that the Chinese garden was gradually drawn out of the realm of the fantastic and the exotic to acquire a real physiognomy, susceptible to comparison with European gardens and thus finally capable of contributing, albeit indirectly, to their evolution. Travelers insisted on the reliability of their accounts as sources of information on Chinese gardens. The Jesuits and other missionaries like Matteo Ripa, employed at court in various roles, were at the time the only Europeans to have had the opportunity of entering the imperial gardens. They proposed themselves as privileged observers and as the only ones able to offer a unique insight into those parks' design.[18] Travel narratives of China, written by several members of different diplomatic delegations, were often entitled "An Authentic Account . . . ," emphasizing the accuracy and reliability of their writings.

The limitation of movement imposed by the Chinese authorities, and the way travel was organized within China, significantly influenced Western observers' experiences of gardens. While Jesuits serving at the imperial court resided in Beijing, other Western travelers had to stay in the ports on the southeastern coast. Those who were allowed imperial audience were obliged to follow more or less the same route, which included the southern ports of Macao or Guangzhou—principal accesses to mainland China for Westerners—and the capital city Beijing, seat of the imperial court from the time of Kublai Khan. Thus the travelers' accounts always ended up describing the same stops along the route, since a standard itinerary elicited standard repetitions. Gardens were featured on this itinerary both for their general importance and as subjects of special interest to the Western readers. In reporting on these gardens, writers were certain that their accounts would satisfy a wide public.

After the first fragmentary descriptions of the imperial parks of Kublai Khan by Marco Polo, travelers' accounts focused mainly on the large complexes developed by the Qing emperors: Changchun yuan, "Garden of Joyful Spring," and Yuanming yuan, "Garden of Perfect Brightness," both built in the northwestern outskirts of Beijing (see Fig. 6), as well as Bishu shanzhuang, constructed near the northern border of the empire. These imperial estates of palaces and gardens, where Qing emperors resided for long periods during the year, were developed to serve as the primary effective centers of imperial power.[19] Jesuits serving at the imperial court often accompanied the emperors during their travels to the imperial residences, and Western diplomats were received there.

Following the restrictions in the Qing policy toward foreigners, from 1757 to 1842, trade with Westerners was limited to the single port city of Guangzhou. Accounts written by those travelers involved in the China trade thus focused mainly on the private gardens of local Qing officials, or of the wealthy hong merchants on the island of Honam, or Henam, in Guangzhou (see Figs. 15 and 18). The Chinese hong merchants, a select group of traders authorized by the Chinese government who held the monopoly on trade in the major export commodities with foreigners, played an important role in cultural relations between China and Westerners. Western travelers and traders often visited the suburban residences of Chinese merchants and were entertained in their gardens, which were the stage for festivities and elaborate banquets. These gardens were also the preferred places to search for botanical specimens to enrich European gardens (see Figs. 9 and 21).[20] The monopoly of the hong merchants of Guangzhou on foreign trade was abolished in 1842, at the end of the First Opium War (1839–42), with the Treaty of Nanjing, which forced China to cede Hong Kong to the British Crown and to grant five southeastern coastal cities to trade with Westerners—the treaty ports of Guangzhou, Shanghai, Xiamen (Amoy), Fuzhou, and Ningbo.[21] This geographical extension of Westerners' movement in China opened areas of the country that had earlier been inaccessible, offering Western traders new possibilities for their commerce, and travelers other gardens to describe.

Four main themes emerge from accounts of the gardens of China by Western travelers over time, reflecting the characteristics these observers gave preference to in their investigations. The Chinese garden was first presented as an evocation of the natural landscape; then as the image of the countryside; later as a choreography of varied sequences; and finally in a derogatory way, as a deformation of nature. These themes cannot be strictly associated with the chronology of Western travelers' descriptions, because, particularly in the accounts written in the second half of the eighteenth century, the first three concepts all tend to be present in the writings, with varying degrees of consideration. However, they do characterize the evolution of Western perceptions of Chinese gardens and allow a thematization of the Western travelers' interpretation of Chinese garden design principles.

EVOCATIONS OF NATURE

In his narrations of the parks of Kublai Khan, compiled at the end of the thirteenth century, Marco Polo described a "hill which has been made by art from the earth dug from the Lake" and which was "entirely covered with trees" brought from faraway places of the empire.[22] Almost four centuries later, in the seventeenth century, the Jesuits Matteo Ricci (1552–1610), Álvaro Semedo (ca. 1586–1658), Martino Martini (1614–61), Gabriel de Magalhães (1610–77), and the Dutch envoy Johannes Nieuhof (1618–72) continued, in their short accounts, to emphasize the natural appearance of the gardens of China. They also emphasized the ability of the Chinese in shaping the ground of their gardens by constructing an artificial topography that reproduced elements of the natural landscape—its hills, lakes, and groves. Among the range of natural forms reconstructed in the gardens of China, artificial mountains were a specific feature that travelers considered an essential element of those gardens' natural quality (see Fig. 2). Western observers appreciated the skills necessary to build them, along with the inventiveness and ingenuity that the creation of these topographic forms entailed. In his *Novus atlas sinensis*, published in 1655, the Italian Jesuit Martini wrote that in the garden of the emperor there were "many mountains, raised by skilled hand, which can arouse envy among the real ones for the quality of the craft [with which they are built]."[23] Likewise when Nieuhof, in 1665, came to describe the same gardens, he admired the "Rocks or Artificial Hills, which are so curiously wrought, that Art seems to exceed Nature."[24]

Artificial hills were not completely alien to Western garden tradition. In European Renaissance gardens they were constructed as symbolic references to mythical settings, such as Mount Parnassus, the home of the Muses and of Apollo, built, for instance, in the garden of Villa Medici in Rome; while in Chinese gardens manufactured mountains and compositions of rockeries and stones, evoking the original forms of the natural landscape, were constructed to suggest an ideal connection with nature.[25] The cunning imitation of elements of the landscape through artifice thus produced gardens that stimulated mental associations in the visitors: the artificial hills evoked the jagged landscape of a mountainous chain. The Portuguese Jesuit Magalhães, in his general description of China published in 1688, described a garden within the Imperial City in Beijing as dominated by a "Mountain made with hands like a Sugarloaf environ'd with Rocks . . . so dispos'd as to counterfeit the high out-juttings, and steep and rugged Precipices of Rocks; so that at a moderate distance the whole seems to represent some craggy wild Mountain, the first work of Nature."[26]

In the gardens of China, travelers were confronted with mountains that were apparently not imbued with any allusive meanings but were displayed as geological formations providing an explicit reference to the natural landscape (see Fig. 17). Just as in nature, artificial mountains in Chinese gardens organized their surrounding space and provided the scenic backdrops against which all the garden's compositional elements associated with the natural landscape were set: streams, ponds, plains, and woods. As the French Jesuit Jean-François Gerbillon (1654–1707) explained, artificial mountains served to subdivide the space in the gardens of the Kangxi emperor, where two large ponds were "surrounded almost all around with little rises made by hand out of the earth thrown there while digging out the pools."[27]

The presence of the manufactured hills thus revealed the artificiality of the garden and indicated the strategy behind the garden composition: they proved that the gardens of China were carefully designed and skillfully constructed in an attempt to reproduce the forms of an articulated natural landscape.

However generic and limited in detail, earlier accounts by Western travelers reported a garden that was the result of both a sensitivity to landscape, expressed in the representation of an intricate topography through a synthetic approach, and the skills necessary to construct it. The artificial mountains and the rocky compositions that the earlier Western observers emphasized to convey the character of the gardens of China suggested a sense of natural appearance and general irregularity in the garden's composition and implied that Chinese garden design principles contrasted with the Baroque symmetrical arrangements, which at the time dominated the gardens of the European courts.

At the turn of the seventeenth century, the discovery that the design strategy behind Chinese gardens consisted in the imitation of the forms of a natural landscape through artifice led to a division of opinions about the Chinese attitude toward garden design, among both the direct eyewitnesses and the readers of their accounts. Some French Jesuits considered the apparent simplicity and the natural quality of the parks of the Kangxi emperor to be inappropriate as a representation of imperial regality and political power, which in French regular gardens was expressed by the imposition of order over the natural environment through the rigorous geometry of the spatial composition.[28] On the contrary, in opposition to French ideas, the hints of Chinese garden design given by earlier travelers' descriptions, in addition to the growing European admiration for Chinese culture and government, appealed to English intellectuals, who were debating about the development of a new, natural garden freed from the geometries of the French garden.[29]

The English landscape garden represented a radical change in eighteenth-century European garden design. Its apparently random disposition of natural and architectural elements, with gentle hills, irregular bodies of water, meandering paths, and clumps of trees, characterized the new national garden aesthetic, emblematic of English political liberty and its mercantile society. The new garden style was seen as the ideological expression of a natural nation, liberated from monarchical absolutism and from the formalism of the past. The legitimization of the new landscape garden came from a range of cultural references that mixed ancient Rome with China. This apparently bizarre combination manifested the intention of constructing, around the landscape garden, an ideal genealogy of a great nation with an ancient history. The rediscovery of Roman and Greek architecture, in addition to the allure of classical landscape scenes depicted by Nicolas Poussin and Claude Lorrain, offered England the opportunity of representing itself as a new republican Rome, on its way to imperial greatness.[30] The Chinese garden, in turn, though an exotic novelty, had the merit of being completely unrelated to the continental tradition, while offering an association with a great and ancient empire. It proposed a typological reference, since the irregularity and naturalness of the gardens of China foreshadowed the direction in which the garden aesthetic in England was already moving, driven by a new appreciation of the natural landscape.

The Chinese garden supported the possibility of countering the manifest artificiality of the great regular gardens of Europe with the different design approach used in China. Beginning in the last decades of the seventeenth century, to support their earlier theoretical formulation of a garden inspired by the natural landscape, English intellectuals evoked the presumed irregularity of the gardens of China as perceived from the reading of the accounts of Western travelers.[31] The erudite public discussion of the evolution of garden design toward a more "natural" or "irregular" form, in the style used by the Chinese, was initiated by the essayist William Temple. In 1690, Temple praised the strikingly different aesthetic of the Chinese gardens, designed "without any Order or Disposition of Parts," as he learned mainly from Marco Polo and the Jesuits, whom he defined as "others, who lived much among the *Chineses.*"[32] His remarks were elaborated in the following decades. In 1712, the poet, essayist, and literary critic Joseph Addison, for example, expressed his appreciation for the natural appearance of Chinese gardens, which he learned from "writers who have given us an Account of China," ridiculing at the same time the still prevalent taste among British gardeners who "on the contrary, instead of humouring Nature, love to deviate from it as much as possible."[33] Addison's position was recalled by Stephen Switzer: in his *Iconographia rustica* (1718), an influential work in the development of the English landscape garden, Switzer considered Chinese gardens a valuable model for the new garden style.[34] Later, Robert Castell, in *The Villas of the Ancients Illustrated* (1728), praised the "close Imitation of Nature" in Chinese gardens and their "artful Confusion, where there is no Appearance of that Skill which is made use of," as he had learned from "Accounts which we have of the present Manner of Designing in China."[35]

The possible contribution of Western travelers' accounts of Chinese gardens to the early development of the English landscape garden was suggested by Christian Cajus Lorenz Hirschfeld, one of the most important German garden theorists at the time. In his lengthy work on garden history and theory, *Theorie der Gartenkunst* (1779–85), published at the same time in both German and French, Hirschfeld noted that "reflection and genius no doubt did not need particular examples to discover the new manner adopted in England, and which from there began to spread everywhere: it is nonetheless probable that the reports that were made of Chinese gardens contributed much."[36] But he had reservations about the idea of Chinese gardens these accounts conveyed.

However, the gardens of China offered English intellectuals more than antithetical aesthetic terms to French regular gardens; they offered the expression of a different political vision. European intellectuals held the Kangxi emperor in high regard as an enlightened and wise ruler, governing a country managed not by aristocratic families, as Europe was, but by scholar-officials, as they had learned through the Jesuits' writings.[37] The natural appearance of Kangxi's gardens, as described by Western travelers, strengthened the European view of China's political wisdom and moral integrity. In fact, as explained by the Jesuit Gerbillon, Kangxi preferred a modest simplicity to elaborated ornaments, even in his gardens, because he intended to show that "he does not want to dissipate the finances of the Empire for his private amusements."[38]

THE PLANNED IRREGULARITY OF THE RURAL LANDSCAPE

In the eighteenth century, the largest number of commentaries about Chinese gardens came from Jesuit missionaries. From the beginning of the century, they initiated a new approach in their observations of the Chinese garden, intended to codify the design principles of that garden inspired by the forms of the natural landscape. Jesuits turned to an image that was much different than rough nature, expressed by the artificial mountains, to convey their perception of the gardens of China: the countryside (see Fig. 3). The image of the countryside the Jesuits proposed served to interpret a series of aspects of Chinese garden design. It represented the gardens' apparent natural simplicity and, at the same time, it expressed a complex composition that consisted of a great variety of natural and architectural elements within the articulated topography of the gardens. Furthermore, the countryside, intended as an ideal landscape, ordered and organized but also irregular and varied, served to express the design principles behind Chinese gardens: it indicated that Chinese gardens were carefully designed spaces and that their composition was based on a planned irregularity, which offered a diversity of spaces and elements.

The connection between Chinese gardens and rural landscape appeared in the Jesuits' accounts as early as 1705, in a letter written by Gerbillon, but it was given authority by the French Jesuit Jean-Denis Attiret (1702–68) in a letter written in 1743 and published in 1749. Describing the imperial residence of Yuanming yuan, located near Beijing, Attiret, who had served as court painter under the Qianlong emperor, wrote that Chinese gardens "go entirely on this Principle, 'That what they are to represent there, is a natural and wild View of the Country; a rural Retirement.'"[39] The countryside was the Jesuits' formula to interpret what other Western travelers, like the Swedish naturalist Olof Torén (1718–53), had called the "agreeable natural confusion" of Chinese gardens. In his travelogue, published in 1757, Torén used that expression to present the gardens of China as completely different to the "trees trained up by art . . . walks . . . flower-pieces of several figures"[40] of Western regular gardens. The concept of the countryside became a persistent key to interpret the main characteristics of the Chinese garden by Western travelers. In the 1770s, the French Jesuit Pierre-Martial Cibot (1727–80) used it often in his writings to present Chinese garden design principles.

The acknowledgment of an affinity between the gardens of China and the rural landscape represents a crucial moment in Western travelers' understanding of Chinese garden design. It indicated a new, enhanced sensitivity of eyewitnesses toward the natural appearance of the gardens of China, in line with the emergence, in early eighteenth-century Europe, of an arcadian and pastoral taste that informed the theoretical debate on garden design and that oriented the later stylistic innovation in Western garden art. The innovation, at the time, was to blur the boundaries between the garden and the rural landscape around it. Both Italian Renaissance gardens and French gardens had valued the aesthetic pleasure of visually including the countryside in the garden, establishing a juxtaposition between the geometry in the garden and the surrounding landscape. It was only in England, during the first half of the eighteenth century, that intellectuals had begun to advocate an integration of the garden and the rural landscape, which would later constitute the major character of the English landscape garden. For the promoters of the new garden style, the aesthetic appreciation of the countryside was the appreciation of the diversification of rural landscape; the idea of the garden that was derived from this was based on the representation of that diversity.[41]

From the beginning of the eighteenth century, it was exactly this aspect of a garden designed as a varied rural landscape that began to emerge from Western travelers' accounts of Chinese gardens (see Fig. 10). The blending of rural simplicity and variety that travelers reported in their descriptions offered support to the theoretical discussion under way in continental Europe in the mid-eighteenth century regarding the development of new garden models, a discussion that was based on a growing critique of the predominant garden style: the Baroque garden, epitomized by the park of Versailles. Among the authors who criticized the inadequacy of Versailles's design was the theorist Jacques-François Blondel, whose *Architecture françoise* (1752) judged the royal park as sad and without variety.[42] Marc-Antoine Laugier, one of the earliest and most important theorists of neoclassicism, held the same opinion and argued for the emulation of the simplicity and variety of Chinese gardens, after learning about them through reading the letter of the Jesuit Attiret. In his *Essai sur l'architecture* (1753), which played an influential role in neoclassical architecture theory, Laugier valued both "*la belle nature* amidst the open country adorned with artless naiveté" and "Chinese taste in gardens," contrasting them with Versailles's regularity and symmetry.[43] He praised the Chinese for the "great naiveté in the decoration of their gardens. The asymmetry they are fond of, the capricious way in which they design and lay out the bosquets, the canals and everything surrounding these must, because of the rustic character, be all the more attractive."[44] Laugier concluded his comments on the Chinese garden with an invitation: "By ingeniously fusing Chinese conceptions with ours we would succeed in creating gardens to which nature with all its charm has returned again."⁴⁵ The new garden style Laugier envisioned for France did not completely exclude regularity: according to him, it should be a harmonious composition of "selection, order and harmony but nothing which is too constricted and too formal," and what he called "nature's pleasant carelessness and piquant *bizarreries*," which Chinese garden design captured fully.⁴⁶

In England as well, the Chinese garden was considered the prototype not only of a natural garden but of a pleasing, varied garden and, for this reason, a distinguished example to follow. Isaac Ware, an English architect who was famous for his English translation of Andrea Palladio's *I quattro libri dell'architettura*,⁴⁷ also proposed an integration of Western and Chinese principles of garden design. In *A Complete Body of Architecture* (1756), Ware countered the monotonous formality of the royal gardens on both sides of the Channel—Versailles and Kensington—with the diversity, the "rural wildness and open simplicity" of the gardens of the Chinese, praising the "happy extravagance of their fancy in the indisposition of their gardens" that he learned from Western travelers' accounts.⁴⁸ Following Laugier, Ware proposed to "adopt their [Chinese] reverence for nature with our own excellence in art," suggesting a combination of regular and irregular design, to develop a new garden style.⁴⁹

This critique of Versailles epitomized a more general reaction against the autocratic system and the moral decline of the ancien régime, supported by the favorable view of China and its government that the Jesuits' writings conveyed. Both Laugier and Ware turned to the image of the "natural" Chinese garden, as proposed in Western travelers' accounts, in reaction to the manifest artificiality, elaborate ornaments, and absence of variety of Baroque gardens, and to advocate simplicity—that "artless naiveté" of the countryside that Laugier praised. That ideal and natural simplicity in garden design represented the sobriety and frugality in the sociopolitical system that intellectuals of the Enlightenment wished for. This attitude was recovered in the 1770s, when the Jesuit missionaries in China emphasized the ethical dimension of Chinese gardens, compared to the costly monumentality of French regular gardens.

The concept of the countryside applied by the Jesuits to their reading of the gardens of China implied a simplicity of compositional forms and, indirectly, suggested a lack of purely decorative ornaments in gardens. In the 1770s, Jesuits presented the Chinese garden, with its design inspired by the rural landscape, as less expensive in terms of design and maintenance than the Baroque garden.[50] In his "Essai sur les jardins de plaisance des Chinois," written in 1774 and published in 1782, the Jesuit Cibot, missionary to the imperial court of Beijing, followed Laugier and Ware by advocating the Chinese garden as a model to reinvent the European garden. His proposal was based not only on matters of aesthetics but also on the assumption that the adoption of Chinese garden design principles in Western gardens would diminish "the expenses for creating and maintaining them." Cibot concluded his essay explaining the social advantages of such a choice in garden design: "The more they follow Chinese taste, the easier it will be; and they could get such a system adopted which would free thousands of hands for agriculture now so uselessly occupied in raking avenues where no one walks, and clipping or shaping trees that no one sees."[51] Cibot's appeal for a more modest garden style was in line with the then severe criticism of French garden style, reflecting the polemics under way in France during the second half of the eighteenth century with regard to the maintenance costs for the park of Versailles, despite the country's serious financial crisis.

A SEQUENCE OF SCENES

One of the main detractors of the Baroque garden was the philosopher Jean-Jacques Rousseau. His works, in which he countered the artificiality of his contemporary society with an ethical vision of nature, oriented not only the moral convictions of the European elites but also their taste, which was directed toward naturalistic arcadias, setting the intellectual context for the successful diffusion of the English landscape garden in France and continental Europe.

However, an important role in shaping the original character of the landscape garden in France was played by Western travelers' accounts of Chinese gardens. Their emphasis on the Chinese aesthetic manipulation of natural forms contributed to the discussion of the French picturesque, and earlier theoretical formulations of the "natural" garden in late eighteenth-century France made explicit references to these travelers' reports.

The first theorist who used the accounts of Western travelers to frame discussions on the landscape garden in France was François de Paul Latapie, an erudite botanist from Bordeaux. In 1771, Latapie published *L'art de former les jardins modernes ou l'art des jardins anglais*, his French translation of Thomas Whately's *Observations on Modern Gardening* (1770), a book that was considered the most comprehensive theoretical discussion on the

English landscape garden.[52] Latapie added to Whately's *Observations* an extended preface, the *Discours préliminaire*, which played an influential role in the theoretical discourse on the irregular garden in France. It included lengthy extracts from Attiret's letter and reproduced the French version of the successful short essay, entitled "Of the Art of Laying Out Gardens Among the Chinese," written by the British architect William Chambers (1723–96) a few years after his return from China and first published in 1757. Latapie turned to Western travelers' accounts to imply a correspondence between the new landscape style developed in England and the gardens of China. The earliest theoretical formulation of the English landscape garden in France thus was associated with Chinese garden design as it was described in the writings of Western travelers.

In the second half of the eighteenth century, Western travelers presented the Chinese garden as characterized by a constructed irregularity. But it was not only an image of a serene rural landscape that their texts conveyed; they focused progressively more on the visual seduction offered by the garden's variety. Both Attiret and William Chambers, as well as the Jesuit Michel Benoist (1715–74) and later the captain of the Swedish East India Company Carl Gustav Ekeberg (1716–84), Pierre-Martial Cibot, and the Dutch-American diplomat André Everard van Braam Houckgeest (1739–1801), emphasized the considerable diversity and the striking contrasts of the Chinese garden, as well as the sense of surprise they elicited, which were amplified by the garden's layout. Attiret described the imperial park of Yuanming yuan as a sequence of unexpected situations merged in an articulated composition of artificial mountains, valleys, and lakes. Numerous disparate structures, like the Chinese city reproduced in the park for the emperor's amusement, contributed to the continuous variety that, Attiret acknowledged, "is not only to be found in their Situations, Views, Disposition, Sizes, Heights, and all the other general Points; but also in their lesser Parts, that go to the composing of them."[53]

Western travelers introduced in their accounts the emotional and aesthetic response that the garden's spatial composition elicited from visitors. In a letter written from Beijing in 1767, the Jesuit Benoist expressed the visual lure of the Chinese garden, describing it as a place where the visitor was fascinated and intrigued by continuous discoveries: "You see a sort of ensemble whose beauty strikes and enchants you, and after a few hundred steps, some new objects present themselves to you, eliciting new admiration."[54] Benoist, as well as Attiret and Chambers and, later, Cibot emphasized the visual and emotional experience in a garden organized as a variety of elements and episodes to be discovered along a set itinerary that guided the visitor through the grounds, gradually revealing its composition. To explain this design method Western observers turned to the concept of the "scene." By using the term "scene," travelers explicitly expressed the artificiality of the Chinese garden's composition as a sequence of carefully composed views, each characterized by a specific identity, to be seen from specific places and pavilions (see Fig. 12). In his letter written in 1743, Attiret described the different "vues" (views) the imperial park offered, thus implying an association between the Chinese garden design and painting. His description of the miniature city built within Yuanming yuan as the setting for representing all the bustle of a real city, however, suggests more the atmosphere of a theater performance than a painting. A few years later, in 1757, Chambers used the term "scenes" to denote the varied prospects the gardens presented to visitors and discussed three different types of scenes. In 1771 Ekeberg talked about "many various scenes" and the role of paths in progressively revealing them. Cibot, in his essay written in 1774, used the term "tableau," suggesting a more dramatic conception of the garden episodes. Attiret showed that the Chinese design method in gardens consisted in the arrangement of a sequence of separate sites, each of which focused on architectural elements set in a backdrop of natural elements: buildings placed in the middle of valleys and framed by artificial hills, or at the summit of a rocky island rising from bodies of water. Cibot, in his essay entitled "Observations sur les plantes, les fleurs et les arbres de Chine qu'il est possible de se procurer en France" (1786), read the scenic possibilities of the Chinese gardens in the spectacle of the rich variety of nature they offered, displaying also "her caprices, her negligence even her faults and forgetfulness," to create a surprising garden composition.[55] The concept of the passage of time, which both Attiret and Chambers, and later Cibot, introduced while discussing the role of plants in Chinese gardens, as well as the changes of vegetation the garden presented during the course of the year, contributed to the apparently infinite possibilities in the construction of the scenes that the Chinese garden was able to create.

In the wake of Western travelers' writings expressing the variety offered by Chinese garden design, the landscape garden in France evolved in the direction of more dynamic and playful forms. New parks were configured as real landscape adventures to be enjoyed by following a set itinerary along which a sequence of varied spaces unfolded, with curious and surprising arrangements and occasionally extravagant *fabriques* (garden buildings).

creating an assortment of scenes capable of awakening diverse emotions and states of mind in the visitor. This new type of garden, the setting for a sort of dramatic narrative of nature, took the name *anglo-chinois* in honor of the fusion of the English landscape garden style and the ingenious Chinese design method it proposed. As the end of the ancien régime approached, France rediscovered a nature hitherto constrained in the absolute power of geometry, and this nature was presented in the form of scenic evocations tinged with exoticism.[56]

The *jardin anglo-chinois* spread rapidly through Europe. One of its more evident characteristics was the proliferation of pavilions and other structures in an extravagant "Chinese" style scattered through the gardens, which evoked the Oriental point of reference of the new garden type. Partially responsible for the fashion for "Chinese" architecture in Western gardens was William Chambers's publication *Design of Chinese Buildings, Furniture, Dresses, Machines, and Utensils* (1757), which included his drawings of Chinese structures and objects (see Fig. 7). Between 1761 and 1762, Chambers himself designed one of the first garden buildings in a Chinese taste, the ten-stories-high pagoda that was erected in the Royal Botanic Gardens at Kew in London.[57] Structures in an inventive "Chinese" style quickly appeared in European gardens, ranging from the Chinese bridge and Chinese tent in the garden of Bagatelle, near Paris, completed in 1775, and the pagoda in the park of Chanteloup, created in the same year, to the Chinese House built in the eclectic Désert de Retz near Chambourcy around 1775, to the Chinese village commissioned for Tsarskoye Selo by Catherine I in the 1780s, and the Chinese Tower, built in 1789–90, in the Englischer Garten in Munich.[58]

What contributed to the diffusion of "Chinese" garden structures throughout continental Europe were pattern books that proliferated during the eighteenth and early nineteenth centuries and that presented a range of the most varied and often fanciful garden arrangements.[59] But a more important role was played by the collections of engravings published by Georges-Louis Le Rouge, architect, engineer, and cartographer, who was among the first to use the term *jardins anglo-chinois*. Between 1775 and 1789, Le Rouge produced twenty-one albums of engravings, or *cahiers*, documenting the most notable European as well as Chinese gardens, collected under the general title of *Détails de nouveaux jardins à la mode*. The Chinese examples were presented through accounts and illustrations by Western travelers. The cahier number 5 contains a French translation of the 1757 essay by Chambers, while cahiers 14 to 17 were dedicated specifically to presenting the Chinese garden.[60] In order to illustrate three of these four cahiers, Le Rouge borrowed images of Chinese gardens sent back to Europe by the Jesuit missionaries in Beijing (see Fig. 8).[61]

Those fanciful visions of distant places contributed to the evolution of gardens in France and continental Europe toward models far removed from the formalism of Baroque gardens. The canon of the past was surpassed thanks also to the apparent opportunity for unruliness and eccentricity that the playful *anglo-chinois* garden offered. As Janine Barrier, Monique Mosser, and Che Bing Chiu have commented, "In the name of a China which was at the same time wise, poetical and reinvented, everything becomes possible, even the greatest license. In a word, Cathay is not only 'à la mode', she is then above all a carrier of modernity."[62]

A QUESTION OF PROGENITURE

The spread of *anglo-chinois* gardens throughout Europe, with their fanciful *fabriques*, engendered obvious perplexities about how much was authentically Chinese in those compositions. The question must have even reached China, if the Jesuit Cibot decided to bring clarity to the matter and compose a treatise on Chinese garden design, "Essai sur les jardins des plaisance des Chinois" (1782), which aimed to "set aside all the false Western ideas about the pleasure gardens now in China."[63] In that essay there was a glaring omission of any reference to garden structures, buildings, and pavilions, which the Jesuit apparently considered secondary elements compared to the general design mechanism that determined the garden's composition.

Christian Cajus Lorenz Hirschfeld, in *Theorie der Gartenkunst*, expressed his sense that the garden Europe was defining as "Chinese" was nothing other than a product of Western imagination, an invention that he believed the writings of William Chambers had helped to create.[64] Hirschfeld considered Chambers's works to have been written more to illustrate, validate, and make more seductive his garden theories than as a serious theoretical analysis of Chinese design principles. To convince his readers, Hirschfeld reproduced in his work Chambers's essay "Of the Art of Laying Out Gardens Among the Chinese," and included lengthy quotations from Chambers's second work on the gardens of China, *A Dissertation on Oriental Gardening* (1772). To discredit Chambers's writings, Hirschfeld also cited as sources of his knowledge of the gardens of China other travelers' accounts: those by Attiret, the French Jesuit Louis Le Comte (1655–1728), Olof Torén, and Carl Gustav Ekeberg. In opposition to Hirschfeld's position toward Chambers, the French theorist and critic Antoine-Chrysostome Quatremère de Quincy wrote in defense of the Western travelers' accounts as reliable sources of knowledge of the gardens of China. In his article "Chinois jardins," written in 1788 and published in the "Architecture" section of the *Encyclopédie méthodique* (the expanded edition of Diderot and D'Alembert's famous work), Quatremère de Quincy pointed out that if Hirschfeld had read the Jesuits' accounts of Chinese gardens—especially Cibot's "Essai"—he would not have cast doubt on the truthfulness of Chambers's affirmations.[65] Thus Quatremère de Quincy assigned Cibot's and Chambers's accounts a fundamental role in Western knowledge of the gardens of China. Following Laugier and Cibot, Quatremère de Quincy expressed the wish that the Chinese taste in gardens be introduced into French modern gardens.[66]

If finally, as the fashion for the *anglo-chinois* garden spread, only a few were interested in the question of authenticity regarding information received in Europe about Chinese gardens and on the Western conception of Chinese garden design, there was a much more lively dispute between the two sides of the English Channel concerning the primogeniture of the irregular garden model. Chinese gardens played a crucial role in this debate. In fact, the major controversy was about something apparently entirely abstract: whether it was in England or China that the landscape garden had been invented. The polemic of each side was nourished by Western travelers' reports of Chinese gardens. English intellectuals used these accounts to demonstrate the difference between the Chinese and English approaches to garden design, to prove the absolute originality of the landscape garden they had elaborated, and to defend the national garden style as an expression of their political liberty. For French intellectuals, the Chinese garden served to undermine English innovation in garden design. The adjective *anglo-chinois* applied to irregular garden design, combining the Chinese reference and English landscape gardens, constituted a subtle way to discredit England as the original inventor of the landscape garden.[67] In the reports compiled by the Western travelers, French intellectuals read the evidence that the origin of landscape gardens lay in the much more ancient Chinese garden tradition. The Jesuit missionaries and William Chambers were the authors most quoted by the intellectuals involved in the controversy. Some considered them to be authoritative sources, while others saw them as mendacious babblers, befogged by their enthusiasm.

The writer Horace Walpole, in *On Modern Gardening*, first published in 1771, based his statement that the English landscape garden was independent from the Chinese model on Attiret's letter, questioning the natural appearance of Yuanming yuan it conveyed.[68] François de Paul Latapie, in his long introduction to the French translation of Whately's *Observations on Modern Gardening*, wrote that the English freed themselves from the regular garden "to follow nature alone" in only about 1720, and that this liberation had come when a very few authors, like William Temple, made reference to Chinese garden design. Latapie used the descriptions of the gardens of China by Western observers to testify to the fact that "the most natural method of composing gardens" was not a British invention. With the aim of "furnishing a complete proof of the perfect resemblance of the English gardens to those of the Chinese," he cited Chambers's 1757 essay and the description of Yuanming yuan written by the Jesuit Attiret.[69] The argument was carried forward by Le Rouge, who stated boldly that "the whole world knows that the English Gardens are nothing but an imitation of those of China."[70]

A more nuanced but equally rigid position toward his neighbors on the channel's opposite shore was that of Jacques-François Blondel. In his *Cours d'architecture* (1771), he stated that the British had no doubt attempted to imitate the Chinese style in their gardens, but that they were hardly successful since the gardens of China were a lesson in gaiety and vivacity that was not in line with the spirit of the British, a "serious People." Therefore, for Blondel, the Chinese model transplanted in England had engendered gardens characterized by a "simplicity that was certainly praiseworthy, but often sad and monotonous"; gardens that were, for this reason, useful for encouraging religious meditation but certainly not appropriate to complement the residences of "men of the world."[71] Mirroring Blondel's position, but with an opposite intention, the participants of the British embassy to the Qianlong emperor, led by Lord Macartney in 1792–94, recognized that precisely a diffused cheerfulness was indicative of the difference between English and Chinese garden aesthetic (see Fig. 13). The catalogue of the characteristics of the Chinese garden they observed and highlighted seemed to evoke the elements of the picturesque garden: "serpentine walks, a narrow winding river forming an island, with a summer-house in the middle of it, a grove of various trees, interspersed with a few patches of grass-ground, diversified with inequalities and roughened with rocks."[72] However, for the first British travelers who visited the great Qing imperial parks,

Chinese gardens, with their gaily painted pavilions, were too cheerful and exuberant to be authentic picturesque parks.

It was Lord Macartney who tried, with sensible words, to put an end to the dispute between French and British intellectuals. As ambassador, he had been received in 1793 in both the imperial residences of Yuanming yuan and Bishu shanzhuang and visited their parks (see Fig. 11). Because he was one of the few people acquainted with English landscape gardens to view the Chinese gardens, he was able to provide evidence of the actual similarity between the two styles. He associated the English and Chinese garden designs because, according to him, they exemplified the same aesthetic principles: they were different applications of the ideas of irregularity, variety, diversity, surprise, and imitation of nature, intended as freedom from formal patterns. "There is certainly a great analogy between our [English] gardening and the Chinese," he wrote, but evidently aware of the contemporary debate, he felt the need to add, "Whether our style of gardening was really copied from the Chinese, or originated with ourselves, I leave for vanity to assert, and idleness to discuss. A discovery which is the result of good sense and reflection may equally occur to the most distant nations, without either borrowing from the other."[73]

That scholarly quarrel about the origin of the English landscape style reflected a far wider question than a discussion of garden aesthetics: the steady intellectual, economic, and political decline of France in favor of England. The island was becoming an industrial and colonial power with a great overseas empire, while France, weakened by continental wars and suffering from a financial crisis, was overwhelmed by the Revolution. Thus, the Chinese garden was used in the imperial rivalry between France and England, and it is impossible not to recognize the validity of the sarcastic but eloquent conclusion that the Englishman William Marshall drew in his practical treatise entitled *Planting and Rural Ornament* (1796): the idea that the English landscape garden was nothing more than an imitation of the Chinese garden was "founded in Gallic envy rather than in truth."[74]

That change of equilibrium was also indicated by the increasingly important role played by British travelers, beginning in the last decade of the eighteenth century, in acquainting Europe with China and its gardens. Jesuits' accounts had greatly influenced the seventeenth- and eighteenth-century European perception of China. But, when Jesuits were expelled from the principal European countries and their colonies in the second half of the eighteenth century, and when in 1773 Pope Clement XIV suppressed the Society of Jesus, the Jesuit missionaries' reading of Chinese culture, proposed in their writings, had already begun to be considered distorted, a result of their propaganda for their mission. Probably provoked by the awareness of that prejudice, Cibot, one of the last Jesuits in China, wished to reassure his readers about the truthfulness of his "Essai sur les jardins de plaisance des Chinois," affirming that he drew exclusively on Chinese historical documents and literary sources. Cibot's "Essai" was the last extensive contribution by a Jesuit to Western knowledge of the Chinese garden aesthetic. From the last decade of the eighteenth century, travel narratives by participants in diplomatic, botanical, and military missions offered a new perception of China and Chinese gardens. Moving away from the viewpoints offered by the Jesuits, these accounts were regarded as being capable of offering a more realistic and authentic picture of the Chinese empire.[75]

DEFORMING NATURE

Near the end of the eighteenth century, the Far East, whose adjacent seas were constantly plied by Western vessels, was becoming ever more a land of conquest. The reverence that travelers in preceding centuries had shown for the Chinese empire was dissolving in an awareness of the technical and economic gap that by then separated China from the rest of the advanced world. During his 1793 diplomatic mission, Lord Macartney had refused to submit to the ceremony of repeated kowtowing to the emperor, feeling that he represented an empire just as powerful as the one in China.[76] Macartney's refusal reflected a change in the Western view of China's form of government. While Voltaire, the West's most illustrious Sinophile, saw it as a form of enlightened absolutism, other Europeans followed Montesquieu in opposing all forms of absolute power as being corrupt and corrupting. They began to consider China to be an example of despotism with an absence of political liberty.

Critiques of China found expression in judgments on its gardens. The discussion about Chinese taste in gardens, a taste Europeans were by that time familiar with, was used to highlight the aesthetic but also the political and social differences between Europe, particularly England, and China.[77] In England, the publication in 1772 of William Chambers's *Dissertation on Oriental Gardening* had resulted in a severe critical reaction by British intellectuals against Chinese garden design, which they saw as the image of a despotic regime.[78] The political meaning behind Chinese garden design

[handwritten annotation: presumably chinese garden style itself evolved over the period — how?]

was later suggested by the participants in the Macartney embassy through their accounts of that diplomatic mission.[79] Lord Macartney perceived and confirmed the similarity of Chinese and English gardens, but at the same time he also emphasized a difference: "Our [English] excellence seems to be rather in improving nature; theirs [the Chinese] to conquer her, and yet produce the same effect."[80] Although this diverging relationship with nature in the two countries brought about similar results, the compositional intentions relied on distinctly different design methods and indicated an essential political difference.[81] Even if Lord Macartney was favorably impressed by the Chinese gardens he visited, his apparently minor comment on the Chinese attitude toward nature showed an important difference between the English landscape garden and the Chinese garden, consisting in how much the apparent naturalness of the garden manifested the human transformation of the environment. This difference, and the explicit artificiality of Chinese garden design, was later the basis of the Western critique of the gardens of China, both by direct eyewitnesses and the readers of their accounts.

Travelers' perceptions of the Chinese attitude toward nature as expressed by the excessive artificiality in the gardens paradoxically made Chinese gardens comparable to the formal gardens in France, as the two different garden styles were both seen as expressions of similar forms of government. The English writer William Marshall, who never visited China, wrote in his *Planting and Rural Ornament* (1796) that the Chinese "style of Gardening . . . has as little to do with natural scenery as the garden of an ancient Roman, or a modern Frenchman: THE ART of *assisting* NATURE is, undoubtedly, all our own [English]."[82] Like French gardens, Chinese gardens manifested an intention to impose themselves on nature, only they refrained from doing so in the transparent manner of symmetry and regular geometry.

Again, considerations of the Chinese garden turned to the theme that had originally provoked European enthusiasm: the naturalness of their forms. Now, however, the judgment changed dramatically. The time was long past when Chinese gardens had constituted an exemplary model to follow because they were based on the imitation of natural forms, as so many eyewitnesses had testified. The fascination that Robert Castell, in the 1720s, had felt for the gardens of China, because they were composed of "*Rocks, Cascades, and Trees,* bearing their natural Forms" had disappeared.[83] With the beginning of the nineteenth century, the rocks, water features, and scattered plantings considered to be the main characteristics of Chinese garden design were devalued by Western observers as being too elaborate, forced, distant from the simplicity of nature itself, and therefore finally unnatural or possibly even monstrous: a clear manifestation of an antidemocratic civilization and its moral degeneration (see Fig. 20).

This association, which led to the denigration of the gardens of China, was common to many accounts compiled by Western, mainly British, travelers in the nineteenth century, and influenced the perception of those intellectuals who had never visited China. John Claudius Loudon made this assumption the central argument of his discussion on Chinese garden design. A Scottish botanist and garden designer, Loudon had theorized the Gardenesque as a gardening style joining the aesthetic approach of the landscape garden with attention to the form and appearance of single plants. He was also a prolific author of theoretical and practical treatises on garden design. In the revised edition of his *Encyclopaedia of Gardening* (1835), Loudon commented on the descriptions that various observers had given of the gardens of China and included in his work extensive quotations, although expanded by himself, from the travel journal of the Scottish botanist James Main (c. 1765–1846).[84] Echoing Main's criticism, and amplifying his comments, Loudon concluded that Chinese gardens were nothing more than "a little world of insignificant intricacy . . . an incongruous combination of unnatural associations," which contained "the most striking features of uncultivated nature: such as antique trees, rugged rocks, mossy caves, etc.; but these are all imitated on such a diminutive scale, that the attempts are truly ridiculous" (see Fig. 16).[85] In the composition of those gardens, Loudon perceived the Chinese "love of the grotesque and the monstrosities" to be an expression of the degenerating character of Chinese society, which was far removed from "enlightened views and liberal sentiments, which are almost always found combined with simplicity."[86] The paradigm was explicit; if gardens reflected the general spirit of a people, the deviation from natural simplicity was an expression of deviate political arrangements.[87]

The Chinese garden, seen in the past as nature's paladin, had now become its tyrant in Western eyes. Nineteenth-century observers' accounts describing the gardens of China in derogatory ways reinforced this change of opinion. The British naturalist George Bennett, who traveled through Australia and Southeast Asia between 1832 and 1834, was prompted to make a drastic conclusion after a visit to Guangzhou, which was recorded in his travel journal published in 1834: "As far as gardening, or laying out a garden, is concerned, these people possess any thing but the idea of beauty or true taste, neither being in the least degree attended to in the arrangement of their gardens; every thing bears the semblance of being stiff, awkward, and perfectly unnatural. To distort nature a Chinese seems to consider the attainment of perfection."[88] Chinese gardens had thus become little more than perversions of nature. Any attempt to understand what might have motivated the reason for the Chinese approach to nature and garden design was abandoned, since the whole garden art was condemned as a symptom of an inferior and degenerate culture. When Lord Macartney wrote about the differences between English and Chinese gardens, he noted that in the latter he had "observed no artificial ruins, caves, or hermitages."[89] He was referring to the buildings and structures used in the English landscape garden to integrate a sense of history into the garden's natural arrangement, a reference to the past, intended as a sequence of historic events, that he believed was missing in Chinese gardens. But Chinese gardens did have components meant to convey a broader sense of history: a geological history. When Loudon stigmatized the presence of "antique trees, rugged rocks, mossy caves" he was offering an image of a tired nature, worn out by time, revealed in bent plants and scarred rocks.[90] Just as Macartney before him, he did not understand the sophisticated intent of suggesting the passage of time in gardens through contorted trees and jagged rocks. Even a liberal and progressive man like Loudon fell victim to the prejudice that now overshadowed Chinese culture and interpreted these aspects of garden composition simply as a distortion of nature.

The overall layout of the garden, aimed at influencing the visitor's perception of the space, contributed to the effect of artificiality in the gardens of China, at least according to the many nineteenth-century Western observers who pondered the spatial strategy behind Chinese garden design. They focused in particular on the "fanciful devices of the East,"[91] the visual devices used to control the sight and alter the perception of the garden's real dimension.[92] The British diplomat John Francis Davis, in the account of his 1816 journey to Beijing with the British embassy led by Lord Amherst, published in 1841, painted a picture of the contrivances of Chinese gardens in his description of the gardens of a Qing imperial traveling palace in southern China: "The ground which they covered was far from extensive, but by the usual intricacies and tricks of Chinese gardening, an artificial appearance of extent was given with the help of winding walks among pavilions, bridges, rocks and groves; the whole being embellished with the addition of a piece of water, in which was situated a little island."[93] A few years later, Robert Fortune (1813–80), probably the most famous of the British plant hunters sent to China, synthesized this spatial strategy aimed at distorting the apparent dimension of the garden space, writing that Chinese garden design was characterized by "an endeavour to make small things appear large, and large things small."[94]

The contorted and unpredictable narrative form that the Chinese had introduced into their gardens seemed, in the nineteenth century, to diverge hopelessly from the clarity of the perfect, natural design that was ushering world civilization into a new epoch. While Loudon was publishing his *Encyclopaedia* and Bennett was sailing toward China, another English ship, the *Beagle*, was traversing the ocean with an English traveler on board who was to put a definitive end to the certainty concerning the "simplicity" of the natural world.

In the mid-nineteenth century the Chinese garden, as described by Western observers, dissolved in two stereotypes of generic and popular exotic settings: the romantic orientalism depicted in *One Thousand and One Nights* and the landscapes represented on mass-produced blue-and-white patterned plates.[95] If allusions to the *Arabian Nights* were used to describe China as a place of marvels, both references were used to express the travelers' perception of the gardens of China.[96] The American writer Brantz Mayer (1809–79), in his travelogue published in 1847, described the garden of a hong merchant in Guangzhou, which he had visited a few years earlier, as an "exquisite picture of Oriental fantasy and taste," with "miniature vallies, lakelets spread out filled with lillies . . . coquettish summer-houses . . . light bridges, whose airy lines seemed spun of gossamer, were hung over the narrow streams."[97] At the same time, however, these images contained a satire of Chinese garden design. While the *Arabian Nights* were used by Western travelers to elicit the excessive luxury of the Chinese imperial parks,[98] patterned porcelain evoked the immutable character of the gardens of China, which, just as the invariable plate designs, could be summarized in a few general and generic elements.

Western rejection of Chinese garden design culminated first in harsh criticism and then in the physical destruction of the ideal model reference for irregular gardens in the West, the park of Yuanming yuan (see Fig. 23). In many accounts by Western travelers, Yuanming yuan was presented as the finest expression of Chinese garden art.[99] With its destruction in 1860,

1860 – end – date for book – the decline of the imperial park

China was deprived of one of its most powerful symbols of cultural identity and political unity. At the same time, the aggression also damaged Europe's own history by eliminating the park that more than any other had influenced the evolution of Western garden art, thanks to the accounts of those who had had the privilege of seeing it. The gardens of China were never again to be taken as models.

The chronological frame of this anthology is defined by two very different texts. The book opens with the fragmentary descriptions of the imperial parks of Kublai Khan by Marco Polo, the first accounts of Chinese gardens by a Western traveler to reach Europe. The last text is the account of the Qing imperial park of Yuanming yuan just before its destruction in 1860 written by the British officer Garnet Joseph Wolseley (1833–1913). The devastation of Yuanming yuan has been chosen as a chronological limit not only for its symbolic significance but also because it represents a dramatic change in the history of China and of the Sino-Western relationship.[100] It marked the decline of the Qing dynasty and the acquisition of extended trading rights and territorial sovereignties for Western powers in China. It marked the decrease of Europeans' curiosity about China and the progressive rise of their interest in Japan and Japanese art, which followed the reopening of Japanese ports to trade with the West in 1853. It also represented the beginning of a new phase of traveling through China and of writing on China. After the Second Opium War, greater concessions were granted regarding foreign trade activities, movement, and residence within China's interior. The presence of Westerners in China increased and printed guidebooks were published, for both permanent residents and visitors, with descriptions of sites and cities and information to explore the country.[101]

The anthology comprises published accounts composed by travelers from European nations, with the exception of two texts by American travelers Osmond Tiffany, Jr. (1823–95) and Charles Taylor (1819–97), which are included in the selection because they are of interest to the discourse on Western perceptions of the Chinese garden.[102] They are also included as testimony to the increasing presence of American merchants in China beginning in the late eighteenth century.[103] The selected texts are organized chronologically according to their year of publication, with the exception of the accounts by Jean-François Gerbillon, Matteo Ripa, Michel Benoist, and François Bourgeois. These texts were composed much earlier than their publication dates and the narratives' tone, language, and approach used to

Euro + 2 USA.

describe the Chinese garden are characteristic of an epoch prior to the time of their publication. The sequence of excerpts ends with an appendix containing William Chambers's *Dissertation on Oriental Gardening*. There are two main reasons for separating this influential text from the others constituting the anthology. First, Chambers's *Dissertation* is a very different text in terms of contents and is also considerably longer than the other selected extracts; second, more than being an account of Chinese garden design, the *Dissertation* shows how Chambers used the Chinese garden to promote a new picturesque garden style.

Descriptions of Chinese gardens appear in a variety of documents, including journals, letters, essays, travel accounts, and missionary reports. These differ in genre, style, and length, as well as in the information about Chinese gardens that they provide. With varying levels of understanding and some naiveté, Westerners in China furthered their investigation by elaborating memories of their visits that were mainly concerned with the visible aspects of the garden: spatial organization, systematically winding paths, arrangement of vegetation, and the constant presence of water and rocks. What they did not perceive were the less apparent aspects beyond Chinese garden design, such as the link between garden design and landscape painting, the influence of Chinese literary tradition in the composition of the garden's scenes, the role of the principles of feng shui (geomancy) in guiding the disposition of volumes and voids and the conformation of paths, or the reference to Daoism and Buddhism that created the palimpsest of meanings implicit to Chinese gardens.

In focusing on the spatial articulation of Chinese gardens, not all of the accounts show the same narrative quality or depth; commentaries on different gardens also vary from fragmentary information to detailed descriptions. Some authors, lacking the appropriate vocabulary to describe the gardens of China, focused their attention on specific elements of the composition, such as artificial mountains; others presented Chinese garden design as juxtaposed to Western garden styles, following the developments of garden aesthetic in Europe, to facilitate their distant readers' understanding of the gardens of China. Matteo Ripa, in the 1720s, described Changchun yuan, "Garden of Joyful Spring," created for the Kangxi emperor in suburban Beijing, as radically different from Baroque gardens, recording that "this and all the other lordly villas that I saw are of the same taste, exactly the contrary of our European taste, since we here artfully attempt to distance ourselves from the natural, making the hills plain, draining out the dead waters of lakes, uprooting spontaneous trees, straightening roads . . . the Chinese, on the other hand, work with art to imitate nature, transforming the terrain into a web of little mountains and hills."[104] In the last years of the eighteenth century, the British diplomats George Leonard Staunton (1737–1801), John Barrow (1764–1848), and George Macartney showed the similarities of approach between Chinese garden design and the English landscape garden. Their views, however, were to be contradicted a few decades later by their compatriots James Main, Robert Fortune, and Garnet Joseph Wolseley, who all emphasized the differences between the two traditions.

Some authors made an honest intellectual effort to interpret Chinese garden design principles, providing texts intended to be authoritative treatises, such as the essays by Chambers and Cibot; others tended toward sketchy simplification. The barriers and restrictions that Westerners experienced, along with the difficulty in describing the spatial articulation of Chinese gardens, perceived as fragmentary and designed apparently without any order, as well as the memory of European chinoiserie, all encouraged simplistic interpretations, so that the Chinese garden aesthetic was associated with recurring elements that seemed to convey a sort of shared image of Chineseness. In 1797, Johann Christian Hüttner (1765?–1847), who joined the Macartney embassy to the Qing court, summarized the main characteristics of Chinese garden design in a repertory of typical elements that he believed could be perceived in almost every garden: "The Chinese, in their gardens, prefer artificial rocks, little hills, groups of wild trees, water, houses built in the shade."[105] The British physician Julius Berncastle (?–1870), in 1850, confirmed that Chinese gardens were exactly like the landscapes represented on "Chinese paintings, familiar to everybody," with "artificial lakes and rivers, with light bridges across them, leading to caverns, kiosks, pagodas, grottoes, and imitation precipices, with a path leading to the summit: fruit-trees, flowers, and porcelain ornaments of all descriptions, too numerous to examine separately, altogether forming one of the most curious and interesting sights it is possible to imagine."[106] Similarly, Charles de Mutrécy, who took part in the North China Campaign of 1860, made a list of the compositional elements of Chinese garden design, which consisted of "clumps of trees, grottoes, miniature mountains, gorges, lakes and other marvels of an artificial nature," confirming the contrived naturalness of the gardens' arrangement.[107] It is interesting to note that even the few Western travelers who were able to see extremely different gardens, such as the imperial parks in Beijing and in Chengde, toward the northern border of the empire, in addition to the gardens of the wealthy merchants and officials on the southeastern coast of China, did not remark on the clear differences in their style. Laurence Oliphant (1829–88), who joined the British military expedition to China in 1857–59 as private secretary to Lord Elgin, after having visited part of Yuanming yuan and the garden of the suburban residence of the official known as Pontinqua in Guangzhou concluded that "all Chinese gardens partake of much the same character," defined by "tangles thickets, and shady walks, and little islands in the middle of ponds, approached by rustic bridges, and surrounded by ornamental rock-work; summer-houses and cool grottoes."[108] These elements were, according to Oliphant, emblematic of the "quaint character peculiar to Chinese taste [in garden design], and which is not without a certain charm."[109] To Western eyes, the confirmation of a Chinese homogeneity in the recurrence of a repertory of elements was more important than stylistic differences.

The reception of such descriptions, which inevitably contained a simplification of the design and a synthesis of Chinese gardens' formal vocabulary, was clearly of concern to the many Western travelers who had pondered the varying opportunities offered by verbal and visual accounts in conveying the spatial arrangement of Chinese gardens. The Jesuit Attiret was convinced that an image would have enhanced his description, while Van Braam Houckgeest affirmed that neither a written nor a graphic account would have been able to supply a sure representation for understanding the complexity of Chinese garden design. The architecture theorist Laugier, who learned about Chinese garden design through Attiret's account, agreed with the Jesuit and wished for a plan of Yuanming yuan because he was convinced that it would have made an important reference for those wishing to evoke Chinese garden design principles in Western gardens.[110]

The reception of Chinese gardens in Europe was the product of both a prolonged period of field investigation and mental construction by travelers and their readers, which varied as the wealth of reports from direct witnesses increased. Despite its imprecise results, this process had a prolonged seminal role: it gave European intellectuals, from the early eighteenth century until the mid-nineteenth century, the wider perspective they needed to justify the new ideas on garden aesthetics that were being developed in western Europe.

NOTES

1   On Europe's fascination for China see, for instance, William W. Appleton, *A Cycle of Cathay: The Chinese Vogue in England During the Seventeenth and Eighteenth Centuries* (New York: Columbia University Press, 1951); H. Belevitch-Stanevitch, *Le goût chinois en France au temps de Louis XIV* (Geneva: Slatkine Reprints, 1970); David Porter, *Ideographia: The Chinese Cipher in Early Modern Europe* (Stanford, Calif.: Stanford University Press, 2001); David Porter, "Monstrous Beauty: Eighteenth-Century Fashion and the Aesthetics of the Chinese Taste," *Eighteenth-Century Studies* 35, no. 3 (2002): 395–411.

2   On the influence of Chinese gardens on eighteenth-century European garden aesthetics my sources were Arthur O. Lovejoy, "The Chinese Origin of a Romanticism," in *Essays in the History of Ideas* (Baltimore: Johns Hopkins University Press, 1948), 99–135; Osvald Sirén, *China and Gardens of Europe of the Eighteenth Century* (New York: Ronald Press, 1950); Dora Wiebenson, *The Picturesque Garden in France* (Princeton, N.J.: Princeton University Press, 1978), especially chapters 3 and 4; Jurgis Baltrušaitis, "Land of Illusion: China and the Eighteenth Century Garden," *Landscape* 11, no. 2 (1961–62): 5–11; Jurgis Baltrušaitis, "Gardens and Lands of Illusion," in *Aberrations: An Essay on the Legend of Forms* (Cambridge, Mass.: MIT Press, 1989), 138–81; Janine Barrier, Monique Mosser, and Che Bing Chiu, *Aux jardins de Cathay: L'imaginaire anglo-chinois en Occident* (Besançon: Les Éditions de l'Imprimeur, 2004), 74–84. See also the works cited in notes 29 and 56 that discuss the influence of China on the English landscape garden and eighteenth-century French gardens.

3   For an overview of Western travelers' accounts of the gardens of China see Sirén, *China and Gardens of Europe*, 3–9, 165–66; Maggie Keswick, *The Chinese Garden: History, Art and Architecture*, rev. ed. (London: Frances Lincoln, 2003), 16–37; Bianca Maria Rinaldi, "Die Reise nach China: Die chinesischen Gärten in den Beschreibungen westlicher Reisender," in *Reisen in Parks und Gärten: Umrisse einer Rezeptions- und Imaginationsgeschichte*, ed. Hubertus Fischer et al. (Munich: Meidenbauer, 2012), 291–308. For an overview of Western traveler's descriptions up to the twentieth century see Peter Valder, *Gardens in China* (Portland, Ore.: Timber Press, 2002). For a study on the Jesuits' accounts of Chinese gardens see Bianca Maria Rinaldi, "Borrowing from China: The Society of Jesus and the Ideal of Naturalness in XVII and XVIII Century European Gardens," *Die Gartenkunst* 17, no. 2 (2005): 319–37; and also Bianca Maria Rinaldi, *The "Chinese Garden in Good Taste": Jesuits and Europe's Knowledge of Chinese Flora and Art of the Garden in the Seventeenth and Eighteenth Centuries* (Munich: Meidenbauer, 2006). Craig Clunas, "Nature and Ideology in Western Descriptions of Chinese Gardens," in *Nature and Ideology: Natural Garden Design in the Twentieth Century*, ed. J. Wolschke-Bulmahn (Washington, D.C.: Dumbarton Oaks Research Library and Collection, 1997), 21–33, that offers a discussion of the concept of nature in Western descriptions of Chinese gardens. These studies were important sources that informed my discussion.

4   On reception of gardens see John Dixon Hunt, *The Afterlife of Gardens* (Philadelphia: University of Pennsylvania Press, 2004). A brief discussion of the reception of the imperial park of Yuanming yuan through verbal accounts is on pp. 22–34.

5   On the perception of Chinese gardens by eighteenth- and nineteenth-century British travelers, see the recent and important study by Elizabeth Hope Chang, *Britain's Chinese Eye: Literature, Empire, and Aesthetics in Nineteenth-Century Britain* (Stanford, Calif.; Stanford University Press, 2010), 23–70. Chang focuses mainly on William Chambers's *Dissertation on Oriental Gardening*, on the reports produced by the participants to the Macartney embassy to the Qianlong emperor, and on the accounts by Robert Fortune.

6   The garden of Versailles was the model of a compositional concept based on regularity and geometry shared by all of European culture; it represented the example to imitate in every royal palace in Europe. Suggesting an analogy between Yuanming yuan and Versailles, Jesuits implied that Yuanming yuan was the greatest model of Chinese garden design. For a parallel between Yuanming yuan and Versailles see Greg M. Thomas, "Yuanming Yuan/Versailles: Intercultural Interactions Between Chinese and European Palace Cultures," *Art History* 32, no. 1 (2009): 117–25.

7   Marcia Reed, "A Perfume Is Best from Afar: Publishing China in Europe," in *China on Paper: European and Chinese Works from the Late Sixteenth to the Early Nineteenth Century*, ed. Marcia Reed and Paola Demattè (Los Angeles: Getty Research Institute, 2011), 9–27.

8   Reed, "A Perfume Is Best from Afar," 18–20.

9   John Barrow, *Some Account of the Public Life, and a Selection from the Unpublished Writings, of the Earl of Macartney*, vol. 2 (London: T. Cadell and W. Davies, 1807), 305–6.

10   In writing this summary of the evolution of Western perception of China, I have relied on the following studies: Basil Guy, *The French Image of China Before and After Voltaire*, Studies on Voltaire and the Eighteenth Century 21 (Geneva: Institut et Musée Voltaire, 1963); Sergio Zoli, "L'immagine dell'Oriente nella cultura italiana da Marco Polo al Settecento," in *Il Paesaggio*, ed. Cesare de Seta, vol. 5 of *Storia d'Italia: Annali*, ed. Ruggiero Romano and Corrado Vivanti (Turin: Einaudi, 1982), 47–123; Colin Mackerras, *Western Images of China* (Oxford: Oxford University Press, 1989); Thomas H. C. Lee, ed., *China and Europe: Images and Influences in Sixteenth to Eighteenth Centuries* (Hong Kong: Chinese University Press, 1991); Julia Ching and Willard G. Oxtoby, eds., *Discovering China: European Interpretations in the Enlightenment* (Rochester, N.Y.: University of Rochester Press, 1992); J. J. Clarke, *Oriental Enlightenment: The Encounter Between Asian and Western Thought* (London: Routledge, 1997), 37–53; David E. Mungello, *The Great Encounter of China and the West, 1500–1800* (1999; reprint, Lanham, Md.: Rowman and Littlefield, 2013).

11   For a recent study on the destruction of Yuanming yuan and its implications in the European image of China see Greg M. Thomas, "The Looting of Yuanming and the Translation of Chinese Art in Europe," *Nineteenth-Century Art Worldwide: A Journal of Nineteenth-Century Visual Culture* 7, no. 2 (Autumn 2008) (http://www.19thc-artworldwide.org/index.php/autumn08/93-the-looting-of-yuanming-and-the-translation-of-chinese-art-in-europe). On the looting of Yuanming yuan see James L. Hevia, *English Lessons: The Pedagogy of Imperialism in*

Nineteenth-Century China (Durham, N.C.: Duke University Press, 2003), 74–111; and also Erik Ringmar, *Liberal Barbarism: The European Destruction of the Palace of the Emperor of China* (New York: Palgrave Macmillan, 2013).

12 Among the significant literature on chinoiserie see Madeleine Jarry, *Chinoiseries: Le rayonnement du goût chinois sur les arts décoratifs des XVIIᵉ et XVIIIᵉ siècles* (Fribourg: Office du livre, 1981); Dawn Jacobson, *Chinoiserie* (London: Phaidon, 1993); and, most recently, David Porter, *The Chinese Taste in Eighteenth-Century England* (Cambridge: Cambridge University Press, 2010), especially chapters 3 and 5.

13 David Porter, "Writing China: Legitimacy and Representation, 1606–1773," *Comparative Literature Studies* 33, no. 1 (1996): 110.

14 On Matteo Ripa and the influence of his engravings on English garden aesthetics my sources were Basil Gray, "Lord Burlington and Father Ripa's Chinese Engravings," *British Museum Quarterly* 22, nos. 1–2 (1960): 40–43; Rudolph Wittkower, *Palladio and English Palladianism* (London: Thames and Hudson, 1974), 185–86; Yu Liu, "Transplanting a Different Gardening Style into England: Matteo Ripa and His Visit to London in 1724," *Diogenes* 55, no. 2 (2008): 83–96. A new publication on Ripa and his engravings of Bishu shanzhuang is currently in preparation, edited by Stephen H. Whiteman and Richard E. Strassberg, to be published by Dumbarton Oaks Research Library and Collection. The essay by Stephen H. Whiteman, "Translating the Landscape: Genre, Style and Pictorial Technology in the Thirty-Six Views of the Mountain Estate for Escaping the Heat," offers a detailed and innovative study of Ripa's views.

15 Joseph Spence, "Letter to the Rev. Mr Wheeler," 1751. Quoted in John Dixon Hunt and Peter Willis, eds., *The Genius of the Place: The English Landscape Garden, 1620–1820* (Cambridge, Mass.: MIT Press, 1988), 269.

16 *The Emperor of China's Palace at Peking, and His Principal Gardens, as well as in Tartary, as at Peking, Gehol and the Adjacent Countries; with the Temples, Pleasure-Houses, Artificial Mountains, Rocks, Lakes, etc. as Disposed in Different Parts of Those Royal Gardens* (London: Sayer, Overton, Bowles, and Bowles and Son, 1753).

17 Joseph Disponzio, introduction to *Essay on Gardens: A Chapter in the French Picturesque*, by Claude-Henri Watelet, ed. and trans. Samuel Danon (Philadelphia: University of Pennsylvania Press, 2003), 5–6.

18 The Jesuit Jean-Denis Attiret explained that due to his work as a painter at the court of the Qianlong emperor, he had the opportunity to visit the imperial residences extensively, writing that he was admitted "every where" inside the compound. Jean-Denis Attiret, *A Particular Account of the Emperor of China's Garden near Pekin*, trans. Sir Harry Beaumont [Joseph Spence] (London: Dodsley, 1752), 47–48.

19 Stephen H. Whiteman, "From Upper Camp to Mountain Estate: Recovering Historical Narratives in Qing Imperial Landscapes," *Studies in the History of Gardens and Designed Landscapes*, 33, no. 4 (2013): 249–50. In his 1743 letter describing Yuanming yuan, the Jesuit Jean-Denis Attiret noted that the Qianlong emperor "usually resides here [at Yuanming yuan] Ten Months in each Year." Attiret, *A*

Particular Account, 48–49. In a letter written in 1773, the Jesuit Michel Benoist confirmed Attiret's observations, explaining that Yuanming yuan was a favorite residence of the Qianlong emperor, who spent only about three months in Beijing and lived at Yuanming yuan the rest of the year, with the exception of hunting trips to Tartary and occasional trips to ceremonies in the capital city. Michel Benoist, "Troisième Lettre du P. Benoit. A Pékin, le 4. Nov. 1773," in *Lettres édifiantes et curieuses, écrites des Missions étrangères par quelques Missionnaires de la C.[Compagnie] de J.[Jesus]*, vol. 33 (Paris: Berton, 1776), 177–79. From 1722 until its destruction, Yuanming yuan served as the effective center of imperial power for five successive Qing rulers. Richard E. Strassberg, "War and Peace: Four Intercultural Landscapes," in Reed and Demattè, *China on Paper*, 104–5.

20 As shown by Fa-ti Fan, *British Naturalists in Qing China: Science, Empire and Cultural Encounter* (Cambridge, Mass.: Harvard University Press, 2004), 31–35.

21 Paul A. Van Dyke, *The Canton Trade: Life and Enterprise on the China Coast, 1700–1845* (Hong Kong: Hong Kong University Press, 2005). On the opening of treaty ports see John King Fairbank, *Trade and Diplomacy on the China Coast: The Opening of the Treaty Ports 1842–1854* (Cambridge, Mass.: Harvard University Press, 1953).

22 Marco Polo, *The Book of Ser Marco Polo, the Venetian, Concerning the Kingdoms and Marvels of the East*, trans. and ed. Henry Yule, vol. 1 (London: Murray, 1871), 326.

23 Martino Martini, *Novus atlas sinensis* (Amsterdam: Blaeu, 1655), 31: "artifice manu exstructos montes, qui veris ipsis invidiam quodammodo ob artis praestantiam facere possint."

24 Johannes Nieuhof, *An Embassy from the East-India Company of the United Provinces, to the Great Tartar Cham, Emperor of China*, trans. John Ogilby (London: Macock, 1669), 129. In chapter 11 of the account of his journey to the Far East with the Dutch East India Company (Vereenigde Oostindische Compagnie, VOC), *Orientalisch-Indianische Kunst- und Lust-Gärtner* (1692), the German George Meister (1653–1713), royal court gardener in Dresden, gave information on East Asian gardens focusing on the artificial mountains and on some aspects of the techniques to construct them. Though his account of Asian gardens is entitled "Von der Jappaner und Chineser zierlichen Gartenbau, und was dem anhängig" (On Japanese and Chinese Ornamental Gardening, and What Is Related to That), it is uncertain whether he had ever visited any garden in China. He traveled to the Cape of Good Hope, where he did research in the VOC's garden, and to Jakarta (Batavia), Malacca, and Japan. As Wybe Kuitert has shown in his study of Meister's travel account, a few gardens that seem to be in accordance with Meister's text can be found in Nagasaki. Wybe Kuitert, "Georg Meister: A Seventeenth Century Gardener and His Reports on Oriental Garden Art," *Japan Review*, no. 2 (1991): 125–43.

25 For a summary of the concept of artificial mountain in both Eastern and Western cultures see Michael Jacob, "On Mountains: Scalable and Unscalable," in *Landform Building: Architecture's New Terrain*, ed. Stan Allen and Marc McQuade (Baden: Lars Müller, 2011), 136–64.

26 This quote comes from the first English translation of Magalhães's work: Gabriel de Magalhães, *A New History of China* (London: Newborough, 1688), 324–25.

27 Jean-François Gerbillon, "Seconde voyage fait par ordre de l'Empereur de la Chine en Tartarie par les Peres Gerbillon et Pereira en l'année 1689," in Jean-Baptiste Du Halde, *Description géographique, historique, chronologique, politique et physique de l'empire de la Chine et de la Tartarie chinoise*, vol. 4 (Paris: Le Mercier, 1735).

28 See, for instance, the comment by the French Jesuit Louis Le Comte included in this anthology. The French Jesuit Joachim Bouvet (1656–1730), who served as Kangxi's instructor in mathematics and Euclidean geometry, describing Kangxi's Changchun yuan, wrote: "Excepting two great fountains, and some canals that he [Kangxi] had had dug, there is nothing that reflects the magnificence of a so rich and so powerful Monarch. Everything is extremely neat: but the buildings, the gardens, the disposition of the terrain are much inferior to those of many *maisons de plaisance* belonging to private Gentlemen, in particular those seen around Paris." Joachim Bouvet, *Portrait historique de l'Empereur de la Chine* (Paris: Michallet, 1697), 81–82. The Austrian Jesuit Johann Grueber (1623–80) was disappointed by the lack of ornaments he perceived in Chinese gardens, which he considered as simple enclosed meadows "to play football." "Voyage du P. Grueber a la Chine," in Melchisédec Thévenot, *Relations de divers voyages curieux . . .* , 2 vol., 3rd part (Paris: Moette, 1696), 15.

29 On the Chinese influence on the development of the English landscape garden, important sources that informed my discussion are Patrick Conner, "China and the Landscape Garden: Reports, Engravings, and Misconceptions," *Art History* 2, no. 4 (1979): 430–40; David Jacques, "On the Supposed Chineseness of the English Landscape Garden," *Garden History* 18, no. 2 (1990): 181–87; Liangyan Ge, "On the Eighteenth-Century Misreading of the Chinese Garden," *Comparative Civilizations Review* 27 (1992): 106–26; more recently, Yu Liu, "The Inspiration for a Different Eden: Chinese Gardening Ideas in England in the Early Modern Period," in *Comparative Civilizations Review*, no. 53 (2005): 86–106; and also Yu Liu, *Seeds of a Different Eden: Chinese Gardening Ideas and a New English Aesthetic Ideal* (Columbia: University of South Carolina Press, 2008), especially 1–41.

30 In writing this summary, I have used the following general histories of gardens and of the English landscape garden: John Dixon Hunt, *Gardens and the Picturesque: Studies in the History of Landscape Architecture* (Cambridge, Mass.: MIT Press, 1997); Franco Panzini, *Progettare la natura: Architettura del paesaggio e dei giardini dalle origini all'epoca contemporanea* (Bologna: Zanichelli, 2005).

31 For a recent study on the role of the gardens of China, descriptions of Chinese gardens by Western travelers, and the development of the English landscape gardens see Christina Kallieris, *Inventis addere: Chinesische Gartenkunst und englische Landschaftsgärten: Die Auswirkungen von Utopien und Reisebeschreibungen auf gardentheoretische Schriften Englands im 18. Jahrhundert* (Worms-am-Rhein: Wernersche Verlagsgesellschaft, 2012).

32 William Temple, "Upon the Gardens of Epicurus," in *Miscellanea, the Second Part: In Four Essays*, 4th ed. (London: Simpson, 1696), 132. Temple constructed

his knowledge of China mainly on the book of Marco Polo and on Jesuits' writings; see William Temple, "Upon Heroick Virtue," in *Miscellanea, the Second Part*, 171–80, 197.

33   Joseph Addison, *The Spectator*, no. 414, 25 June 25, 1712. Quoted in Hunt and Willis, *The Genius of the Place*, 142.

34   Stephen Switzer, *Iconographia rustica*, vol. 1 (London: Browne, Barker, King, Mears, Gosling, 1718), xxxviii.

35   Robert Castell, *The Villas of the Ancients Illustrated* (London: By the author, 1728), 116–17.

36   Christian Cajus Lorenz Hirschfeld, *Théorie de l'art des jardins*, vol. 1 (Leipzig: Weidmann and Reich, 1779), 93: "La réflexion et le génie n'avoient sans doute pas besoin d'exemples particuliers pour découvrir la nouvelle manier adoptée en Angleterre, et qui de là commence à se répandre partout: il est cependant probable que les relations qu'on a faites des jardins Chinois, y ont beaucoup contribué."

37   The work by Joachim Bouvet, *Portrait historique de l'Empereur de la Chine* (1697), contributed much to the European image of Kangxi. Bouvet's account was an editorial success and was quickly translated and published in other languages: a Latin version edited by Leibniz came out in Hanover in 1699; English and Dutch translations appeared the same year in London and Utrecht. In 1710, an Italian translation was published in Padua.

38   Gerbillon, "Seconde voyage . . . en Tartarie," 228.

39   Attiret, *A Particular Account*, 38–39.

40   The quote is taken from the first English translation of the travelogue: Olof Torén, "Letter V," in *Peter Osbeck, A Voyage to China and the East Indies*, vol. 2 (London: B. White, 1771), 230. To his very brief comments on the gardens of China, Torén added, "Instead of grottoes they [the Chinese] throw a heap of a porous sort of stones together, which look like rocks and mountains. This taste of the romantic in gardens extends even to the small flower-beds, and flower-pots in houses." Ibid., 230.

41   For this short summary on the relationship between the garden and the landscape in the Italian Renaissance garden, in the French garden tradition, and in the English landscape style, I drew upon John Dixon Hunt, *A World of Gardens* (London: Reaktion, 2012), 160–85.

42   Jacques-François Blondel, *Architecture françoise*, vol. 1 (Paris: Jombert, 1752), 46.

43   Marc-Antoine Laugier, *An Essay on Architecture*, trans. Wolfgang and Anni Herrmann (Los Angeles: Hennessey and Ingalls, 1977), 138. All the quotes from Laugier are from the English translation by Wolfgang and Anni Herrmann.

44   Laugier, *An Essay on Architecture*, 139.

45   Ibid., 139.

46   Ibid., 138.

47   Isaac Ware, *The Four Books of Andrea Palladio's Architecture* (London: Ware, 1738). The work was dedicated to Richard Boyle, the Third Earl of Burlington and the Fourth Earl of Cork.

48   Isaac Ware, *A Complete Body of Architecture* (London: T. Osborne and J. Shipton, 1756), 646 and 645.

49 Ibid., 646.

50 Chinese gardens shared this characteristic with the English landscape garden. See Hunt and Willis, introduction to *The Genius of the Place*, 23–25.

51 Pierre-Martial Cibot, "Essai sur les jardins de plaisance des Chinois," in *Mémoires concernant l'histoire, les sciences, les arts, les mœurs, les usages, & c. des Chinois: Par les Missionnaires de Pekin*, vol. 8 (Paris: Nyon, 1782), 326. The series will be hereafter cited as *Mémoires . . . des Chinois*.

52 Thomas Whately, *Observations on Modern Gardening* (London: Exshaw, 1770).

53 Attiret, *A Particular Account*, 41.

54 Michel Benoist, "Lettre du Père Benoist à Monsieur Papillon d'Auteroche. A Péking, le 16 novembre 1767," in *Lettres édifiantes et curieuses écrites des missions étrangères, Mémoires de la Chine*, vol. 23 (Paris: Merigot, 1781), 536–37.

55 Pierre-Martial Cibot, "Observations sur les plantes, les fleurs et les arbres de Chine qu'il est possible de se procurer en France," in *Mémoires . . . des Chinois*, vol. 11 (Paris: Nyon, 1786), 216: "copier ses caprices, ses négligences, ses fautes même et ses oublis."

56 On the French picturesque gardens see *Jardins en France, 1760–1820: Pays d'illusion, terre d'expériences* (Paris: Caisse Nationale des Monuments Historiques et des Sites, 1977); Wiebenson, *The Picturesque Garden in France*; Sophie Le Ménahèze, *L'invention du jardin romantique en France, 1761–1808* (Neuilly-sur-Seine: Éditions Spiralinthe, 2001); John Dixon Hunt, *The Picturesque Garden in Europe* (London: Thames and Hudson, 2002), 88–139. On the role of Chinese gardens in eighteenth-century French gardens see Antoine Gournay, "Jardins chinois en France à la fin du XVIIIe siècle," *Bulletin de l'Ecole Française d'Extrême-Orient* 78 (1991): 259–73.

57 The literature on Chambers and his writings on Chinese gardens is profuse. Important sources include Robert C. Bald, "Sir William Chambers and the Chinese Garden," *Journal of the History of Ideas* 2, no. 3 (1950): 287–320; Eileen Harris, "Design of Chinese Buildings and the Dissertation on Oriental Gardening," in *Sir William Chambers, Knight of the Polar Star*, ed. John Harris (University Park: Pennsylvania State University Press, 1970), 144–62; David Porter, "Beyond the Bounds of Truth: Cultural Translation and William Chambers's Chinese Garden," *Mosaic* 37, no. 2 (2004): 41–58; Barrier, Mosser, and Chiu, *Aux jardins de Cathay*.

58 On garden architectures in a "Chinese" style in eighteenth-century European gardens, important works include Eleanor von Erdberg, *Chinese Influence on European Garden Structures* (Cambridge, Mass.: Harvard University Press, 1936); Patrick Conner, *Oriental Architecture in the West* (London: Thames and Hudson, 1979); Gerd-Helge Vogel, "Wunderland Cathay: Chinoise Architekturen in Europa, Teil 1," *Die Gartenkunst* 16, no. 1 (2004): 125–72; Gerd-Helge Vogel, "Wunderland Cathay: Chinoise Architekturen in Europa, Teil 2," *Die Gartenkunst* 16, no. 2 (2004): 339–82; and more recently, Stefan Koppelkamm, *The Imaginary Orient: Exotic Buildings of the Eighteenth and Nineteenth Centuries in Europe* (Fellbach: Menges, 2014).

59 See, for instance, William and John Halfpenny, *Chinese and Gothic Architecture Properly Ornamented* (London: Sayer, 1752); Matthew Darly, *A New Book of*

Chinese Designs (London: By the author, 1754); Charles Over, *Ornamental Architecture in the Gothic, Chinese and Modern Taste* (London: Sayer, 1758); Paul Decker, *Chinese Architecture, Civil and Ornamental* (London: By the author, 1759). On the role of pattern books in the design of garden structures see Hunt, *A World of Gardens*, 221–23.

60 William Chambers, "Traité des édifices, meubles, habits, machines et ustensiles des Chinois . . . ," in George-Louis Le Rouge, *Détails de nouveaux jardins à la mode "jardins anglo-chinois,"* cahier 5 (Paris: By the author, 1776). The cahiers dedicated to the Chinese garden are 14 (1785), 15 (1786), 16 (1786), and 17 (1786), respectively with 11, 28, 30, and 30 plates.

61 Le Rouge, *Détails de nouveaux jardins,* cahier 14, *Des jardins chinois* (1785), was illustrated with the eleven engravings of imperial palaces visited by the Qianlong emperor in the course of his travels through the southern Chinese province of Jiangsu, contained in an album sent to France by French Jesuit Jean Joseph Marie Amiot, and kept since 1770 in the Cabinet des Estampes de la Bibliothèque du Roi in Paris. Le Rouge used the images included in a second album of forty-six views of imperial palaces and scenic landscapes of southern China, which Amiot had sent to France in 1765, to illustrate part of cahier 16, "Des jardins chinois: Jardins de l'Empereur de la Chine" (1786), and cahier 17, "Des jardins anglo-chinois: Maisons de plaisance de l'Empereur de la Chine" (1786). Véronique Royet, ed., *Georges Louis Le Rouge: Les jardins anglo-chinois* (Paris: Bibliothèque Nationale de France, 2004), 202. The plates included in cahier 15 and in part of cahier 16 reproduced a series of Western copies of forty woodcuts illustrating the imperial park of Yuanming yuan. Le Rouge borrowed them from Swedish Count Carl Fredrik Scheffer, a significant figure in supporting the enthusiasm for China in Sweden. Scheffer became managing director of the East India Company and had probably procured the set of images thanks to his mercantile connections. Sirén, *China and Gardens of Europe,* 166–69.

62 Barrier, Mosser, and Chiu, *Aux jardins de Cathay,* 83: "Au nom d'un Chine à la fois savante, poétique et réinventée tout devient possible, même les plus grandes licences. En un mot, Cathay n'est pas seulement 'à la mode', elle est alors surtout porteuse de modernité."

63 Cibot, "Essai," 316: "Ecartons toutes les fausses idées de l'Occident sur les jardins de plaisance qui sont actuellement en Chine."

64 Hirschfeld, *Théorie,* vol. 1, 93–118.

65 Antoine-Chrysostome Quatremère de Quincy, "Chinois jardins," in *Encyclopédie méthodique: Architecture,* vol. 1 (Paris: Panckoucke, 1788), 644–53. Published between 1782 and 1832, the *Encyclopédie méthodique* was a revised version of the *Encyclopédie* edited by Denis Diderot and Jean Le Rond d'Alembert and published between 1751 and 1772.

66 Quatremère de Quincy, "Chinois jardins," 653.

67 Hunt, *Picturesque Garden,* 92–95. On the role of the Chinese garden in the theoretical debate in England see also Liu, *Seeds of a Different Eden,* 1–14; Qian Zhongshou, "China in the English Literature of the Eighteenth Century," in Hsia, *The Vision of China,* 128–32.

68 Walpole based his comment on Joseph Spence's English translation of the description of Yuanming yuan by Attiret. Horace Walpole, "On Modern Gardening," in *Anecdotes of Painting in England*, vol. 4 (Strawberry Hill: Kirgate, 1771), 134–35. Wiebenson, *The Picturesque Garden in France*, 60–61. For a comprehensive analysis of the different positions of the British authors see Liu, *Seeds of a Different Eden*, 2–41.

69 Thomas Whately, *L'art de former les jardins modernes, ou l'art des jardins anglois*, trans. François de Paul Latapie (Paris: Jombert, 1771), Discours préliminaire, iv; vj; ix: "pour ne suivre que la nature . . . la méthode la plus naturelle de composer des jardins . . . fournir une preuve complette de la parfaite ressemblance des jardins Anglois avec les jardins Chinois." The French version of Chambers's "Of the Art of Laying Out Gardens Among the Chinese" published in 1757 is on p. ix–xxiij, and a substantial part of the description of the imperial garden of Yuanming yuan written by Attiret and published in 1749 is on p. xxiij–xxxvij. Concerning the letter of Attiret, nonetheless, Latapie wrote, "Malgré tout le merveilleux qu'elle présente, je crois qu'il y aura très-peu de gens qui ne jugent que ces jardins sont trop magnifiques, et trop remplis de palais, pour que l'imagination s'y peigne une solitude. Tant de richesses étonnent plus qu'elles ne plaisent, et excluent toute idée d'un séjour de paix et de bonheur (Despite all that is marvelous that it presents, I believe that there would be very few people who do not judge that these gardens are too magnificent, and too full of palaces, for the imagination to picture solitude there. So many riches astonish more than they please, and exclude any idea of a sojourn of peace and contentment)" (Latapie, Discours, xxxvij).

70 Le Rouge, *Détails de nouveaux jardins à la mode*, cahier 5, plate 1: "tout le monde sait que les Jardins Anglais ne sont qu'une imitation de ceux de la Chine."

71 Jacques-François Blondel, *Cours d'architecture*, vol. 1 (Paris: Desaint, 1771), 150, 153: "Peuple sérieux . . . simplicité, louable sans doute, mais souvent triste et monotone . . . hommes du monde." On Blondel and his idea of Chinese and English gardens see also Wiebenson, *The Picturesque Garden in France*, 32–34.

72 Barrow, *Some Account of the Public Life*, 213.

73 John Barrow, *Travels in China* (London: T. Cadell and W. Davies, 1804), 134–35. The design similarity between English and Chinese gardens was confirmed by James Bruce, the eighth Earl of Elgin (1811–63), British high commissioner to China and commander of the English troops engaged at Beijing in the Arrow War (1856–60). Concerning Yuanming yuan he wrote: "It is really a fine thing, like an English Park." Elgin's appreciation for the imperial complex did not keep him from ordering its destruction. James Bruce, Earl of Elgin, *Extracts from the Letters of James, Earl of Elgin to Mary Louisa, Countess of Elgin, 1847–1862* (Edinburgh: Constable, 1864), 220.

74 William Marshall, *Planting and Rural Ornament*, vol. 1, 2nd ed. (London: Nicol, Robinson and Debrett, 1796), 195–96. Quoted in Conner, "China and the Landscape Garden," 429. Western observers' descriptions of Chinese gardens continued to be used in the debate about the origin of the English landscape garden that continued in the following century. In 1845, in *Kosmos*, Alexander von Humboldt confirmed the similarities of the between the Chinese and English garden traditions: "The Chinese gardens appear to have approached most nearly to what we

are now accustomed to regard as English parks." He based his discussion on Chinese garden design on the accounts by Cibot, Amiot, George Leonard Staunton, and Lord Macartney. Alexander von Humboldt, *Cosmos: Sketch of a Physical Description of the Universe*, transl. C. Otté, vol 2 (London: Bohn, 1849), 462. A few years later, in 1848, the British writer Gilbert Lewis, in his review of the first account of Robert Fortune's travels in China, rejected any idea of the Chinese origin of the English landscape garden: "But whatever aid our gardens may have received or may be destined to receive from this quarter [China] in the vegetable *matériel*, or the plants themselves, the other very improbable notion that the peculiar style of character of the English garden, as distinguished from that of the European continent, had been copied from the Chinese, is plainly without foundation." To support his argument, he offered an analysis of the descriptions of Chinese gardens by Western observers considering those compiled by the Jesuits as too vague, or too general, or too rhetorical for being relevant. Gilbert Lewis, "Fortune's China: Gardening," in *Edinburgh Review*, vol. 88 (London: Longman, Brown, Green, and Longmans, 1848), 411.

75 Jonathan D. Spence, *The Chan's Great Continent: China in Western Minds* (New York: W. W. Norton, 1998), 41–42. Chang, *Britain's Chinese Eye*, 41–42. Peter J. Kitson, *Forging Romantic China: Sino-British Cultural Exchange, 1760–1840* (Cambridge: Cambridge University Press, 2013), 13–14.

76 For a recent, important study on the Macartney embassy as an encounter between two empires see James L. Hevia, *Cherishing Men from Afar: Qing Guest Ritual and the Macartney Embassy of 1793* (Durham, N.C.: Duke University Press, 1995), chapters 3 and 4.

77 As shown by Elizabeth Hope Chang, who analyzes the role Chinese garden played as a tool to discuss the political and aesthetic differences between England and China; Chang, *Britain's Chinese Eye*, 23–70.

78 Stephen Bending, "A Natural Revolution? Garden Politics in Eighteenth-Century England," in *Refiguring Revolutions: British Politics and Aesthetics, 1642–1789*, ed. Kevin Sharpe and Steven Zwicker (Berkeley: University of California Press, 1998), 241–66.

79 Chang, *Britain's Chinese Eye*, 40–50.

80 Barrow, *Travels in China*, 135.

81 As shown in Chang, *Britain's Chinese Eye*, 40–42, 52–53.

82 Marshall, *Planting and Rural Ornament*, 195–96.

83 Castell, *The Villas of the Ancients*, 117.

84 In the first edition of the *An Encyclopaedia of Gardening* (1824) Loudon had quoted and made skeptical comments on the descriptions of those gardens given by the Jesuits Le Comte, Du Halde, and Attiret; the few lines written by the travelers Olof Torén, Sir Henry Ellis, and Peter Dobell; and the extended observations by the controversial and famous Chambers and Lord Macartney. These quotations and comments were repeated in the 1835 edition.

85 John Claudius Loudon, *An Encyclopaedia of Gardening* (London: Longman, Rees, Orme, Brown, and Green, 1835), 386.

86 Ibid., 388.

87 Clunas, "Nature and Ideology," 23–25. Clunas offers a discussion on the position of Loudon toward Chinese garden design and China.

88 George Bennett, *Wanderings in New South Wales, Batavia, Pedir Coast, Singapore and China*, vol. 2 (London: Bentley, 1834), 90.

89 Barrow, *Travels in China*, 135. A few years later, Henry Ellis (1777–1855), who in 1816 had accompanied the British diplomatic mission to the Qing court led by Lord Amherst, commented in his travel journal that "the Chinese are certainly good imitators of nature, and their piles of rocks are not liable to the same ridicule as some modern Gothic ruins in England; indeed they are works of art on so great a scale that they may well bear a rivalship with the original." Henry Ellis, *Journal of the Proceedings of the Late Embassy to China* (London: J. Murray, 1817), 286.

90 Loudon, *An Encyclopaedia of Gardening*, 386.

91 Brantz Mayer, "China and the Chinese," *Southern Quarterly Review* 23, no. 12 (1847): 18.

92 Elizabeth Hope Chang has argued that the visual devices in Chinese gardens were seen as a proof of the "divergence between British naturalism and Chinese artificiality." Chang, *Britain's Chinese Eye*, 27.

93 John Francis Davis, *Sketches of China*, vol. 2 (London: Knight and Co., 1841), 2–3. Ellis confirmed that a Chinese garden is "so disposed as to appear more extensive than it really is." Ellis, *Journal of the Proceedings*, 286.

94 Robert Fortune, *A Residence Among the Chinese* (London: J. Murray, 1857), 218.

95 See John R. Haddad, "Imagined Journeys to Distant Cathay: Constructing China with Ceramics, 1780–1920," *Winterthur Portfolio* 41, no. 1 (Spring 2007): 53–80, particularly 69–73. See also Chang, *Britain's Chinese Eye*, 71–97.

96 The American merchant Osmond Tiffany, Jr., concluding his travelogue of his sojourn in Guangzhou, wrote: "In the Arabian Tales the central flowery kingdom is considered the land of enchantments; and though I did not fall in love with a princess of China, yet to my vision there were as many wonders displayed as were unveiled by the genii of the lamp of Aladdin." Osmond Tiffany, *The Canton Chinese; or, The American's Sojourn in the Celestial Empire* (Boston: J. Munroe and Co., 1849), 271. Quoted in Haddad, "Imagined Journeys," 71. On the influence of the *Arabian Nights* in the American perception of China see Haddad, "Imagined Journeys," 70–71.

97 Mayer, "China and the Chinese," 18–19. Quoted in Haddad, "Imagined Journeys," 71.

98 Thomas, "The Looting of Yuanming," 5–7.

99 For a recent discussion on Western accounts of Yuanming yuan and its destruction, see Erik Ringmar, "Malice in Wonderland: Dreams of the Orient and Destruction of the Palace of the Emperor of China," *Journal of World History* 22, no. 2 (2011): 273–97.

100 Hevia, *English Lessons*, 74.

101 Valder, *Gardens in China*, 32 and 34–35.

102 Very short accounts, below two hundred words, are not included in the anthology as separate entries but are instead quoted in this introductory essay or in the notes accompanying some of the entries.

103 On North American perceptions of China and on accounts of China written by North American travelers see John Rogers Haddad, *The Romance of China: Excursions to China in U.S. Culture, 1776–1876* (New York: Columbia University Press, 2009).

104 Matteo Ripa, *Storia della fondazione della Congregazione e del Collegio de' Cinesi*, vol. 1 (Naples: Manfredi, 1832), 401: "Questa e tutte le altre ville di signori da me vedute, sono tutte di un medesimo gusto, tutto diverso dal nostro Europeo, poiché siccome noi qui coll'arte proccuriamo di allontanarci dal naturale, ponendo in piano le colline, disseccando le acque morte de' laghi, sbarbicando gli alberi silvestri, raddrizzando le strade . . . i Cinesi, al contrario, proccurano coll'arte imitare la natura, facendo di terra un intreccio di monticelli, e colline."

105 Johann Christian Hüttner, *Voyage à la Chine par J. C. Hüttner*, trans. T. F. Winckler (Paris: J. J. Fuchs, 1798), 41: "Les Chinois aiment, dans leurs jardins, les rochers artificiels, les petites collines, les groups d'arbres sauvages, l'eau, et les maisons situées à l'ombre." Originally written in German, Hüttner's travel account was first published in 1797: Johann Christian Hüttner, *Nachricht von der Brittischen Gesandtschaftsreise durch China und einen Theil der Tartarei* (Berlin: Voss, 1797).

106 Julius Berncastle, *A Voyage to China*, vol. 2 (London: Shoberl, 1850), 170.

107 Charles de Mutrécy, *Journal de la campagne de Chine, 1859–1860–1861*, vol. 1 (Paris: Bourdilliat, 1861), 137: "Un jardin décoré dans le goût chinois, avec des bouquets d'arbres, des grottes, des montagnes en miniature, des défilés, des lacs et autres merveilles d'une nature artificielle."

108 Laurence Oliphant, *Narrative of the Earl of Elgin's Mission to China and Japan in the Years 1857, '58, '59*, vol. 1 (Edinburgh: Blackwood and Sons, 1859), 181 and 161.

109 Ibid., 161.

110 Laugier wrote, "I wish the author of the pretty description had given us the actual plan of this delightful country seat which, no doubt, could serve us as a good model." Laugier, *Essay on Architecture*, 139.

CHAPTER 1

Marco Polo (c. 1254–1324)

The Venetian merchant and explorer Marco Polo was to become the emblematic figure of a traveler. His widely read *Book of the Marvels of the Modern World* (later known in English as *The Travels of Marco Polo*), a geographical description of Far Eastern countries and the regions of the Mongol Empire presented as a travel account, influenced European knowledge of China for centuries.[1] Polo's book was still being used in the late eighteenth century as an essential reference by Western travelers undertaking the long journey to China.[2]

Polo spent seventeen years, from 1275 to 1292, working as an imperial officer in Mongol China. The work was probably written in 1298, when Polo was imprisoned in Genoa along with his companion in misfortune Rustichello (or Rusticiano) da Pisa; it originated in the account Polo made to Rustichello of his 1271 journey to reach the court of Kublai Khan (r. 1260–94), the first ruler of the Yuan dynasty (1271–1368), of his experience of Asia during the period of 1271 to 1295, and of his long, adventurous residence in China.[3] The encounter of the two men from very different backgrounds—Marco Polo, a merchant and traveler, and Rustichello, an author of courtly romance—produced a work in which information about the geography and characteristics of the countries Polo traversed in an effort to reach "Cathay" were enriched by observations about local products, customs and uses, famous people, and historical events, along with anecdotes. The outcome was a sort of guide to medieval Asia that was both fed by and fed into the late medieval Europe collective imagination, giving substance to the notion of a fabled Orient, which remained rooted in European culture for many years to come. Starting with Polo's narrative, based on the things "he saw . . . with his own eyes" and on what "he heard from men of credit and veracity,"[4] Rustichello composed the text in an archaic French mixed in with Venetian and Italian terms, enriching the literary style of Polo's descriptions.[5] The use of that mixed language from trade and romance suggests a conscious intent to reach a wider audience; and this is exactly what happened. Under various titles, such as *Le devisement du monde*, *Le livre des merveilles du monde*, and *Il milione*, the work was immensely successful from the beginning of the fourteenth century and was circulated in many languages, in more or less faithful translations.

Marco Polo was the first Westerner to mention the gardens of China. The following two extracts, taken from the 1871 English translation of Polo's travelogue by the Scottish Orientalist Henry Yule, contain his short accounts of the imperial complex in Shangdu, the Mongolian upper capital, and of the imperial park Kublai Khan constructed in Dadu (Great Capital), the new city he built on the site of what is now Beijing.[6] These first fragmentary descriptions are influenced by European medieval garden culture. Polo's presentation of the imperial parks as large wooded precincts, populated with wild and tame animals, with fish pools and fountains, recalls the Western courtly hunting preserves. At the same time, Kublai Khan's parks, as described by Polo, appear as symbolic microcosms, a well-tended nature with an abundance of water, a variety of animals and plants from distant places, thus evoking the Middle Age topos of the Garden of Eden, which, according to medieval lore, was hidden in some remote place in the Orient. Polo's descriptions of Kublai Khan's parks became the Europeans' primary source of knowledge of the gardens in China and informed the sparse commentary about Chinese gardens in later medieval travel literature. Both the Franciscan missionary Odorico da Pordenone, in the narrative of his travels through Asia compiled in the 1330s, and John Mandeville, in his popular fictional descriptions of the Orient written around 1356, based their short accounts of imperial parks of China on those compiled by Polo.[7]

Polo was the first Western traveler who perceived the Chinese ability to contrive the forms of the natural landscape in the artificial context of a park. In describing the hilly, wooded island that Kublai Khan had built in the western part of Dadu with the material excavated in enlarging an artificial lake, Polo began a long tradition of accounts emphasizing the artificially natural quality common to Chinese gardens.

* * *

From *The Book of Ser Marco Polo, the Venetian, Concerning the Kingdoms and Marvels of the East*, translated and edited by Henry Yule, vol. 1 (1871)

OF THE CITY OF CHANDU [SHANGDU], AND THE KAAN'S PALACE THERE

And when you have ridden three days from the city last mentioned,[8] between north-east and north, you come to a city called Chandu, which was built by the Kaan [Khan] now reigning. There is at this place a very fine marble Palace, the rooms of which are all gilt and painted with figures of men and beasts and birds, and with a variety of trees and flowers, all executed with such exquisite art that you regard them with delight and astonishment.

Round this Palace a wall is built, inclosing a compass of 16 miles, and inside the Park there are fountains and rivers and brooks, and beautiful meadows, with all kinds of wild animals (excluding such as are of ferocious nature), which the Emperor has procured and placed there to supply food for his gerfalcons and hawks, which he keeps there in mew. Of these there are more than 200 gerfalcons alone, and without reckoning the other hawks. The Kaan himself goes every week to see his birds sitting in mew, and sometimes he rides through the park with a leopard behind him on his horse's croup; and then if he sees any animal that takes his fancy, he slips his leopard at it, and the game when taken is made over to feed the hawks in mew. This he does for diversion.

CONCERNING THE PALACE OF THE GREAT KAAN

Between the two walls of the enclosure which I have described, there are fine Parks and beautiful trees bearing a variety of fruits. There are beasts also of sundry kinds, such as white stags and fallow deer, gazelles and roebucks, and fine squirrels of various sorts, with numbers also of the animal that gives the musk, and all manner of other beautiful creatures, insomuch that the whole place is full of them, and no spot remains void except where there is traffic of people going and coming. The parks are covered with abundant grass; and the roads through them being all paved and raised two cubits above the surface, they never become muddy, nor does the rain lodge on them, but flows off into the meadows, quickening the soil and producing that abundance of herbage.

From that corner of the enclosure which is towards the north-west there extends a fine Lake, containing foison of fish of different kinds which the Emperor hath caused to be put in there, so that whenever he desires any he can have them at his pleasure. A River enters this Lake and issues from it, but there is a grating of iron or brass put up so that the fish cannot escape in that way.

Moreover on the north side of the Palace, about a bow-shot off, there is a hill which has been made by art from the earth dug from the Lake; it is a good hundred paces in height and a mile in compass. This hill is entirely covered with trees that never lose their leaves, but remain ever green. And I assure you that wherever a beautiful tree may exist, and the Emperor gets news of it, he sends for it and has it transported bodily with all its roots and the earth attached to them, and planted on that hill of his. No matter how big the tree may be, he gets it carried by his elephants; and in this way he has got together the most beautiful collection of trees in all the world. And he has also caused the whole hill to be covered with the ore of azure, which is very green. And thus not only are the trees all green, but the hill itself is all green likewise; and there is nothing to be seen on it that is not green; and hence it is called the GREEN MOUNT; and in good sooth 'tis named well.

On the top of the hill again there is a fine big palace which is all green inside and out; and thus the hill, and the trees, and the palace form together a charming spectacle; and it is marvellous to see their uniformity of colour! Everybody who sees them is delighted. And the Great Kaan had caused this beautiful prospect to be formed for the comfort and solace and delectation of his heart.

You must know that beside the Palace (that we have been describing) *i.e.* the Great Palace, the Emperor has caused another to be built just like his own in every respect, and this he hath done for his son when he shall reign and be Emperor after him. Hence it is made just in the same fashion and of the same size, so that everything can be carried on in the same manner after his own death. It stands on the other side of the Lake from the Great Kaan's Palace, and there is a bridge crossing the water from one to the other.

NOTES

1   On the role Marco Polo's book played in European knowledge of Far East Asia's geography, see John Larner, *Marco Polo and the Discovery of the World* (New Haven, Conn.: Yale University Press, 1999). To define Polo's book, Larner uses the term "chorography." For a recent study of Marco Polo's book and its reception see Suzanne Conklin Akbari and Amilcare Iannucci (eds.), *Marco Polo and the Encounter of East and West* (Toronto: University of Toronto Press, 2008).

2   In his travel account of the British Embassy to China led by Lord George Macart-
     ney in 1792–94, George Leonard Staunton refers to Marco Polo as "the first
     European who published any account of that empire [China]" and shows deep
     knowledge of his book. George Leonard Staunton, *An Authentic Account of an
     Embassy*, vol. 1 (London: Nicol, 1797), 454; vol. 2 (London: Nicol, 1797), 42;
     184–85, 514.

3   Spence, *The Chan's Great Continent*, 1.

4   Marco Polo, *The Book of Ser Marco Polo, the Venetian, Concerning the Kingdoms
     and Marvels of the East*, trans. and ed. Henry Yule, vol. 1 (London: John Murray,
     1871), 1.

5   On the language in Marco Polo's book and the role of both Polo and Rustichello
     in the development of the book, the sources I have relied on are Jennifer Robin
     Goodman, *Chivalry and Exploration, 1298–1630* (Woodbridge: Boydell Press,
     1998), 83–103; and F. Regina Psaki, "The Book's Two Fathers: Marco Polo, Rus-
     tichello da Pisa, and *Le Devisement du Monde*," *Mediaevalia* 32 (2011): 69–97.
     For a more recent philological study see Simon Gaunt, *Marco Polo's "Le Devise-
     ment du Monde": Narrative Voice, Language and Diversity* (Cambridge: Brewer,
     2013).

6   When Kublai Khan decided to move his capital city to Dadu, Shangdu became
     his summer capital. On Kublai Khan's Dadu see Nancy Shatzman Steinhardt,
     Chinese Imperial City Planning (Honolulu: University of Hawaii Press, 1990),
     154–60.

7   For the descriptions of the imperial parks by Odorico da Pordenone and Mande-
     ville see Odorico da Pordenone, *The Travels of Friar Odoric*, trans. Henry Yule
     (Grand Rapids, Mich.: W. B. Eerdmans, 2002), 136; John Mandeville, *Mandeville's
     Travels*, ed. Maurice Charles Seymour (London: Oxford University Press, 1968),
     163.

8   A city called "Chagannor" by Polo.

CHAPTER 2

200 yrs later

Matteo Ricci (1552–1610)

Matteo Ricci was the earliest Western traveler to present the complexity of the Chinese gardens' spatial composition. One of the founders of the Jesuit mission in China, Ricci reached Ming China in 1582 and remained there until his death in 1610, in Beijing. During the later years of his life, Ricci was dedicated to the compilation of his journals, in which a report about the beginning and progress of the Jesuit mission in China was accompanied by an account of Chinese culture and customs. Ricci's unfinished manuscript, entitled *Della entrata della Compagnia di Giesù e Christianità nella Cina*, was integrated and edited by the Belgian Jesuit missionary Nicolas Trigault (1577–1628), who brought Ricci's journal to Europe on his way back from China, translated it into Latin, and published it with the title *De Christiana expeditione apud Sinas* (1615).[1] Within a few years, Trigault's work underwent numerous editions and translations that made it accessible to a wider public, contributing decisively to the European image of China in the seventeenth century.[2]

This work includes the extract presented here: Ricci's brief account of a garden in Nanjing belonging to Xu Hongji, duke of Weiguo, which the Jesuit visited in 1599. The garden to which Ricci referred has never been identified more specifically. It has, in any case, long since disappeared, along with the other historical gardens that formed the rich heritage of Nanjing, which had served as the imperial capital city numerous times and was as many times destroyed. The description, however, suggests that the garden was (or included) a rock garden, dominated by a rockwork arranged to convey the idea of a mountainous landscape. A notable surviving example of this compositional formula is the garden Shizi lin (Lion Grove) in Suzhou, which today still presents all the elements Ricci noted in the private Ming garden in Nanjing: ponds, trees, pavilions, and elaborated artificial hills. Just as in the garden sketched by Ricci, in Shizi lin the artificial rocky landscape, traversed by an intricate network of paths, helps dissimulate the distinct functional areas of the garden and their concatenation.³

In addition to seeing the evocation of a mountainous landscape in Xu Hongji's garden, Ricci perceives the role of the paths in concealing the real dimension of the garden and in distorting the visitor's perception of space. The Jesuit describes the structure of the garden as labyrinthine, suggesting not only the able manipulation of space and a general sense of irregularity, but also an intriguing sense of playfulness, surprise, and variety that the garden prompted.⁴ Regarding the idea of space that it implied, Ricci's choice of the labyrinth as a key to interpreting the compositional mechanism of the Chinese garden was adopted by subsequent Western travelers in describing the gardens of China, testimony to the role that Ricci's short account had in terms of future reference.⁵

*   *   *

From Nicolas Trigault, *De Christiana expeditione apud Sinas* (1615), translated by Bianca Maria Rinaldi

The head of this family in Nanking [Nanjing] is the only one distinguished by the splendor in which he lives.⁶ Each time he leaves his residence he is carried in an open chair on the shoulders of eight porters; he possesses gardens, palaces, furniture, all regal things. This man one day invited Padre Matteo to his house after having sent his paternal uncle to pay him a visit. When he went there, he greeted him in the most beautiful garden of the whole city. In that garden, leaving aside many other things which cannot be seen nor perhaps described without pleasure,⁷ he saw an artificial mount made of various rough stones, which was artfully excavated into grottos, and contained chambers, rooms, stairs, fish ponds, trees, and many other things where art competed with pleasure. [The Chinese] do all this for the purpose of evading the summer heat in cool grottos, when they are working hard studying or organizing banquets. Its gracefulness was accentuated by its labyrinthine form: in fact, even though it occupies an area which is not too extensive, someone wanting to go through it all needed two or three hours, coming out then through another door.

Figure 1. Frontispiece of Athanasius Kircher, *China monumentis . . . illustrata* (Amsterdam: van Waesberge and Weyerstraet, 1667). Biblioteca Mozzi-Borgetti, Macerata.

NOTES

1   Nicolas Trigault, *De Christiana expeditione apud Sinas suscepta a Societate Jesu, ex P. Matthaei Riccii eiusdem Societatis commentariis Libri V* (Augsburg: Mangius, 1615).

2   Trigault's book was reprinted four times between 1616 and 1684 and reissued in several European languages: French (1616, republished twice in 1617 and 1618), German (1617), Spanish (1621), and Italian (1622). A partial English version appeared in Samuel Purchas, *Hakluytus Posthumus or Purchas His Pilgrimes* (1625). An unabridged English translation of Trigault's book was published in 1953: *China in the Sixteenth Century: The Journals of Matthew Ricci, 1583–1610*, trans. Louis J. Gallagher (New York: Random House, 1953). See David E. Mungello, *Curious Land: Jesuit Accommodation and the Origins of Sinology* (Honolulu: University of Hawaii Press, 1989), 48. For a comprehensive discussion of *De Christiana expeditione apud Sinas* see Mungello, *Curious Land*, 46–49.

3   Designed in the fourteenth century during the Yuan dynasty, Shizi lin was originally part of an adjacent temple and was renowned for its fantastically shaped rocks. Following his first visit to the garden in 1757, during his second inspection tour in southern China, the Qianlong emperor used Shizi lin as model for two rocky gardens constructed within his northern imperial parks. The first one was completed around 1772 in the section of Yuanming yuan (Garden of Perfect Brightness) called Changchun yuan (Garden of Everlasting Spring), in the outskirts of Beijing; a second replica of Shizi lin was built in 1774 within Bishu shanzhuang (Mountain Estate to Escape the Summer Heat), in Chengde. Often altered in the course of the centuries, the original Shizi lin was bought in 1917 by the family of the Sino-American architect I. M. Pei and restored by them until 1926. Some features of the garden date to that period. Shizi lin was opened to the public in 1954. Since 2000, it has been registered as a UNESCO World Heritage Site. Bianca Maria Rinaldi, *The Chinese Garden: Garden Types for Contemporary Landscape Architecture* (Basel: Birkhäuser, 2011), 147.

4   The 1625 English translation of Trigault's book omitted the reference to a labyrinth. See Samuel Purchas, *Hakluytus Posthumus or Purchas His Pilgrimes: Containing a History of the World in Sea Voyages and Lande Travells by Englishmen and Others*, vol. 12 (Glasgow: MacLehose and Sons, 1906; first edition 1625), 323.

5   In his detailed treatise on Chinese geography, the Jesuit Martino Martini faithfully transcribed Ricci's description of the Chinese garden included in Trigault's volume. See Martino Martini, *Novus atlas sinensis* (Amsterdam: Blaeu, 1655), 31. The Dutch emissary Johannes Nieuhof associated Chinese gardens and labyrinths. See Johannes Nieuhof, *Het gezantschap der Neêrlandtsche Oost-Indische Compagnie, ann den grooten Tartarischen Cham* (Amsterdam: Jacob van Meurs, 1665), 178. The Jesuit Jean-Baptiste Du Halde, who never visited China, clearly took Ricci's general outline of the garden in Nanjing as a reference when writing that the rock compositions which characterized Chinese gardens were crossed by intricate paths "parcées de tous côtez, avec divers détours, en forme de labyrinthes, pour y prendres le frais" (with several deviations in the form of labyrinths where

one could enjoy the cool air). Jean-Baptiste Du Halde, *Description . . . de la Chine*, vol. 2 (Paris: Le Mercier, 1735), 85. In his account of the last Dutch embassy to the Qing court, which took place in the years 1794 and 1795, André Everard van Braam Houckgeest linked the concept of a labyrinth with the way the different buildings were distributed and connected in the gardens. See André Everard van Braam Houckgeest, *An Authentic Account of the Dutch East-India Embassy*, vol. 2 (London: R. Phillips, 1798), 8. Antoine Julien Fauchery who, in 1860, followed the French military expedition to China during the Arrow War as a writer and photographer, used the metaphor of the labyrinth in a derogatory way. He wrote that in the imperial park of Yuanming yuan the endless waterways were like a "labyrinthe aquatique" (aquatic labyrinth) whose effect is "plus étrange que pittoseque" (stranger than the picturesque). Antoine Julien Fauchery, "Lettres de Chine," *Le Moniteur universel* 362, December 28 (1860): 1534, quoted and translated in Thomas, "The Looting of Yuanming." A later use of the metaphor of the labyrinth was given by the field marshal Garnet Joseph Wolseley, who served in the British forces during the Arrow War. He likened the garden paths in Yuanming yuan to a maze, writing that walking in that imperial park, "you then found yourself in a labyrinth of neatly laid out walks." Garnet Joseph Wolseley, *A Narrative of the War with China in 1860* (London: Longman, Green, Longman, and Roberts, 1862), 235.

6   Ricci refers to Xu Hongji (?–1643), who had inherited the title of Weiguo gong of the city of Nanjing in 1595. Matteo Ricci, *Della entrata della Compagnia di Giesù e Cristianità nella Cina*, ed. Maddalena Del Gatto (Macerata: Quodlibet, 2001), 307.

7   Trigault's text, in this part, is less detailed than the original manuscript in which Matteo Ricci writes that in the garden of Xu Hongji, one had to pass through "the hall, chambers, loggias, towers, courtyards and other magnificent edifices" before reaching the "hill of stone made artificially." Ricci, *Della entrata . . . nella Cina*, 307.

CHAPTER 3

Álvaro Semedo (1585/1586–1658)

The two passages that follow are from the 1655 English version of one of the first and most successful works promulgating China and the Jesuit mission there: the *Imperio de la China* (1642), written by the Portuguese Álvaro Semedo.[1] Semedo reached Nanjing in 1613, during the last years of the reign of the Wanli emperor (r. 1572–1620), thirteenth ruler of the Ming dynasty, but stayed mainly in the southern part of China and died in Guangzhou. His work is a general description of the Chinese empire narrated through a series of thematic chapters and focusing on various aspects of Chinese culture, including government and religion, language and literature, and the arts and sciences. The piece concludes with chapters about the history and progress of the Jesuit mission in China.[2]

Semedo's brief accounts of the gardens of China focus on both those in private residences and the green spaces scattered throughout the imperial palaces in Nanjing and Beijing. The emphasis on the presence of artificial mountains and on the effort to construct them places Semedo's observations in the tradition that began with Marco Polo, who highlighted the crafted natural appearance of the Chinese garden.[3] Semedo's descriptions are also reminiscent of Polo's text in his reference to the presence within the garden of live animals, both domestic and wild, which provided amusement and intensified the natural quality of the garden.

* * *

From Álvaro Semedo, *The History of That Great and Renowned Monarchy of China* (1655)

The houses, where they inhabit, are not so sumptuous and lasting, as ours: yet are they more convenient for the good contrivance, and more pleasant for the exquisite neatnesse. They use much in their houses *Charam*, an excellent varnish, and painting of an accurate diligence. They build them not very high, esteeming them more convenient for being low, as well for habitation, as for good accommodation. The richer sort of people doe plant the courts and approaches to their houses with flowers and small trees; and, towards the North, they use fruit trees. In like manner, where they have room enough, they set greater trees, and raise artificiall mountaines; to which end they bring from farre, great pieces of rocks. They keep there severall sorts of fowl; as Cranes and Swannes, and other beautifull birds, and also wild beasts, as Stagges, and fallow Deare. They make many fish-ponds, where are to be seen gliding up and downe painted fish with gilded finns, and other things likewise of curiositie and delight.

All the rest of his time he [the Wanli emperor] staieth at home in his *Palace*, like a King of Bees, without either seeing or being seen. Many are perswaded, that this is not to live like a King, but like a criminall Person condemned to perpetuall imprisonment. How ever, it seemeth to me a great matter, that a man, without being seen, by his power only should be the most reverenced, the most obeyed and feared, of all the Kings in the world. And as for the prison, if we will call his *Palace* so, it is very large and pleasant for to give him delight, besides that he hath the libertie to go out whensoever he pleaseth, and his habitations therein are so commodious, and full of all manner of entertainment, of pleasure and recreation, that he hath no need to seek abroad wherewith to content himself.

His *Palaces*, laying every thing together that is contained in them, I think are the best that are to be found in the world. Those of *Nankim* [Nanjing], which are the biggest, containe about five miles in circuit. Those of *Pekim* [Beijing], are somewhat lesse, but much the better. These are not all one *Palace*, but many, at a good distance from the other. . . . The structure of the *Palaces* is very exact, having many things in it after the manner of ours, as *Arches*, *Balausters*, *Columnes* and, such like, of Marble excellently wrought, with severall little works and curious enrichments, as also embossements, or figures in *relieve*, so well raised and standing out, that they seem to hang in the aire. That which is wrought in wood, is all varnished over with their *Charam*, painted and guilded very exquisitely.

The *Halls* and Roomes, although they are not, as it is here reported, one of Gold, another of Silver, another of precious stones, neither do they use hangings; yet the hand of the Architect, and the pensil of the painter doth supply all other ornaments. The Base Courts are very neat and spacious. There are also many pleasant Gardens, and a River which runneth among the *Palaces*, and yeeldeth them much delight with his windings and turnings. There are many artificiall mounts with very rare Beasts and Birds, many Gardens made of exquisite diligence, and all manner of curiositie. There was a certaine King among them, who being discontented at the spoile which the winter made in the beauty of the trees, depriving them both of leaves and flowers, commanded that many artificiall ones should be made, with great labour and expence, and little satisfaction of the Magistrates, who did much blame him.

The whole fabrique is encompassed with two walls that have foure gates opening to the foure windes, *East, West, North, and South,* and this last is the chiefest, and maketh a beautifull and sightly *facciata* or aspect to the *Palaces*.

NOTES

1   Álvaro Semedo, *The History of That Great and Renowned Monarchy of China* (London: E. Tyler, 1655). Semedo's work, written in Portuguese in 1640, was printed for the first time in 1641 and then in 1642 with the title *Relaçao de fé regno da China e outros adjacentes*. A Spanish translation was published in 1642 with the title *Imperio de la China*; an Italian version was published in 1643, a French one in 1645, and an English translation appeared in 1655. The frontispiece of the 1655 edition reads: "put into English by a Person of quality." Mungello, *Curious Land*, 75.

2   Mungello, *Curious Land*, 74–76.

3   Two other Jesuit missionaries in China, the Italian Martino Martini and the Portuguese Gabriel de Magalhães, appreciated the natural appearance of Chinese gardens. In their accounts of China written in the mid-seventeenth century, they provided intriguing descriptions of the compositions of rocks and rough stones arranged to resemble natural mountains. In his description of the imperial palace in Beijing, Martini wrote of a "palatium permeat fluvius arte introductus magnarum etiam navium patiens, per interiores palatii partes in varios distributus canales ad comoda domestica, ac amoenitatem. Multos his illic lambit artifice manu exstructos montes, qui veris ipsis invidiam quodammodo ob artis praestantiam facere possint, qua in re Sinae mire sunt curiosi, ut ne dicam superstiziosi: hos ex ruderibus pulcherrime efformant, ad intuentium voluptatem ac admirationem: arbores floresque in iis cinserunt raro ordine ac eleganza" (a river introduced artificially, in which boats can navigate, crosses through the palace; it branches into various canals within the different parts of the palace for domestic necessities and for pleasure. These [canals] lap at many mountains, raised by skilled hand, which can arouse envy among the real ones for the quality of the

craft [with which they are built]. In such things, the Chinese are extraordinarily accurate . . . they shape these [mountains] beautifully, with regard to delight and surprise, and tastefully surround them with scattered trees and flowers). Martino Martini, *Novus atlas sinensis* (Amsterdam: Blaeu, 1655), 31. Martini was certainly influenced by Ricci, whose description of the rock garden in Nanjing he reported fully in his work. Magalhães described a temple in the Imperial City built "upon a Mountain made with hands like a Sugarloaf environ'd with Rocks which were brought thither in former times from the Sea side, though far remote, with great labour and expence. These Rocks are for the most part full of holes and hollownesses, occasion'd by the continual dashing of the waves; the *Chineses* taking great delight to behold those unpolish'd works of nature. And they are so dispos'd as to counterfeit the high out-juttings, and steep and rugged Precipices of Rocks; so that at a moderate distance the whole seems to represent some craggy wild Mountain, the first work of Nature." Gabriel de Magalhães, *A New History of China . . .* (London: Newborough, 1688), 324–25.

CHAPTER 4

Johannes Nieuhof (1618–72) Dutch

The Dutch emissary Johannes Nieuhof, as a steward, accompanied the first Dutch embassy to the Qing court, a journey undertaken during the years 1655–57 for the purpose of developing trade relations between the Dutch East India Company and China.[1] That mission resulted in a travel account with rich illustrations, entitled *Het gezantschap der Neërlandtsche Oost-Indische Compagnie, ann den grooten Tartarischen Cham, den tegenwoordigen Keizer van China* (1665), which became a great editorial success.[2] Nieuhof's evocative descriptions of the country, together with the numerous copperplates accompanying the volume representing landscapes, cityscapes, architecture, and costumes, as well as Chinese plants and animals, were influential in shaping the perception of China in seventeenth-century Europe. The engravings had been commissioned by the publisher Jacob van Meurs to make the work more appealing to the European public and more marketable, and were based on sketches produced by Nieuhof during the voyage. They depict fantasy scenes placed in a pictorial framework of palms and pagodas, according to a formula that the European public recognized as a representation of faraway, exotic lands.[3]

The book was based upon the notes that Nieuhof took during the journey to compile a report for the Company directors and was augmented with information on China as drawn from Jesuit sources.[4] The observations of Chinese gardens contained in Nieuhof's travelogue seem to reveal this hybridization. The following text, taken from the first English version of Nieuhof's account, published in 1669, is an extract of the description of the Imperial City in Beijing, concluding with some notes on the gardens of China. Nieuhof's comments recall Matteo Ricci's description of the garden in Nanjing and Martino Martini's outline of the green spaces within the imperial palace in Beijing.[5] Like Ricci and Martini, Nieuhof considered the most relevant characteristic of the Chinese garden to be the artificial hills,

Figure 2. *Clippen door Const gemaakt, Rupes arte factae* (Mountain made by art). In Johannes Nieuhof, *Legatio batavica ad magnum Tartariae chamum Sungteium, modernum Sinae imperatorem*, trans. Georg Horn (Amsterdam: Jacob Van Meurs, 1668), p. 73. Biblioteca Mozzi-Borgetti, Macerata.

carefully designed to evoke a natural mountain landscape. Showing his appreciation for the skills necessary to obtain such a contrivance, Nieuhof wrote that in the design of these artificial rocky mountains in Chinese gardens, "Art seems to exceed Nature."

*　*　*

From Johannes Nieuhof, *An Embassy from the East-India Company of the United Provinces, to the Great Tartar Cham, Emperor of China*, translated by John Ogilby (1669)

This Imperial Court, which is exactly square, contains three miles in circumference, within the second Wall of the City on the North side, being fortified also with strong stone Battlements fifteen foot high; in this Wall are four Gates, (in the middle of each side one) which have their Prospects toward the four Angles of the world, and so named after the four Cardinal winds; but that which stands toward the South, is the chiefest and most used. We past, from thence into a Base Court, which had a well paved cross way of 400 paces, with a Water-Trench cut through the middle, and over a stone bridge of fourteen paces, very curiously built, but the water was in some places covered over with weeds. Before this Graff or Channel stands also drawn up upon the Plain, a great number of *Tartars*, Horse and Foot, who as Sentinel, suffer none to pass through; when you are over the Bridge you come to the first Gate, guarded with three Black Elephants; through this Porch, being fifty paces long, and built upon five stately Arches, you come into the first quadrangle, which is also 400 paces large, and whither we were brought by *Pinxenton*[6] (as hath been already said) to expect with the other Embassadours the coming of the Emperor. This Plaino [*sic*] is well built with uniform and stately houses, standing amidst three more lofty and fortified Edifices, which are so strong with thick Walls and Bulwarks, that they are able to defend the place. From this Court there are passages underneath the three great Structures, which leads into a second quadrangle also 400 paces wide, built and adorned with brave buildings as the former; from hence you pass into the third and last Plain, also square, and of the same bigness with the former; this quadrangle which lyes directly in the Cross, and paved with Grey stone, the Great *Cham* chose himself for his own Residence. Here also are most sumptuous and costly Buildings, but the chiefest among these are four, which exceed all the rest in Magnificence, Art, and Beauty, and take up as least a third part of the three sides of the Court.

Directly forward appears the Building, where his Imperial Majesty sat upon his Throne, and which are far more stately and sumptuous then the former, into which you enter through three ample and curious Arches. In this third Court reside only the Emperour and Empress, and none is permitted to enter here but their Attendants.

The Emperour, according to the custom of the Heathen Princes, maintains several Women in this his Seraglio; but amongst all those only one assumes the Title of Empress, all the rest are his Concubines, performing duties in several degrees; these wait on the King himself, other look to the keeping of Rooms and Chambers decent and clean; some take care of the Children, and these only of the Emperours Bed-chamber, his Kitchen, and Table: of these Concubines in their several Attendancies are at least five thousand, most of them no more than Maid-servants.

Such shews this Palace within, if you go through the South Gate strait to the third Plaino, or the Emperours abode; the same Courts, and as many appear, going through the other Gates with all such buildings and adornments; for the whole circumference of the Court, is cut through in the middle in the form of a Cross, and in several places equally and orderly divided. Without the third Plain, which lyes in the middle of the Court, and upon which stand the Emperours Buildings, are several pleasant Gardens, Palaces, Woods, Pools, Rivers, and delicate Summer-Houses, which the Emperour caused to be made for his Pleasure; and each is so large, that it is fit enough for any Prince to live in; so that this his Palace contains several Courts for Kings within the Walls. . . .

Beside the above-mentioned Channel or Graff, which is very shallow and grown over with Weeds; there is yet another in this Palace, which runs through the whole Court, with several windings and turnings, and serves to water the Gardens and Woods. This receives its water from the River *Yo*, which springs from a Pool called *Si*, near to the Mountain *Faciven*,[7] and is within the Emperours Court so broad and deep, that it will bear great Vessels which come laden in, to the great convenience of the Inhabitants. This River sends also in its Streams to such Rocks or Cliffs made by Art, whereof we formerly mentioned. There is not any thing wherein the *Chineses* shew their Ingenuity more, then in these Rocks or Artificial Hills, which are so curiously wrought, that Art seems to exceed Nature. These Cliffs are made of a sort of Stone, and sometimes of Marble, and so rarely adorned with Trees and Flowers, that all that see them are surprized with admiration. Rich and Wealthy People, especially the great Lords and *Mandorines*, have for the most part such Rocks in their Courts and Palaces, upon which they squander good part of their Estates. It was told me of a certainty, that somewhere about *Peking* there are some Rocks, which contain Chambers, Closets, Parlours, Vyvers [fishponds],[8] and all manner of Trees so curiously wrought and adorned by Art, that the like is not to be seen in the whole world.[9] These Artificial Mountains or Cliffs are commonly contrived with Chambers and Anti-chambers, for a defence against the scorching heat in Summer,[10] and to refresh and delight the Spirits; for they commonly make their great entertainments on these Grots, and the Learned seek to study in them rather than any other place.[11]

If I should relate all the other Artificial Ornaments, as of Gardens, Wildernesses, Pools, and other particulars which adorn this Court, I should far exceed the bounds of what I intend, and perhaps to some of belief; this shall only suffice to set forth the wonders of this most Magnificent Palace.

Great endeavours were used by me to observe what was most remarkable and worth taking notice of, as far as the shortness of our stay would permit, especially concerning its situation.

NOTES ― Useful .

1 The embassy, led by Peter de Goyer and Jacob de Keyzer, was received in Beijing in 1656. The Dutch never managed to establish a regular direct trade with mainland China. In 1624 they were permitted to reside on Taiwan but their very limited trading privileges were revoked in 1666, and in 1668 the Dutch abandoned their last outpost in Taiwan. John E. Wills, Jr., *Embassies and Illusions: Dutch and Portuguese Envoys to K'ang-hsi, 1666–1687* (Cambridge, Mass.: Council on East Asian Studies, Harvard University, 1984), 38–82.

2 Johannes Nieuhof, *Het gezantschap der Neërlandtsche Oost-Indische Compagnie, ann den grooten Tartarischen Cham* . . . (Amsterdam: Jacob van Meurs, 1665). The volume was translated into the main European languages: a French translation was published in Leiden in 1665, a German one in Amsterdam in 1666, with a Latin one following in 1668. Two versions in English were published by John Ogilby (1600–76), "King's Cosmographer and Geographic Printer" under Charles II, in London in 1669 and 1673.

3 For a study of the illustrations in Nieuhof's travelogue, see Friederike Ulrichs, *Johan Nieuhofs Blick auf China (1655–1657): Die Kupferstiche in seinem Chinabuch und ihre Wirkung auf den Verleger Jacob van Meurs* (Wiesbaden: Harrassowitz, 2003); Leonard Blussé and R. Falkenburg, *Johan Nieuhofs beelden van een Chinareis 1655–1657* (Middelburg: Stichting VOC Publicaties, 1987); and also Jing Sun, "The Illusion of Verisimilitude: Johan Nieuhof's Images of China" (Ph.D. diss., Leiden University, 2013).

4 Donald F. Lach and Edwin J. Van Kley, *Asia in the Making of Europe*, vol. 3, *A Century of Advance*, book 1, *Trade, Missions, Literature* (Chicago: University of Chicago Press, 1993), 483.

5 For Martini's text see note 3 to the extract by Álvaro Semedo presented in this anthology.

6 A mandarin accompanying the Dutch embassy.

7 The mountain is named Jociven in the original Dutch version. Nieuhof, *Het gezantschap der Neërlandtsche Oost-Indische Compagnie*, 173.

8 The second edition of the English version, translated by John Ogilby and published in London in 1673, adds "stairs" to this list of elements that compose the artificial rocks. Johannes Nieuhof, *An Embassy from the East-India Company of the United Provinces, to the Grand Tartar Cham, Emperor of China* (London: Printed by the author, 1673), 122.

9 The original Dutch version presents a more emphatic comment on the beauty and uniqueness of the artificial mountains, comparing them to artistic productions in Europe: "'t welk alles zo net en kunstig gemaakt was, dat de treffelijkste kunststukken der schranderste Europische kunstenaars, by deze Sineesche kunst-werken geenzins halen mochten" (Everything is so beautifully made and so aesthetically pleasing, that similar works of art by the most ingenious European artists are

inferior to these Chinese works of art). Nieuhof, *Het gezantschap der Neërlandt-sche Oost-Indische Compagnie*, 178.

10 The original Dutch version adds here: "en steeken der Zonne" (and the sting of the sun). Nieuhof, *Het gezantschap der Neërlandtsche Oost-Indische Compagnie*, 178.

11 The original Dutch version presents at this point another comment on the complexity of Chinese gardens and, especially, of the structure of the artificial mountains: "In zommige zijn ook heele Dool-hoven gemaakt, die dikwils met hunne ommewegen en dwaal-paden zo verre en krom omlopen, dat men drie uuren aan 't omdoolen van doen heft" (In some of these [rocks], entire labyrinths are also made, complicated by so many turnings, that with difficulty you can walk through them in three hours of time). Nieuhof, *Het gezantschap der Neërlandtsche Oost-Indische Compagnie*, 178. This comment was omitted by John Ogilby, both in the first English version of Nieuhof's work (1669) and in the second (1673). It did appear in the French version (Leiden: Jacob van Meurs, 1665, 217) and in the Latin (Amsterdam: Jacob van Meurs, 1668, 159), while it was omitted in the German edition (1666).

*more from —
1600 s —
chronological*

Jean-François Gerbillon (1654–1707)

Jean-François Gerbillon was one of the first six French Jesuits who, given the formal title of "Mathématiciens du Roy," were sent to China by Louis XIV in 1687 to establish a French China mission.[1] Promoted by the minister Jean-Baptiste Colbert, who aimed at increasing France's political and colonial prestige internationally, the French Jesuit mission was established in Beijing in 1688 with the task of spreading the Catholic faith, as well as facilitating the development of diplomatic and commercial relations between France and China. The "Mathématiciens du Roy" were also to work as corresponding members for the newly established Académie Royale des Sciences in Paris, which had provided the Jesuits with a list of themes they should investigate to increase French knowledge of China. That catalogue, comprised of widely different subjects, included, "The forms of . . . gardens . . . allées, fountains, parterres."[2]

In 1688, Gerbillon entered the Kangxi emperor's service as his tutor in mathematics and Euclidean geometry, spending the rest of his life at the Qing court and dying in Beijing.[3] He made eight trips to Tartary (Manchuria and Mongolia), often following Kangxi, recording his experiences in a series of journals, which contain detailed descriptions of the events that occurred and observations of a geographical, topographical, scientific, and cultural nature, as had been requested by the Académie des Sciences.[4] The two extracts that follow are taken from Gerbillon's chronicle of his second voyage to Tartary.[5]

The first text contains a brief description of the emperor's *maison de plaisance* on the lake Nanhai (Southern Sea), within the Imperial City in Beijing; the second is a description of Changchun yuan (Garden of Joyful Spring), the complex of palaces and gardens constructed beginning in 1687 by Kangxi in suburban Beijing.[6] Gerbillon's depiction of the modest, natural simplicity of the emperor's quarters in the Imperial City made it possible for him to underline what a wise and enlightened monarch Kangxi was,

one who did not indulge in luxury and excesses but <u>preferred frugality,
even in his gardens. In</u> his account of Changchun yuan, Gerbillon provided
his synthesis of "the genius of the Nation" in the art of the garden, which
consisted, according to the missionary, in the juxtaposition of a variety
of compositional elements: green spaces, pavilions, large rocks of fantastic
shapes, pools of water, and the pathways that linked them. Gerbillon
appreciated the general layout of the garden; his education in the canons of
Western classicism, however, inevitably conditioned his attitude toward
some characteristic features, such as the curiously shaped rockeries, which
he considered to be as bizarre and puzzling as the Chinese fondness for
them. Gerbillon failed to perceive the evocative quality and the aesthetic
value of the rocks, pierced by the winds or shaped by the erosion of the
water, which were used in the garden as evocations of nature and as allusions to the passage of time.[7]

Gerbillon's travel journals, written in 1688–98, were published in 1735
by the French Jesuit Jean-Baptiste Du Halde, who included them in his
four-volume encyclopedic work entitled *Description . . . de la Chine*.[8] Du
Halde, who never left Europe, compiled his work on the basis of reports,
texts, and letters sent by Jesuit missionaries in China. The *Description . . .
de la Chine* was a very successful publication. It was of great importance to
eighteenth-century intellectuals, who used the favorable image of China it
presented to criticize the despotic French political system and contemporary French society.[9]

*   *   *

From Jean-François Gerbillon, "Seconde voyage . . . en
Tartarie . . . en l'année 1689," in Jean-Baptiste Du Halde,
Description . . . de la Chine, vol. 4 (1735) translated by
Bianca Maria Rinaldi

The 27th (March 1690) on his way to the pleasure house he has on the
Lake near his Palace, and that is called *Yntai* [Yingtai, or Sea Terrace
Island],[10] His Majesty [Kangxi] passed through the apartment of *Yang sin
tien* [Yangxin dian, or <u>Hall of Mental Cultivation</u>][11] where he remained
very briefly, he was content to consider the Breviary of Father Thomas,[12]
which he found accidentally in a corner, and he went out quickly, ordering

that we be brought to his pleasure house in the afternoon to give our explanation, which was done even though it rained heavily all day long.

After we had completed our explanation, and he again had completed proofs on his little segmented circle, he ordered one of the Eunuchs who are in his presence, and who has the most spirit and is most in his good graces, to show us the neatest and most agreeable apartment in this entire pleasure house, which they told us was a very special favor because it is not the custom to let anyone enter these interior places, which are reserved solely for the person of the Emperor.

This apartment is neat, but without having anything either grand or magnificent: there are some little quiet places that are very pleasant, some little groves of a very neat type of bamboo, some pools and some reservoirs of spring-fed water, but all small and covered with stones alone, without any richness: this comes in part from the fact that the Chinese have no idea of what we call Building and Architecture, and in part from what the Emperor intends to show, which is that he does not want to dissipate the finances of the Empire for his private amusements.

On this I cannot help but remark in passing, that either naturally or by affectation, the Emperor is extremely reserved in relation to his private expenditure, and to the gratuities he gives, even though he is without doubt the richest Prince in the world; but it must be affirmed that as far as public expense is concerned, and the execution of what he undertakes for the good of the State, he spares nothing and does not complain about the expense, however big it is: he is also very liberal in diminishing the people's taxes when the occasion presents itself, as when he travels in some Provinces, or when there is dearth of food.

Before we left the Emperor, he told us that the next day he was going to his pleasure house called *Tchang tchunyuen* [Changchun yuan], which is two and a half leagues from *Peking* [Beijing] toward the west, and he ordered that we go to see him there every two days to continue the explanation of the elements of Geometry: he also had us informed that that same day he had intended to fish in the Lake, and to give us the fish that he caught, but that the rain had impeded that.

The 28th. [March 1690] The Emperor went in the morning to his pleasure house. The 29th. we went according to His Majesty's order to the pleasure house named *Tchang tchunyuen* [Changchun yuan], which means, garden of perpetual Spring, of long-lasting Spring.[13]

We entered first in the innermost part of this house, and shortly after we had arrived, His Majesty sent us several dishes from his table, all in porcelain very fine and yellow on the outside, of the sort that only the Emperor can use. Afterwards he had us come into the apartment where he was lodged, which is the gayest and most agreeable of all in this house, even though it is neither rich nor magnificent. It is situated between two great pools of water, one on the south, and the other on the north: the one and the other surrounded almost all around with little rises made by hand out of the earth thrown there while digging out the pools: all these rises are planted with apricot trees, peach trees, and other trees of this nature; that makes this view attractive enough when the trees are covered with green.

When our explanation was finished, the Emperor had us led through this whole apartment. There was a little gallery on the northern side, immediately on the edge of the pool which is on that side, with a very pleasant view: they showed us other chambers, where the Emperor sleeps in winter and in summer; this was regarded as a unique favor; those who approach closest to His Majesty never go that far: everything there was quite modest, but extremely neat in the Chinese manner; they [the Chinese] make the beauty of their pleasure houses and gardens consist in a great neatness, and in certain pieces of extraordinary rocks such as one sees in the wildest deserts; but above all they love to have numerous little rooms, and numerous little parterres enclosed by rows of plants which create little paths: there lies the genius of the Nation.[14]

The rich people among them go to any expense for this sort of bagatelle: they will pay far more for some old rock which has something grotesque or extraordinary, as, for example, if it has several cavities, or if it is pierced through to the other side, than they would for a block of jasper or some beautiful statue in marble. If they do not use marble at all in their buildings it is not because they do not have it; the mountains near *Peking* are full of very beautiful white marble, that they use only to adorn their graves.[15]

NOTES

1   In addition to Jean-François Gerbillon, the "Mathématiciens du Roi" included the Jesuits Jean de Fontaney (1643–1710), Claude de Visdelou (1656–1737), Joachim Bouvet (1656–1730), and Louis Le Comte (1655–1728). They had also been accompanied by Father Guy Tachard (1648–1712), who remained in Siam.

2   Virgile Pinot, *Documents inédits relatifs à la connaissance de la Chine en France de 1685 à 1740* (Geneva: Slatkine Reprints, 1971), 7–8. Compiled in 1684, the list

included a vast variety of subjects to investigate, ranging from mathematics, medicine, social organization, types of fortifications, and the botanical world to the art of gardens.

3   In the 1690s, the Jesuits Tomás Pereira, Antoine Thomas, Joachim Bouvet, and Gerbillon were Kangxi's instructors in Western science. For a recent discussion see Catherine Jami, *The Emperor's New Mathematics: Western Learning and Imperial Authority During the Kangxi Reign (1662–1722)* (New York: Oxford University Press, 2012), 139–59.

4   Mme Yves de Thomaz de Bossiere, *Jean-François Gerbillon, S.J. (1654–1707): Un des cinq mathématiciens envoyés en Chine par Louis XIV* (Leuven: Ferdinand Verbiest Fondation, 1994), 30.

5   Jean-François Gerbillon, "Seconde voyage fait par ordre de l'Empereur de la Chine en Tartarie par les Peres Gerbillon et Pereira en l'année 1689," in Du Halde, *Description . . . de la Chine*, vol. 4, 163–251. The diary of the "Seconde voyage . . . en Tartarie" includes the account of the diplomatic mission Gerbillon took part in to participate in the negotiations which led to the Treaty of Nerchinsk, which defined the frontier between China and Russia.

6   Changchun yuan (Garden of Joyful Spring) was constructed by the Kangxi emperor on the site where gardens had already existed during the Ming period. Perhaps it was the landscapes and private gardens of the region of Jiangnan, in southern China, which Kangxi had visited for the first time in 1684, which inspired the design of Changchun yuan, later to become his major suburban residence. It occasionally served as a location for audiences and for administrative duties. The Russian embassy sent by Peter the Great to China and led by Count Leon Vasilievich Izmailov in 1719–22 was received there in late 1720 and early 1721. Kangxi died at Changchun yuan in 1722, the sixty-first year of his reign.

7   On the role of rocks in the Chinese aesthetic and on Western perceptions of those rocks, see Porter, *The Chinese Taste*, 95–114.

8   Du Halde, *Description . . . de la Chine*, vol. 4, 87–421. The journals of Gerbillon's travels in Tartary were included in the second English version of Du Halde's work, entitled *A Description of the Empire of China and Chinese-Tartary* and published in 1738. An abridged English translation of Gerbillon's journals appeared in John Green, *A New General Collection of Voyages and Travels . . .*, vol. 4 (London: for T. Astley, 1747), 664–751.

9   David E. Mungello, "Confucianism in the Enlightenment: Antagonism and Collaboration Between the Jesuits and the Philosophes," in *China and Europe: Images and Influences in Sixteenth to Eighteenth Centuries*, ed. Thomas H. C. Lee (Hong Kong: Chinese University Press, 1991), 106–7.

10   Yingtai (Sea Terrace Island) is an islet emerging from Nanhai (Southern Sea), the smallest of three artificial lakes linked to one another but separated by narrow strips of land, which formed the spine of a vast imperial park situated on the west side of the Forbidden City in Beijing, named Xiyuan (Western Garden). Created during the Ming dynasty by expanding the lake excavated by Kublai Khan, the system of the three lakes was called Three Seas and consisted of Beihai (Northern Sea), Zhonghai (Middle Sea), and Nanhai (Southern Sea). The area around Beihai

is the only part of the extensive Western Garden that is open to the public; it became a large urban park in 1925. Zhonghai serves as the central headquarters for the Communist Party of China, while Nanhai is the seat of the government of the People's Republic of China. The Kangxi emperor often stayed at Yingtai. Linked to the larger park by a strip of land, the wooded island featured different pavilions connected by covered walkways. Liyao Cheng, *Imperial Gardens* (Vienna: Springer, 1998), 137; and Valder, *Gardens in China*, 130–31.

11 The Yangxin dian (Hall of Mental Cultivation) was the Qing emperors' preferred residence in the Forbidden City, as both the Kangxi emperor and the Yongzheng emperor and, later, the Qianlong emperor chose to reside there. Kangxi used also the Qianqing gong (Palace of Heavenly Purity), the largest of the three halls on the central axis of the inner court in the Forbidden City, as his residence. Frances Wood, "Imperial Architecture of the Qing: Palaces and Retreats," in *China, the Three Emperors, 1662–1795,* ed. Evelyn S. Rawsky and Jessica Rawson (London: Royal Academy of Arts, 2005), 57–58. A description of the Yangxin dian compound is recorded by Gerbillon in his diary on January 16, 1690. Jean-François Gerbillon, "Seconde voyage . . . en Tartarie," 217.

12 Antoine Thomas (1644–1709), a Belgian Jesuit who arrived in China in 1682.

13 Gerbillon refers to Kangxi's Changchun yuan, the "Garden of Joyful Spring." It is interesting to note that Gerbillon, like the Jesuit Jean-Denis Attiret and later the missionary Matteo Ripa, translated the name of Kangxi's garden Changchun yuan as "Garden of Perpetual Spring" or "Garden of Everlasting Spring." This translation recalls a second imperial garden called Changchun yuan, whose name was written with different characters and usually translated as "Garden of Eternal Spring." It was built in 1747 by Kangxi's grandson, the Qianlong emperor, as part of Yuanming yuan. As Stephen H. Whiteman suggested, in trying to express in a European language the symbolic meaning of the name Kangxi gave to his garden—that of an unrestricted spring—the Jesuits chose a name that happens to be the literal translation for Qianlong's Changchun yuan. Stephen H. Whiteman, personal communication, January 8, 2013. For Kangxi's explanation of why he named his garden Changchun yuan see Kangxi's *Record of Changchun yuan* in Hui Zou, *A Jesuit Garden in Beijing and Early Modern Chinese Culture* (West Lafayette, Ind.: Purdue University Press, 2001), 169. I am grateful to Stephen H. Whiteman for bringing this passage to my attention. The Italian traveler Giovanni Francesco Gemelli Careri, who journeyed to China during the mid-1690s, in *Giro del Mondo* (1699–1700), offered his explanation of the meaning of the name of Kangxi's garden: "It is call'd, *Shian-Sciun-Yuen* [Changchun yuan]; *Yuen*, signifying a garden; *Sciun*, always; and *Shian*, spring; that is, The garden where there is continual spring. It consists of fine little houses, separated from one another . . . with gardens and fountains after the *Chinese* manner." Giovanni Francesco Gemelli Careri, "A Voyage Round the World," in Awnsham and John Churchill, *A Collection of Voyages and Travels . . .*, vol. 4 (London: J. Walthoe, T. Whotton, S. Birt, D. Browne, T. Osborn, J. Shuckburgh, H. Lintot, 1732), 306.

14 The 1738 English translation of Gerbillon's travel journal altered the original text adding to the description the evocation of a Renaissance nymphaeum, a garden

feature familiar to English readers as a symbolic representation of nature: "The Beauty of their Houses and Gardens consists in a great Propriety, and Imitation of Nature, as Groto's, Shell-Work, and craggy Fragments of Rocks, such as are seen in the wildest Desarts." Jean-François Gerbillon, "The Second Journey of the PP. Gerbillon and Pereyra into Tartary, in 1689," in Du Haide, *A Description of the Empire of China and Chinese-Tartary. . .* , vol. 2 (London: printed for Cave, 1738), 326.

15 A similar comment on the lack of statuary in Chinese gardens was expressed by John Bell in his account of the Russian embassy led by Izmailov in 1719–22 to the court of Kangxi. Relating to Kangxi's Changchun yuan, Bell wrote, "They have many quarries of fine marble, of different colours; but not so much as a single statue is to be seen in the Emperor's garden." John Bell, *Travels from St. Petersburg in Russia to Diverse Parts of Asia*, vol. 2 (Glasgow: Robert and Andrew Foulis, 1763), 103.

————— ❧⚜❧ —————

CHAPTER 6

Louis Le Comte (1655–1728)

FRANCE

Louis Le Comte was one of the "Mathématiciens du Roy" who arrived at the Qing court in Beijing in 1688. He was not chosen by the Kangxi emperor for service at court but was allowed to undertake missionary activity anywhere in China.[1] He returned to France in 1691 and a few years later published his account of China, *Nouveaux mémoires sur l'état présent de la Chine* (1696).[2] Le Comte's narrative took the form of a collection of fourteen letters addressed to notable French personalities. His letters offer a vivid picture of Chinese culture and society and include comments about the government, history, geography, culture, language, religion, architecture, and vegetation of the Chinese empire, as well as information about the Catholic mission in China.[3]

The extract that follows is taken from the letter to the Duchess of Bouillon, in which Le Comte speaks of architecture and furnishings, paintings and porcelain, and festivities, in addition to discussing gardens.[4] Showing a rather different attitude than Gerbillon, in this letter Le Comte is openly critical of the aesthetic of Chinese gardens, which he considers modest and poorly cared for compared to Western gardens. Le Comte's judgment on the aesthetic superiority of the gardens of France over those of China are reiterated in his other writings;[5] but in this letter he even gives practical advice on possible improvements to the Chinese gardens' irregular layout, proposing regular dispositions of ornamental plants and fruit trees to design *allées*. The Jesuit's critical judgment is determined by his cultural background. Finding no trace of the geometrical arrangements of French formal gardens, Le Comte minimizes the aesthetic quality of Chinese gardens, writing that they are simply aimed at the "imitation of nature."[6] It is ironic that only a few decades later, "imitate nature" was the most favored slogan in the campaign to transform European gardens.

* * *

From Louis Le Comte, "Letter VI. To the Duchess of
Bouillon. Of the Œconomy and Magnificence of the
Chineses," in *Memoirs and Observations . . . Made in a Late
Journey Through the Empire of China* (1697)

By all that I have said, you may judge, *Madam*, that these People have
shut themselves up within the Bounds of Necessity and Profit, without
being over solicitous about Magnificence, which is very regular, tho' but
very indifferent in their Houses. They likewise seem more negligent as to
their Gardens, they have in that respect Conceptions much different from
ours; and setting aside places designed for the Sepulchre of their Ancestors,
which they leave untilled, they would think themselves out of their Wits, to
put the Ground to no other use than to make Alleys and Walks, to cultivate
Flowers, and plant Groves of unprofitable Trees.[7] The benefit of the Com-
monweal commands that all should be sowed; and their own particular
Interest, that more nearly concerns them than the Publick Good, doth not
permit them to prefer Pleasure to Profit.

'Tis true, the Flowers of the Country do not deserve their looking after;
they have none curious; and tho' many may be met with like those in
Europe, yet do they cultivate them so ill, that one has much ado to know
them. Nevertheless there are Trees to be seen in some places, that would
afford great Ornament in their Gardens, if they knew how to dispose them.
Instead of Fruit they are almost all the year long laden with Flowers of a
florid Carnation; the Leaves are small, like those of the Elm, the Trunk
irregular, the Branches crooked, and Bark smooth. If Alleys were made of
them mixing therewith (which might easily be done) some Orange Trees,
it would be the most pleasant thing in the World: But seeing the *Chineses*
walk not much, Alleys do not agree with them.[8]

Amongst other Trees they might dispose of in Gardens, there is one
they call *Outom-chu*,[9] resembling the Sycomore; the Leaves are in Diameter
between 8 or 9 Inches, fasten'd to a Stalk a foot long; it is extreamly tufted,
and laden with Clusters of Flowers so thick set, that the Sun cannot inter-
squeeze a Ray. The Fruit which is extraordinary small not withstanding the
Tree be one of the biggest, is produced after the manner I am about to
relate: Towards the Month of *August*, or the end of *July*, there Springs out

of the very point of the Branches, little bunches of Leaves different from the other, they are whiter, softer, and as broad, and are in lieu of Flowers, upon the border of each of these Leaves grow three or four small Grains, or Kernels as big as green Peas, that inclose a white Substance, very pleasant to the taste, like to *that* of an Hazle Nut that is not yet ripe. This Tree being fruitful, and the manner of bearing its Fruit being something extraordinary, I was apt to believe, *Madam*, you might be desirous to see the Description of it, which I have caused to be engraven.[10]

The *Chineses*, who so little apply themselves to order their Gardens, and manage the real Ornaments, are nevertheless taken with them, and are at some cost about them; they make Grotto's in them, raise little pretty Artificial Eminences, transport thither by piecemeal whole Rocks, which they heap one upon another, without any further design, than to imitate Nature. If they could, besides all this, have the convenience of so much Water as is necessary to water their Cabbage and Ligumenous Plants, they would think they could desire no more as to that point. The Emperor hath *Jets d'eau*, or Fountains, of *European* Invention, but private Persons content themselves with their Ponds and Wells.

NOTES

1   On their arrival in Beijing, the French Jesuits were received by the Kangxi emperor who retained Joachim Bouvet and Jean-François Gerbillon at the court.

2   Louis Le Comte, *Nouveaux Mémoires sur l'état présent de la Chine*, 2 vols. (Paris: Jean Anisson, 1696). Le Comte's work was a notable success and was published in various versions with numerous reprintings, and translated into the primary Western languages. Second and third French editions were published in Paris in 1697; the English edition appeared in the same year (the source of the extract included in this anthology). In 1698, a new third edition was published in French, as well as a first version in Dutch. A German edition was published in Frankfurt in 1699–1700. For a recent edition see Louis Le Comte, *Un jésuite à Pékin: Nouveaux mémoires sur l'état présent de la Chine, 1687–1692*, texte établi, annoté et présenté par Frédérique Touboul-Boyeure (Paris: Phébus, 1990).

3   The literary form of the letter was used by Le Comte as the most appropriate for supporting, in a concealed way, the Jesuits' missionary strategy in China and their policy of accommodation toward the Chinese rites, which was not of secondary importance in Le Comte's publication. Lach and Van Kley, *Asia in the Making of Europe*, Vol. 3, book 1, 427–28 and Vol. 3, book 4, 1679–80. On Le Comte and the reception of his publication in Europe see Mungello, *Curious Land*, 329–40.

4   Louis Le Comte, "Letter VI. To the Duchess of Bouillon. Of the Œconomy and Magnificence of the Chineses," in *Memoires and Observations . . . Made in a Late*

Journey Through the Empire of China (London: Benj. Tooke and Sam Buckley, 1697), 150–78.

5 In his letter to the Count de Crécy, Le Comte writes, "Si nous sommes plus magnifiques qu'eux dans nos jardins, par les differens ornemens dont nous les embellissons; il faut avoûër qu'ils nous surpassent dans leurs potagers." Louis Le Comte, "Lettre a Monsieur Le Comte de Crécy. Du climat, des terres, des canaux, des rivieres et des fruits de la Chine," in *Nouveaux mémoires*, vol.. 1, 221. The more concise and immediate English translation reads: "If our *Parterre* excels theirs, they exceed us in their Kitchin Garden." Louis Le Comte, "Letter IV. To the Count de Crécy. Of the Clime, Soil, Canals, Rivers and Fruits of China," in *Memoires and Observations*, 103.

6 Robert Kinnaird Batchelor, Jr., "The European Aristocratic Imaginary and the Eastern Paradise: Europe, Islam and China, 1100–1780" (Ph.D. diss., University of California, 1999), 759–64. The Jesuit has the same critical attitude toward Chinese architecture. Describing the Forbidden City, Le Comte writes, "Chiefly the great number of different Pieces of Architecture which they consist of, dazle the Beholders Eye, and truly look great, becoming the Majesty of so great a Monarch. But still, the imperfect Notion the *Chinese* have of all kind of Arts, is betrayed by the unpardonable Faults they are guilty of. The Apartments are ill contrived, the Ornaments irregular, and the former wants the Connexion which makes the Beauty and Coveniency of our Palaces. In a word, there is as it were an unshapenness in the whole, which renders it very unpleasing to Foreigners, and must needs offend any one that has the least Notion of true Architecture." Louis Le Comte, "Letter III. To his Highness the Cardinal of Furstemberg. Of the Cities, Houses, and Chief Building of China," in *Memoires and Observations*, 60–61. Le Comte cannot accept the adoption of irregularity as a compositional criterion and makes no effort to hide his irritation about this. As Robert Batchelor has shown, "'Irregularity,' which had no place in the geometrically ordered Versailles of Louis XIV, also had no place in the aesthetic of Le Comte." Batchelor, "The European Aristocratic Imaginary," 758.

7 The original French version is here slightly different: "Ils croiraient manquer au bon sens d'occuper uniquement la terre en parterres, à cultiver des fleurs, à dresser des allées, à planter des bosquets d'arbres inutiles." Louis Le Comte, "Lettre VI. À Madame la duchesse de Bouillon. De la propreté et de la magnificence des Chinois," in *Nouveaux mémoires*, 334.

8 The comment concerning the supposed laziness of the Chinese or habit of the Far East, considered by Le Comte the main cause of the lack of long avenues for walking in their gardens, was repeated by William Chambers, who wrote, "As the Chinese are not fond of walking, we seldom meet with avenues or spacious walks as in our European plantations." William Chambers, "On the Art of Laying Out Gardens Among the Chinese," in *Design of Chinese Buildings, Furniture, Dresses, Machines and Utensils . . . to which is annexed a Description of their Temples, Houses, Gardens* (London: Published for the author, 1757), 15. George Leonard Staunton confirms this Chinese habit and writes: "The Chinese, especially men of business, such as are most of the mandarines, have little idea of the use or

pleasure of walking abroad, merely for the sake of exercise, or for seeing prospects, or the situation of countries, unless with military, and, consequently, suspicious views." George Staunton, *An Authentic Account of an Embassy from the King of Great Britain to the Emperor of China*, 2 vols. (London: G. Nicol, 1797), 215.

9   Le Comte refers to the large-leaved Chinese parasol tree (*Firmiana simplex* [L.] W. Wight). The tree is known in China as *wutong* and is planted as an ornamental. Francine Fèvre and Georges Métailié, *Dictionnaire Ricci des plantes de Chine* (Paris: Cerf, 2005), 470.

10   The engraving representing the "Outom-Chu A Tree in China" is between page 162 and 163 in the 1697 English version of Le Comte's book.

CHAPTER 7

Jean-François Gerbillon (1654–1707)

In the following passage, taken from the 1714 English translation of a letter written from Beijing in 1705 and first published in 1713 in the collection *Lettres édifiantes et curieuses*,[1] the French Jesuit Jean-François Gerbillon shows his understanding of Chinese garden design, explaining that the emperor of China has, as a pleasure garden, a fragment of fertile countryside. The Jesuit provides a short description of that serene landscape, which included ponds, grasslands, clumps of trees, orchards, and lawns. Showing that a design for a great imperial park may encompass features of a rural landscape, Gerbillon emphasizes the natural quality of the Chinese garden. He therefore foreshadows the development of a taste for the arcadian and pastoral landscape in eighteenth-century Europe, which will influence the evolution of European garden art toward a natural design. Gerbillon's text also anticipates other contributions by Western travelers, especially French Jesuits, who will describe the Chinese garden as rural and irregular, using the countryside as a key for reading its design.

* * *

From "Extract of a Letter from F. Gerbillon, at Peking 1705, Giving an Account of a Country House of the Emperor of China . . . ," in *The Travels of Several Learned Missioners of the Society of Jesus* . . . (1714)

Some Leagues from *Peking* [Beijing] towards the East and West are Two Rivers, neither deep nor wide, and yet they do infinite Mischief, when they happen to overflow. Their Sources are at the Foot of the Mountains of *Tartary*, and they meet together at a Place call'd *Tien-Tsin-ouci* [Tianjin?],[2]

Figure 3. Samuel Smith, after William Alexander, *A View in the Gardens of the Imperial Palace in Pekin*. In George Leonard Staunton, *An Authentic Account of an Embassy from the King of Great Britain to the Emperor of China*, vol. 3, pl. 29, April 12, 1796 (London: printed for G. Nicol, 1797). Beinecke Rare Book and Manuscript Library, Yale University.

about Fifteen Leagues below the Capital, when they run together with many Windings to discharge themselves in the Eastern Ocean.

All the Country between those Two Rivers is flat, well cultivated, planted with Trees full of large and small Game, and so delightful, that the Emperors us'd to reserve it for their own Diversion; but the Inundations have so entirely destroy'd it, that notwithstanding the several Dikes which have been made to restrain the Rivers, within their Channel, there is scarce any thing to be seen but the ruinous Remains of Castles, Pleasure Houses, Towns and Villages there were formerly in it.

The Emperor [Kangxi] order'd the Jesuits to go take an exact Draught of all the Country between those Two Rivers, by an actual Survey upon the Spot; to the End that having it continually before his Eyes, he might consider of Means for retrieving of what had been ruin'd, making new Dikes at the convenient Distances, and digging in the proper Places vast Trenches to carry off the Water. The making of this Draught was by the Emperor committed to the Fathers *Thomas, Bouvet, Regis* and *Parrenin*.³ His Majesty funish'd them with all Necessaries for that Work and oder'd Two *Mandarines*, One of whom belong'd to the Palace, and the other is President of the Mathematicians, to see his Commands speedily obey'd, and to find out good Measurers, able Draughtsmen, and such Persons as were perfectly acquainted with the Country. This was all perform'd in such orderly Manner, that the said Plan, being perhaps the Greatest that has been seen in *Europe* was taken in Seventy Days. It has been since finish'd at Leasure and adorn'd with curious Cuts, that nothing may be wanting in it.

In the first Place has been drawn the Capital of the Empire, with the Walls that enclose it, not according to the Common Notion of the People, but agreeably to the most exact Rules of Geometry.

In the second Place there is the Pleasure House of the ancient Emperors. It is of a prodigious Extent, being full Ten *French* Leagues in Compass; but very unlike the Royal Palaces in *Europe*. There is no Marble, no Fountains, nor Stone Walls. It is water'd by four little Rivers of excellent Water, the Banks whereof are planted with Trees. There are Three handsome Structures of a great Extent; there are also several Ponds, Pasture Ground for Stags, wild Goats, and Mules, and other Sorts of Game, Stalls for Cattle, Kitchin Gardens, Grass Plats, Orchards and some Pieces of Till'd Land. In a Word, there is every Thing that makes the Country Life Pleasant. There, formerly the Emperors casting off the Burden of the publick Affairs, and laying aside for a while that Air of Majesty which is so great a Confinement, us'd to partake of the Pleasures of a private Life.

NOTES

1   "Extract of a Letter from F. Gerbillon, at Peking 1705, Giving an Account of a Country House of the Emperor of China; Inundation of a vast Country; Conversions of Infidels and Honesty of Converts," in *The Travels of Several Learned Missioners of the Society of Jesus into Divers Parts of the Archipelago, India, China, and America* (London: Printed for R. Gosling, 1714), 226–30. The letter was first published in French as "Lettre du Père Gerbillon. A Peking en l'année 1705," in *Lettres édifiantes et curieuses, écrites des missions étrangères, par quelques Missionnaires de la Compagnie de Jésus*, vol. 10 (Paris: Barbou, 1713), 412–28. The text was reprinted in several later editions of the *Lettres édifiantes et curieuses*: "Lettre du Père Gerbillon à Peking en l'année 1705. Maison de plaisance de l'Empereur de la Chine à quelques lieues de Pekin," in *Lettres édifiantes et curieuses, écrites des missions étrangères, par quelques Missionnaires de la Compagnie de Jésus*, vol. 10 (Paris: Le Clerc, 1732), 412–19; "Lettre du Père Gerbillon. A Pekin, en l'année

1705," in *Lettres édifiantes et curieuses, écrites des missions étrangères*, vol. 18 (Paris: Merigot, 1781), 67–77; "Lettre du Père Gerbillon, Supérieur-Général des missions de la Chine. A Pekin, en l'année 1705," in *Lettres édifiantes et curieuses, écrites des missions étrangères: Mémoires de la Chine*, vol. 12 (Lyon: Vernarel et Cabin, 1819), 38–44; "Lettre du Père Gerbillon. A Pekin, année 1705," in *Lettres édifiantes et curieuses, concernant l'Asie, l'Afrique et l'Amerique: Chine*, vol. 3 (Paris: Panthéon Littéraire, 1843), 157–60. The *Lettres édifiantes et curieuses* was a successful series that collected and presented letters written by Jesuit missionaries in China, containing their observations on the state of their mission and on various aspects of Chinese culture. Published between 1702 and 1776 in thirty-six volumes, it had several editions.

2   In the original French version it is spelled as *Tien-Tsin-ouei*.

3   Antoine Thomas (1644–1709), Joachim Bouvet (1656–1730), Jean-Baptiste Régis (1663?–1738), and Dominique Parrenin (1665–1741).

CHAPTER 8

Matteo Ripa (1682–1746)

Matteo Ripa, a Neapolitan missionary belonging to the Sacred Congre-
gation of Propaganda Fide, arrived in China in 1710 and served at
the imperial court in Beijing as a painter and engraver from 1711 to 1723.[1]
Ripa's contribution to Europe's understandings of Chinese gardens lies
mainly in the series of engravings that depicted thirty-six scenic views of
Kangxi's imperial summer residence of Bishu shanzhuang (Mountain
Estate to Escape the Summer Heat), located in modern Chengde.[2] However,
Ripa also provided descriptions of the imperial parks that he had visited.

During his stay at the Qing court, Ripa kept a meticulous journal, which
he organized only after his return to Italy in 1724,[3] expanding the chronicle
of his experience as a missionary and artist in China with autobiographical
information and reports on the foundation of the Collegio dei Cinesi that
he established in Naples.[4] His memoirs, from which the two extracts that
follow are taken, were only published posthumously in 1832, in three volumes, with the title *Storia della fondazione della Congregazione e del Collegio
de' Cinesi*.[5]

In the first extract, Ripa describes Kangxi's Changchun yuan (Garden of
Joyful Spring), near Beijing, which the missionary takes as an exemplary
model of Chinese garden design.[6] The text opens with a synthesis of the
aesthetic difference between Western and Chinese garden traditions: while
Western gardens distance themselves from nature through art, used to
organize the garden space in regular forms and through linear perspective,
the Chinese gardens use art to reproduce nature. Ripa's account depicts
Changchun yuan as a placid microcosm of wooded hills and brooks gur-
gling through little valleys, with lakes traversed by happy boating parties
and marked by islets adorned with pavilions. Ripa recognizes the essence
of the Chinese garden in a lively yet serene variety and chooses a popular
image, another microcosm familiar to him, to convey his perception of the

garden to his readers: the Neapolitan crèche. With its multitude of scenes and figures, and mixture of architecture and nature, the crèche became for Ripa the emblematic representation of Chinese gardens.

In the second extract, Ripa gives a lively account of Bishu shanzhuang, focusing on the spatial composition of the vast park according to its topographical situation.[7] Ripa describes the park as a natural landscape of high wooded hills, valleys, plains, forests, lakes, and rivers, scattered with pavilions and temples. These were the architectural subjects of the engravings Ripa was commissioned by Kangxi to produce, all relative to single buildings, often overlooking water and inserted in the context of the forested hills. The missionary brought copies of these engravings with him back to Europe as the first veritable graphic representation of a Chinese garden.

Both extracts close with the evidence of Ripa's presence in the imperial gardens he describes. In the proliferation of writings on China, whose authors had often no experience of the country, Ripa intends to give his readers proofs of the reliability of his accounts.

*   *   *

From Matteo Ripa, *Storia della fondazione della Congregazione e del Collegio de' Cinesi*, vol. 1 (1832), translated by Bianca Maria Rinaldi

The imperial villa called *Ccin-Cciun-Juen* [Changchun yuan], which means "continuous spring," was created by this same Emperor *Kanghi* [Kangxi] for his pleasure. It stands, as I said, at a distance of about three of our miles from the Royal Palace, in a big plain surrounded by several villas, all of them walled, belonging to his various sons and other gentlemen. Its gates are always guarded by Tartar soldiers, because except for the Eunuchs, they permit entry to no one, except those to whom entry has been expressly conceded by the Emperor. . . . This and all the other lordly villas that I saw are of the same taste, exactly the contrary of our European taste, since we here artfully attempt to distance ourselves from the natural, making the hills plain, draining out the dead waters of lakes, uprooting spontaneous trees, straightening roads, creating fountains with great effort, planting flowers in good order, and the like; the Chinese, on the other hand, work

Figure 4. Views of Jehol, the Seat of the Summer Palace of the Emperors of China / thirty-six etchings by Matteo Ripa, f. 2. [Chengde, China: s.n., 1713?]. © Dumbarton Oaks Research Library and Collection, Rare Book Collection, Washington, D.C.

with art to imitate nature, transforming the terrain into a web of little mountains and hills, with pathways that in some places are broad and straight, in others tortuous, and that are interspersed with diverse paths that in some places are narrow and in others wider, flat and steep, straight and crooked, through mountains (some of which are connected by rough stone formations placed to look natural) and through valleys; thence over varied bridges on rivers and streams created with water brought in by art, and on these one goes from one side to the other, and also to some islets in the middle of the lakes, on the heights of which can be seen pavilions for recreation, where they go by way of the bridges or little boats for amusement with the women, especially when they are tired from the fishing they

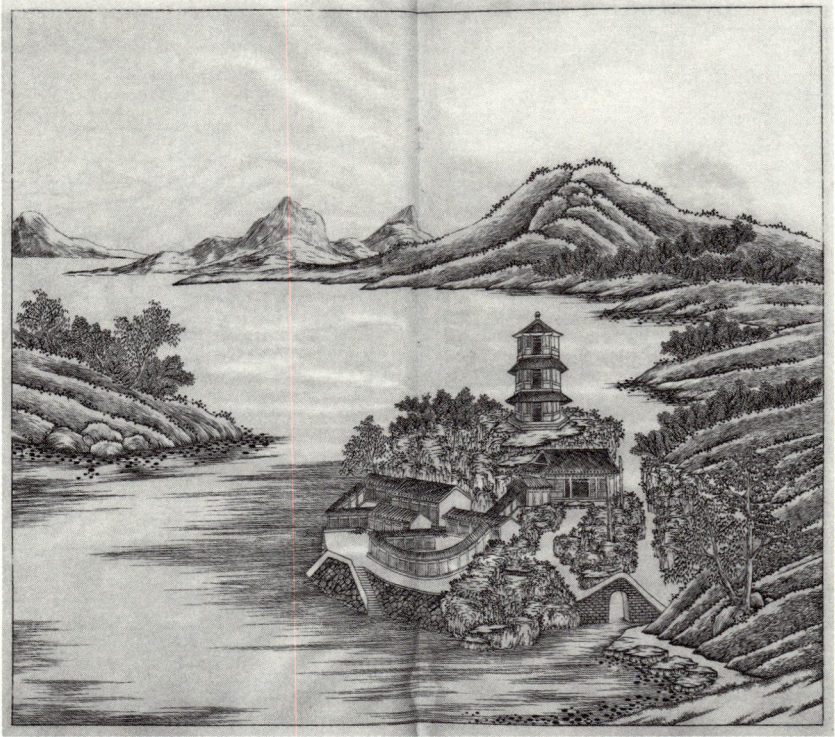

Figure 5. Views of Jehol, the Seat of the Summer Palace of the Emperors of China / thirty-six etchings by Matteo Ripa, f. 18. [Chengde, China: s.n., 1713?]. © Dumbarton Oaks Research Library and Collection, Rare Book Collection, Washington, D.C.

do there, since those waters are full of fish, which were brought there at the beginning to breed, as they do wonderfully, and they do not disappear because there are iron nets placed on purpose at the mouths in the walls where the water discharges. They have also brought in mother-of-pearl, which they view with pleasure on the artificial rocks, or rock formations made cunningly with different stones arranged artfully to look natural, beyond these little mountains and hills, some of which are denuded of trees, and others all wooded and wild. There are also groves, in which there are many deer, hares, and some animals very similar to little deer, which produce musk, and plains; and so that everything might imitate nature, in some of these they plant grain and vegetables. There are also gardens of fruit trees, and with flowers and odoriferous herbs, and moving forward little by little in good settings one sees various pleasure pavilions, lodging for the eunuchs and then the seraglio of the women, in front of which there is a great space where for amusement once a month they hold a fair, and the merchants are the eunuchs themselves, who sell every sort of things, the rarest and most precious. To describe this complex in a few words, I will say that it has much of the taste of the good crèche scenes here in Naples made to represent the nativity of Our Lord naturally.

And all the other [villas] of so many gentlemen are done in the same taste because this is the taste of the Chinese in their villas and their pleasure gardens. I went into this villa every day, but only twice did I see all of it, and it was when, by order of the Emperor, I went to serve as interpreter for Monsignor Mezzabarba, Apostolic Legate, and signor Ismailof [Izmailov], ambassador of Peter, Czar of Moscow.[8]

His Majesty Kanghi [Kangxi], to avoid the excessive summer heat of Peking [Beijing], used to travel every year toward the south of China partly by land and partly by river. But because of the excessive expense that this pleasure brought with it, his subjects were heavily burdened, and he decided to go for that period to Tartary, specifically to the place called *Ge-hol* [Jehol], about one hundred fifty Italian miles from Peking, where he immediately built a villa. Here he remained from the end of the month of May or the beginning of June until the end of September or the beginning of October with thirty thousand soldiers, and great numbers of merchants and other Chinese people also came there as though to a fair, which often made it look like one of the most populous cities of Italy, and here he brought a physician with him every year, and a Jesuit mathematician. . . .

In *Ge-hol* one day I had the pleasure of climbing a mountain which dominated the others because of its height, from which one could see all around what appeared to be a sea of agitated mountains, whose peaks looked like so many rolling waves.[9] This panorama was truly most curious, and unique in the whole World. On the top of this same mountain, there is a good view of one of nature's portentous tricks, which is the elevation from its peak of another height similar to those of which I spoke in reference to my travel from Canton [Guangzhou] to Peking, but much higher, and different in shape, resembling the mythical club of Hercules. . . .

The Imperial villa of *Ge-hol*, which is in Tartary, stands about one hundred fifty Italian miles from Peking, and is situated on a plain completely surrounded by mountains, from the slopes of which runs a river which can usually be crossed on foot, but when it rains and when the ice and snow melt it swells so much that it is frightening to look at it. . . . A high and spacious hill rises gently from the plain, on whose slopes houses were built for the use of those who follow the Emperor, as well as others who gather there from the various provinces of China so as to purvey their merchandise. [This hill] then ends down on the plain where the wall around the villa begins. From this plain another one slopes into the valley below the hill, and from it rises an elevation crowned with other delicious hills, with abundant water springing forth in the same place, which, aided by art, then flows around those hills like a river and finally forms quite a large lake, with an abundance of good fish. In addition to the well-disposed site, what nature made most delectable, rendering the place even more jocund, is the flora. It is rare to see a tree throughout the vast plain beneath those Tartar mountains: and yet in Ge-hol not only the plain and the hills but the very mountain itself are thick with trees, and many of these bear fruit, that is nuts, corianders, pears, and apples. These, even though they are wild, are nonetheless so good to eat that they take them to the table of the Emperor himself. Now this plain, enclosed with its mountain and hills by the Emperor Kanghi, is so extensive that to go around it, as I did more than once on horseback, although at a slow pace, takes more than an hour of riding. In various places here, at a distance from one another, stand numerous dwellings, more or less spacious depending on the use they are intended for, namely, one for His Majesty: behind this, another for the harem of his concubines, so many in number that they are three or four in a room: another for his Mother: some others, more distinguished, for the Queens of His Majesty: and others for Eunuchs. In addition there was a *Miao*, or Temple of Idols, which night and day was served by many *Tausci* [Daoshi, or Daoist masters], I say Priests of the Demon, and they are all Eunuchs, dressed in yellow: and it is to that *Miao* that the Emperor goes with his women to do sacrifice and adoration while he is dwelling in Ge-hol. In addition, one sees there various lodges and pleasure pavilions. These pavilions are all constructed in good taste and with great care: their structures are different, and they can be closed on all sides with silk curtains, so that those within cannot be seen. They contain various seats around and within, in some there is a table, and in others a bed all made up. The Emperor goes to these lodges and pavilions with his Queens and concubines, since the whole time that he is dwelling in the villa he deals only with his women and the Eunuchs. With the women, he goes in an open litter carried by the Eunuchs on their shoulders, and they go on foot, and they have fun moving about here and there through the villa grounds. He also goes fishing with them in numerous little boats in the lakes and along the canals. He eats with the women who are dearer to him, although not at the same table, since he always eats alone, seated on a platform two palms high, while the women are seated on the floor on Tartar-style cushions, having each her own table before her, eating in his sight. Even when he studies, he is surrounded by the Queens dearest to him; and I was eyewitness of all these things in the year 1721 and 22.

NOTES

1   Matteo Ripa was chosen to take to the papal legate in China, Carlo Tommaso Maillard de Tournon, his nomination as cardinal.

2   Built in a mountainous area about 250 km northeast of Beijing, near the city of Chengde, Bishu shanzhuang was begun in 1703 during the reign of the Kangxi emperor, and its construction lasted for almost the whole century. However, a first phase must already have been completed by 1713, when Kangxi commissioned Matteo Ripa to make thirty-six engravings of the most characteristic scenes of the imperial property. From 1741 onward, Qianlong further developed the imperial complex. The site chosen for the construction of the park was a valley with many undulations covered with evergreen trees. In its southern part, the valley opened into a flat area where the imperial palaces were built. Beyond the palace, the park was organized into three main areas characterized by different topography: lakes, lowland, and mountains. North of the palace stretched a vast artificial lake punctuated by islands, and further north a vast wooded plain extended from the lake area to the foothills of the mountains in the northwestern part of the park. Pavilions and temples were scattered around the lake and on the mountains enclosing the park. On Bishu shanzhuang and Chengde see, for instance, Philippe Forêt, *Mapping Chengde: The Qing Landscape Enterprise* (Honolulu: University of Hawaii Press, 2000); Patricia Berger, *Empire of Emptiness: Buddhist Art and Political Authority in Qing China* (Honolulu: University of Hawaii Press, 2003); Cary Y. Liu, "Archive of Power: The Qing Dynasty Imperial Garden-Palace at Rehe," *Meishushi yanjiu jikan* 28 (2010): 43–66. For a discussion on Bishu shanzhuang during the Kangxi period, see Stephen H. Whiteman, "Creating the Kangxi Landscape: Bishu shanzhuang and the Mediation of Qing Imperial Identity" (Ph.D. diss., Stanford University, 2011); see also Stephen H. Whiteman, "From Upper Camp to Mountain Estate: Recovering Historical Narratives in Qing Imperial Landscapes," *Studies in the History of Gardens and Designed Landscapes* 33, no. 4 (2013): 249–79.

3   The journal, or "Giornale," of Matteo Ripa was published only recently as Matteo Ripa, *Giornale (1705–1724)*, introduzione, testo critico e note di Michele Fatica,

2 vols. (Naples: Istituto Universitario Orientale, 1991–96). The first volume relates to the years 1705 and 1711, the second volume to the years 1711–16. Ripa's manuscript is part of the collection of the Biblioteca Nazionale of Naples, with the collocation number ms. I.G.75.

4   The Collegio dei Cinesi (Chinese College) aimed to give religious training and ordination as priests to young Chinese converts, who were then to propagate Catholicism in their country. It was given official recognition in 1732.

5   Matteo Ripa, *Storia della fondazione della Congregazione e del Collegio de' Cinesi.* . . . 3 vols. (Naples: Manfredi, 1832).

6   A first partial English translation of this passage appeared in *Memoirs of Father Ripa, During Thirteen Years' Residence at the Court of Peking*, selected and trans. by Fortunato Prandi (London: Murray, 1844), 62–63.

7   A first, partial English translation of this passage was made by Fortunato Prandi and was published in *Memoirs of Father Ripa*, 72–73.

8   Cardinal Carlo Ambrogio Mezzabarba (1685–1741) arrived in China in 1720 as head of a papal legation sent by Pope Clement XI, with the task of settling the delicate question of the Chinese rites with the Kangxi emperor and the Jesuit missionaries in China. Ripa was the interpreter during the audiences of the cardinal with the emperor. Count Leon Vasilievich Izmailov led the Russian embassy sent by Peter the Great to Kangxi in 1719–22.

9   A similar comparison was later expressed by George Leonard Staunton. Describing the mountainous landscape around Chengde, he wrote that the hills surrounding the area "were neither steep nor lofty. They consisted, at least near the surface, of clay and gravel. They presented no salient and retiring angles, such as are produced by powerful torrents making their way through mountains; nor did they form any regular range; but, taken collectively, resembled a confused sea, in which the broken billows lie in different directions, as tossed by opposite gales succeeding suddenly to each other." George Staunton, *An Authentic Account of an Embassy*, vol. 2, 216–17.

CHAPTER 9

Jean-Denis Attiret (1702–68)

Jean-Denis Attiret arrived in China in 1738 to join the French Jesuit mission and from 1739 spent the remainder of his life serving at the Qing court as a painter. He was the first Western traveler to perceive the spatial mechanism that determined the design of Chinese gardens. In a letter written from Beijing in 1743 and published in 1749,[1] Attiret offered an enthusiastic description of the imperial park of Yuanming yuan (Garden of Perfect Brightness) under the reign of the Qianlong emperor.[2] The description is composed as a visual narrative, guiding the readers in the discovery of a great variety of elements and carefully composed scenes and views, each endowed with a specific formal and aesthetic identity. In the initial part of his letter, Attiret declares his difficulty with describing Yuanming yuan "because there is nothing in the Whole, which has any Likeness to our manner of Building, or our Rules of Architecture." He subtly invites the reader to avoid recalling familiar images of the Western canon of formality to interpret the different, and still unfamiliar, complexity of the Qing imperial park. The Chinese garden that Attiret described was characterized by an elaborate composition of hills, valleys, lakes, sinuous streams, and architectural elements, scattered with masses of trees and traversed by winding paths. It was dominated by a "beautiful Disorder," the term Attiret chose to express the park's irregular design, obtained through a planned sequence of spaces and settings that revealed themselves slowly along the paths.[3] Attiret understood the apparent confusion of the garden's spatial articulation as a compositional device to increase the visual fascination of the park. In the absence of perspective scenes constructed from specific vanishing points, as were common in Baroque gardens, Attiret understood that vision, in Chinese gardens, melted into a sequence of emotional moments engendered by aesthetic seduction and a sense of discovery.[4]

Attiret's account is the most detailed description of a Chinese imperial park to reach Europe in the eighteenth century and thus provided an essential source for Western knowledge of the gardens of China. His narration of the irregular design of Yuanming yuan, of its continuous variety, and of the sense of surprise that it elicited, as well as its composition as a sequence of episodes, constituted an influential reference for the development, in late eighteenth-century continental Europe, of the picturesque garden toward livelier forms and surprising features.[5] Attiret described Yuanming yuan as a kaleidoscope of unexpected situations suggestive of theatrical settings, offering intriguing references for enriching Western gardens. His description of the Chinese city reproduced in the imperial park prefigures the Chinese village built in Tsarskoye Selo, commissioned by the Empress Catherine I in the 1780s; there members of the court dressed as Chinese and pretended to live in a Chinese city. The atmosphere of "rural Simplicity" and the "Scene of . . . Agriculture" included in the imperial precinct of Yuanming yuan, which Attiret described, foreshadows the Hameau, the elegant rural village built in 1782 for Marie Antoinette in the park of Versailles, and more generally possibly contributed to the rural aesthetic of the ferme ornée.[6]

The letter written by Attiret contributed enormously to the fortune of the Chinese garden in Europe and was widely quoted and translated at the time. The text that follows is its first abridged English translation by Joseph Spence (under the pseudonym Sir Harry Beaumont), who published it with the title A Particular Account of the Emperor of China's Garden near Pekin (1752).[7] Spence, a professor of modern history at Oxford at the time, did not always reflect the original vocabulary in his translation. He altered the original text in some parts, omitting passages related to the state of the mission of the French Jesuits in China, probably considering them of little interest to British readers and distant from the principal purpose of his booklet, which was the description of the imperial park. He also omitted some of Attiret's comments, perhaps because he considered them too emphatic, permeated as they were with a somewhat emotional attitude that might have caused the British public to doubt the objectivity of the account.

*   *   *

Jean-Denis Attiret, *A Particular Account of the Emperor of China's Garden near Pekin*, translated by Sir Harry Beaumont [Joseph Spence] (1752)

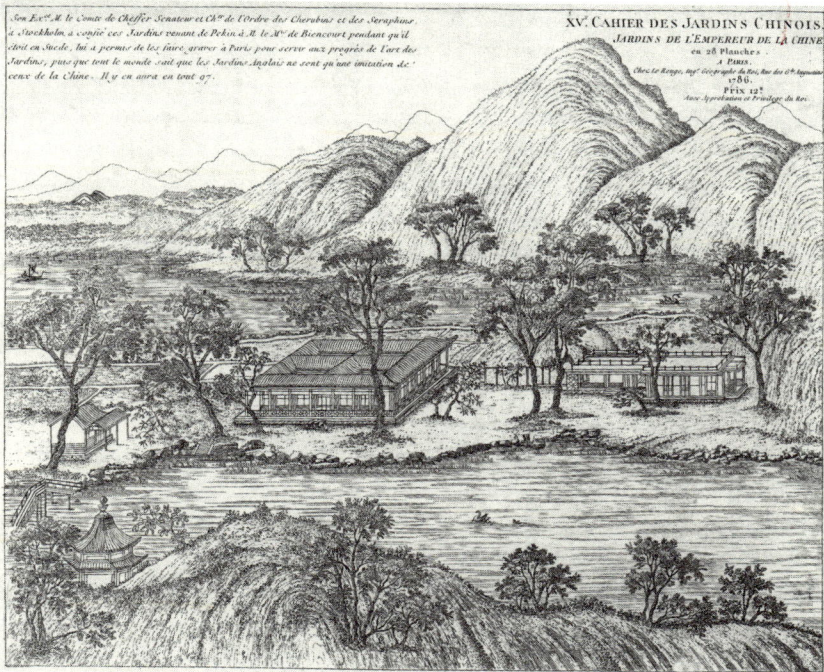

Figure 6. Title page of Cahier 15, "Des jardins chinois. Jardins de l'Empereur de la Chine." In George-Louis Le Rouge, *Détails de nouveaux jardins à la mode "jardins anglo-chinois"* (Paris: By the author, 1786). © Dumbarton Oaks Research Library and Collection, Rare Book Collection, Washington, D.C.

Sir,

It was with the greatest Pleasure that I received your Two last Letters; one of the 13th of *October*, and the other of the 2d of *November*, 1742. I communicated the very interesting Account of the Affairs of *Europe*, which you gave me in them, to the rest of our Missionaries; who join with me in our sincere Thanks. I thank you too in particular for the Box full of Works in Straw, and Flowers, which came very safe to me: but I beg of you not to put yourself to any such Expence for the future; for the *Chinese* very much exceed the *Europeans*, in those kinds of Works; and particularly, in their Artificial Flowers.[8]

We came hither by the Command, or rather by the Permission of the Emperor.[9] An Officer was assign'd to conduct us; and they made us believe, that he would defray our Expences: but the latter was only in Words, for in

Effect the Expence was almost wholly out of our own Pockets. Half of the Way we came by Water; and both eat, and lodg'd in our Boats: and what seem'd odd enough to us, was; that, by the Rules of Good-breeding received among them, we were not allow'd ever to go ashore, or even to look out of the Windows of our Cover'd boats to observe the Face of the Country, as we passed along. We made the latter Part of our Journey in a sort of Cage, which they were pleas'd to call a Litter. In this too we were shut up, all Day long; and at Night, carried into our Inns; (and very wretched Inns they are!) and thus we got to *Pekin* [Beijing]; with our Curiosity quite unsatisfy'd, and with seeing but very little more of the Country, than if one had been shut up all the while in one's own Chamber.

Indeed they say, that the Country we passed is but a bad Country; and that, tho' the Journey is near 2000 Miles, there is but little to be met with on the Way that might deserve much Attention: not even any Monuments; or Buildings, except some Temples for their Idols; and those built of Wood, and but one Story high: the chief Value and Beauty of which seem'd to consist in some bad Paintings, and very indifferent Varnish-works. Indeed any one that is just come from seeing the Buildings in *France* and *Italy*, is apt to have but little Taste, or Attention, for whatever he may meet with in the other Parts of the World.

However I must except out of this Rule, the Palace of the Emperor of *Pekin*, and his Pleasure-houses; for in them every thing is truly great and beautiful, both as to the Design and the Execution: and they struck me the more, because I had never seen any thing that bore any manner of Resemblance to them, in any Part of the World that I had been in before.

I should be very glad, if I could make such a Description of these, as would give you any just Idea of them; but that is almost impossible; because there is nothing in the Whole, which has any Likeness to our manner of Building, or our Rules of Architecture. The only way to conceive what they are, is to see them: and if I can get any time, I am resolved to draw some Parts of them as exactly as I can, and send them into *Europe*.

The Palace is, at least, as big as *Dijon*;[10] which City I chuse to name to you, because you are so well acquainted with it. This Palace consists of a great Number of different Pieces of Building; detach'd from one another, but dispose with a great deal of Symmetry and Beauty. They are separated from one another by vast Courts, Plantations of Trees, and Flower-gardens. The principal Front of all these Buildings shines with Gilding, Varnish-work, and Paintings; and the Inside is furnish'd and adorn'd with all the most beautiful and valuable Things that could be got in *China*, the *Indies*, and even from *Europe*.

As for the Pleasure-houses, they are really charming. They stand in a vast Compass of Ground. They have raised Hills, from 20 to 60 Foot high; which form a great Number of little Valleys between them. The Bottoms of these Valleys are water'd with clear Streams; which run on till they join together, and form larger Pieces of Water and Lakes. They pass these Streams, Lakes, and Rivers, in beautiful and magnificent Boats. I have seen one, in particular, 78 Foot long, and 24 Foot broad; with a very handsome House raised upon it. In each of these Valleys, there are Houses about the Banks of the Water; very well disposed: with their different Courts, open and close Porticos, Parterres, Gardens, and Cascades: which, when view'd all together; have an admirable Effect upon the Eye.

They go from one of the Valleys to another, not by formal strait Walks as in *Europe*; but by various Turnings and Windings, adorn'd on the Sides with little Pavilions and charming Grottos: and each of these Valleys is diversify'd from all the rest, both by their manner of laying out the Ground, and in the Structure and Disposition of its Buildings.

All the Risings and Hills are sprinkled with Trees; and particularly with Flowering-trees, which are here very common.[11] The Sides of the Canals, or lesser Streams, are not faced, (as they are with us,) with smooth Stone, and in a strait Line; but look rude and rustic, with different Pieces of Rock, some of which jut out, and others recede inwards; and are placed with so much Art, that you would take it to be the Work of Nature. In some Parts the Water is wide, in others narrow; here it serpentizes, and there spreads away, as if it was really push'd off by the Hills and Rocks. The Banks are sprinkled with Flowers; which rise up even thro' the Hollows in the Rock-work, as if they had been produced there naturally. They have a great Variety of them, for every Season of the Year.[12]

Beyond these Streams there are always Walks, or rather Paths, pav'd with small Stones; which lead from one Valley to another. These Paths too are irregular; and sometimes wind along the Banks of the Water, and at others run out wide from them.

On your Entrance into each Valley, you see its Buildings before you. All the Front is a Colonnade, with Windows between the Pillars. The Wood-work is gilded, painted, and varnish'd. The Roofs too are cover'd with varnish'd Tiles of different Colours; Red, Yellow, Blue, Green, and Purple: which by their proper Mixtures, and their manner of placing them, form an agreeable Variety of Compartiments and Designs. Almost all these Buildings are only one Story high; and their Floors are raised from Two to Eight Foot above the Ground. You go up to them, not by regular Stone Steps, but by a rough Sort of Rock-work; form'd as if there had been so many Steps produced there by Nature.[13]

The Inside of the Apartments answers perfectly to the Magnificence without. Beside their being very well disposed, the Furniture and Ornaments are very rich, and of an exquisite Taste. In the Courts, and Passages, you see Vases of Brass, Porcelain, and Marble, fill'd with Flowers: and before some of these Houses, instead of naked Statues, they have several of the Hieroglyphical Figures of Animals,[14] and Urns with Perfumes burning in them, placed upon Pedestals of Marble.

Every Valley, as I told you before, has its Pleasure-house: small indeed, in respect to the whole Inclosure; but yet large enough to be capable of receiving the greatest Nobleman in Europe, with all his Retinue. Several of these Houses are built of Cedar; which they bring, with great Expence, at the Distance of 1500 Miles from this Place. And now how many of these Palaces do you think there may be, in all the Valleys of the Inclosure? There are above 200 of them: without reckoning as many other Houses for the Eunuchs; for they are the Persons who have the Care of each Palace, and their Houses are always just by them; generally, at not more than Five of Six Foot Distance. These Houses of the Eunuchs are very plain: and for the Reason are always concealed, either by some Projection of the Walls, or by the Interposition of their artificial Hills.

Over the running Streams there are Bridges, at proper Distances, to make the more easy Communication from one Place to another. These are most commonly either of Brick or Free-stone, and sometimes of Wood; but are all raised high enough for the Boats to pass conveniently under them. They are fenced with Ballisters [balusters] finely wrought, and adorned with Works in Relievo [relief]; but all of them varied from one another, both in their Ornaments, and Design.

Do not imagine to yourself, that these Bridges run on, like ours, in strait Lines: on the contrary, they generally wind about and serpentize to such a Degree, that some of them, which, if they went on regularly, would be no more than 30 or 40 Foot long, turn so often and so much as to make their whole Length 100 or 200 Foot. You see some of them which, (either in the Midst, or at their Ends,) have little Pavilions for People to rest themselves in; supported sometimes by Four, sometimes by Eight, and sometimes by

Sixteen Columns. They are usually on such of the Bridges, as afford the most engaging Prospects. At the Ends of other of the Bridges there are triumphal Arches, either of Wood, or white Marble; form'd in a very pretty Manner, but very different from any thing that I have ever seen in *Europe*.[15]

I have already told you, that these little Streams, or Rivers, are carried on to supply several large Pieces of Water, and Lakes. One of these Lakes is very near Five Miles round; and they call it a Meer, or Sea. This is one of the most beautiful Parts in the whole Pleasure-ground. On the Banks, are several Pieces of Building; separated from each other by the Rivulets, and artificial Hills above mentioned.

But what is the most charming Thing of all, is an Island or Rock in the Middle of this Sea; rais'd, in a natural and rustic Manner, about Six Foot above the Surface of the Water. On this Rock there is a little Palace; which however contains an hundred different Apartments. It has Four Fronts; and is built with inexpressible Beauty and Taste; the Sight of it strikes one with Admiration. From it you have a View of all the Palaces, scattered at proper Distances round the Shores of this Sea; all the Hills, that terminate about it; all the Rivulets; which tend thither, either to discharge their Waters into it, or to receive them from it; all the Bridges, either at the Mouths or Ends of these Rivulets; all the Pavilions, and Triumphal Arches, that adorn any of these Bridges; and all the Groves, that are planted to separate and screen the different Palaces, and to prevent the Inhabitants of them from being overlooked by one another.

The Banks of this charming Water are infinitely varied: there are no two Parts of it alike. Here you see Keys of smooth Stone; with Porticoes, Walks, and Paths, running down to them from the Palaces that surround the Lake; there, others of Rock-work; that fall into Steps, contrived with the greatest Art that can be conceived: here, natural Terraces with winding Steps at each End, to go up to the Palaces that are built upon them; and above these, other Terraces, and other Palaces, that rise higher and higher, and form a sort of Amphitheatre. There again a Grove of Flowering-trees presents itself to your Eye; and a little farther, you see a Spread of wild Forest-trees, and such as grow only on the most barren Mountains: then, perhaps, vast Timber-trees with their Under-wood; then, Trees from foreign Countries; and then, some all blooming with Flowers; and others all laden with Fruits of different Kinds.

There are also on the Banks of this Lake, a great Number of Network-houses, and Pavilions; half on the Land, and half running into the Lake, for all sorts of Water-fowl: as farther on upon the Shore, you meet frequently with Menageries for different sorts of Creatures; and even little Parks, for the Chace. But of all this sort of Things, the *Chinese* are most particularly fond of a kind of Fish, the greater Part of which are of a Colour as brilliant as Gold; others, of a Silver Colour; and others of different Shades of Red, Green, Blue, Purple, and Black: and some, of all Sorts of Colours mixt together.[16]

There are several Reservoirs for these Fish, in all Parts of the Garden; but the most considerable of them all is at this Lake. It takes up a very large Space; and is all surrounded with a Lattice-work of Brass-wire: in which the Openings are so very fine and small, as to prevent the Fish from wandering into the main Waters.

To let you see the Beauty of this charming Spot in its greatest Perfection, I should wish to have you transported hither when the Lake is all cover'd with Boats; either gilt, or varnish'd: as it is sometimes, for taking the Air; sometimes, for Fishing; and sometimes, for Justs [jousts],[17] and Combats, and other Diversions, upon the Water: but above all, on some fine Night, when the Fire-works are play'd off there; at which time they have Illuminations in all the Palaces, all the Boats, and almost on every Tree. The *Chinese* exceed us extremely in their Fire-works: and I have never seen any thing of that Kind, either in *France* or *Italy*, that can bear any Comparison with theirs.

The Part in which the Emperor usually resides here, with the Empress, his favourite Mistresses,[18] and the Eunuchs that attend them, is a vast Collection of Buildings, Courts, and Gardens; and looks itself like a City. 'Tis, at least, as big as our City of *Dole*.[19] The greater Part of the other Palaces is only used for his walking; or to dine or sup in, upon Occasion.

This Palace for the usual Residence of the Emperor is just within the grand Gate of the Pleasure-ground. First are the Ante-chambers; then the Halls for Audience: and then, the Courts, and Gardens belonging to them. The Whole forms an Island; which is entirely surrounded by a large and deep Canal. 'Tis a sort of Seraglio; in the different Apartments of which you see all the most beautiful things that can be imagin'd, as to Furniture, Ornaments, and Paintings, (I mean, of those in the *Chinese* Taste;) the most valuable Sorts of Wood; varnish'd Works, of China and Japan; antient Vases of Porcelain; Silks, and Cloth of Gold and Silver. They have there brought together, all that Art and good Taste could add to the Riches of Nature.

From this Palace of the Emperor a Road, which is almost strait, leads you to a little Town in the Midst of the whole Inclosure. 'Tis square; and

each Side is near a Mile long. It has Four Gates, answering the Four princi-
pal Points of the Compass; with Towers, Walls, Parapets, and Battlements.
It has it's Streets, Squares, Temples, Exchanges, Markets, Shops, Tribunals,
Palaces, and a Port for Vessels. In one Word, every thing that is at *Pekin* in
Large, is there represented in Miniature.[20]

You will certainly ask, for what Use this City was intended? Is it that the
Emperor may retreat to it as a Place of Safety, on any Revolt, or Revolution?
It might indeed serve well enough for that Purpose; and possibly that
Thought had a Share in the Mind of the Person, who at first design'd it:
but it's principal End was to procure the Emperor the Pleasure of seeing all
the Bustle and Hurry of a great City in little, whenever he might have a
Mind for that sort of Diversion.

The Emperor of *China* is too much a Slave to his Grandeur ever to shew
himself to his People, even when he goes out of his Palace. He too sees
nothing of the Town, which he passes through. All the Doors and Windows
are shut up. They spread wide Pieces of Cloth every where, that no body
may see him. Several Hours before he is to pass through any Street, the
People are forewarned of it; and if any should be found there whilst he
passes, they would be handled very severely by his Guards. Whenever he
goes into the Country, two Bodies of Horse advance a good Way before
him, on each Side of the Road; both for his Security, and to keep the Way
clear from all other Passengers. As the Emperors of *China* find themselves
obliged to live in this strange sort of Solitude, they have always endeavoured
to supply the Loss of all public Diversions, (which their high Station will
not suffer them to partake,) by some other Means of Inventions, according
to their different Tastes and Fancies.

This Town therefore, in these Two last Reigns, (for it was this Emperor's
Father who order'd it to be built,) has been appropriated for the Eunuchs
to act in it, at several times in the Year, all the Commerce, Marketings, Arts,
Trades, Bustle, and Hurry, and even all the Rogueries, usual in great Cities.
At the appointed Times, each Eunuch puts on the Dress of the Profession
or Part which is assigned to him. One is a Shopkeeper, and another an
Artisan; this is an Officer, and that a common Soldier: one has a Wheel-
barrow given him, to drive about the Streets; another, as a Porter, carries a
Basket on his Shoulder. In a word, every one has the distinguishing Mark
of his Employment. The Vessels arrive at the Port; the Shops are open'd;
and the Goods are exposed for Sale. There is one Quarter for those who
sell Silks, and another for those who sell Cloth; one Street for Porcelain,

and another for Varnish-works. You may be supply'd with whatever you want. This Man sells Furniture of all sorts; that, Cloaths and Ornaments for the Ladies: and a third has all kinds of Books, for the Learned and Curious. There are Coffee-houses too, and Taverns, of all Sorts; good and bad: beside a Number of People that cry different Fruits about the Streets, and a great Variety of refreshing Liquors. The Mercers, as you pass their Shops, catch you by the Sleeve; and press you to buy some of their Goods. 'Tis, all a Place of Liberty and Licence; and you can scarce distinguish the Emperor himself, from the meanest of his Subjects. Every body bauls [bawls] out what he has to sell; some quarrel, others fight: and you have all the Confusion of a Fair about you. The public Officers come and arrest the Quarrellers; carry them before the Judges; in the Courts for Justice; the Cause is try'd in form; the Offender condemn'd to be bastinado'd; and the Sentence is put in Execution: and that so effectually, that the Diversion of the Emperor sometimes costs the poor Actor a great deal of Pain.

The Mystery of Thieving is not forgot, in this general Representation. That noble Employ is assign'd to a considerable Number of the cleverest Eunuchs; who perform their Parts admirably well. If any one of them is caught in the Fact he is brought to Shame; and condemn'd (at least they go through the Form of condemning him,) to be stigmatiz'd, bastinado'd, or banish'd; according to the Heinousness of the Crime, and the Nature of the Theft. If they steal cleverly, they have the Laugh on their Side; they are applauded, and the Sufferer is without Redress. However, at the End of the Fair, every thing of this Kind is restor'd to the proper Owner.

This Fair, (as I told you before,) is kept only for the Entertainment of the emperor, the Empress, and his Mistresses. 'Tis very unusual for any of the Princes, or Grandees, to be admitted to see it: and when any have that Favour, it is not till after the Women are all retired to their several Apartments. The Goods which are expos'd and sold here, belong chiefly to the Merchants of *Peking*; who put them into the Hands of the Eunuchs, to be sold in reality: so that the Bargains here are fast from being all pretended ones. In particular, the Emperor himself always buys a great many things; and you may be sure, they ask him enough for them. Several of the Ladies too make their Bargains; and so do some of the Eunuchs. All this trafficking, if there was nothing of real mixt with it, would want a great deal of that Earnestness and Life, which now make the Bustle the more active, and the Diversion it gives the greater.

To this Scene of Commerce, sometimes succeeds a very different one; that of Agriculture. There is a Quarter, within the same Inclosure, which is set apart for this Purpose. There you see Fields, Meadows, Farm-houses, and little scatter'd Cottages; with Oxen, Ploughs, and all the Necessaries for Husbandry. There they sow Wheat, Rice, Pulse, and all other sorts of Grain. They make their Harvest; and carry in the Produce of their Grounds. In a Word, they here imitate every thing that is done in the Country; and in every thing express a rural Simplicity, and all the plain Manners of a Country Life, as nearly as they possibly can.

Doubtless you have read of the famous Feast in *China*, call's *The Feast of the Lanthorns* [lanterns]. It is always celebrated on the 15th Day of the first Month. There is no Chinese so poor, but that upon this Day he lights up his Lanthorn. They have of them of all sorts of Figures, Sizes, and Prices. On that Day, all *China* is illuminated; but the finest Illuminations of all are in the Emperor's Palaces; and particularly in these Pleasure-grounds, which I have been describing to you. There is not a Chamber, Hall, or Portico, in them, which has not several of these Lanthorns hanging from the Cielings. There are several upon all the Rivulets, Rivers, and Lakes; made in the Shape of little Boats, which the Waters carry backward and forward. There are some upon all the Hills and Bridges, and almost upon all the Trees. These are wrought mighty prettily, in the Shapes of different Fishes, Birds, and Beasts; Vases, Fruits, Flowers; and Boats of different Sorts and Sizes. Some are made of Silk; some of Horn, Glass, Mother of Pearl, and a thousand other Materials. Some of them are painted; others embroider'd; and of very different Prices. I have seen some of them which could never have been made for a thousand Crowns. It would be an endless thing, to endeavour to give you a particular Account of all their Forms, Materials, and Ornaments. It is in these, and in the great Variety which the *Chinese* shew in their Buildings, that I admire the Fruitfulness of their Invention; and am almost tempted to own, that we are quite poor and barren in Comparison of them.

Their Eyes are so accustom'd to their own Architecture, that they have very little Taste for ours. May I tell you what they say when they speak of it, or when they are looking over the Prints of some of our most celebrated Buildings? The Height and Thickness of our Palaces amazes them. They look upon our Streets, as so many Ways hollowed into terrible Mountains; and upon our Houses, as Rocks pointing up in the Air, and full of Holes like Dens of Bears and other wild Beasts. Above all, our different Stories, piled up so high one above another, seem quite intolerable to them: and they cannot conceive, how we can bear to run the Risk of breaking our Necks, so commonly, in going up such a Number of Steps as is necessary to climb up to the Fourth and Fifth Floors. "Undoubtedly, (said the Emperor *Cang-hy* [Kangxi], whilst he was looking over some Plans of our *European* Houses,) this *Europe* must be a very small and pitiful Country; since the Inhabitants cannot find Ground enough to spread out their Towns, but are obliged to live up this in the Air." As for us, we think otherwise; and have Reason to do so.

However I must own to you, without pretending to decide which of the two ought to have the Preference, that the Manner of Building in the Country pleases me very much. Since my Residence in *China*, my Eyes and Taste are grown a little *Chinese*. And, between Friends, is not the *Duchess* of *Bourbon*'s House opposite to the *Tuilleries*, extremely pretty? Yet that is only of one Story, and a good deal in the *Chinese* Manner.[21] Every Country has it's Taste and Customs. The Beauty of our Architecture cannot be disputed: nothing is more Grand and Majestic. I own too, that our Houses are well dispos'd. We follow the Rules of Uniformity, and Symmetry, in all the Parts of them. There is nothing in them unmatch'd, or displaced: every Part answers it's Opposite; and there's an exact Agreement in the Whole. But then there is this Symmetry, this beautiful Order and Disposition, too in *China*; and particularly, in the Emperor's Palace at *Pekin*, that I was speaking of in the Beginning of this Letter. The Palaces of the Princes and great Men, the Court of Justice, and the Houses of the better sort of People, are generally in the same Taste.

But in their Pleasure-houses, they rather chuse[22] a beautiful Disorder, and a wandering as far as possible from all the Rules of Art.[23] They go entirely on this Principle, "That what they are to represent there, is a natural and wild View of the Country; a rural Retirement, and not a Palace form'd according to all the Rules of Art."[24] Agreeably to which, I have not yet observ'd any Two of the little Palaces in all the grand Inclosure, which are alike, tho' some of them are places at such considerable Distances from one another. You would think, that they were form'd upon the Ideas of so many different foreign Countries; or that they were all built at random, and made up of Parts not meant for one another. When you read this, you will be apt to imagine such Works very ridiculous; and that they must have a very bad Effect on the Eye: but was you to see them, you would find it quite otherwise; and would admire the Art, with which all this Irregularity is conducted. All is in good Taste; and so managed, that it's Beauties appear gradually, one after another. To enjoy them as one ought, you should view every Piece by itself; and you would find enough to amuse you for a long while, and to satisfy all your Curiosity.[25]

Beside, the Palaces themselves (tho' I have called them little, in Comparison of the Whole,) are very far from being inconsiderable Things. I saw them building one in the same Inclosure, last Year, for one of the Princes of the Blood; which cost him near Two hundred thousand Pounds:[26] without reckoning any thing for the Furniture and Ornaments of the Inside; for they were a Present to him from the Emperor.

I must add one Word more, in relation to the Variety which reigns in these Pleasure-houses.[27] It is not only to be found in their Situations, Views, Disposition, Sizes, Heights, and all the other general Points; but also in their lesser Parts, that go to the composing of them. Thus, for instance, there is no People in the World who can shew such a Variety of Shapes and Forms, in the Doors and Windows, as the *Chinese*. They have some round, oval, square, and in all Sorts of angled Figures; some in the shape of Fans; others in those of Flowers, Vases, Birds, Beasts, and Fishes; in short, of all Forms, whether regular or irregular.

It is only here too, I believe, that one can see such Portico's, as I am going to describe to you. They serve to join such Parts of the Buildings in the same Palace, as lie pretty wide from one another. These are sometimes raised on Columns only, on the Side toward the House; and have Openings, of different Shapes, thorough the Walls on the other Side: and sometimes have only Columns on both Sides; as in all such as lead from any of the Palaces, to their open Pavilions for taking the fresh Air. But what is so singular in these Portico's or Colonnades is, that they seldom run on in strait Lines; but make an hundred Turns and Windings: sometimes by the Side of a Grove, at others behind-a Rock, and at others again along the Banks of their Rivers: or Lakes. Nothing can be conceiv'd more delightful: they have such a rural Air, as is quite ravishing and inchanting.

You will certainly conclude from all I have told you, that this Pleasure-place must have cost immense Sums of Money; and indeed there is no Prince, but such an one as is Master of so vast a State as the Emperor of *China* is, who could either afford so prodigious an Expence, or accomplish such a Number of great Works in so little time: for all this was done in the Compass of Twenty Years. It was the Father of the present Emperor who began it; and his Son now only adds Conveniences and Ornaments to it, here and there.[28]

But there is nothing so surprising, or incredible, in this: for besides that the Buildings are most commonly but of one Story, they employ such prodigious Numbers of Workmen, that every thing is carried on very fast. Above half the Difficulty is over, when they have got their Materials upon the Spot. They fall immediately to disposing them in Order; and in a few Months the Work is finish'd. They look almost like those fabulous Palaces, which are said to be raised by Inchantment, all at once, in some beautiful Valley, or on the Brow of some Hill.

This whole Inclosure is called, *Yuen-ming Yuen* [Yuanming yuan], The Garden of Gardens; of the Garden, by way of Eminence. It is not the only one that belongs to the Emperor; he has Three others, of the same Kind: but none of them so large, or so beautiful, as this. In one of these lives the Empress his Mother, and all her Court. It was built by the present Emperor's Grandfather, *Cang-hy* [Kangxi];[29] and is called *Tchamg tchun yuen* [Changchun yuan], or The Garden of perpetual Spring.[30] The Pleasure-places of the Princes and Grandees are in Little, what those of the Emperor are in Great.

Perhaps you will ask me, "Why all this long Description? Should not I rather have drawn Plans of this magnificent Place, and sent them to you?" To have done that, would have taken me up at least Three Years; without touching upon any thing else: whereas I have not a Moment to spare; and am forced to borrow the Time in which I now write to you, from my Hours of Rest. To which you may add, that for such a Work, it would be necessary for me to have full Liberty of going into any Part of the Gardens whenever I pleas'd, and to stay there as long as I pleas'd: which is quite impracticable here. 'Tis very fortunate for me, that I had got the little Knowledge of Painting that I have: for without this, I should have been in the same Case with several other *Europeans*, who have been here between Twenty and Thirty Years, without being able ever to set their Feet on any Spot of this delightful Ground.

There is but one Man here; and that is the Emperor. All Pleasures are made for him alone. This charming Place is scarce ever seen by any body but himself, his Women, and his Eunuchs. The Princes, and other chief Men of the Country, are rarely admitted any farther than the Audience-Chambers. Of all the *Europeans* that are here, none ever enter'd this Inclosure, except the Clock-makers and Painters; whose Employments make it necessary that they should be admitted every where. The Place usually assign'd us to paint in, is in one of those little Palaces above-mentioned; where the Emperor comes to see us work, almost every Day: so that we can never be absent. We don't go out of the Bounds of this Palace, unless what we are to paint cannot be brought to us; and in such Cases, they conduct us to the Place under a large Guard of Eunuchs. We are obliged to go quick, and without any Noise; and huddle and steal along softly, as if we were going upon some Piece of Mischief. 'Tis in this Manner that I have gone through, and seen, all this beautiful Garden; and enter'd into all the Apartments. The Emperor usually resides here Ten Months in each Year. We are about Ten Miles from *Pekin*.[31] All the Day, we are in the Gardens; and have a Table furnished for us by the Emperor: for the Nights, we are bought us a House, near the Entrance to the Gardens. When the Emperor returns to *Pekin*, we attend him; are lodg'd there within his Palace; and go every Evening to the *French* Church.[32]

I think it is high time, both for you and me, that I should put an End to this Letter; which has carried me on to a greater Length, than I at first intended. I wish it may give you any Pleasure; and should be very glad if it was in my Power to do any thing more considerable, to shew you the perfect Esteem I have for you. I shall always remember you, in my Prayers; and beg you would sometimes remember me in yours.

I am,

With the greatest Regards,

Sir,

Your most obedient,

Humble Servant,

Attiret.

NOTES

1   Jean-Denis Attiret, "Lettre du frère Attiret de la Compagnie de Jésus, peintre au service de l'empereur de Chine, à M. d'Assaut. A Pékin le Iᵉʳ novembre 1743," in *Lettres édifiantes et curieuses, écrites des missions étrangères, par quelques Missionnaires de la Compagnie de Jésus,* vol. 27 (Paris: Guerin, 1749), 1–57.

2   Yuanming yuan was begun in 1709 by the Kangxi emperor as a summer palace for his fourth son, the future Yongzheng emperor. Once on the throne, in 1725 Yongzheng began expansion of the complex, which became his principal residence. Under the reign of the Qianlong emperor, Yuanming yuan was expanded further and became a park of over three hundred hectares. Qianlong added two

more gardens to the original nucleus: to the east, Changchun yuan, "Garden of Everlasting Spring," designed between 1745 and 1751, and to the south Qichun yuan, "Garden of Variegated Spring," added to the complex in 1772 and in the 1870s renamed Wanchun yuan, "Garden of Ten-Thousand Springs." Yuanming yuan was the biggest of the three gardens and gave its name to the whole complex. The three gardens were separate from one another, yet connected through an intricate network of waterways and winding paths. In 1747, Qianlong commissioned the Jesuit missionaries at court to design a further extension of the park, a Western-style formal garden called Xiyang lou, "European Palaces." On the profuse literature concerning Yuanming yuan see, for instance, Che Bing Chiu, *Yuan ming yuan: Le jardin de la clarté parfaite* (Besançon: Les Éditions de l'Imprimeur, 2000); Young-tsu Wong, *A Paradise Lost: The Imperial Garden Yuanming Yuan* (Honolulu: University of Hawaii Press, 2001).

3   The concept of "beautiful disorder," used by Attiret to define Chinese garden design, was later borrowed by the French traveler Pierre Poivre (1719–86). In his travelogue entitled *Voyage d'un philosophe*, published in 1768, describing Chinese gardens, Poivre wrote: "That which constitutes their principal beauty, is their delightful situation, judiciously improved, where, in the disposition of the various parts which form the whole, there every where reigns a happy imitation of that beautiful disorder of nature, from whence art has borrowed all her charms." Pierre Poivre, *Travels of a Philosopher: or, Observations on the Manners and Arts of Various Nations in Africa and Asia* (Glasgow: Urie, 1770), 153.

4   Rinaldi, *The Chinese Garden: Garden Types*, 44–45.

5   On the influence of Attiret's letter on the development of European gardens see George Loehr, "L'artiste Jean-Denis Attiret et l'influence exercée par sa description des jardins impériaux," in *La mission française de Pékin aus XVIIe et XVIIIe siècles: Actes du Colloque international de Sinologie, Chantilly 20–22 sept. 1974* (Paris: Les Belles Lettres, 1976), 77–80. For a recent discussion of Attiret's description of Yuanming yuan see Thomas, "Yuanming Yuan/Versailles," 125–28.

6   On the *ferme ornée* and the role of the French views of China on its development see Wiebenson, *The Picturesque Garden in France*, 98–104.

7   Jean-Denis Attiret, *A Particular Account of the Emperor of China's Garden near Pekin*, trans. Sir Harry Beaumont [Joseph Spence] (London: Dodsley, 1752). During the same year, portions of Spence's translation of Attiret's letter were published in some important periodicals: in the cultural journal *London Magazine* 21 (1752), the literary journal *Monthly Review* 7 (1752), and *Scots Magazine* 14 (1752); Loehr, "L'artiste Jean-Denis Attiret," 69. A second English translation of Attiret's letter was completed by the Anglican bishop Thomas Percy, who was an important figure in shaping the image of China in Britain; it was published ten years after the rendition by Joseph Spence in the second volume of Percy's *Miscellaneous Pieces Relating to the Chinese* (1762) with the title "A Description of the Emperor of China's Gardens and Pleasure-Houses Near Pe-king." Percy translated Attiret's letter in its entirety. His English version of Attiret's letter is perhaps less refined in language than that of Joseph Spence but more faithful to the original. In the "Advertisement" to his version of Attiret's letter, Percy writes: "A great

part of this translation was finished before the editor was apprized that a former one had been published in 1752 under the name of Sir Harry Beaumont. Whatever advantages that version may have over this, it may be necessary to mention that the last twenty pages of the original are omitted in it, and some other passages elsewhere: which, tho' they only relate to the affairs of the mission, were judged too curious to be wholly suppressed, as the Reader will be apt to inquire upon what footing the Jesuits remain at present in China." Jean-Denis Attiret, "A Description of the Emperor of China's Gardens and Pleasure-Houses Near Peking," trans. Thomas Percy, in *Miscellaneous Pieces Relating to the Chinese*, ed. Thomas Percy, vol. 2 (London: Dodsley, 1762), 147. On the contribution of Percy on British perception of China see Kitson, *Forging Romantic China*, 26–44.

8 Note by Joseph Spence about his translation: "These are chiefly made of Feathers; colour'd and form'd, so exactly like real Flowers, that one Is often apt to forget one's self, and smell to them. The famous *Signora Vannimano*, at *Rome*, (so many of whose Works in this kind are continually brought Home by our Gentlemen who travel to that City,) at first learn'd her Art from some which were sent from *China*, by the Jesuits; as a Present to the then Pope." And he goes on explaining that his translation at this point differs from the original letter as, "Here is a Page or two omitted, as relating only to their private Affairs." Attiret, *A Particular Account of the Emperor of China's Garden*, 2.

9 Attiret refers to the Qing dynasty Qianlong emperor (r. 1735–96).

10 The note by Joseph Spence about his translation reads: "A handsome City in *France*; and the Capital one, in the Province of *Burgundy*: between Three and Four Miles round." Attiret, *A Particular Account of the Emperor of China's Garden*, 6.

11 The green and fertile appearance of the imperial complex, given by the great variety of trees and flowering trees, suggested a slightly rhetorical comparison to Attiret; in his letter, the Jesuit said of the park, "C'est un vrai Paradis terrestre" (It is indeed a terrestrial paradise). See Attiret, "Lettre," 10. This comment, part of the original French text at this point in the description, was omitted by Joseph Spence, who must have found the affirmation too emphatic, or perhaps even more, considering that it offered an image associated with Catholic culture, hardly in harmony with Anglo-Saxon culture and therefore, less appealing for the public for whom the translation was intended. The comment was included in Percy's translation; see Attiret, "Description of the Emperor of China's Gardens," 157.

12 Attiret emphasized an important aspect of Chinese garden composition: the fact that it should propose a certain variety in the flora over the course of the year. Evidence of the change of seasons, which alluded to the dimension of the passage of time, was in fact one of the effects sought after in the botanical character of the gardens.

13 At this point of his letter, Attiret added a personal comment on the scene just described: "Rien ne ressemble tant à ces Palais fabuleux de Fées, qu'on suppose au milieu d'un désert élevés sur un roc dont l'avenue est raboteuse et va en serpentant." See Attiret, "Lettre," 12. Spence decided not to translate this comparison, perhaps considering it too hyperbolic. The comment was included in the

more literal and complete translation by Percy: "They resemble nothing so much as those fabulous palaces of the fairies, which are supposed to be seated in the midst of a desert, or some craggy rock, whose ascent is rugged and goes winding up by degrees." See Attiret, "Description of the Emperor of China's Gardens," 159.

14 In the original French, Attiret speaks more simply of "figures en bronze ou en cuivre d'animaux symboliques," which is translated literally by Percy with "figures of symbolical animals in bronze or copper." See Attiret, "Description of the Emperor of China's Gardens," 160. It is interesting to note that here Spence uses the adjective "hieroglyphical" to translate the French term "symboliques." In translating Attiret's letter, Spence uses the then (before the discovery of the Rosetta stone in 1799) current interpretation of Egyptian hieroglyphs as symbolic pictures rather than phonetic writing. Thus Spence is making an erudite association of the "animaux symboliques," the symbolical animals mentioned by Attiret, to the symbols of hieroglyphs. Also in this phrase from Attiret, Spence perhaps sees proof of the theory that the Chinese were supposed to descend from ancient Egyptians, which had been formulated by another Jesuit, Athanasius Kircher (1602–80). Kircher, famous for being one of the first Westerners to try to decipher the hieroglyphical writing of the ancient Egyptian language, had gathered studies of that language in two important works: *Lingua Aegyptiaca Restituta* (1643) and the third volume of *Oedipus Aegyptiacus* (1654). In his work *China monumentis . . . illustrata* (1667), Kircher affirmed that the Chinese were related to the Egyptians as common descendants of Ham, one of the three sons of Noah, and he considered Chinese characters to be a proof of this theory, believing that they were derived from Egyptian hieroglyphs. See Athanasius Kircher, *China monumentis . . . illustrata* (Amsterdam: van Waesberge and Weyerstraet, 1667), 233–35. On this topic, see Mungello, *Curious Land*, 153; Adrian Hsia, *Chinesia: The European Construction of China in the Literature of the 17th and 18th Centuries* (Tübingen: Max Niemeyer, 1998), 27.

15 The description of the imperial complex in Attiret's letter often assumes the character of a Europe-China comparison through their different ways of conceiving architecture, decorative arts, and the art of the garden.

16 Attiret refers to different specimens of goldfish.

17 Note by Joseph Spence about his translation: "I have seen of this sort of Justs upon the Water, in our Parts of the World; and particularly at Lions in France. The Champions stand, as firmly as they are able, on the Prows of two Boats; with a Shield in their left Hands, and a blunted Spear in their Right, There is an equal Number of Rowers in each of the Boats, who drive them on with a great deal of Impetuosity. The two Combatants charge each other with their Spears: and often both, but almost always one or other of them, is driven backward on the Shock; either down into his Boat, or (which often happens) into the Water: which latter makes one of the principal Parts in this odd sort of Diversion." Attiret, *A Particular Account of the Emperor of China's Garden*, 20–21.

18 Note by Joseph Spence about his translation: "The Original says: 'Les *Koucifeys*, les *Feys*, les *Pines*, les *Kouci-gins*, et les *Tchangtfays*': and informs us in a Note,

that these are so many different Titles of Honour, for the different Classes of such of the Emperor's Mistresses, as are most in his Favour. I did not think it worth while to set down all these hard Names in the Text; and perhaps, they might as well have been omitted even here." Attiret, *A Particular Account of the Emperor of China's Garden*, 22.

19   Note by Joseph Spence about his translation: "The second City for Size in the *Franche Comté.*" Attiret, *A Particular Account of the Emperor of China's Garden*, 22. The city of Dole, which Attiret referred to, was his birthplace. The Jesuit compares the residential area in Yuanming yuan with the whole city of Dole in scale and vastness but also in the complexity of the spatial organization of the diverse architectural structures composing the imperial compound, where the volumes of buildings are opposed to the voids of open courts, and are interspersed with different gardens, according to a hierarchical logic, which Attiret explains in the lines immediately following.

20   In the following lines, Attiret describes the surprising playful space of the miniature city that the emperor had built within the precinct of Yuanming yuan. Attiret presents it as a sort of amusement park created especially for the court. The Chinese city reproduced in the imperial garden offered the emperor the chance to satisfy his curiosity among the urban features of a real little city, with the liveliness of its daily life and even its confusion. This description of the miniature city must have struck the imagination of those European travelers who, after Attiret, described Chinese gardens. William Chambers, who had never seen the imperial parks near Beijing, included this portion of the letter of Attiret in his *Dissertation on Oriental Gardening* (1772); also, George Leonard Staunton, who accompanied the first British embassy to Qianlong led by Lord George Macartney, in his report on that voyage wrote of the miniature city—of whose existence he had learned from Attiret's letter—as a place "where the scenes of common life, and the transactions and confusion of the capital, are faithfully represented, according to the accounts of a missionary." See William Chambers, *A Dissertation on Oriental Gardening* (London: Griffin, 1772), 31–33; Staunton, *An Authentic Account of an Embassy*, 245–46.

21   Though at the beginning of his letter, Attiret affirmed that Chinese architecture might seem modest if compared with French or Italian architecture, his assessment of it is generally positive. Attiret's insistence on his genuine appreciation had also, perhaps, the intent of promoting Chinese taste in architecture in Europe and resulted in an imaginative comparison of a typical Chinese building with a building in Paris, Palais Bourbon. Built between 1722 and 1728 for Louise Françoise de Bourbon (1673–1743), the recognized daughter of Louis XIV and Françoise-Athénaïs, Marquise de Montespan, Palais Bourbon was situated on the left bank of the Seine, overlooking the river and the Tuileries to the east. The parallel Attiret proposed between Palais Bourbon and Chinese architecture is due to the original plan of the Parisian building. Its simple axial and symmetrical plan and its one-story structure accessed through a sequence of two courts enclosed by walls or edifices were, for Attiret, reminiscent of the architecture of Chinese imperial palaces and their spatial arrangement.

22 Note by Joseph Spence about his translation: "The Author of this Letter seems here to have form'd his Opinion, only from the Garden in which he was employ'd; for this is not universally the Case in the Pleasure-houses of the Emperor of *China*. I have lately seen some Prints of another of his Gardens, (brought from that Kingdom, and which will very soon be publish'd here,) in which the Disposition of the Ground, Water, and Plantations, is indeed quite irregular; but the Houses, Bridges, and Fences, are all of a regular Kind. Those Prints will give the truest Idea, we can have, of the *Chinese* Manner of laying out Pleasure-grounds." Attiret, *A Particular Account of the Emperor of China's Garden*, 38. Spence is referring to the set of views of palaces and gardens in the imperial summer residence of Bishu shanzhuang (Mountain Estate to Escape the Summer Heat), prepared by the missionary Matteo Ripa in 1713 for the Kangxi emperor.

23 In the French original, Attiret writes that "dans les maisons des plaisance, on vuet que presque partout il regne un beau désordre, une anti-symmétrie" (in pleasure houses one sees almost everywhere a fine disorder, an antisymmetry). See Attiret, "Lettre," 34.

24 In the original text Attiret writes: "C'est une campagne rustique et naturelle, qu'on veut représenter; une solitude, non pas un Palais bien ordonné dans toutes le regles de la symmétrie e du rapport." Attiret, "Lettre," 34–35. Percy's translation of this paragraph is more literal than the one by Spence and reads: "It is a rural landscape (they say) a face of nature, that we would represent, a solitude, and not a palace leid out in all the rules of symmetry and proportion." Attiret, "Description of the Emperor of China's Gardens," 180.

25 The idea of the Chinese garden as a place that opens to view slowly, which entices the visitor to traverse it in the constant lure of discovering something new, is also expressed in the letter written from Beijing in 1767 by the French Jesuit Michel Benoist to Monsieur Papillon d'Auteroche, included in this anthology.

26 Note by Joseph Spence to his translation: "The Original says, *Soixante Ouanes*: and adds in a Note that one *Ouane* is worth Ten thousand *Taëls*; and each *Taël* is worth Seven Livres and a Half; so that Sixty Ouanes make Four Millions and a Half of Livres. Which is equal to 196,875 Pounds Sterling." Attiret, *A Particular Account of the Emperor of China's Garden*, 40.

27 In the original, Attiret does not write simply "variety" but "admirable variété" (admirable variety). The English translation shows yet again the cleansing work done by Spence, which frees, if not deprives, Attiret's writing from all traces of passionate appreciation, which Spence evidently considers redundant. Attiret, "Lettre," 36.

28 See note 2.

29 Note by Joseph Spence about his translation: "*Cang-hy* [Kangxi] began his Reign in 1660; his Son, *Yongtching* [Yongzheng], succeeded him in 1722; and his Grandson, *Kien-long* [Qianlong], in 1735." Attiret, *A Particular Account of the Emperor of China's Garden*, 45. Spence is rather accurate in his biographical notes on the three emperors of the Qing dynasty: Kangxi ruled over China from 1661 to 1722; Yongzheng, Kangxi's fourth son, reigned from 1722 to 1735; Qianlong, Yongzheng's fourth son, reigned from 1735 to 1796.

30   Attiret is referring to Changchun yuan (Garden of Joyful Spring), built in the Northwestern outskirts of Beijing for the Kangxi emperor from 1684. Both the Yongzheng emperor and his son, the Qianlong emperor, adapted it as a residence for their mothers. Attiret, like Jean-François Gerbillon before him and like Matteo Ripa afterward, translates the name of Kangxi's garden Changchun yuan as "Garden of Perpetual Spring." In a letter written from Beijing in 1773, the French Jesuit Michel Benoist gives further details on the imperial gardens built in the outskirts of Beijing: "La maison de plaisance de l'Empereur se nomme *yven ming yven* (jardin d'une clarté parfaite). La maison de plaisance de l'Impératrice mère, tout proche celle de S.M., s'appelle *Tchang tchun yven*, (jardin où regne un agréable printems.) Une autre maison de plaisance peu éloignée de celle-ci se nomme *ouan cheou chan*, (montagne de longue vie). Une autre à quelque distance de là a nom, *tsing ming yven*, (jardin d'une brillante tranquillité). Au milieu de la maison de plaisance de l'Empereur est une montagne appellée *yu tsiven chan*, (montagne d'une précieuse source)." (The pleasure house of the Emperor is named *yven ming yven*, garden of perfect clarity [Yuanming yuan, "Garden of Perfect Brightness"]. The pleasure house of the Empress-mother, very near to that of H.M., is called *Tchang tchun yven*, garden where a pleasurable spring reigns [Changchun yuan, "Garden of Joyful Spring"]. Another pleasure house not much distant from this one is named *ouan cheou chan*, montagne de longue vie [Wanshou shan, "Longevity Hill"]. Another one at some distance from that one has the name of *tsing ming yven*, garden of a bright tranquility [Jingming yuan, "Garden of Tranquil Brightness"]. In the middle of this pleasure house of the Emperor there is a mountain called *yu tsiven chan*, mountain of a precious spring [Yuquan shan, "Jade Spring Hill"]). Michel Benoist, "Troisième Lettre du P. Benoit. A Pékin, le 4. Nov. 1773," in *Lettres édifiantes et curieuses, écrites des missions étrangères, par quelques Missionnaires de la Compagnie de Jésus*, vol. 33 (Paris: Berton, 1776), 180–82. In addition to Yuanming yuan and Changchun yuan, Benoist recorded two other gardens: Qingyi yuan, "Garden of Clear Ripples," expanded by the Qianlong emperor from 1750 and based on the harmonious juxtaposition of Wanshou shan, "Longevity Hill" and the large Kunming Hu, "Vast Bright Lake," both artificial; Jingming yuan, "Garden of Tranquil Brightness," which was begun by the Kangxi emperor in 1680 on the southern slope of Yuquan shan, "Jade Spring Hill," and further enlarged by the Qianlong emperor in 1750. Zou, *A Jesuit Garden in Beijing*, 11; Valder, *Gardens in China*, 116–17, 172–73.

31   In the original, Attiret makes another comparison of Beijing and France, in the form of an analogy between the distance between the capital city and the residence of the court. Attiret writes that Yuanming yuan "n'y est éloigné de Pékin qu'autant que Versailles l'est de Paris" (is not as far from Beijing as Versailles is from Paris). Attiret, "Lettre," 36. Spence, however, makes a correct synthetic evaluation as the approximate distance between Paris and Versailles in a straight line is in fact ten miles.

32   Note by Joseph Spence about his translation: "Here follow 14 or 15 Pages in the Original which treat only of the Author's private Affairs, or of the Affairs of the Mission, without any thing relating to the Emperor's Garden; and are therefore omitted by the Translator." Attiret, *A Particular Account of the Emperor of China's Garden*, 49.

CHAPTER 10

William Chambers (1723–96)

The writings of British architect William Chambers were influential in the eighteenth-century European perception of the Chinese garden and in the introduction of Chinese-inspired elements in Western gardens. In addition to the letter of the Jesuit Jean-Denis Attiret, Chambers's writings were considered an important source of inspiration for the development of the *jardin anglo-chinois*.

On the two journeys he took to Guangzhou with the Swedish East India Company, in 1743–44 and then in 1748–49, Chambers gathered information about Chinese architecture and gardens that informed his two successful works on the subject, published several years after his return to England: *Design of Chinese Buildings, Furniture, Dresses, Machines, and Utensils* (1757) and *A Dissertation on Oriental Gardening* (1772 and 1773). The former, which was published simultaneously in English and French, is a collection of twenty-one engravings representing architectural details, interior views, furniture and decorations, boats, utilitarian objects, and figures dressed according to rank and work, all based on Chinese paintings and the sketches Chambers himself had made in Guangzhou.[1] The illustrations are introduced by brief essays on Chinese public and private architecture, on "Machines and dresses," and by a short treatise on the Chinese garden entitled "Of the Art of Laying Out Gardens Among the Chinese," which became extremely popular in both England and France.[2] Unlike accounts about the gardens of China composed by other Western travelers, who inserted their descriptions of gardens into a wider cultural and historical context, the "Chinese garden" Chambers describes is decontextualized. This form of abstraction is instrumental to the theoretical construction of his essay, concerned solely with garden composition. Chambers's text, reproduced here in its entirety, aimed at divulging Chinese garden design principles and thus at contributing to the evolution of the English landscape style.[3]

Though his own direct acquaintance with Chinese gardens was modest, limited to some small private gardens that he visited in Guangzhou, Chambers gives quite an accurate reading of Chinese gardens' spatial composition. He perceives the articulation of the garden as a visual construct generated by—as Attiret had already suggested—a sequence of carefully planned scenes capable of arousing different emotions in the visitor. Chambers explains the "artifices they [the Chinese] employ to surprize"; he emphasizes the aesthetic of variety, based on contrasts and on the dialectic of an alternation of opposite spatial qualities, such as narrow and wide, closure and openness, used to alter the visitor's perception of the garden space and at the same time to arouse curiosity. In addition to the importance of engendering an emotional response in the observer, Chambers introduces the role of pauses in the appreciation of the garden's space. He indicates that an essential quality of the spatial strategy behind Chinese garden design is the positioning of specific vantage points, marked by a seat or a pavilion, for the contemplation of the individual scenic views.

Chambers's understanding of the gardens of China had been informed by earlier accounts by Jesuit missionaries. Their narratives supplied the British architect the details that his short visits to China would not have provided him. References to the Jesuits' writings are not always explicit in Chambers's texts.[4] As an authoritative source of his knowledge, Chambers mentions an elusive yet "celebrated Chinese painter" Lepqua. By invoking the testimony of a Chinese source as a guarantee of the reliability of the information he was presenting, Chambers aims at proposing his essay as an accurate and impartial account of the gardens of China.[5] At the same time, a reference to a painter in the very opening lines of his essay, and the repeated allusions to painting that follow, suggest that Chambers may have derived the idea of the scenes he describes as characteristic features of the gardens of China from Chinese landscape paintings instead of real gardens.

Chambers also drew on the Western garden tradition in his account. The three categories of scenes he identified in the Chinese garden—the beautiful, the enchanted, and the horrid—which represent the main argument of his essay, had precedents in the history of Western garden aesthetics. They paralleled the three categories proposed by Joseph Addison—the beautiful, the uncommon, and the great—as early as 1712 in his essay *On the Pleasures of the Imagination*.[6] They also recalled the opposition between beautiful and sublime proposed by Edmund Burke in his *A Philosophical Enquiry into . . . the Sublime and the Beautiful*, published in 1757.[7] The catalogue of scenes

Figure 7. Edward Rooker, after William Chambers, pl. 9 from William Chambers, *Designs of Chinese Buildings, Furniture, Dresses, Machines, and Utensils* (London: Published for the author, 1757). Yale Center for British Art, Paul Mellon Collection.

Chambers proposed in his short essay was developed further in *A Dissertation on Oriental Gardening* (1772), reproduced in its entirety in the Appendix.

* * *

William Chambers, "Of the Art of Laying Out Gardens Among the Chinese," in *Design of Chinese Buildings, Furniture, Dresses, Machines, and Utensils* (1757)

The gardens which I saw in China were very small; nevertheless from them, and what could be gathered from Lepqua, a celebrated Chinese painter, with whom I had several conversations on the subject of gardening, I think I have acquired sufficient knowledge of their notions on this head.

Nature is their pattern, and their aim is to imitate her in all her beautiful irregularities. Their first consideration is the form of the ground, whether it be flat, sloping, hilly, or mountainous, extensive, or of small compass, of a dry or marshy nature, abounding with rivers and springs, or liable to a scarcity of water; to all which circumstances they attend with great care, chusing such dispositions as humour the ground, can be executed with the least expence, hide it's defects, and set it's advantages in the most conspicuous light.

As the Chinese are not fond of walking, we seldom meet with avenues or spacious walks, as in our European plantations:[8] the whole ground is laid out in a variety of scenes, and you are led, by winding passages cut in the groves, to the different points of view, each of which is marked by a seat, a building, or some other object.

The perfection of their gardens consists in the number, beauty, and diversity of these scenes. The Chinese gardeners, like the European painters, collect from nature the most pleasing objects, which they endeavour to combine in such a manner, as not only to appear to the best advantage separately, but likewise to unite in forming an elegant and striking whole.

Their artists distinguish three different species of scenes, to which they give the appellations of pleasing, horrid, and enchanted. Their enchanted scenes answer, in a great measure, to what we call romantic, and in these they make use of several artifices to excite surprize. Sometimes they make a rapid stream, or torrent, pass under ground, the turbulent noise of which strikes the ear of the new-comer, who is at a loss to know from whence it proceeds: at other times they dispose the rocks, buildings, and other objects that form the composition, in such a manner as that the wind passing through the different interstices and cavities, made in them for that purpose, causes strange and uncommon sounds. They introduce into these scenes all kinds of extraordinary trees, plants, and flowers, form artificial and complicated ecchoes, and let loose different sorts of monstrous birds and animals.

In their scenes of horror, they introduce impending rocks, dark caverns, and impetuous cataracts rushing down the mountains from all sides; the trees are ill-formed, and seemingly torn to pieces by the violence of tempests; some are thrown down, and intercept the course of the torrents, appearing as if they had been brought down by the fury of the waters; others look as if shattered and blasted by the force of lightning; the buildings are some in ruins, others half consumed by fire, and some miserable huts dispersed in the mountains serve, at once to indicate the existence and wretchedness of the inhabitants. These scenes are generally succeeded by pleasing ones. The Chinese artists, knowing how powerfully contrast operates on the mind, constantly practise sudden transitions, and a striking opposition of forms, colours, and shades. Thus they conduct you from limited prospects to extensive views; from objects of horrour to scenes of delight; from lakes and rivers to plains, hills, and woods; to dark and gloomy colours they oppose such as are brilliant, and to complicated forms simple ones; distributing, by a judicious arrangement, the different masses of light and shade, in such a manner as to render the composition at once distinct in it's parts, and striking in the whole.

Where the ground is extensive, and a multiplicity of scenes are to be introduced, they generally adapt each to one single point of view: but where it is limited, and affords no room for variety, they endeavour to remedy this defeat, by disposing the objects so, that being viewed from different points, they produce different representations; and sometimes, by an artful disposition, such as have no resemblance to each other.

In their large gardens they contrive different scenes for morning, noon, and evening; erecting, at the proper points of view, buildings adapted to the recreations of each particular time of the day: and in their small ones (where, as has been observed, one arrangement produces many representations) they dispose in the same manner, at the several points of view, buildings, which, from their use, point out the time of day for enjoying the scene in it's perfection.

As the climate of China is exceeding hot, they employ a great deal of water in their gardens. In the small ones, if the situation admits, they frequently lay almost the whole ground under water; leaving only some islands and rocks: and in their large ones they introduce extensive lakes, rivers, and canals. The banks of their lakes and rivers are variegated in imitation of nature; being sometimes bare and gravelly, sometimes covered with woods quite to the water's edge. In some places flat, and adorned with flowers and shrubs; in others steep, rocky, and forming caverns, into which part of the waters discharge themselves with noise and violence. Sometimes you see meadows covered with cattle, or rice-grounds that run out into the lakes, leaving between them passages for vessels; and sometimes groves, into which enter, in different parts, creeks and rivulets, sufficiently deep to admit boats; their banks being planted with trees, whose spreading branches, in some places, form arbours, under which the boats pass. These generally conduct to some very interesting object; such as a magnificent building, places on the top of a mountain cut into terrasses; a casine [casino, small pavilion] situated in the midst of a lake; a cascade; a grotto cut into a variety of apartments; an artificial rock; and many other such inventions.

Their rivers are seldom streight, but serpentine, and broken into many irregular points; sometimes they are narrow, noisy, and rapid, at other times deep, broad, and slow. Both in their rivers and lakes are seen reeds, with other aquatic plants and flowers; particularly the *Lyen Hoa* [lian hua], of which they are very fond.[9] They frequently erect mills, and other hydraulic machines, the motions of which enliven the scene: they have also a great number of vessels of different forms and sizes. In their lakes they intersperse islands; some of them barren, and surrounded with rocks and shoals; others enriched with every thing that art and nature can furnish most perfect. They likewise form artificial rocks; and in compositions of this kind the Chinese surpass all other nations. The making them is a distinct profession; and there are at Canton, and probably in most other cities of China, numbers of artificers constantly employed in this business. The stone they are made of comes from the southern coasts of China. It is of a bluish cast, and worn into irregular forms by the action of the waves. The Chinese are exceeding nice in the choice of this stone; insomuch that I have seen several Tael given for a bit no bigger than a man's fist, when it happened to be of a beautiful form and lively colour. But these select pieces they use in landscapes for their apartments: in gardens they employ a coarser sort, which they join with a bluish cement, and form rocks of a considerable size. I have seen some of these exquisitely fine, and such as discovered an uncommon elegance of taste in the contriver. When they are large they make in them caves and grottos, with openings, through which you discover distant prospects, They cover them, in different places, with trees, shrubs, briars, and moss; placing on their tops little temples, or other buildings, to which you ascend by rugged and irregular steps cut in the rock.

When there is a sufficient supply of water, and proper ground, the Chinese never fail to form cascades in their gardens. They avoid all regularity in these works, observing nature according to her operations in that mountainous country. The waters burst out from among the caverns, and windings of the rocks. In some places a large and impetuous cataract appears; in others are seen many lesser falls. Sometimes the view of the cascade is intercepted by trees, whose leaves and branches only leave room to discover the waters, in some places, as they fall down the sides of the mountain. They frequently throw rough wooden bridges from one rock to another, over the steepest part of the cataract; and often intercept it's passage by trees and heaps of stones, that seem to have been brought down by the violence of the torrent.

In their plantations they vary the forms and colours of their trees; mixing such as have large and spreading branches, with those of pyramidal figures, and dark greens, with brighter, interspersing among them such as produce flowers; of which they have some that flourish a great part of the year. The Weeping-willow is one of their favourite trees, and always among those that border their lakes and rivers, being so planted as to have it's branches hanging over the water. They likewise introduce trunks of decayed trees, sometimes erect, and at other times lying on the ground, being very nice about their forms, and the colour of the bark and moss on them.

Various are the artifices they employ to surprize. Sometimes they lead you through dark caverns and gloomy passages, at the issue of which you are, on a sudden, struck with the view of a delicious landscape, enriched with every thing that luxuriant nature affords most beautiful. At other times you are conducted through avenues and walks, that gradually diminish and grow rugged, till the passage is at length entirely intercepted, and rendered impracticable, by bullies, briars, and stones: when unexpectedly a rich and extensive prospect opens to view, so much the more pleasing as it was less looked for.

Another of their artifices is to hide some part of a composition by trees, or other intermediate objects. This naturally excites the curiosity of the spectator to take a nearer view; when he is surprised by some unexpected scene, or some representation totally opposite to the thing he looked for. The termination of their lakes they always hide, leaving room for the imagination to work; and the same rule they observed in other compositions, wherever it can be put in practice.

Though the Chinese are not well versed in opticks, yet experience has taught them that objects appear less in size, and grow dim in colour, in proportion as they are more removed from the eye of the spectator. These discoveries have given rise to an artifice, which they sometimes put in practice. It is the forming prospects in perspective, by introducing buildings, vessels, and other objects, lessened according as they are more distant from the point of view; and that the deception may be still more striking, they give a greyish tinge to the distant parts of the composition, and plant in the remoter parts of these scenes trees of a fainter colour, and smaller growth, than those that appear in the front or fore-ground; by these means rendering what in reality is trifling and limited, great and considerable in appearance.

The Chinese generally avoid streight lines; yet they do not absolutely reject them. They sometimes make avenues, when they have any interesting object to expose to view. Roads they always make streight; unless the un-evenness of the ground, or other impediments, afford at least a pretext for doing otherwise. Where the ground is entirely level, they look upon it as an absurdity to make a serpentine road: for they say that it must either be made by art, or worn by the constant passage of travellers; in either of which cases it is not natural to suppose men would chuse a crooked line when they might go by a streight one.

What we call clumps, the Chinese gardeners are not unacquainted with; but they use them somewhat more sparingly than we do. They never fill a whole piece of ground with clumps: they consider a plantation as painters do a picture, and groupe their trees in the same manner as these do their figures, having their principal and subservient masses.

This is the substance of what I learnt during my stay in China, partly from my own observation, but chiefly from the lessons of Lepqua: and from what has been said it may be inferred, that the art of laying out grounds, after the Chinese manner, is exceedingly difficult, and not to be attained by persons of narrow intellects. For though the precepts are simple and obvious, yet the putting them in execution requires genius, judgment, and experience; a strong imagination, and a thorough knowledge of the human mind. This method being fixed to no certain rule, but liable to as many variations, as there are different arrangements in the works of the creation.

NOTES

1   William Chambers, *Design of Chinese Buildings, Furniture, Dresses, Machines and Utensils . . . to which is Annexed a Description of their Temples, Houses, Gardens* (London: Published for the author, 1757); William Chambers, *Desseins des edifices, meubles, habits, machines, et ustenciles des Chinois: Gravés sur les originaux dessinés à la Chine . . . Auxquels est ajoutée une description de leurs temples, de leurs maisons, de leurs jardins, &c* (London: Haberkorn, 1757).

2   Immediately after its publication, "Of the Art of Laying Out Gardens Among the Chinese" was reproduced in widely read eighteenth-century periodicals, such as the *Gentleman's Magazine* and, the following year, in the *Annual Register*. See *Gentleman's Magazine* 27 (May 1757): 216–19; *Annual Register* 1 (1758): 319–23. Bishop Thomas Percy, who edited several collections of texts related to Chinese culture, inserted Chambers's essay into his *Miscellaneous Pieces Relating to the Chinese* (1762), along with his translation of the letter of Jean-Denis Attiret. William Chambers, "Of the Art of Laying Out Gardens Among the Chinese," in *Miscellaneous Pieces Relating to the Chinese*, ed. Thomas Percy, vol. 2 (London: Dodsley, 1762), 125–144. In 1776, Georges-Louis Le Rouge published a French version of Chambers's essay in cahier 5 of *Détails de nouveaux jardins à la mode*

(1775–89): William Chambers, "Traité des édifices, meubles, habits, machines et ustensiles des Chinois . . . Compris une description de leurs temples, maisons, jardins, etc." (Paris: Chez le Sieur Le Rouge, 1776). On the reception of Chambers's essay on the Chinese garden in Europe, see Eileen Harris, "Design of Chinese Buildings and the Dissertation on Oriental Gardening," in *Sir William Chambers, Knight of the Polar Star*, ed. John Harris (University Park: Pennsylvania State University Press, 1970), 152.

3   In the preface to the *Design of Chinese Buildings, Furniture, Dresses, Machines and Utensils* (1757), Chambers writes that "the Chinese excel in the art of laying out gardens. Their taste in that is good, and what we have for some time past been aiming at in England, though not always with success, I have endeavoured to be distinct in my account of it, and hope it may be of some service to our Gardeners." Chambers, *Design*, iii–iv.

4   On the dependence of Chambers's writings on the Jesuits' reports, especially those of Jean-Baptiste du Halde and Attiret, see, Harris, "Design," 146, 150–51, 157.

5   On Lepqua and Chambers's writings see Janine Barrier, Monique Mosser, and Che Bing Chiu, eds., *Aux jardins de Cathay: L'imaginaire anglo-chinois en Occident. William Chambers* (Besançon: Editions de l'imprimeur, 2004), 59–60.

6   Richard Quaintance, "Toward Distinguishing Among Theme Park Publics: William Chambers's Landscape Theory vs. His Kew Practice," in *Theme Park Landscapes: Antecedents and Variations*, ed. Terence Young and Robert Riley (Washington, D.C., Dumbarton Oaks Research Library and Collection, 2002), 27; Porter, *The Chinese Taste*, 48–49. Dora Wiebenson suggests Noël-Antoine Pluche's *Le spectacle de la nature* (1732) as another possible source for the categories of scenes described by Chambers; Wiebenson, *The Picturesque Garden in France*, 40n7, see also 39–43.

7   Burke's *Philosophical Enquiry* was to be an important reference for Chambers's later *Dissertation on Oriental Gardening*. On Chambers and Burke, see Eileen Harris, "Burke and Chambers on the Sublime and the Beautiful," *Essays in the History of Architecture Presented to Rudolf Wittkower*, ed. Douglas Fraser, Howard Hibbard, and Milton J. Lewine (London: Phaidon, 1967), 207–13. See also Wiebenson, *The Picturesque Garden in France*, 40–41 and 53–54.

8   Chambers probably drew this affirmation from the Jesuit Le Comte's letter to the Duchess of Bouillon, where Le Comte explained the lack of alleys by the supposed laziness of the Chinese and wrote: "seeing the *Chineses* walk not much, Alleys do not agree with them." Le Comte, *Memoires and Observations*, 162. This indebtedness to Le Comte represents an example of the role that the Jesuit writings played in Chambers's knowledge of Chinese gardens and on the formulation of his theories on garden design.

9   The aquatic plant Chambers is referring to is the lotus (*Nelumbo nucifera* Gaertn.), whose Chinese name is *lian*. Lotus flowers are called *huehua* in Chinese but when they are used for medical purposes they are given the name *lian hua*. Fèvre and Métailié, *Dictionnaire Ricci*, 272–73.

CHAPTER 11

Jean Joseph Marie Amiot (1718–93)

In a letter written from Beijing in 1752 and published in 1758 in the collection *Lettres édifiantes et curieuses*, the French Jesuit Jean Joseph Marie Amiot describes the festivities on the occasion of the sixtieth birthday of the Qianlong emperor's mother, the Dowager Empress Chongqing.[1] The event had been celebrated by Qianlong with a grand project, the complete reconfiguration of a vast landscaped area, which was later going to become the imperial park currently known as Yihe yuan (Garden of the Preservation of Harmony), which the Jesuit, arrived in Beijing in 1751, had probably not yet had the opportunity to see. Amiot's letter focuses on the ephemeral structures erected along the route that the empress was to take in January 1752, on her way to the capital from the imperial parks in the outskirts of Beijing. The epistle is an important documentation of the use, and significance, of temporary constructions set up in the city's open spaces and surroundings on particular occasions to mark ceremonial solemnities of the court. Temporary structures were also erected in European cities for important events, such as the visits of illustrious persons or noble weddings. But while in the West preference was given to architectonic structures used to emblematize the solemnity of the ceremony, in China, as Amiot observed, a benign nature was artfully staged around festive pavilions. Along the route embellished for the dowager empress, there were open spaces and buildings intended to welcome the members of the retinue, arranged among the visual seductions of little valleys and lakes, animated by a nature that displayed, exuberantly, her gifts before the august parent.

The extract presented below is taken from the English translation of Amiot's letter made by the Anglican bishop Thomas Percy, who published it in the second volume of his *Miscellaneous Pieces Relating to the Chinese* (1762).[2]

Amiot, who remained at service at the Qing court for nearly forty years, was held in high esteem by the Qianlong emperor for his musical expertise and linguistic abilities, as he spoke both fluent Tartar, the language of the Manchu-Qing emperors, and Chinese. He was a prolific author and wrote extensively on different aspects of Chinese culture, including music, military art, history, and language.[3] He also kept an extensive regular correspondence with European intellectuals, among them Henri-Léonard-Jean-Baptiste Bertin, French statesman and minister and noted Sinophile. During his long stay in China, where he remained until his death, Amiot sent the minister a remarkable number of books, objects, prints, and illustrations, enriching his private collections.[4]

＊　＊　＊

From Jean Joseph Marie Amiot, "A Description of the Solemnities Observed at *Pe-king* on the Emperor's Mother Entering on the Sixtieth Year of Her Age, from the French of P. *Amyot*, Jesuit," translated by Thomas Percy (1762)

It is in *China* an ancient custom to celebrate with great pomp the day when the Emperor's mother enters upon the sixtieth year of her age. Some months before that day arrived, all the Tribunals of the capital, all the Viceroys and great Mandarines of the empire, had orders to prepare themselves for the aforementioned ceremony, the most splendid, that is observed in these parts. All the painters, engravers, architects, and joiners of *Pe-king* [Beijing] and the neighbouring provinces, were without intermission employed for more than three months, together in making, everyone, the nicest works, of his respective art. Many other kinds of artists had also employment. The business was to construct something that might charm the eyes of a delicate and voluptuous court, accustomed to see whatever is most beautiful in the works of art brought from the four quarters of the globe. The decorations were to begin at one of the Emperor's houses of pleasure, which is at *Yuen-min-yuan* [Yuanming yuan], and to terminate at the palace which is at *Pe-king* in the center of the *Tartarian* city: these distant from each other, about four leagues.

There are two roads which lead from one of these palaces to the other. The Emperor ordered that the procession should be made along that which runs by the river side. . . . On the two banks of the river were erected buildings of different forms. Here was a house either square, triangular, or polygon,[5] with all its apartments. There was a rotunda or some other edifice of a similar kind. As one went along, others appeared, whose construction (varied in a hundred different manners) engaged, amused and charmed the sight, wherever one fixed it. In such places as the river, by growing wider, had departed from a right line, were built houses of wood supported by pillars fixed in the water, and which appeared above its surface, some two feet, and others three or four, or even higher, according to the plan of the *Chinese* architect. The greatest part of these buildings formed islands, the passage to which was over bridges built for that purpose. There were some intirely detached and separate, others were contiguous, and had a communication between them by covered galleries, built much in the same manner as the houses and bridges which I have described above. All these edifices were gilt and embellished in the most splendid taste of the country. They were every one devoted to a particular use. In some were bands of music: in others companies of comedians; in the greatest part were refreshments and magnificent thrones to receive the Emperor and his mother, supposing they should have an inclination to stop and rest themselves there for a few moments.

In the city was another sight still finer in its kind, than that I have been describing. From the western gate, by which the court was to make its entrance, to the gate of the palace, there were nothing but superb buildings, peristyles,[6] pavilions, colonnades, galleries, amphitheatres, with trophies and other works of *Chinese* architecture all equally splendid. These were embellished with festoons, garlands, and many other ornaments of a similar kind, which being composed of the finest silk of different colours, afforded a charming sight. Gilding, mock-diamonds, and other stones of the same kind, glittered on all sides. A large quantity of mirrours made of metal highly polished, greatly added to the shew.[7] Their construction and arrangement, by multiplying objects on all sides, and re-assembling them in miniature, formed every thing that could enrich the eyes.

These brilliant edifices were interrupted from time to time by artificial mountains and valleys, made in imitation of nature, which one would have taken for agreeable deserts and for real places of the most delightful solitude. They had contrived brooks and fountains, had planted trees and thickets, and stuck on deer, to which they had given attitudes so natural, that one would have said they were alive. Upon the summits or declivities of some of these mountains, were seen *Bonzaries* or *Chinese* convents with their little temples and idols, to which they had made little paths. In other places they had made orchards and gardens. In the greatest part of these were seen vines with their tendrils and clusters, in different degrees of maturity. In others were planted all sorts of trees, so as to exhibit the fruits and flowers of the four seasons of the year. They were not to be distinguished from the true ones, altho' they were only artificial.

This was not all. In diverse places by which the procession was to pass, they had distributed lakes, meres, and reservoirs with their several kinds of fish and aquatic fowls. In other places they had children disguised like apes and other animals, who acted the several parts assigned them. As these were cloathed in the very skins of the animals they were to represent, the deception was complete. Other children made to resemble birds and fowls, and acted their parts upon pillars or lofty poles, these poles and pillars were covered with pieces of silk, which concealed men underneath: whose business it was to put the children stationed above in motion. In other places they had laid fruits of an enormous size, in which they had also inclosed children. These fruits opened from time to time, so far as to shew the spectators what they contained. I am not able to inform you, reverend father, whether there was any symbolical meaning in all this, or whether it was merely the production of a whimsical and extravagant fancy. The bands of music, the companies of comedians, juggler, and others, were places at intervals, all along the side of the river, and endeavoured every one, according to his ability, his skill, and his address, to do something which might please, if not the Emperor and his mother, at least some of the grandees of the retinue, into whose service they might hope to be admitted.

NOTES

1   Jean Joseph Marie Amiot, "Lettre du Pere Amyot, Missionnaire de la Compagnie de Jesus, au Pere Allart de la même Compagnie. Pékin le 20 Octobre 1752," in *Lettres édifiantes et curieuses*, vol. 28 (Paris: Guerin et De la Tour, 1758), 171–215.
2   "A Description of the Solemnities observed at *Pe-king* on the Emperor's Mother Entering on the Sixtieth Year of Her Age, from the French of P. *Amyot*, Jesuit," trans. Thomas Percy, in *Miscellaneous Pieces Relating to the Chinese*, ed. Thomas Percy, vol. 2 (London: Dodsley, 1762), 209–48.
3   Many of Amiot's writings were included in the series *Mémoires concernant l'histoire, les sciences, les arts, les mœurs, les usages, & c., des Chinois: par les Missionnaires de Pékin*, a monumental fifteen-volume collection edited by the Jesuits and published in Paris between 1776 and 1791, to which Amiot was one of the main

contributors. A sixteenth, and final, volume of the series was published in 1814. Amiot wrote a biography of Confucius included in volume 12 of the *Mémoires . . . des Chinois* (Paris, 1786), a grammar of the Manchu language, *Grammaire tartare-mantchou* (Paris, 1787), as well as a Manchu-French dictionary, *Dictionnaire tartare-mantchou-français* (Paris, 1789).

4 Louis Pfister, *Notices biographiques et bibliographiques sur les Jésuites de l'ancienne mission de Chine 1552–1773*, vol. 2 (Shanghai: Imprimerie de la Mission Catholique, 1934), 837–60; Michel Hermans, "Joseph-Marie Amiot, Une figure de la rencontre de 'l'autre' au tems des Lumières," in *Les Danses rituelles chinoises d'après Joseph-Maria Amiot*, ed. Yves Lenoir and Nicolas Standaert (Namur, Presses Universitaire de Namur, 2005), 11–62. On the correspondence between Amiot and Bertin see also Emmanuel Davin, "Un éminent sinologue toulonnais du XVIIIᵉ siècle, le R. P. Amiot, S.J. (1718–1793)," *Bulletin de l'Association Guillaume Budé* 1, no. 3 (1961): 380–95.

5 Note of Percy about his translation: "i.e. of many angles." Percy, "Description of the Solemnities," 227.

6 Note of Percy about his translation: "A *peristyle* is a circular range of pillars. Any series of pillars is a *colonnade*." Percy, "Description of the Solemnities," 229.

7 Note of Percy about his translation: "The *Chinese* mirrours are not of glass but polished metal. See P. Du Halde." Percy, "Description of the Solemnities," 229. Percy refers here to the popular *Description . . . de la Chine* by the Jesuit Jean-Baptiste du Halde published in Paris in 1735.

CHAPTER 12

John Bell (1691–1763)

The Scottish physician John Bell accompanied the Russian embassy on a diplomatic mission led by Count Leon Vasilievich Izmailov and sent to the Kangxi emperor by Peter the Great in 1719–22. During late 1720 and early 1721, the Russian delegates were received several times in the urban and suburban imperial residences; they participated in banquets, emperor's hunts, Chinese New Year celebrations, firework displays, as well as theatrical and musical performances that occurred there and which Bell details in his account entitled *Travels from St. Petersburg in Russia to Diverse Parts of Asia* (1763).[1]

The following extracts from Bell's travel account contain the descriptions of three gardens and parks that Bell visited: the private garden of the "Prime Minister's house" in Beijing, the green areas within the Imperial City, and the emperor's vast hunting park near the capital. In his descriptions of these three green spaces, which were very different from one another for dimension, use, and, surely, layout, Bell focuses instead on the characteristic aspects that they have in common. He emphasizes "imitating nature" as the design principle inspiring the whole composition, as well as the entirely artificial construction of the various elements evoking the forms of a natural landscape.

Bell also notes the role of the private residence and its garden as preferred places for the collection and exhibition of particularly valuable objects, presented to the diplomats to convey the owner's intellectual and scientific curiosity in addition to his social and political status, similarly to *Wunderkammern* in Europe. The prime minister's residence in Beijing housed a collection of natural and artificial objects, including a fine selection of Chinese and Japanese porcelains. Its garden featured the tea plant, native to southeastern regions of China and consequently a rarity in Beijing, where, Bell wrote, it could be found solely "in the gardens of the curious."

| 126 |

The Russian delegation was received and entertained several times at the Changchun yuan, but Bell gave no description of the imperial park other than stating that it "abounded with shaded walks, arbours, and fish ponds, in the Chinese taste."[2]

* * *

From John Bell, *Travels from St. Petersburg in Russia to Diverse Parts of Asia* (1763)

About ten o'clock in the morning, chairs were sent for the ambassador and gentlemen of the retinue, and horses for the servants, though the prime minister's house was very near our lodgings. The chairs were carried through two courts, and set down at the entry into a hall, where the aleggada [prime minister] waited to receive the ambassador. After entering the hall, we were seated on neat cane chairs, with japanned frames, inlaid with mother of pearl. The apartment itself was very simple, open to the south, and the roof supported, on that side, by a row of well turned wooden pillars. It had no ceiling; but the rafters appeared finely polished, and perfectly clean. The floor was paved with a checker-work of white and black marble; and in the middle of it stood a large brass chafing-dish, in shape of an urn, full of charcoal. At the entry were placed two large CHINA-cisterns, filled with pure water, in which played some scores of small fishes, catching at crumbs of bread thrown into the water. These fishes are about the size of a minnow, but of a different shape, and beautifully varied with red, white, and yellow spots; and therefore called the gold and silver fish. . . .

We were now conducted through all the different apartments of his house, excepting only those of the ladies, to which none have access but himself, and the eunuchs who attend them. We saw a noble collection of many curiosities, both natural and artificial; particularly a large quantity of old porcelain or in CHINA-ware, made in CHINA and JAPAN; and, at present, to be found only in the cabinets of the curious. They consisted chiefly of a great number of jars of different sizes. He took much pleasure in telling when and where they were manufactured; and, as far as I can remember, many of them were above two thousand years old. He added, that, both in CHINA and JAPAN, they had lost the art of making porcelain in that perfection they did in former times; and the fault, in his opinion, lay in the preparation of the materials. These curiosities were piled up on shelves to the very roof of the house, and in such order and symmetry as had a pretty effect.

From the house we went into a little garden, enclosed with a high brick-wall. In the middle of it stood a small basin, full of water, surrounded with several old crooked trees and shrubs; among which I saw that which produces the famous tea. The climate about PEKIN [Beijing] being too cold for this shrub, there are only a few bushes of it to be found in the gardens of the curious. I shall not at present enlarge on this useful plant, which appears like a currant-bush, as an opportunity will occur of giving a fuller account of it before I leave this place. There was a walk round the garden, which, together with that in the middle, was covered with small gravel. At each end of the middle-walk was a piece of artificial rock-work, with water running under it, through holes so natural they looked as if made by the current of the stream. The rocks were about seven feet high, and shaded with some old bended trees. This garden, and many other things in CHINA, display the taste of the inhabitants for imitating nature.

The 12th [of January 1721], the Emperor came from Tzan-shu-yang [Changchun yuan], to his palace in the city. . . . This palace occupies a large space of ground, encompassed with an high brick-wall. There are several streets, for servants and officers of the household. Many of the houses are high, and covered with yellow varnished tiles, which appear like gold in the sun. Northward from the palace is a large canal, of an irregular figure, where the imperial family divert themselves by fishing. This canal is artificial; and the earth dug out of it has raised an high bank, from whence you have a full view of the city, and the country adjacent, to a considerable distance. This mount rises to a ridge, which is planted with trees; resembling the wild and irregular scenes of nature that frequently present themselves in this country.[3] The canal and mount are of an equal length, which I compute to be about an ENGLISH mile. This must have been a work of vast expence and labour; and, it must be confessed, contributes greatly to the beauty of the place.

The 21st [of February, 1721], being the day appointed for hunting with the Emperor, at one of the clock in the morning, horses were brought to our lodgings, for the ambassador and those who attended him. We immediately mounted, and, after riding about six miles, to the south-west of the city, at break of day, we reached the gates of the park called CHAYZA; where we were received by an officer, and conducted, through the forest, to a summer-house, about a mile from the gate, in which the Emperor had slept the preceding night. This was a small but neat building, having a double row of galleries, open to the forest, on all sides, and an avenue leading to it from the gate, planted with several rows of trees. At some distance from the house, we dismounted, and were met by the master of the ceremonies, who conducted us into a gallery. As soon as we entered, the good old Emperor, who had risen long before our arrival, sent one of his eunuchs to salute the ambassador, and ordered us tea and other victuals. On the south side of the house is a canal, filled with clear water, and several large fish-ponds, which make a great addition to the beauties of this charming place. . . . After proceeding about two or three miles farther into the forest, we came to a tall wood, where we found several sorts of deer. . . . We had now been six hours on horse-back, and, I reckon, had travelled about fifteen ENGLISH miles; but no end of the forest yet appeared. We turned short from this wood southwards, till, coming to some marshes, overgrown with tall reeds, we roused a great many wild boars. . . .

We continued to sport till about four o'clock, when we came to a high artificial mount, of a square figure, raised in the middle of a plain, on the top of which were pitched about ten or twelve tents, for the imperial family. This mount had several winding paths leading to the top, planted, on each side, with rows of trees, in imitation of nature. To the south was a large bason of water, with a boat upon it; from whence, I suppose, the earth has been taken that formed this mount. At some distance from the mount, tents were erected for the people of distinction, and officers of the court. About two hundred yards from it, we were lodged in some clean huts, covered with reeds. The Emperor, from this situation, had a view of all the tents, and a great way farther into the forest. The whole scene made a very pretty appearance. . . .

Next morning, the sport was resumed and varied little from that of the preceding day. About three o'clock, afternoon, we came to another summer-house, in the middle of the forest, where the Emperor lodged the following night; while we lay in a small neat temple in the neighbourhood. . . . I shall only observe further, that this forest is really a most delightful place; is well stored with variety of game; and is of great extent, as will easily be conceived from the account I have given of our two days hunting. It is all inclosed with a high wall of brick. The value of this park, so near the capital, shows the magnificence of this powerful monarch.

NOTES

1   John Bell, *Travels from St. Petersburg in Russia to Diverse Parts of Asia*, 2 vols. (Glasgow: Robert and Andrew Foulis, 1763). On Bell's perception of China as emerged from his travel account, see Spence, *The Chan's Great Continent*, 44–51. On Bell's description of the reception of the Russian delegation at the court of Kangxi, see Carroll Brown Malone, *History of the Peking Summer Palaces Under the Ch'ing Dynasty* (Urbana: University of Illinois, 1934), 37–42.

2   Bell, *Travels*, vol. 2, 35.

3   Bell describes a similar scene, commenting on the area of Changchun yuan imperial park where the Russian delegation was staying: "The 29th, chairs were sent from court to carry the ambassador, and gentlemen of the retinue; we arrived there in the evening, and lodged in a house near the palace. Near our lodgings was a pretty garden with a canal, on which was a small pleasure-boat. In the middle of the canal was raised an artificial mount, planted with some barren trees, in imitation of nature. We ascended by a winding path to the top of the mount, from whence we had a fine view of all the country around." Bell, *Travels*, vol. 2, 59.

CHAPTER 13

Michel Benoist (1715–74)

long standing...

A rriving in China in 1745, the French Jesuit Michel Benoist remained
at the service of the Qianlong emperor for nearly thirty years. He was
one of the Jesuit missionaries working at the Qing court to whom Qianlong
entrusted the design and the construction of the Western-style garden
called Xiyang lou, "European Palaces," within the precincts of Yuanming
yuan in 1747.[1] That particular landscaping adventure is mentioned in the
last lines of the following extract taken from a letter written in 1767 from
Beijing, in which Benoist presents the main characteristics of Chinese garden design, derived from his perception of the imperial park of Yuanming
yuan.[2]

Benoist emphasizes the ability of the Chinese in using and concealing
"art to improve nature" to recreate its variety in their gardens, making it
more accessible to the spectator. He introduces the role of the garden's
spatial organization in creating curiosity and a delightful sense of surprise
for the visitor. Probably because he supervised the design and the construction of the fountains and waterworks in Xiyang lou, Benoist focuses, more
than other descriptions of the period, on the central role of water, in the
form of lakes, streams, and waterfalls, in the overall composition and in the
articulation of a variety of scenes.[3] In fact, Yuanming yuan emerged from a
connective tissue of lakes and meandering streams that subdivided the garden's space, making it appear as a kind of island cluster.

In noting the differences between the imperial parks and the great
French gardens, beyond the obvious ones of composition and aesthetic,
Benoist adds their accessibility to the list. While imperial parks in China
were strictly reserved for use by the emperor, since the seventeenth century
aristocratic gardens in France had been generally open to city residents;
Benoist, therefore, proudly notes that French gardens can be considered
"almost public."

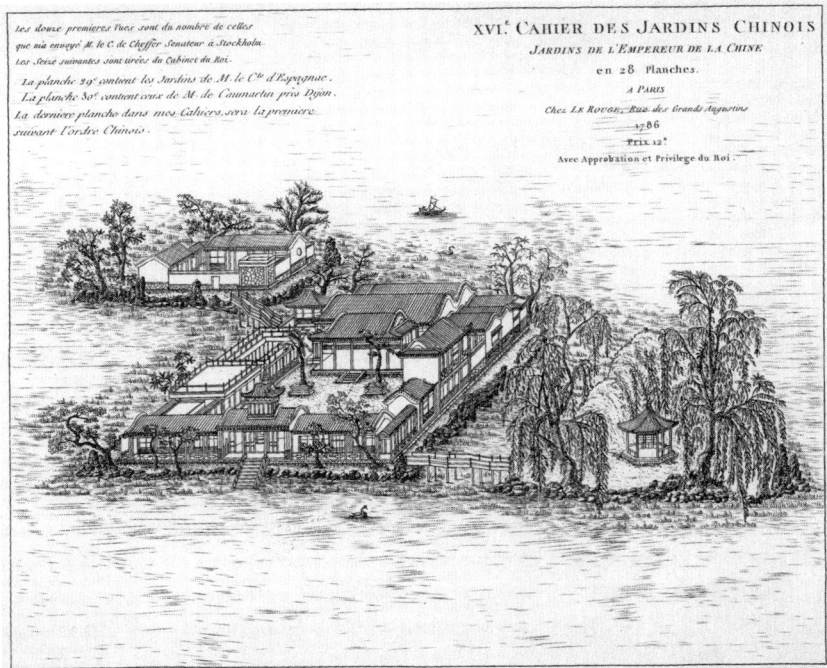

les douze premieres Vues sont du nombre de celles
que m'a envoyé M. le C. de Cheffer Sénateur à Stockholm.
les Seize suivantes sont tirées du Cabinet du Roi.
La planche 29.ᵉ contient les Jardins de M. le C.ᵗᵉ d'Espagnac.
La planche 30.ᵉ contient ceux de M. de Caumartin près Dijon.
La derniere planche dans mes Cahiers, sera la premiere
suivant l'ordre Chinois.

XVI.ᵉ CAHIER DES JARDINS CHINOIS
JARDINS DE L'EMPEREUR DE LA CHINE
en 28 Planches.
A PARIS
Chez LE ROUGE, Rue des Grands Augustins
1786
Prix 12.ᵗ
Avec Approbation et Privilege du Roi.

Figure 8. Title page of Cahier 16, "Des jardins chinois. Jardins de l'Empereur de la Chine." In Georges-Louis Le Rouge, *Détails de nouveaux jardins à la mode "jardins anglo-chinois"* (Paris: By the author, 1786). © Dumbarton Oaks Research Library and Collection, Rare Book Collection, Washington, DC.

*   *   *

From Michel Benoist, "Lettre du Père Benoist à Monsieur Papillon d'Auteroche. A Péking, le 16 novembre 1767," in *Lettres édifiantes et curieuses*, vol. 23 (1781), translated by Bianca Maria Rinaldi

It was in the year 1745 that, by order of the emperor, I arrived in Peking [Beijing] with the title of mathematician. Two years later, I was called by His Majesty to direct some hydraulic works. Two leagues from the capital, the emperor has a house of delight where he spends a great part of the year, and he works to embellish it all the time.[4] To give you an idea of it, if we do not have a little description in our *Lettres édifiantes et curieuses*, I will remind you of these enchanted gardens, of which the brilliant imagination of some authors has given so attractive a description, which becomes reality in the gardens of the emperor.[5] The Chinese, in arranging their gardens, use art to improve nature with such success that an artist wins praise to the degree that his art does not show at all, and he has, rather, imitated nature. There are not, as in Europe, alleys open to view, terraces where one can discover an infinitude of magnificent objects in the distance, such a multitude that doesn't allow the imagination to focus on one in particular. In the gardens of China, the view is never fatigued, because it is almost always confined to a space proportionate to the extent of the viewer's glances. You see a sort of ensemble whose beauty strikes and enchants you, and after a few hundred steps, some new objects present themselves to you, eliciting new admiration.

All these gardens are divided up by various channels of water winding their way through artificial mountains, in some places going over rocks and forming waterfalls, sometimes accumulating in the valleys and creating bodies of water which take the name of lake or of sea, according to their different sizes. The irregular banks of these channels and these bodies of water are ornamented with parapets; but quite different from ours, which are made of stones cut with art from which the natural has been eliminated; these parapets are made of rocks which seem untouched, solidly placed on supports. If the laborer takes a great deal of time to work them, it is only to increase their irregularities and to give them an even more country-like appearance.

On the banks of the channels, on different places, these stones are so arranged as to create a very comfortable stairs to board the boats on which they wish to take a ride. On the mountains, these stones are sometimes polished to form rocks as far as you can see; other times, despite the solidity of their positions, they look as though they might tumble down and crush anyone approaching them. Still other times they form grottos which, winding underneath the mountains, lead to delightful palaces. Amongst the rocks, both along the water's edge and in the mountains, openings have been arranged. Great trees sometimes grow out of these openings, at other times there are bushes which flower in season. Elsewhere, the openings present different species of plants and flowers which are carefully changed with the seasons.

The palace destined as lodging for the emperor and all his court is immense in size, and it unites in its interior all from the four parts of the world that is most precious and most curious. In addition to this palace, there are many others in the gardens, some situated around a vast body of water, or in the islands created in the middle of these lakes; others stand on the slope of some mountain or in pleasant valleys. There are places for keeping wheat, rice and other sorts of grains. To work and cultivate these lands, there are villages whose inhabitants never go out of their enclosures. There one sees a type of street made up of shops which during different times of the year gather, as though in a fair, what is most precious from China, Japan, and even the kingdoms of Europe.[6]

But I notice, sir, that I am passing beyond the limits which I prescribed for myself this year. I will be able to speak to you later of those enchanted places which are not solely for the emperor and his court; because here it is not as in France, where the palaces and the gardens of the great are open and almost public. Here princes of the blood, ministers of State, mandarins, no one can get into them, excepting those who make up the household of the emperor. On occasion, either for a comedy or some other spectacle, the emperor invites the princes of the blood, tributary kings, etc.; but they are led solely to parts of the garden.

It is in these gardens that the emperor, having wanted to construct a European palace, thought of adorning it within and without with hydraulic works, which he put into my hands despite all my protests of my incapacity.[7]

NOTES

1   Destroyed by French and English troops in October 1860, Xiyang lou rose in a narrow T-shaped piece of land, surrounded by a wall, in the northern part of Changchun yuan (Garden of Everlasting Spring), situated to the east of the bigger Yuanming yuan. It was built in two phases between 1747 and 1759. The team of Jesuits who took part in the project was composed of Giuseppe Castiglione (1688–1766), who was entrusted with the overall plan and architecture; Jean-Denis Attiret and Ignaz Sichelbart (1708–80), who designed the building details and painted decoration; Pierre d'Incarville (1706–57), who was responsible for the landscaping; Gilles Thébault (1703–66), who took charge of the iron work; and Michel Benoist, who together with Pierre-Martial Cibot was in charge of the hydraulics and design of fountains. The European Palaces presented an inventive contamination between the European and the Chinese art of the garden. The Jesuits designed a compendium of elements typical of Western gardens—

including a rectangular stone labyrinth dominated by a central belvedere, fountains with jets of water, and an open-air theater—that were presented as a collection of single scenes, autonomous rooms separated by walls, in the spatial framework typical of Chinese gardens. At the same time, however, the architectural structures, paths, and decorative elements were articulated according to symmetry and rigorous geometry in the Western Baroque tradition, in order to produce calculated effects of perspective. A new building was added in 1768 to display some Beauvais tapestries woven according to designs of François Boucher and presented to Qianlong by the missionaries. The European Palaces became a sort of *Wunderkammer* where Qianlong collected the gifts from European missionaries or ambassadors. Xiyang lou, an ideal evocation of a European garden, constituted one of the settings in Yuanming yuan, whose overall composition was characterized by different scenes, many of them were inspired by famous gardens or landscapes in China. On the profuse literature discussing the European Palaces and the work of the Jesuits, see Michèle Pirazzoli-t'Serstevens, "Les Palais Européens, histoire et légendes," in *Le Yuanmingyuan: Jeux d'eau et palais européens du XVIII siècle à la cour de Chine*, ed. Michèle Pirazzoli-t'Serstevens (Paris: Éditions Recherche sur les Civilizations, 1987), 6–10; Vincent Droguet, "Les Palais Européens de l'empereur Qianlong et leurs sources italiennes," *Histoire de l'Art* 25–26 (May 1994): 15–28; Victoria M. Siu, "China and Europe Intertwined: A New View of the European Sector of the Chang Chun Yuan," *Studies in the History of Gardens and Designed Landscapes* 19 (1999): 376–93; Strassberg, "War and Peace," 104–20; and, more recently, Zou, *A Jesuit Garden in Beijing*, especially 103–38. For a discussion of landscaping in Xiyang lou, see Gilles Genest, "Les Palais Européens du Yuanmingyuan: Essai sur la végétation des jardins," *Arts Asiatiques* 49 (1994): 82–90.

2   Michel Benoist, "Lettre du Père Benoist à Monsieur Papillon d'Auteroche. A Péking, le 16 novembre 1767," in *Lettres édifiantes et curieuses écrites des missions étrangères: Mémoires de la Chine*, vol. 23 (Paris: J. G. Merigot, 1781), 534–47. This letter by Benoist was published for the first time in the second edition of the series of the *Lettres édifiantes et curieuses* (1780–83), edited by Yves Mathurin Marie Tréaudet de Querbeuf and printed in Paris in twenty-six volumes. Benoist's letter was reprinted in three later editions of the *Lettres édifiantes et curieuses*, edited by De Querbeuf: Michel Benoist, "Lettre du Père Benoit, Missionnaire, à Monsieur Papillon d'Auteroche. A Péking, le 16 novembre 1767," in *Lettres édifiantes et curieuses écrites des missions étrangères: Mémoires de la Chine*, vol. 23 (Toulouse: Sens et Gaude, 1811), 427–37; Michel Benoist, "Lettre du père Benoist, missionnaire, à M. Papillon d'Auteroche. A Péking, le 16 novembre 1767," in *Lettres édifiantes et curieuses écrites des missions étrangères: Mémoires de la Chine*, vol. 13 (Lyon: Vernarel et Cabin, 1819), 176–84; Michel Benoist, "Lettre du Père Benoist a M. Papillon d'Auteroche. Sur les jardins, les palais, les occupations de l'empereur. Pékin le 16 novembre 1767," in *Lettres édifiantes et curieuses concernant l'Asie, l'Afrique et l'Amérique, avec quelques relations nouvelles des missions, et des notes géographiques et historiques*, vol. 4 (Paris: Panthéon littéraire, 1843), 120–23.

3   Just a few years after the letter by Benoist was published in France, another Western traveler noted with disapproval the liberal use of water in Chinese gardens.

The merchant Samuel Shaw (1754–94) was in 1786 appointed American consul in Guangzhou and was one of the first Americans to reach that major Chinese trading port. In his travelogue of his voyages between the United States and China, published only in 1847, Shaw described the gardens of the wealthy merchant Chowqua in Guangzhou, observing: "The gardens belonging to Chowqua are extensive; much art and labor are used to give them a rural appearance, and in some instances nature is not badly imitated. Forests, artificial rocks, mountains, and cascades, are judiciously executed, and have a pleasing effect in diversifying the scene. The Chinese, however, discover a vitiated taste in their fondness for water. Every garden must have abundance of this element, and where it does not flow naturally, large, stagnant ponds, in the middle of which are summer-houses, supply the deficiency. Chowqua says that his house and gardens cost him upwards of one hundred thousand teals." Josiah Quincy, *The Journals of Major Samuel Shaw, the First American Consul at Canton* (Boston: W. Crosby and H. P. Nichols, 1847), 179.

4   Benoist refers here to the imperial complex of Yuanming yuan.

5   Benoist alludes to the description of Yuanming yuan written in 1743 by Jean-Denis Attiret and published in 1749 as part of the twenty-seventh volume of the *Lettres édifiantes et curieuses*.

6   Benoist makes references to the space for play and recreation, with a clearly commercial and urban nature, reproduced by the emperor within the confines of Yuanming yuan, described in detail by the Jesuit Attiret in his letter.

7   Benoist refers to the task that he was entrusted with concerning the design of Xiyang lou. A detailed description of the European palaces was given by the French Jesuit François Bourgeois in one of his letters written from Beijing in 1786 and addressed to the publisher Louis-François Delatour, who included selected passages from them in his treatise on Chinese architecture and garden design. The description accompanied a set of the twenty copperplates representing the European palaces, commissioned by Qianlong in 1783 and made by court artist Yi Lantai, which the Jesuit sent to Delatour in 1786. Delatour, who defined the architectural language of the European palaces as "Italo-Gothic-Chinois," used Bourgeois's depictions as the source for his chapter on the twenty views of Xiyang lou. In a letter to Delatour written in October 1786, Bourgeois briefly described the imperial complex of Changchun yuan (Garden of Everlasting Spring) as well, and wrote that the park was dominated by a mountain, covered with several buildings and pavilions, overlooking a large lake. See Louis-François Delatour, *Essais sur l'architecture des Chinois, sur leurs jardins, leurs principes de médecine, et leurs mœurs et usages* (Paris: Clousier, 1803), 170–86 and 167–68.

CHAPTER 14

Travel account.

François Bourgeois (1723–92)

In a letter written in 1768 containing an account of his journey from Guangzhou to Beijing, François Bourgeois, one of the French Jesuits at the service of the Qianlong emperor, describes the landscapes and cities encountered along the route, as well as the gardens he visited. While he very briefly mentions the gardens of the urban residences in Nanjing, describing them as simple and natural grounds, his account of the park of an imperial traveling palace in the city of Yangzhou suggests a highly dynamic composition, constructed through the juxtaposition of multiple parts and elements. Its intricate design must have produced an effect of great magnificence. In fact, in the aesthetic and functional diversification of the spaces constituting the garden, the Jesuit recognizes a strategy aimed at representing the regality of the emperor. Published only in 1782, the letter was included in the collection of *Mémoires . . . des Chinois.*[1]

The second extract presented here is taken from a letter written from Beijing in 1786 in which Bourgeois gives further details on the imperial complex in Yangzhou, describing its "rural air," its variety, and its visual appeal. The letter was published by Louis-François Delatour in his *Essais sur l'architecture des Chinois, sur leurs jardins, leurs principes de médecine, et leurs mœurs et usages* (1803).[2] Delatour compiled the section of his essays related to Chinese garden on the basis of the Jesuits' accounts, including lengthy quotations from the letters by Bourgeois, Jean François Gerbillon, Jean-Denis Attiret, Michel Benoist, and the writings by Pierre-Martial Cibot and Jean Joseph Marie Amiot. He also included selected passages from William Chambers's writings and the travel account of André Everard van Braam Houckgeest.

*   *   *

From François Bourgeois, "Lettre d'un missionnaire a
M. l'Abbé G. [Gallois] contenant une relation de son voyage
de Canton à Pé-king. Péking, le 15 Septembre 1768," in
Mémoires . . . des Chinois, vol. 8 (1782), translated by
Bianca Maria Rinaldi

We arrived in Nankin [Nanjing] the 2nd of June. I wanted to see that
city which is considered the largest in the world. The suburb through which
we passed is of considerable extent, but it is not highly populated; the
houses are distant from each other, and have within their enclosure reeds,
pools of water, and groves of bamboos. . . .

Finally, we arrived at the most beautiful place in China: it is the country
that lies between the two great rivers, the Kian [Changjiang, Yangtze River]
and the Huang-ho [Huanghe, Yellow River]; it measures fifty miles from
south to north. Here there is no more question of mountains; the terrain is
level like a mirror as far as the eye can see. The lands yield harvests several
times each year, and all at the same time; this affords a view altogether
absent in Europe, where a portion of the soil is always at rest. This country
is singularly populated. It is also in this part of China that one sees the most
beautiful cities of the Empire. Son-tcheou [Suzhou?] is paradise on earth,
as the Chinese say. Yan-tcheou [Yangzhou], which we passed through, is
one of the biggest and most beautiful cities which we saw. There, the salt
tax collectors have built for the Emperor a pleasure house which is all the
more a surprise since we had seen nothing so fine before.

It is the copy of Hai-tien [Haidian], another suburban residence two
leagues from Peking [Beijing], where the Emperor usually resides, and
which Father Attiret, that excellent painter who dared to refuse the badge
of Mandarin, gave a fine description of in the twenty-seventh volume of
the *Lettres édifiantes & curieuses*.[3]

The pleasure house in Yan-tcheou occupies more space than the city of
Rennes. It is a mass of little mountains and rocks built by hand; of valleys;
of watercourses sometimes wide, sometimes narrow, sometimes lined with
cut stone, sometimes with rough rock scattered without order; of a crowd
of buildings each different from the other; of rooms; of courts; of open and
closed galleries; of gardens; of parterres; of cascades; of well-built bridges;
of pavilions; of groves; of triumphal arches. Each piece is pretty and in
good taste; but it is the multiplicity of objects which is striking, and which
eventually make you say: this is for quite a grand Master.

From "Description d'une Maison de plaisance de
l'Empereur, à Yang-tchéou, par M. Bourgois, selon sa lettre
de novembre 1786," in Louis-François Delatour, *Essais sur
l'architecture des Chinois, sur leurs jardins, leurs principes de
médecine, et leurs mœurs et usages* (1803), translated by
Bianca Maria Rinaldi

Yang-tchèou [Yangzhou] of which I will tell you Sir *ex visu*, is one of the
finest and largest cities of China; I was surprised to see there houses of
several stories, which are quite similar to our ordinary European houses.
They say it contains a million inhabitants: what I know is that the population is prodigious in those neighborhoods: near the big city, along the
Imperial Canal, I saw villages of more than a league of expanse, and that
are swarming with inhabitants. The country is open, so full of houses and
scattered farmsteads, surrounded by their land, that from a distance one
could believe one is seeing absolutely contiguous villages. Not much land
is required for the maintenance of a family, because every year the land is
harvested at least twice, and it never lies fallow.

It is nearby, and partly beyond *Yang-tchèou,* that the pleasure house of
the emperor is located: it was built at the time of *Kang-hi* [Kangxi], not at
the expense of that prince, but at that of the company of salt farmers, who
wanted to give him this token of gratitude. . . .

This [pleasure] house is like a public promenade: a prodigious crowd
of idlers goes, at their ease, into these gardens where it might take three
quarters of an hour of walking to traverse its length; I can not say the
width, but with the naked eye I have estimated from the top of the mountain which is at its end, that the perimeter can be compared to that of the
city of Nancy. One goes from one part to the other by boats and gondolas.
As soon as one arrives at the entrance, one sees a great number of them
that are truly beautiful: they are varnished, gilded, painted, and very convenient, one can rent them for several hours and inexpensively. From the
boats you can see, as you advance, almost what you see at *Yuen-ming-
Yuen* [Yuanming yuan], but what is missing in *Yang-tchèou,* in that
regard, is compensated by other advantages. After having read the letter
from Brother Attiret, and after having seen *Yuen-ming-Yuen* several
times, if I had to make a choice between these two beautiful imperial
pleasure houses, I would choose *Yang-tchèou.*

Yueng-ming-Yuen is situated in a depression, so one discovers only what
is within the precinct of the park; yet one sees it all in succession, because

there are always mounds, detours, etc. In *Yang-tchèou*, you sail on beautiful waters, you go from right to left, as you wish, and you discover at once a multitude of pleasant, charming things: here is a forest of tall trees; there groves; further there is a shore covered with nicely built Chinese pavilions, in front of these small houses there are a number of people drinking tea and watching the passersby, and they make a very nice sight for those who sail.

The high bridges that one sees from afar vary and beautify the scene: you pass under one of these bridges which consists of a single arch. Everything is full of ornaments, but so natural, that you would not say that it involved labor. A letter as long as that of brother Attiret would be necessary to go into more specific detail; but as I have not seen *Yang-tchèou* for twenty years, I do not quite remember all things, and I recall only the most essential. It is true that the palaces of *Yuen-ming-Yuen* are much more extensive, more beautiful and more numerous than those of *Yang-tchèou*, but also the latter have a certain rural air which makes them more enjoyable. I got off the boat several times to explore them without haste; I was enchanted: instead of beautiful and stunning staircases, you go from a small rock to another, and you are in a building on a height without having climbed stairs.

But the main beauty of *Yang-tchèou* is the conclusion of the promenade. You arrive by boat at the foot of a beautiful mountain, the only one in the country: it is dotted with Chinese buildings of different heights, and its summit is a platform of great extent also covered with several beautiful buildings, and in particular, with a palace of the Emperor which is connected to a Miao [temple] of great magnificence.

It is from this platform that you have the most beautiful view in the world. You dive into *Yang-tchèou* which is only half a league away, you see the great river *Kiang* [Yangtze River] and the Imperial Canal lined with all kinds of buildings: beyond, as far as you can see, you discern cities, villages and vast fields everywhere, rich with all sorts of crops; the land never lies fallow.

NOTES

1   "Lettre d'un missionnaire a M. l'Abbé G. [Gallois] contenant une relation de son voyage de Canton à Pé-king. Péking, le 15 Septembre 1768," in *Mémoires . . . des Chinois*, vol. 8 (Paris: Nyon, 1782), 291–300.

2   "Description d'une Maison de plaisance de l'Empereur, à Yang-tchéou, par M. Bourgois, selon sa lettre de novembre 1786," in Delatour, *Essais sur l'architecture des Chinois*, 216–19.

3   The Jesuit refers to Jean-Denis Attiret's refusal to be elevated to the mandarinate, an honor that the Qianlong emperor had offered him. He also refers to the letter in which Attiret described the imperial park of Yuanming yuan, located in the district of Haidian, northwest of Beijing.

CHAPTER 15

Carl Gustav Ekeberg (1716–84)

travel booklet.
Scandinavian.

O f Carl Linnaeus's many followers who explored various parts of the world observing and describing native flora, as well as collecting specimen and seeds, it was the Swede Carl Gustav Ekeberg who first managed to carry a living tea plant to Sweden. A naturalist, friend of Linnaeus, captain of the Swedish East India Company and, later, member of the Royal Swedish Academy of Science, Ekeberg made several journeys to southeastern China in 1742–78.[1] He assembled some of his observations recorded during those travels in a booklet entitled *Kort berättelse om den chinesiska landt-hushåldningen*. It was published in 1757 as an appendix to the travelogue of the 1750–52 travels in China of the Swedish naturalists and disciples of Linnaeus Pehr Osbeck (1723–1805) and Olof Torén (1718–53), which was concentrated mainly on Chinese plants.[2] The extract that follows is taken from the first English version of Ekeberg's report, entitled "A Short Account of the Chinese Husbandry" and published in 1771.[3]

Ekeberg's remarks are organized in brief thematic chapters, each describing Chinese agriculture and horticulture and focusing on a variety of subjects, including "Rice-fields," "Monsoons and Weather," "Dungs," "Beasts and Birds," "The Fishery," and "Kitchen Gardens." The chapter from Ekeberg's account presented here, entitled "Gardens for Diversion," is related to Ekeberg's understanding of the key design principles of Chinese gardens. Ekeberg insists on the extraordinary compositional variety of the garden's layout, in which "no part must be similar to another," and on the role of twisting paths in revealing that variety and in influencing the perception of the garden's space. He also emphasizes the presence of live animals in the garden. In explaining how plants were used in the composition of the garden, both as masses and as single exemplars, Ekeberg sheds light on the role of vegetation in contributing to the character of the garden's scenes.

Figure 9. Thomas Daniell and William Daniell, *View in a Chinese Garden*. In Thomas Daniell and William Daniell, *A Picturesque Voyage to India, by the Way of China* (London: Printed for Longman, Hurst, Rees, and Orme, 1810), p. 81. Hand-colored aquatint. Yale Center for British Art, Paul Mellon Collection.

* * *

From Carl Gustav Ekeberg, "A Short Account of the Chinese Husbandry," in *A Voyage to China and the East Indies by Peter Osbeck*, translated from the German by John Reinhold Foster, vol. 2 (1771)

GARDENS FOR DIVERSION

As great a difference as there is between the taste of the *Chinese*, and that of other nations in their customs, dress, and other things, it is full as great with regard to flower gardens and those intended for diversion. They take very little care about flower-pieces, hedges, covered walks, and symmetry; they are better pleased with a naked place, laid with stones of different colours, and sizes in the figure of dragons or flowers, than if they were adorned with pretty designs, and the spaces filled up, with plants or grass.

Their walks must likewise not be open; but generally they are inclosed with walls, on the sides of which vines and other climbing plants are planted; which being strained from wall to wall on poles, by this means form a covered walk. The benches made in those walks, are not lined with walls on the sides, and, by the peculiar construction of the stones, they are provided with several holes in which they place pots with different flowers. The walks have many bendings; sometimes they pass over a little smooth path covered with stones, and lead to an open summer-house, on which there are flower pots, sometimes they form arched walks, which are doubly twisted with thin bamboo, but in an irregular way; and between it a sort of bushy ever-green is planted, which twines in among them, and makes them look like a green wall. Besides this there are many various scenes: hills covered with bushes, below which run some rivulets, surrounded with close standing shady trees; buildings which are three or four stories high, and generally open on the sides; towers, rough grottoes, bridges, ponds, places sown with beans; thick and wild bushes or little thickets, and other varieties which afford a fine landscape. Sometimes they have low stone seats under the shade of some great trees, from whence they can survey a great part of the country.

Though their gardens are very large, yet they appear still greater by their winding walks which turn backwards and forwards. From as much as can be judged of their taste, it appears that no part must be similar to another. In some gardens they dig ditches, round which a walk leads to all the above mentioned places; near them they have many summer-houses, which are all of them of a different construction, and are commonly near a pond on one side, that they may catch the fishes contained in it through the great windows. In the summerhouses they have gold and silver fishes in little ponds; and besides them, birds and other animals, flowers, figures of dragons, with many other objects more pleasing.

NOTES

1   On Ekeberg see Torkel Stålmarck, *Ostindiefararen Carl Gustav Ekeberg, 1716–1784* (Göteborg: Kungl. Vetenskaps-och vitterhets-samhället, 2012); Thommy Svensson and Elisabeth Lind, "Early Indonesian Studies in Sweden: The Linnaen Tradition and the Emergence of Ethnography Before 1900," *Archipel* 33 (1987): 63–64.

2   Pehr Osbeck, Olof Torén, *Dagbok öfwer en ostindisk resa åren 1750, 1751, 1752 . . .* (Stockholm: Lor. Ludv. Grefing, 1757). The travelogue was translated into German and published in 1765: Pehr Osbeck, Olof Torén, C. G. Ekeberg, *Reise nach Ostindien und China . . .*, trans. von J. G. Georgi (Rostock: Koppe, 1765).

3   *A Voyage to China and the East Indies, by Peter Osbeck: Together with A Voyage to Suratte, by Olof Toreen and an Account of the Chinese Husbandry, by Captain Charles Gustavus Eckeberg,* translated from the German by John Reinhold Foster, 2 vols. (London: B. White, 1771). In the same year the first French version of Ekeberg's account was published: *Précis historique de l'économie rurale des Chinois, présenté à l'Académie Royale des Sciences des Suède, en 1754: Par M. Charles Gustave Eckeberg Capitain, publié par M. Linnaeus,* translated from Swedish by Dominique de Blackford (Milan: Reycends, 1771).

CHAPTER 16

Pierre-Martial Cibot (1727–80)

[longuive ·]

As part of the monumental collection of the *Mémoires . . . des Chinois*, in 1777 the Jesuits published a French translation of the poem in which Sima Guang (1019–86), a Song dynasty Confucian scholar and statesman, celebrated his garden Dule yuan (Garden of Solitary Delight), located in the city of Luoyang.[1] This translation, far more elaborate than the original text, was probably the work of the French Jesuit Pierre-Martial Cibot. It must have been fairly well known in France before its publication by the Jesuits because the painter and writer Claude-Henri Watelet had included it to illustrate the forms of Chinese gardens in his *Essai sur les jardins* (1774), a short but influential work that advocated a more natural style in French garden design.[2]

Sima Guang's poem describes an irregular garden inspired by the natural landscape, with a complex layout articulated as a promenade through a series of ever-diverse episodes. To lead the Western reader to an understanding of the Chinese garden as it emerges from the poem of Sima Guang, Cibot adds to it a brief introduction, presented below.[3] In this text, Cibot emphasizes the variety of materials, elements, and design solutions, as well as the visual effects they have on the visitor. He emphasizes the cunning way in which the garden is laid out to distort the visitor's perception of its physical space, disguising its real extent. Cibot is the first Western traveler to perceive and present the contemplative dimension of the Chinese garden and its evocative quality: he describes the garden as a protected and secluded space where a concentrated and allusive naturalness encourages quiet meditation, fostering isolation from the external context.

Cibot reached China in 1759 in order to join the French Jesuit mission in Beijing. He was introduced to the court of the Qianlong emperor to aid the Jesuit Michel Benoist in the planning and construction of the fountains at Xiyang lou (European Palaces), the Western-style garden designed by a team of Jesuits within Yuanming yuan. Skilled in mechanics and botany, Cibot worked at the imperial court for the remainder of his life, first as a fountain- and clockmaker and then as a botanist and gardener. The latter tasks enabled him to gather information about plants, horticultural techniques, and the gardens of China, subjects on which he then wrote extensively.[4] Many of his writings were published in the collection *Mémoires . . . des Chinois*, to which Cibot, along with the French Jesuit Jean Joseph Marie Amiot, was one of the main contributors.

*   *   *

From Pierre-Martial Cibot, "Le jardin de Sée-Ma-Kouang: Pöeme," in *Mémoires . . . des Chinois*, vol. 2 (1777), translated by Bianca Maria Rinaldi

The translation of the verses of the famous *Sée-ma-kouang* [Sima Guang] about his garden has fallen into our hands. But before reading it, it is good to get an idea of the Chinese garden. It must be first assumed that in it [the garden] one seeks only to copy beautiful nature, and to gather in a quite limited space what she had scattered here and there in the countless scenes and views of the countryside. It must also be considered that here one goes to gardens solely to flee the tumult of the world, breathe freely and enjoy his soul and his thoughts thanks to the silence of solitude, which they strive to make so naive and countrified that it can deceive the senses. Finally, one must begin with the principle that in a garden, they like only gardening, and that the least sensitive eye, or the most luxurious, would be wounded by the sight of sumptuous marbles, statues, etc.

The gardens of China are a studied but natural imitation of the various beauties of the countryside, in hills, valleys, gorges, pools, little plains, sheets of water, brooks, isles, rocks, grottoes, old caves, plants and flowers. The great work of art is to extend a small space through a multitude of varying and surprising scenes; to disrobe nature of all her resources, and then to honor her through them. . . . To get an idea of the effect of all these parts (which are shown in the drawings), one must imagine that the hills are so flung, raised, lowered, linked, cut, distributed, covered with bushes, flowering trees, carpeted with lawn, excavated in rock, that they bring extreme variety to the scenes. It must also be assumed that the earth between the hills and the water is adorned with parterres, orchards, carpets of verdure, with parts uncultivated and abandoned to wild herbs. One must also imagine that the waters' edges, which are not made of steep rocks, are here sand and pebbles, there greenery, elsewhere roses, in some places steep as moats, in others walled, and that the waters themselves, more or less deep, have waterfalls, rapids, gurgles, and parts smooth as a mirror. It must be finally assumed that the palaces, buildings, galleries, etc. are in some cases of a fabulous magnificence, while others are simply neat, some like those of a petit bourgeois, and many others are even made of straw, or reeds, or bamboo, as in the villages. All these assumptions, based on the truth, prodigiously vary the scenes of the garden, and double its size in some way, because the same place looks different according to the position of the viewer, etc. This is the general idea of the modern Chinese garden. The poem by Sée-Ma-Kouang proves that this style is not new to the Nation [China], since Sée-Ma-Kouang was prime minister in the year 1086.

NOTES

1   "De Sée-Ma-Kouang: Le jardin de Sée-Ma-Kouang," in *Mémoires . . . des Chinois*, vol. 2 (Paris: Nyon, 1777), 645–50.

2   Claude-Henri Watelet, *Essai sur les jardins* (Paris: Prault, 1774), 125–36. For a recent English translation of Watelet's essay, see Claude-Henry Watelet, *Essay on Gardens: A Chapter of the French Picturesque*, ed. and trans. Samuel Danon (Philadelphia: University of Pennsylvania Press, 2003).

3   Pierre-Martial Cibot, "Le jardin de Sée-Ma-Kouang: Pöeme," in *Mémoires . . . des Chinois*, vol. 2 (Paris: Nyon, 1777), 643–44.

4   Cibot wrote about several aspects of Chinese natural sciences, including geology, mineralogy, zoology, and botany, and sent information and observations on these subjects to the Scientific Academy of Saint Petersburg, of which he became a corresponding member in 1767. Pfister, *Notices biographiques . . .* , vol. 2, 890–902.

CHAPTER 17

Jean Joseph Marie Amiot (1718–93) or Pierre-Martial Cibot (1727–80) (attributed)

The two extracts that follow come from a long essay entitled, "Remarques sur un ecrit de M. P** [Pauw], intitulé: Recherches sur les Egyptiens et les Chinois," written in 1775 by the Jesuit missionaries in Beijing in reaction to European criticism of Chinese culture. It was published in 1777 as part of a collection edited by the Jesuits, *Mémoires . . . des Chinois*.[1] The essay, with 105 specific points, was written to confute the same number of affirmations about China and diverse aspects of its culture, including gardens, made by the Dutch historian and philosopher Cornelis de Pauw (1739–99) in his popular and weighty two-volume work entitled *Recherches philosophiques sur les Égyptiens et les Chinois* (1773).[2] De Pauw published extensively on the origins of ancient peoples—the Greeks, Egyptians, Chinese, and natives of the West Indies—even though he had never visited the countries he wrote about.[3] Precisely as a result of this lack of direct experience, De Pauw's opinions, above all those concerning the Americas and China, were promptly rejected and harshly criticized by the far more experienced Jesuits who lived in those countries. Some scholars attribute the authorship of the essay "Remarques sur un ecrit de M. P**" to the Jesuit Cibot and others to Amiot.[4] The original manuscript, dated July 27, 1775, served at the Bibliothéque Nationale de France in Paris, is not signed, but is included in a folder entitled "Réponses aux *Recherches philosophiques* de M. de P[auw] sur les Chinois, par le P. Amiot."[5] However, the French minister Henri Bertin, who was instrumental in the production of the *Mémoires . . . des Chinois*, in a letter to Cibot dated September 30, 1777, acknowledged that Cibot's response to the *Recherches philosophiques* had been included in the second volume of the *Mémoires . . . des Chinois*.[6]

In the first extract, confuting De Pauw's pronouncement that the disorder of Chinese gardens is engendered by a depraved imagination, the Jesuits explain that the characteristic irregularity of Chinese gardens is the same used by "beautiful nature herself" for arranging her landscapes.[7] In the second extract, the Jesuits counter De Pauw's statement that garden rockeries have no aesthetic quality; once again, they explain that the harmony of Chinese gardens is due precisely to their adherence to the simple disorder nature herself displays in a beautiful countryside. The Jesuits summarized all the compositional elements inspired by the natural and the rural landscape that could be found in the diverse scenes of a "Chinese garden in good taste."

In the two passages, the Jesuits present Chinese gardens as relatively inexpensive compared to the great formal gardens of Europe, whose creation and maintenance, as well as their abundance of decorative elements, imposed an unbearable cost on Western societies. The Jesuits' emphasis on this specific quality of the gardens in China apparently reflects the polemics in France at that time regarding the considerable costs of maintaining the park of Versailles as well as the court's lifestyle, despite the country's serious economic crisis.

* * *

From "Remarques sur un ecrit de M. P**, intitulé: Recherches sur les Egyptiens et les Chinois," in *Mémoires . . . des Chinois*, vol. 2 (1777), translated by Bianca Maria Rinaldi

XXXIXe REM. [Remark] *Only a depraved imagination could have given birth to the idea of Chinese Gardens*, (p. 250).[8] . . . The words *depraved imagination* . . . apply more to the English, the French and the other Nations of Europe who have tasted our manner, than to our poor Chinese who, in the final accounting, are more to pity than to blame, for not having the Author's *penetration*;[9] one could well appeal to beautiful nature herself, if necessary and relate what she teaches man in the places where a fertile soil, a felicitous situation, a temperate climate allow her to display all her beauties. The pleasure gardens that she there creates will have hills and hillocks here and there, winding paths, trees planted one place and another without order and without symmetry, waters which take on different forms and wend their way through the channels they have dug, so that the eye, refreshed and content, views the spectacle with an ever new pleasure. But, having to do with a Philosopher of such rare *penetration*, we really have something else to say to him. Let him take his pen, and calculate the cost of so many flowers, works, efforts and pains as it takes to maintain those gardens which are linear, symmetrical, measured, combed, fashioned, embellished and adorned in such a way as to satisfy his *penetration*: then, with the total sum well and exactly calculated, let him tell us, not how many people would be in a condition to procure such gardens, and to do so without hurting the public good, but simply if men have gathered themselves into society so that some could burden others like themselves in order to procure for themselves, by so many flowers, works, efforts and pains, the idle and sterile pleasure of refreshing their view by a garden in their taste.

CIV^e REM. [Remark] *It is peculiar to see the Architects of China raise artificial rocks, in what they call gardens*, (p. 41).[10] . . . Our garden [the gardens of China] returned to the noble simplicity of the most beautiful days of the ancient *Tcheou* [Zhou], can support the looks of Sages, and deserves to serve as a model for all Nations.[11] Nature alone appears there [in Chinese gardens], and without any other embellishment or adornment than the naiveté, simplicity, carelessness, disorder and anti-symmetry that she shows in the most beautiful countryside, and which are always equally pleasing there. The rules of art take offense, the prejudiced murmur, false taste is scandalized, but the eyes are ravished, reason applauds, and the most jaded soul is sensitive to a thousand impressions of pleasure, of joy, and of delight.

A Chinese garden in good taste is a place where the beauty of the site, the amenities of the situation, and the variety of viewpoints are embellished by a varied but natural mixture of slopes and hills, of valleys and plains, of running water and still water, of islets and bays, of groves and solitary trees, of plants and flowers, of pavilions and grottos, of smiling bowers and wild solitary places, serious and detached, as it were, from the rest of the universe. The compass and rule have not traced anything there, the meter has measured nothing, and symmetry commanded nothing, and, what is even more delightful, luxury and magnificence have not come into the picture. There one enjoys the charms of the countryside and the pleasures of each season without any of the disturbing signs of continuous travail moving or troubling one's feelings. Even Princes and the Great have felt that they owe this to their hearts, and when they have added to the work of nature, it was necessary that art and labor attribute their works to nature, by imitating it. The rocks, grottos and caverns which enflame the zeal of our Author truly demand great art and taste so that the eye is deceived and does not see the hand of man; but what the *penetration* of the Author failed above all to see in his criticism is that a single statue, a single marble vase cost more than all the rough rocks of a garden which, therefore, cannot do damage to the public good.

NOTES

1   "Remarques sur un ecrit de M. P** [Pauw], intitulé: Recherches sur les Egyptiens & les Chinois," in *Mémoires . . . des Chinois*, vol. 2 (Paris: Nyon, 1777), 365–574.

2   Cornelis de Pauw, *Recherches philosophiques sur les Égyptiens et les Chinois* (Amsterdam: Barth. Vlam & J. Murray, 1773). In their confutation, the Jesuits referred to the edition of De Pauw's *Recherches philosophiques* published in Berlin in 1773: Cornelis de Pauw, *Recherches philosophiques sur les Égyptiens et les Chinois*, 2 vols. (Berlin: G. J. Decker, 1773).

3   De Pauw wrote a critical treatise in two volumes entitled *Recherches philosophiques sur les Américains, ou Mémoires intéressants pour servir à l'Histoire de l'Espèce Humaine: Avec une Dissertation sur l'Amérique & les Américains* (Berlin, 1768), in which he discussed the American Indians, presenting them as inferior to the Europeans. Susanne Zantop, *Colonial Fantasies: Conquest, Family, and Nation in Precolonial Germany, 1170–1870* (Durham, N.C.: Duke University Press, 1997), 47–65.

4   In their work on the Jesuit authors and their writings, Augustin and Alois de Backer ascribed the essay "Remarques sur un ecrit de M. P**. . ." to Amiot, while Joseph Dehergne attributed the essay to Cibot, with the cooperation of the Chinese Jesuit Gao Leisi (b. 1732). See Augustin et Alois de Backer, *Bibliothéque des écrivains de la Compagnie de Jésus* (Liege: Grandmont-Donders, 1856), 237; Joseph Dehergne, "Une grande collection: Mémoires concernant les Chinois (1776–1814)," *Bulletin de l'Ecole Française d'Extrême-Orient* 72 (1983): 274. *Mémoires . . . des Chinois* includes another essay written by Amiot that refutes De Pauw's writings about China: Jean Joseph Marie Amiot, "Extrait d'une lettre du P. Amiot à M.*** du 28 septembre 1777: Observations sur un livre de M. P*** [Pauw] intitulé: Recherches philosophiques sur les Égyptiens et les Chinois," in *Mémoires . . . des Chinois*, vol. 6 (Paris: Nyon, 1780), 275–346.

5   "Réponses aux *Recherches philosophiques* de M. de P[auw] sur les Chinois, par le P. Amiot," in *Mélanges sur la Chine et les Chinois*, MS, Bibliothèque Nationale de France, fonds Bréquigny 12.

6   Dehergne, "Une grande collection," 274. I thank Claudia von Collani for her advice on this matter.

7   The position will be adopted also by the Jesuit Cibot in "Essai sur les jardins de plaisance des Chinois" (1782).

8   The Jesuits refer to De Pauw's statement, "On peut croire combien de tels Pein-
    tres on dû être embarrassés, lorsqu'ils vouloient représenter la vue d'un jardin
    Chinois, où il y a des montagnes artificielles, qui en cachent d'autres, des préci-
    pices, des fossés, des allées tortueuses, des arbres plantés sans ordre, sans symmé-
    trie, des canaux qui vont en serpentant, et tant de choses si confuses qu'il n'y a
    qu'une imagination dépravée qui ait pu en enfanter l'idée. Au reste, quoiqu'ils
    maltraitassent singulièrement le paysage, ils maltraitoient encore davantage les
    figures." (One can believe how embarrassed so many Painters must have been
    when they wanted to represent the view of a Chinese garden, where there are
    artificial mountains that hide others, and precipices, moats, tortuous alleys, trees
    planted without order, without symmetry, channels which meander, and so many
    things that are so confused that only a depraved imagination could have engen-
    dered the idea. For what it is worth, however much they singularly maltreat the
    landscape, they maltreat figures even more.) Cornelis de Pauw, *Recherches philo-
    sophiques sur les Égyptiens et les Chinois*, vol. 1 (Berlin: G. J. Decker, 1773), 249.

9   The Jesuits are ironical concerning De Pauw, subtly accusing him of not having
    conducted sufficient research in writing his books on China. Their criticism was
    echoed by another Jesuit missionary in China, Joseph-Anne-Marie de Moyriac de
    Mailla, author of a monumental general history of China: *Histoire générale de la
    Chine ou annales de cet empire*, 12 vols. (Paris, 1777–84). Referring to *Recherches
    philosophiques sur les Égyptiens et les Chinois*, Mailla spoke of "le résumé des asser-
    tions hardies que M. Paw, tranquilement assis dans son cabinet, à Berlin, pro-
    nonce sur un peuple qu'il n'a jamais vu, et qui habite à six mille lieues de lui"
    (the audacious assertions that M. Paw, sitting tranquilly in his study in Berlin,
    pronounces about a people that he has never seen, who live six thousand leagues
    from him). Joseph-Anne-Marie de Moyriac de Mailla, *Histoire générale de la
    Chine ou annales de cet empire*, vol. 1 (Paris: Pierres, Clousier, 1777), xxxvij.

10 De Pauw wrote, "Il est singulier de voir les architectes de la Chine élever des
    rochers artificiels dans ce qu'ils appellent des jardins, et ensuite ils osent de-
    mander aux Européens si nous avons des ouvriers qui pourroient en cela les
    égaler. Mais on devroit leur répondre que pour mettre au hazard des pierres les
    unes sur les autres, il ne faut avoir ni génie, ni art, ni industrie, ni goût, ni enfin
    aucune notion du beau et de l'utile: aussi feroit-on infiniment mieux de semer
    dans ces endroits du ris ou du froment pour rendre moins funestes les famines
    qui désolent si souvent la Chine. On assure que ce pays a bien deux mille montag-
    nes; ainsi c'est une fureur de vouloir encore en augmente le nombre, en rendant
    de plus en plus inégal ce qu'on devroit tacher d'applanir." (It is singular to see
    the architects of China raise artificial rocks in what they call gardens, and then
    they dare ask Europeans if we have workers who could equal them in that. But
    one should respond to them that to put haphazardly some rocks on top of others,
    it is not necessary to have genius, nor art, nor labor, nor taste, nor finally any
    notion of the beautiful and the useful: moreover it would have been infinitely
    better to plant rice or grain in these places to make less fatal the famines that so
    often desolate China. One is assured that that country has two thousand moun-
    tains; thus it is a folly to want to increase their number further, in making more

and more uneven that which one should have worked to make flat.) Cornelis de Pauw, *Recherches philosophiques sur les Égyptiens et les Chinois*, vol. 2 (Berlin: G. J. Decker, 1773), 45.

11 Zhou dynasty (ca. 1046–256 BC). The Zhou dynasty is traditionally divided into Western Zhou (ca. 1046–770 BC) and Eastern Zhou (770–256 BC).

CHAPTER 18

Pierre-Martial Cibot (1727–80)

Jesuit

Pierre-Martial Cibot's "Essai sur les jardins de plaisance des Chinois," written in 1774 and published in 1782, is the first attempt by a Jesuit to treat Chinese garden aesthetics theoretically.[1] Cibot's primary aim of explaining the compositional principles of Chinese garden design is accompanied by his intent to discard "all the false Western ideas about the pleasure gardens now in China" and, at the same time, to propose the Chinese garden as both an ethical and aesthetic model for Europe.

The "Essai" is organized into two parts. The first offers an overview of the development of Chinese gardens through time, which Cibot was the first Western author to compile.[2] He refers to the Chinese historical records and literary sources available to him to document the ancient tradition of garden art in China, placing the Chinese garden into a historical context. At times, Cibot's historical account assumes a moralizing tone: his warning against excess in the decoration of gardens, "fatal to so many dynasties" in ancient China, seems to imply a veiled criticism of French gardens. Likewise, his description of the imposing works that King Zhou of the Shang dynasty commissioned in remote times for "channeling water" into his gardens' artificial lakes, "with enormous dikes and dams" that "burdened his people with the overwhelming weight of their constant maintenance," suggests a reference to the Machine de Marly, the costly and gigantic hydraulic system constructed under the reign of Louis XIV to pump water from the river Seine to supply the numerous fountains in Versailles.

In the second part of the essay, Cibot explains the design strategy behind the Chinese garden as developed during the Ming and Qing dynasties, emphasizing its planned irregularity inspired by the natural landscape, its similarity to the countryside, its variety, and its continual surprises. He offers a vocabulary of compositional elements—mountains, valleys, water features, and vegetation—giving accurate and detailed descriptions of scenes and emphasizing the role of paths in organizing visitors' movement through the garden, leading "to the most smiling viewpoints" and defining the rhythm of the garden as it unfolds, so as "to prepare the visitors for surprises, and to save him from the satiation of habit."

Cibot is a real promoter of the Chinese garden. He explains, and perhaps justifies, his enthusiasm for Chinese garden design as being the result of a long acquaintance with these green spaces, just as Attiret did in a letter written in 1743 that states, "Since my Residence in *China*, my Eyes and Taste are grown a little *Chinese*." Cibot believes that the Chinese garden represents a noble example that could be followed in the reinvention of Western gardens because of its characteristics of being inspired by nature, offering diversity and a variety of compositional arrangements, and, at the same time, being simple and inexpensive to lay out and maintain due to a lack of the costly monumentality of French formal gardens. Though quite vague, his proposal for a very different garden style in Europe combines both Chinese and Western ideas in an effort to engender a garden that is aesthetically beautiful and, above all, economical, designed to reduce the human and financial resources necessary to create and maintain it.

*   *   *

Pierre-Martial Cibot, "Essai sur les jardins des plaisance des Chinois," in *Mémoires . . . des Chinois*, vol. 8 (1782), translated by Bianca Maria Rinaldi

And they shall say, This land is become like the garden of Eden. *Ezech. chap. 35.*[3]

It is generally acknowledged that the Ancients had pleasure gardens. Poets celebrated the gardens of Alcinous, of Adonis and of the Hesperides; historians have spoken admiringly of those of Semiramis, of Ninus and of Cyrus; the Scriptures themselves recount that Solomon brought together an infinity of trees and flowers in his gardens. But how were those ancient gardens organized? According to what rules were they designed? To what point had the art of adorning and embellishing them been perfected? We trusted erudition to answer these questions, but it had to admit that its deepest research cannot take the place of memoires and details. Erudition

Figure 10. Felice Beato, *View of the Gardens and Buddhist Temple of Peking*. October 29, 1860. Wellcome Library, London.

cannot describe what the Ancients barely mentioned in their surviving works.

China is more felicitous in this regard. From earliest times, China has been affected by an uninterrupted heritage of a people [that remained] always the same, and always isolated from the rest of the universe, and China has lost less in the ancient monuments which have been destroyed, and has gained more from those that were preserved. The gardens surviving the reign of *Tsin-chi-hoang* [Qin Shi Huangdi, the Qin First Emperor][4] were an authentic epilogue to those books which the ruler had reduced to ashes, and an excellent commentary on those which had escaped his fury. We will attempt to outline the history of the pleasure Gardens of this extremity of eastern Asia, and to make a sketch of the plan and adornments of such gardens today. We promise to state nothing except what is authorized by the *King* [*Jing*, "Confucian classics"], the annals, and the best-informed Writers.[5] If we neglect to quote them as often as we might, that is only so as not to drag on uselessly.

I

The most ancient garden mentioned in Chinese books is that of the *Kouen-lun* [Kunlun] mountain;[6] but aside from the fact that this mountain is not at all in China, the enchanted description made of these hanging gardens by the *Chan-hai-king* [*Shanhai jing*, "Collection of the Mountains and the Seas"][7] and other ancient books of the *Tao-sée* [Daoshi, "Daoist masters"][8] follows so closely that of the earthly Paradise in Genesis that it would be a sort of profanation to include it in the history of those [gardens] that were the work of men.[9] If nonetheless one wanted to give credence to the accounts of the *Tao-sée*, the gardens of the Emperor *Hoang-ty* [Huangdi],[10] where the *Fong-hoang* [fenghuang] came to perch, the *Ki-ling* [qilin] to take walks,[11] the celestial dragon to unfold its wings, and where one found all that is most beautiful, curious, and rare midst the four seas, they long preceded those of Semiramis and of Ninus, if one were to link them even more to the century of Nimrod than the wisest chronologists have done. But we will adhere to what the *Chou-king* [*Shujing*, "Classic of History" or "Classic of Documents"][12] tells us: that China was in the barren and wild state in which the waters of the deluge had left it, when the colony governed by *Yao*[13] attempted to settle there.

When should the origin of pleasure gardens in China be dated back to? One could date them as early as *Yu*,[14] whose palace was bordered by an orchard and a little park where animals destined to sacrifice to *Chang-ty* [Shangdi, "Lord on High"] were fed.[15] But some research that we undertook, whether in annals or in the most ancient monuments, did not lend itself even to conjectures. In those ancient times, agriculture absorbed public attention; there were very few towns, and what were these? Families, scattered in bunches in the countryside, cultivated at common expense the lands given them by the State, where they kept the flocks in the solitary confines that separated principalities; the arts of necessity were barely known; the empire made up one big family to which each citizen owed his work; and the Emperor had around his palace gardens that were half orchards, half paddock, whose only distinction was their size.

China's Nero was the one who dared introduce the senseless pomp, the ruinous luxury, the insulting magnificence that afterwards was so fatal to the res publica and to Emperors. The delirious passions in which *Tcheou* [Zhou][16] had indulged prevailed, in this as in everything else, over the wisdom of the princes and those of the highest ranks of his council. He uprooted thousands of peasants from their lands to expand to his satisfaction the ancient gardens of his predecessors, changing plains into chains of hills and mountains, excavating immense basins and channeling water to them with enormous dikes and dams, shocking the earth by plants and trees that suddenly appeared in the full size they had reached in the distant regions where they had been dug up, and then finally gathering into them all the pleasures of the countryside in all of its seasons.

Lieou-hiang [Liu Xiang][17] makes an observation on this that is far more satisfying than any detailed description of these gardens that history might have recorded, but did not. "The great *Yu*, the wise man states, opened the road to the throne and founded his dynasty by devoting ten years of efforts and sweat and vigilance to cut down the wild forests the land was covered with, drain the waters it was inundated with, and procure lands and fields for the people to assure them subsistence. *Tcheou*, in the bosom of his pleasures and debauchery, had the crop-covered plains transformed into uncultivated and sterile lands, fake seas, and ruinous channels for water, which burdened his people with the overwhelming weight of their constant maintenance. Therefore he was toppled from his throne, the last sovereign of his dynasty."

Heaven and earth had had their revenge on *Tcheou*. He precipitated into the flames from the fatal tower which had cost such great oppression and where he had amassed so many riches. *Ou-ouang* [Wu Wang] became master of the empire in the year 1222 before Jesus Christ.[18] This prince, more powerful through the love of his peoples than through his armies, and more celebrated for his virtues than for his victories, gave the gardens of *Tcheou* back to agriculture, and his son, to bury even memory [of Zhou], went on to found a new capital at *Lo-yang* [Luoyang].[19]

It was only after more than a century later that *Mou-Ouang* [Mu Wang][20] again took up the idea of adorning the imperial garden. *Lie-tsée* [Liezi?][21] says that this prince, whom Abdalla, a Persian author, mentions, and who seems to have been a contemporary of Solomon, having traveled in the great West, brought back with him some artists who presided over the magnificence of the palaces he had built, and of the gardens in a new style he surrounded them with. But either because this foreign novelty displeased the nation, or because his successors accounted it a type of glory to create their own pleasures, the *Tcheou-ly* [Zhouli, "Rites of Zhou"][22] and history mention only the gardens placed north and west of the palace, where the empress and all her court went to gather mulberry leaves for silk worms, the success of which are demonstrated and illustrated by this grand example. The lines of the *Chi-king* [*Shijing*, "Book of Poetry"][23] do not suggest that the ever increasing luxury of the court had in any way affected the simplicity of the gardens.

But the fatal revolution at the end of the eighth century obliged the emperors to move their court to *Ho-nan* [Henan Province][24] and weakened their authority over the princes of the empire; at that time, either to impress the multitude with ostentatious display, or to keep themselves from feeling their state of decay, they attracted the most celebrated artists to their new capital and occupied them in building magnificent palaces and adorning them with gardens worthy the preeminence they were trying to preserve. In turn the princes, who saw they had the strength to hold on, wanted to compete in grandeur with the emperors, win against them in magnificence and have gardens that were admired more than those of the capital. Their vassals, their high officials, the wealthy, imitated them, and all the areas around the towns, which until then had been fields, were replaced by pleasure gardens and places of delights which the common people, who had been fleeced of their lands, were now obliged to cultivate in order to earn a living. This was not all: while wars became almost continual among the princes, who formed alliances sometimes with the emperor, sometimes against him, the peasants, scattered throughout the countryside, came now to seek shelter near the towns, which expanded and multiplied prodigiously, and little by little sold their inheritances to give themselves relief from public duties, increasing, though their properties, the sumptuousness of the gardens as they went to work for their compatriots as servants and laborers.

What might this sumptuousness have been like? We respond, with the sage *Lu-chi* [Lu Ji?],[25] "What does it matter to the present generation to know how the pleasure gardens of the last centuries of the dynasty of the *Tcheou* [Zhou] were designed, cultivated and adorned? Does luxury need lessons and examples to expand infinitely, to dig an abyss around the throne and to drown it in the tears and blood of the people? What is important for us to know and what can never be studied too much, is the fact that society is sustained only through the labor of agriculture and the wisdom of the administration; agriculture and administration require too much effort and care to interrupt their continuity; it is when agriculture becomes a scourge and a persecution for those who bear the burden of it, and looking after official business becomes merely a pastime for those who have been entrusted with it, that agriculture and government decline daily. Their decadence causes misery, oppression, and the despair of peoples; and the misery, oppression, and despair of peoples inflame them with the fury of revolt, and change gardens from places of delight into places of horror and carnage."

Our man of letters here vigorously reproaches his age, continuing on then as a true disciple of Confucius. "Let us never ask history about what it has destroyed. History has never included the description of the pleasure gardens of the *Tcheou* [Zhou dynasty] in the pictures of this dynasty it has painted with such force and energy; but it has carefully recounted that they grew only at the expense of the best lands and the most fertile fields; that they were embellished only by burdening the peasants with the continual labors that their maintenance required; and that they multiplied only in increasing the misery of the people through inflicting the insulting spectacle of luxury, of idleness, and of the refined pleasures of the great and the rich."

To understand well what these words meant to the Chinese, it is necessary to know that the *Tchun-tsieou* [*Chunqiu*, "Spring and Autumn Annals"],[26] contrasts the famine of the twenty-first year of *Tchoang-kong* [Zhuang Gong, Duke Zhuang of Lu][27] with the immense labors that his gardens cost; that *Mong-tsée* [Mengzi or Mencius] told the prince of *Leang* [Liang][28] that he should adorn his gardens only insofar as was necessary to relax there from the cares of government; that *Lu-chi* had *Tchao* [Zhao?] informed that it was of little importance to the state if the palace gardens were more or less smiling and embellished, but that it was of capital importance that the people enjoy the fruit of their labor and get at least enough out of it to meet their needs; that according to *Koue-yu* [*Guoyu*, "Discourses of the States"],[29] the true magnificence of a prince is to have no poor people in his domains at all; that the prince of *Tsin* [Qin],[30] having taken the orchards of ten thousand families to expand his gardens, was dethroned before he could complete the work; and that finally, according to what *Yang-chi* [Yang Xiong] writes,[31] these gardens of delight and pleasure which had been so often watered with the sweat of the people, ended up by being inundated with blood, delivered to the flames, and changed into places of horror and desolation.

However much research we have done, we have found nothing to clarify ideas on the manner in which the gardens of those times were designed and embellished. But when *Tsin-chi-hoang* [Qin Shi Huangdi],[32] who destroyed

the dynasty of the *Tcheou* [Zhou] toward the end of the third century before
the Christian era, abolished all the separate principalities and invented a
new government, when, *Tsin-chi-hoang*, I was saying, wanted to enjoy his
successes through the beauty of his gardens, as well as by the magnificence
of his palaces and the pomp of his court; what history tells us shows amply
that, being unable to surpass the elegance, refinement and splendor of the
pleasure gardens of the *Tcheou* [Zhou], he aimed simply to surpass them in
dimensions. The ones he ordered to be created had a perimeter of more
than thirty leagues. He filled them with animals, fish, birds, trees, plants,
and flowers from all countries. History specifically reports that he gathered
there *more than three thousand species of trees.* In order to have the pleasure
of enjoying all his victories at the same time and in detail, he built there
[in these gardens] as many palaces as the number of principalities he had
destroyed, and these palaces were built on the model of the most beautiful
of each of these.[33]

However bloody and merciless his tyranny was, one of his ministers
dared tell him, "In your gardens, there are many spaces that are empty and
useless for agriculture. Your Majesty could not put them to a better use
than by giving them to the people to cultivate and augment the harvests
that are the great wealth of the state." Such a personal observation afflicted
his pride; but the power of the thought of the public good was such, that
he didn't dare to appear offended, and he limited himself to answering: "I
enriched my kingdom (the kingdom of *Tsin* [Qin] within the *Chan-si*
[Shaanxi Province]) with the wealth of the rest of the empire; how dare
you ask me to give my garden over to wheat fields?"

But it was less these fields that one asked him for, observes *Tchang-tsien*
[Zhang Liang?],[34] than to bring an end to the immense labors the people
were burdened with to maintain the quality of this *Province-garden*, and
the enormous expenses that increased constantly to make them places more
delicious, more enchanted, and more admirable than those of the *Hien-gin*
[xianren] (the immortals of the *tao-sée*).[35] This prince in fact every day
added new embellishments to the palaces, parterres, woods, pools, canals,
and grottoes. But death ended this rush toward magnificence and buried,
so to speak, his dynasty with him, because his successor, who shared his
vices but none of his good qualities, ascended to the throne only to be
crushed by his fall in the year 206 before the Christian era.[36]

However singular, curious, and interesting may be the events in the history of gardens of the nineteen centuries we still have to cover to come to

our own age, the limits of our purpose, and even more the astonishment they [more complete details] would create in Europe, force us only to outline a light prospect. It might seriously hurt Europe to reveal how far China, however humiliated [that country may be] because of its excesses today, in [the design of] its gardens of pleasure and delight had surpassed and effaced everything that was most magnificent and astonishing in the rest of the universe.

The greatest ones known in the West are but parterres compared to that of the emperor *Ou-ty* [Wudi] of the *Han* [Han dynasty], which had a perimeter of more than fifty leagues and was so scattered with palaces, houses, pavilions, grottoes, that each of its valleys offered scenes and beauties whose magnificence exhausted admiration.[37] Thirty thousand slaves were occupied in cultivating them, and each season the whole empire sent from all the provinces the most beautiful plants and flowers, bushes and trees.

This famous emperor believed that he could increase his gardens in proportion with his empire, whose borders he had expanded as far as the Caspian Sea and into India. He in fact succeeded in creating the biggest garden ever seen, and to flaunt there such magnificence and wealth that, despite the testimony of history, we remain incredulous.

His successors down to the seventh century gave themselves over to excesses even more humiliating to humanity and more dishonorable to the throne, as well as fatal to the res publica.[38] It is true that they gave up the proud folly of transforming entire counties into gardens: their biggest ones were only eighteen or twenty leagues around; but they were still blinded by the thought of extraordinary and gigantesque magnificence and attempted to distinguish themselves by any novelty that they believed might make their power and luxury immortal. Some of them wanted to create their gardens themselves, and chose nature's most arid and graceless places in order to enter into a competition with her by the effort of labor, to conquer her by the resources of work and industry, and thus to surpass her through painstaking cultivation that was even more expensive than it was painful and refined. Others [of this period] completely transformed the places they had chosen: mountains and hills were flattened or even excavated into pools and lakes; valleys and plains were in turn covered with mountains and hills which were rapidly raised, overshadowing lands which shortly before had been brightened by the rays of the sun. These men also had a mania for waters. After having channeled waters to their gardens at great expense from twenty-five or thirty leagues away, they distributed them to the lakes, pools and brooks which kept freshness and greenery, bringing an impression of life and movement all around, and varying at each step the charming perspective from the different points of view that they were embellishing.[39] They undertook to collect in their gardens all that is scattered, dispersed, and disseminated here and there in the most immense territories. Gorges and defiles, plains and valleys, chains of rocks and forests, fields and meadows, lakes and pools, rivers and creeks, towns, villages and hamlets; roads, paths, bridges and passages: the wall of the garden brought all this together; and it made it the epitome of the universe.[40]

Finally, since the emperors could no longer compete for glory with their predecessors in the imitation of nature, they summoned all the arts at once to their gardens, and obtained from them masterpieces and marvels and prodigies of all sorts. Architecture, sculpture, painting vied in genius and invention in the palaces, galleries, towers, salons, pavilions and all the various buildings of all types and sizes, which attracted the eye all around, and which, often built even of aromatic woods or precious marbles, were all the more adorned with porcelains and shiny gold and silver. Some were raised in the distance above the water, others were built on the mountains or rocks, hanging over precipices. Some were brought close together, disposed in such a manner as to add to the beauty of any point of view one saw them from. Others were isolated in delightful valleys, or in a way abandoned in wild and rustic solitary places. All the rest was absorbed into this insane magnificence, to such excess that under the emperor *Yang-ty* [Yangdi][41] silk flowers and foliage supplemented those that fell from the trees, and so as to deceive all the senses at once, they were perfumed as well. But let us spare sensitive souls a more complete account of a luxury so fatal to peoples, which gave rise to such terrible revolutions.

The founder of the *Tang* dynasty,[42] who finally pacified the empire, even midst the fullness of his victories and successes thought as a citizen, to the degree than he ordered the destruction and annihilation of these pleasure gardens that had eaten up the treasures of the state's coffers, impoverishing all segments of the empire and increasing public unhappiness because of the disgust the insulting contrast of their unheard-of magnificence with the extreme poverty of the people aroused. But soon he thought of restoring the luxury of the gardens he had previously sacrificed. All the intrepid zeal of a censor was necessary to keep him from crashing into the rocks already covered with so many shipwrecks.

Under this dynasty and under those of the *Song* and the *Yuen* [Yuan dynasty],[43] which is to say from the seventh to the fourteenth century, it was no longer through taking over the lands of the people, through incredible works, through senseless magnificence that emperors attempted to surpass the pomp of earlier dynasties and to efface the memory of their gardens; it was by the choice of embellishments and by the good taste used in arranging them, by the beauty of the flowers and the rarity of the trees, the spectacle of waters and all other inventions of a studied and delicate luxury. The mild climate of the place where the capital was established lent itself to all the methods through which nature could be led to show herself under new forms and to outdo herself.

Let Europe reconsider its presumptuousness and give up the glory of having first conquered or altered the seasons, subjugated or surpassed the earth's fertility, commanding nature and forcing her efforts to accept the willfulness and the inconstancy of caprice. The West was not even distinguishing pleasure gardens from orchards when the desire to please the emperors or to share their same pleasures gave these men the idea of elevating simple plants to the rank of ornamental shrubs and to lengthen their seasons and increase their beauty: a proof of it is the development of peonies into those majestic *Moutan* [*mu dan*, tree peony] still unknown in Europe;[44] so much so that by dint of efforts they turned the wildest plants into such distinguished and beautiful ones that they effaced more renowned flowers: an example of these is the autumn *Hai-tang*,[45] long unknown by the sea, and now the handsomest decoration of parterres in this season; so much so, finally, as to work on the very foundation and development of flora in varying, embellishing, and perfecting the form of trees and plants, adding to single species all the beauties of others, an example of which are the matricaria, for which florists have not yet found enough names.

The same art, the same care worked together with an equal enthusiasm on all types of trees and flowers in the gardens. There was no more need to expand the enclosure [of the garden], therefore, in order to create an immense show of delight and pleasure. Let no one ask us details about these futile marvels; we will answer with *Lien-chan*: "What difference does it make for the fate of the empire if luxury uses the energies and thoughts of the people in colossal and gigantic magnificence which astonishes, or in a miniature and jewel-like magnificence which dazzles: the latter are not less fatal to agriculture and the arts of necessity, to modesty in display and sobriety in desire, to wise economy and careful administration." All that one can say more favorably about the gardens of the *Tang*, the *Song* and the *Yuen* is that they stole little land from the harvests, and did refine public industry; nonetheless these gardens perhaps employed more hands than those of earlier dynasties: because the less extensive they were the more well-off citizens tried to procure similar ones for themselves.

The pleasure gardens of private individuals were no less objects of curiosity and admiration than those of the emperors. Their very names of *gardens of pleasures, valley of gold, perfume of spring, parterre of waters, wood of peaches, field of pools, theater of matricaria*,[46] and a thousand others like them, proclaimed that public luxury had found the fatal art of piling up more expenses and use more time and employ more hands even though within a smaller enclosure. Our modern emulators of Lucullus in the West are still well behind in the care, attentiveness, precautions, arrangements, practice, attention, and refinement to imagine that millionaires and dilettantes then used in procuring or conserving these flowers of creativity, of fashion or vanity, that made up the glory of their gardens.

When all this had been accomplished, they came to the wish to turn all months into a continual spring, so that flowers from the whole year were available each day. The trees which were forced to grow in pots, and produce more beautiful flowers and bigger fruits than when they were planted in the earth, encouraged new projects. They were treated in a manner that was more bizarre than simply curious. Cedars and pines were shrunken into more graceful and more interesting proportions. They got to the point to reduce them to only a few inches in height, and to perpetuate them in this form by their seeds.[47] Everything in the gardens was proportionate to such refinements. Pools of waters became carpets of flowers vying with the beauty of the parterres; borders of fountains and streams were embellished with shells and covered with the finest sand, or made falling sharply with rocks of bizarre forms; groves were filled with birds remarkable for the brightness of their plumage or the beauty of their song; wild woods and desolate areas and precipices were created to contrast with the magnificent decorations of the parterres, themselves thus becoming spectacles; the very lawn they trod on was remarkable for its green color and for its good smell.

The censors of the empire were not listened to when they compared the magnificence of the greenhouses and the shelter for flowers, to the huts and cabins of the farmers; the selected seeds to feed fish and birds, to the corn and millet fed to the people of the countryside. [They compared] the countless workdays spent on a few acres of sterile land, with those which would have covered an immense plain with crops; the expense which precocious flowers and fruits ripened before time cost, to the amount the state gave citizens who risked their lives in its defense; the number of widows and poor people who could have been fed by taking to the country the fine manure used on parterres, to the idle pleasures of a wealthy dilettante used up an infinity of other people's lives to compensate for the boredom of his own. Mongol Tartars had already taken over half of China, when the discovery of a new exemplar of the matricaria species was the big event in the capital. A controversy about which theater of flowers was best was considered consolation for a defeat. People feared a storm fatal to some fashionable trees more than the invasion of a province. The Tartars advanced towards the capital bringing devastation, slavery and massacre all around, and people were still worried, in more distant provinces, about saving the rarities in their gardens, which had absorbed the attention and exhausted the treasure with which they might have pushed them [the invaders] back. Finally, because we do not pretend and dare to say anything, the articles of capitulation were made to include the rule that soldiers, to whom granaries and treasuries and entire cities had been given up, should respect the gardens and their parterres.

Let no one ask us about the number of ways in which the frivolity and madness of luxury had led to such blindness in a nation that was naturally sage, equitable and moderate. The errors that luxury had led spirits into were at once so seductive and so monstrous that even the Tartars, who had considered the possibility of destroying all the towns and villages of China, to turn their sites into pasturage for their horses, lost their hardiness in the gardens that they had imprudently conserved. They went after the foolish glory of outdoing the *Song* [in their gardens] through a multiplication of machines and gushing waters, so much so that famine, plague and revolts devastated their provinces, and armed against them the despair of people, who chased them away, or who cut their throats as they were a flock of sheep.

It was the destiny and prerogative of the great dynasty of the *Ming* to see pleasure gardens through the eyes of an enlightened and benevolent policy, and to set ideas which endured through the future of the Chinese empire.[48] The one reigning today [the Qing dynasty] adopted their principles.[49]

Wise men should examine how far Europe too should adopt them. We confine ourselves to saying that in China, pleasure gardens were successfully reestablished after their original introduction, not just for the small amount of trouble and expense required in their maintenance, but even more for the natural and pleasing form which they assumed.[50]

I I

Let us set aside all the false Western ideas about the pleasure gardens now in China.

The essence of the constitution of the present government has so clearly set what uses lands are to be put to, has arranged the division of inheritances, marked the boundaries of private holdings, set the proportion of fortunes, has regulated supervision of the administration, and directed all national thoughts toward the public good, that the needs of an agriculture to satisfy the basic subsistence of an immense population have made people hate anything that might diminish its resources or put obstacles before their work. So that, even though the law has not forbidden pleasure gardens, it has irrevocably set [rules concerning] what each individual owes the state annually, and such enticing rewards for clearing land, while the laziness and indolence of those who leave the fields without crops are so punished, that only those of high rank and great fortunes have been able to save some portion of land from the plow and turn it into a pleasure garden. With the exception of the emperor, the princes, and the high dignitaries of the empire, nearly all those who have real gardens claim that they are to serve as the place of their burial, thus calling into play the ancient respect that the eternal dwelling place of the dead demands.

The most extensive gardens of the West have been expanded from those that existed there before, or within the great courtyards, or opposite the last extensions of the palaces. Those in China have been expanded and adorned out of the rustic and artless enclosure where the altar for sacrifices was placed, or out of the field set aside for the tillage owed to the emperor, or the mulberry orchards for the silkworms of the empress. Thus, even though the luxury and magnificence of past centuries exceeded all bounds and piled prodigality on prodigality, the original and basic plan of these pleasure gardens discouraged excesses. Let us judge, from what we are going to say, how it has influenced even those of today.

What is looked for first of all in their situation is the salubrious quality of the air, the goodness of their exposure, the fertility of the soil, an agreeable mélange of little hills and slopes, of little plains and valleys, of groves and meadows, of still waters and brooks.

Mountains are preferred on the northern side to serve as protection, to encourage the cool of summer, ensure the presence of water, pleasantly close the perspective, and show year-round the first and last rays of sun; they are also careful to avoid the risk that these gardens be dominated by neighbors' land, or to be exposed to the glances of the curious public.[51]

The terrain, the position and the placement of Chinese gardens are not dominated by the same choices as those of Europe. The great art of these gardens is to copy nature in all her simplicity, to embellish itself with her disorder, and to hide under the veil of her irregularities.

"What does one look for in a pleasure garden?" writes *Lieou-tcheou* [Liu Zongyan?].[52] "What is their enjoyment through time? All ages acknowledge the same: it is compensation for the painful deprivation of the always lovable, delightful, and ever-new spectacle of the countryside, which is the natural place of man. A garden thus should be the living and animated image of everything one finds there, to engender in the soul the same sentiments, and to satisfy the eyes with the same pleasure. The art of planning them consists therefore in representing so candidly the serenity, the verdure, the shade, the viewpoints, the variety and the solitude of fields, that the eye, deceived, could mistake their simple country air, the ear their silence, or what troubles it, and all the senses feel the impression of enjoyment and peace which makes the time spent there so sweet. So that variety, which is the dominating and eternal beauty of the countryside, should be the first aim of the distribution of the terrain of a garden. And when it is not big enough to suffice for all the models nature uses for placing hills, raising mountains, separating valleys, extending plains, gathering together or isolating trees, making streams fall in cascades or channeling them into a thousand rivulets, displaying pools of waters under the shadow of aquatic flowers, suspending rocks over precipices or leaving them just on the ground, excavating dark caves or constructing pergolas out of foliage: then vary your plans as she does, and let not the false excitement of the first glance make you fall into the constraints and conditioning of a symmetry even more tiring than it is cold and monotonous. If your land is enclosed within too-tight boundaries and does not enable you to put many things there, make your choices and arrange them so that together they bear that imprint of simplicity, negligence and caprice which makes the view of the countryside so graceful and pleasant. Where genius can distinguish itself in competition with nature, or even surpass her, is in arranging its hills, woods, and waters so that their disposition brings out their beauty and augments the effect, and varies the viewpoints in a thousand ways. Nothing can be grand in a little space, but nothing should be pinched, constrained, or exaggerated there. Even in more extensive places, only harmony of proportions can produce this true, touching and invariable beauty which pleases all eyes and ever satisfies the gaze.[53]

"Let us however note that each climate has its needs and proprieties. If one does not keep this in mind, a pleasure garden will not fulfill its purpose. In one place the dryness of summer demands that pools, canals and islets, groves, hills be multiplied endlessly as well as everything that might bring or maintain a peaceful and pleasant coolness. In another, to avoid the unhealthy humidity caused by long rains, it is necessary that the terrain be less covered, more open to the air, cleared, and so disposed that its slopes prevented water from stagnating, yet tempered and irregular enough that the running water does not cause damage. In a situation too exposed to the burning sun and scorching heat, much shade is needed as shelter from the sun, as well as paths, gorges, defiles, promontories cleverly arranged to channel the breeze. Places where the soggy surprise of storms and north winds are feared should have deeper, more protected and less opened valleys, and hills placed against the direction of the most impetuous winds."

Our author, whom we have abridged, here enters into equally curious and instructive details on the varying climates of his province and the type of plan appropriate for the pleasure gardens of each area of it; then he resumes his precepts.

"Whatever choice you make, remember that nothing can later protect you from the mistakes caused by your preferences. If the terrain is badly disposed and badly organized, the cover-up that may seem to hide its defects serves only to point up its disproportions, improprieties and deformities that a better plan would have either repaired or effaced. But even the project that has been most thoroughly studied and happily conceived cannot result in a beautiful garden except insofar as the hand, which puts in the embellishments, disposes them with discernment, distributes them with proportion, varies them with taste, diversifies them without affectation, and combines them, not to efface the caprices and negligence of beautiful nature, but to conserve its simple graces and enhance its pleasing qualities. Let no one say that these are the austere aims that modern policies and philosophy have expressed in the throne room to discourage emperors from seeking the pomp and magnificence which have been fatal to so many dynasties. Disgust, lassitude and irritation have said even more vigorously that anything in a pleasure garden that shows effort and laboriousness, the affectation and refinement of art, is a mask which is all the more disturbing to the view because of its violent contrast with the colors and tones of beautiful nature."

Anyone of spirit will agree that these reflections of the Chinese man of letters are very sage, and come from a man who has a very delicate sense of true beauty. But if we neglect to say, who would believe that the expression *profusion of pomp and magnificence* is indicating peristyles, galleries, statues, reflecting pools, water theaters, cascades, with rich and sumptuous decorations? It is enough to observe that this expression *prodigality of pomp and magnificence*, in the language of the author, is designating only the affluence, the excess and piling up of embellishments which otherwise he accepts: and what are these embellishments? Simple ones such as are appropriate for a garden whose plan is based on the pattern of nature, and all of whose parts are only an imitation of what is charming in the countryside.

All that is alignment and symmetry is far from nature. She never offers trees planted in avenues, flowers gathered in parterres, waters enclosed in basins or regular canals. It is following these ideas that the embellishment of Chinese gardens has been arranged: hills, slopes, little mountains are nearly always entirely covered by different trees, sometimes planted very close together, densely as in the forest; sometimes scattered here and there, isolated as in the fields. The shade of their verdure, the freshness of their foliage, the form of their crowns, the thickness of their trunks, and the height of their stalk decide whether they will be placed north or south, on the summit or on the slopes of the hills, in the gorges or in the defiles that they form.

This arrangement must be a masterpiece of taste, because it should temper what could be too sharp, sustain what would appear too isolated, hide the narrow passages, and support the perspective, whether it cuts off the horizon or is lost in distance. The interests of the single seasons must be balanced and managed so that each has its moment to prevail. Beautifully flowering peaches and cherry trees create an enchanted amphitheater in the spring, acacias, ash, and plane trees create *berceaux de verdure*[54] for summer; autumn has its weeping willows, its satin-leaved poplars and aspens; and winter its cedars, its cypresses and its pines. Since the shape of the hills and the little mountains varies highly, bushes go onto the places where the slope is gentler or brusquely broken by jutting projections or by heaths. In the hillsides which are very steep, or are projecting in a half-arch, or are raised up like a cliff, the scattered rocks leave only space for single bushes, which increase the wild atmosphere and stand out against their bizarre [rock] formations. May the admirers of symmetrical *berceaux*, avenues, porticos, *palissades*,[55] and all the studied shapes of our [Western] gardens, forgive us this avowal: either because the memory we retain of them is too weak, or because the view of [Chinese] gardens here has subjugated our taste by habit, the former seem to us like the eclogues of Fontanelle, the latter like those of Virgil.

A little valley, surrounded by hills and little mountains, itself formed a smiling landscape made to please our eyes. The more the wall of the garden is irregular, indented and tortuous, the more it offers variety according to the different points of view. However one goes around the edges, the design seems different with each step, offering a new tableau. The Chinese Le Nôtres[56] all use this idea in working to create the different shapes that they give to the valleys of the pleasure gardens; and it is also on the basis of this idea that they choose the decoration embellishing them. The bigger a garden is, the more of these little valleys it has; but none resembles another, this one is elongated and as level as our great avenues, then it curves at one end to hide the part where it ends; another extends outward and gets bigger, spreading from its center with openings on all sides; still another seems to contract gradually, and appears to end under the horizon; yet another rounds out into a circle, and seems to isolate and detach itself from everything. The passages leading from one valley to another are so negligently arranged that nothing prepares one for the surprise for the eye and sweet excitement for the soul when one discovers the whole lake. Since their enclosure elongates or shortens, expands or contracts, strengthens or advances, according to the place one approaches it from, one always believes that he is seeing it for the first time. The changing of the seasons adds to the charms of illusion and increases our pleasure just as in the countryside. But it is only in truly seeing them that one can understand how touching meadows carpeted with flowers are, and fields covered with crops, areas of tilled earth, with its rounded furrows, its edges and ditches filled with reeds. If one runs into some regular areas or some edges [planted] with cultivated flowers, their small size seems to express that they are a whim for which one asks pardon. The Chinese dispense with the brilliance and éclat of studied decorations because they have mastered a superior art of animating the scene of their gardens by the waters that they use there, the manner that they use to arrange them, and the excellent results that they obtain.

If the source of a brook is high, and dominates their valleys, they only bring it down by cascades and degrees, that is, by making it fall from one rock to another by detours and falls, where it [water] gets lost to appear again in a way all the more agreeable, the more irregular and capricious it is, and the effect alone [is that] of the escape. When this grand resource is lacking, they use all the slopes on the ground to form little boisterous falls, by stopping the course of the waters by sluices, and by making the waters turn back on themselves by singularly invented detours, or by leading them to even deeper falls. In the West, all our bodies of water are rounded by a compass or aligned by a square. Here, instead, they fear nothing so much as a regularity of shape. They [the bodies of water] are so arranged and open, that it seems that the waters themselves dug their basins, as though the shape of these was the work either of their presence or of their course, which created their shores. These bodies of water sometimes are little pools, or sheets of water, occupying the bottom of a valley, leaving only the most constricted path between the shore and the steep slopes dominating them. Sometimes these waters are brought into a channel that is unusually wide, curved, deepened or deviated by rocks which block it, offering an ensemble charming to see. Sometimes the waters shoot forth, as it were, in the middle of a valley where they seem to have arrived only with effort. Or you have the pleasant sight of a little plain divided into strips and squares for rice! The countless water-filled ditches framing them contrast gracefully with their greenery, bringing out their nuances, and also keeping the air cool. Poets' fiction here must give its prize over to reality. The course of a brook in a pleasure garden is normally a great spectacle. It has its falls, its rapids, its imperfections, its returns: it is the vivid image of the changes in life.

Putting together all that we have said about hills and mountains, valleys, running water and still waters; imagining all this organized and disposed according to a plan drawn imitating nature; envisioning not smooth and spacious avenues, symmetric and aligned, but narrow multiple tracks which expand and contract, advance or detour, climb or descend, according to the character of the places they traversed; but always so happily that they lead pleasantly to the most smiling viewpoints, to the most country-like solitary places, to the coolest shade, while deceiving the first impressions so as to prepare the visitor for surprises, and to save him from the satiation of habit.

We can only describe roughly a part of what we have seen; and Europe's ideas are still so far from the Chinese taste that we might despair of having our account believed.

It would take an entire volume to describe fully all the details. We will limit ourselves to point out that the great features of pleasure gardens in China include: for bodies of water, shores and edges in sand, pebbles, big stones, shells placed randomly, or in earth and turf; carpets of water lilies or of the beautiful *Ki-leou* plant [prickly water lily];[57] wild rushes or reeds; little islands covered with grass or greenery; dikes, sluices, and rustic bridges of all shapes. For the valleys: darkened fields, arid earth, sand, moats, little hedges, grottos, caverns, huts covered either with thatch or palm leaves, or with big stones or tiles, all of a different shape, gay and rustic. For the little mountains: precipices, gorges, terraces, belvederes, ramps and steps of an artless bucolic nature, but clean and graceful. Everywhere masses of rocks, of petrifaction, of rockwork, and of fossil stones of so many shapes and colors, scattered here and there as though by accident.

We must hazard an opinion on what success this taste might have in Europe, not only in embellishing the gardens of the great palaces and villas, but also in the houses of opulent citizens. One visits the former so as simply to breathe freely, far from tumult, and to enjoy the spectacle of the country-side, of which they [the gardens] offer but a simple taste. Even those who are not philosophically inclined might be charmed to find there many features of Chinese gardens, and the more sensitive visitors will easily enjoy the beautiful things that are closest to those [aspects of nature] that make time spent in the country so delicious.

As for the rest, let no one ask us how, with what rules, and to what point the Chinese taste can be introduced into the pleasure gardens of the West, or even to dominate them. Our object in this essay is not to answer those questions, and we have taken care not to burden ourselves with attempts to find answers to questions that are infinitely far beyond us.

The whole world knows that a fine wit of the last century was of the certain opinion that our greatest and most celebrated gardens were provided with serious symmetry and cold monotony which send sentiment to sleep;[58] the ingenious author of an Essay on Architecture later proposed that, by making a happy mixture of Chinese and European ideas, we would succeed in having gay and smiling gardens, where nature would be found with all her graces.[59] Let the sages reason about this matter, working to reconcile all interests, and invent a plan which takes us on the Chinese path in the decoration of our gardens, procuring for us all the pleasures of the beauty of our climates, diminishing only the expenses for creating and maintaining them. The more they follow Chinese taste, the easier it will be;

and they could get such a system adopted which would free thousands of hands for agriculture now so uselessly occupied in raking avenues where no one walks, and clipping or shaping trees that no one sees.

NOTES

1   Pierre-Martial Cibot, "Essai sur les jardins de plaisance des Chinois," in *Mémoires . . . des Chinois*, vol. 8 (Paris: Nyon, 1782), 301–26.

2   Valder, *Gardens in China*, 25–26.

3   (Dicent terra illa facta est velut hortus voluptatis). The quotation is verse 35 of chapter 36 of the Book of Ezekiel: "Dicent: Terra illa inculta, facta est velut hortus voluptatis; et civitates desertae et destitutae atque suffossae, minutae sederunt" (And they shall say, This land that was desolate is become like the garden of Eden; and the waste and desolate and ruined cities are fortified and inhabited). Ezekiel 36:35, American Standard Version, 1901.

4   Qin Shi Huangdi (r. 221–210 BC), first emperor of China, was the founder of the Qin dynasty (221–206 BC). He became king of the Chinese state of Qin in 247 BC and in 221 BC unified China, proclaiming the Empire of Ten Thousand Generations, which he ruled as emperor until 210 BC. See also note 32. For the information on Chinese history and the succession of dynasties and emperors, I have relied on John Keay, *China: A History* (London: Harper, 2008). For pre-imperial China, I have relied on Michael Loewe and Edward L. Shaughnessy, eds., *The Cambridge History of Ancient China: From the Origins of Civilization to 221 B.C.* (Cambridge: Cambridge University Press, 1999).

5   On the Confucian classics or canonical texts, see Endymion Wilkinson, *Chinese History: A Manual*, rev. ed. (Cambridge, Mass.: Harvard University Asia Center for the Harvard-Yenching Institute, 2000), 475–80. My thanks to Alison Hardie for suggesting the translation of the word *Jing* and for pointing out this source to me.

6   Cibot refers here to the fabulous Kunlun Mountain. According to Chinese mythology, it was one of the dwelling places of the Immortals and the home of several deities.

7   Composed between the fourth and first centuries BC, the *Shanhai jing*, commonly translated as "Classic of Mountains and Seas," or "Collection of the Mountains and the Seas," is one of the earliest Chinese texts and an important source of Chinese legends and myths. Compiled as a travel record, it is an account of mythical geography, culture, and natural history of ancient China and includes symbolic descriptions of landscapes, flora and fauna, and legendary figures, as well as information on early medicines. Richard E. Strassberg, ed., *A Chinese Bestiary: Strange Creatures from the Guideways Through Mountains and Seas* (Berkeley: University of California Press, 2003), 1–80. For an English translation of the *Shanhai jing* see Anne Birrell, trans., *The Classic of Mountains and Seas* (London: Penguin, 1999).

8   Cibot is probably referring to two important works of the Daoist canon that are considered the two Daoist classics: the *Daodejing* (Classic of the Dao and of Virtue), known also as the *Laozi*, from the name of the man who was believed to be

the author, Laozi, the Old Master; and the *Zhuangzi*, attributed to the philosopher known as Zhuangzi or Master Zhuang. Alan Chan, "The *Daode jing* and Its Tradition," in *Daoism Handbook*, ed. Livia Kohn (Leiden: Brill, 2000), 1–2; Victor Mair, "The *Zhuangzi* and Its Impact," in *Daoism Handbook*, ed. Livia Kohn (Leiden: Brill, 2000), 30–31.

9   According to tradition, on the top of Kunlun Mountain there was a large hanging garden full of delights, including animals and plants with medicinal properties, and it was considered to be the lower capital of Huangdi, the legendary Yellow Emperor. In the *Shanhai jing* the park took the name of Pingpu (Garden of Peace). For a discussion of this park in relation to ancient myths and the early Chinese texts and for an account of the park, see Shuen-fu Lin, "A Good Place Need Not Be a Nowhere: The Garden and Utopian Thought in the Six Dynasties," in *Chinese Aesthetics: The Ordering of Literature, the Arts, and the Universe in the Six Dynasties*, ed. Zongqi Cai (Honolulu: University of Hawai'i Press: 2004), 129–31. Lin affirms that in popular imagination, this fabulous park represented a sort of paradise.

10   Huangdi, or the Yellow Emperor, is a legendary Chinese sovereign. According to tradition, his reign began in 2697 BC.

11   The *fenghuang* is a mythical bird, often compared to a phoenix; the *qilin* is a mythical hybrid beast with the head of a dragon with two horns, the body of a deer covered with scales, and hooves.

12   The *Shujing*, commonly translated as "Classic of History," "Classic of Documents," or "Book of Documents," is a compilation of documents on the earliest history of China. Together with the *Shijing* (Book of Poetry), the *Liji* (Book of Rites), the *Yijing* (Classic of Changes), and the *Chunqiu* (Spring and Autumn Annals), the *Shujing* formed the *Wujing* (Five Classics), which constituted an essential part of the Confucian canon and were part of the program of examinations to be admitted to the Chinese imperial bureaucracy. The French Jesuit Antoine Gaubil (1689–1759), missionary in China, prepared a translation in French of the *Shujing*, which was edited by the sinologist Joseph de Guignes and published in Paris in 1770 with the title of *Le Chou king, un des livres sacrés des Chinois*. Reed and Demattè, *China on Paper*, 174.

13   Yao was a legendary Chinese ruler who lived in the twenty-fourth century BC.

14   Yu the Great, founder of the Xia dynasty (ca. 2070–1600 BC).

15   *Shangdi* (Lord on High) is the name given the supreme divinity in the most ancient Chinese belief system. Beginning at the time of the Zhou dynasty, this divinity was more commonly referred to as *Tian* (Heaven). In their strategy to express Catholic concepts and definitions in Chinese words, both the notion of *Shangdi* and that of *Tian* were interpreted by the first Jesuit missionaries as possible renditions of the concept of God. The Jesuit accommodation to Chinese terms and rituals provoked a long and ferocious theological debate among the various religious orders, called the Chinese Rites Controversy. David E. Mungello, ed., *The Chinese Rites Controversy: Its History and Meaning* (Nettetal: Steyler, 1994).

16   Zhou was the posthumous name given to Di Xin (r. ca. 1086–1045 BC), the last king of the Shang dynasty (ca. 1570–1045 BC). Along with the preceding Xia

dynasty and the following Zhou dynasty (ca. 1045–256 BC), the Shang formed the first three (pre-imperial) dynasties in Chinese history.

17 Liu Xiang (79–8 BC), Han dynasty scholar and historian, during the reign of the Cheng emperor (r. 32–7 BC) organized an enormous portion of the earliest writings preserved in the imperial library into collections, many of which he collected and edited. He compiled the first systematic catalogue of works in the Han imperial library. Martin Kern, "Early Chinese Literature, Beginnings Through Western Han," in *The Cambridge History of Chinese Literature*, vol. 1, *To 1375*, ed. Kang-i Sun Chang and Stephen Owen (Cambridge: Cambridge University Press, 2010), 60–65.

18 Wu Wang (r. ca. 1045–1043 BC) was the founder and first ruler of the Zhou dynasty (ca. 1046–256 BC), which is traditionally divided into Western Zhou (ca. 1046–771 BC) and the Eastern Zhou (770–256 BC). In the course of the Battle of Muye in ca. 1045 BC, Wu Wang defeated King Zhou of the Shang dynasty; Zhou set his palace on fire and died in the flames. In the copy of the manuscript of Cibot's *Essai* preserved at the Archives des Jésuites in Vanves, the date of the beginning of the Zhou dynasty differs from the printed version. The manuscript reads: "Ou-Ouang, maître de l'Empire en 1122 avant Jésus-Christ" (Ou-ouang [Wu Wang] became master of the empire in the year 1122 before Jesus Christ), Archives des Jésuites Vanves, Mss. Fonds Brotier 130, f. 163r. Due to the lack of real historical documentation, there is uncertainty about the precise dates of the most ancient dynasties. The year 1122 BC as the ending date of the Shang dynasty and, therefore, as the beginning of the Zhou dynasty, was first calculated by the Han scholar Liu Xin (46 BC–AD 23), son of Liu Xiang and his assistant in the compilation of the catalogue of the imperial library. On the basis of archaeological evidence, scholars have only recently revised the beginning date of the Zhou dynasty. David N. Keightley, "The Shang: China's First Historical Dynasty," in Loewe and Shaughnessy, *The Cambridge History of Ancient China*, 247–48.

19 Cheng Wang (ca. 1043–1021 BC), son of Wu Wang and the second ruler of the Zhou dynasty, built an eastern capital in the vicinity of present-day Luoyang.

20 Mu Wang (ca. 1001–946 BC), fifth sovereign of the Zhou dynasty.

21 *Liezi* is an early text of the Daoist tradition. Chapter 3 of the eight chapters it consists of is entitled, "Zhou Mu Wang," from the name of the fifth sovereign of the Zhou dynasty, Mu Wang.

22 The *Zhouli* (Rites of Zhou) is an early Chinese text. It contains a description of an idealized government and also prescriptions for the layout of palaces and cities.

23 *Shijing* (Book of Poetry), one of the Five Classics of the Confucian canon. It consists of 305 poems and hymns from the first period of the Western Zhou dynasty. Edward L. Shaughnessy, "Western Zhou History," in Loewe and Shaughnessy, *The Cambridge History of Ancient China*, 295.

24 With the fall of the Western Zhou in 771 BC, the royal court fled eastward from their previous capital city near present-day Xi'an and moved to present-day Luoyang, in Henan Province, which became the capital city of the Eastern Zhou.

25 Lu Ji (261–303), poet and writer during the Jin dynasty (281–420). Alternatively, as Alison Hardie suggested, Cibot might refer to Master Lü (Lü Buwei) (291–235

BC) and his encyclopedic work *Lüshi Chunqiu* (Master Lü's Spring and Autumn Annals), completed around 239. Alison Hardie, personal communication, March 5, 2014.

26 The *Chunqiu* (Spring and Autumn Annals) is one of the Five Classics of the Confucian canon. Attributed to Confucius, as Martin Kern states, it "provides brief annalistic entries from the perspective of twelve generations of rulers from the small northeastern state of Lu, the home state of Confucius" between 722 and 481 BC. Martin Kern, "Early Chinese Literature, Beginnings Through Western Han," in Chang and Owen, *The Cambridge History of Chinese Literature*, vol. 1, 46.

27 Duke Zhuang of Lu (r. ca. 693–662 BC) was the sixteenth ruler of the state of Lu, a vassal state of the Zhou dynasty, and one of the several small states into which ancient China was divided.

28 King Hui of Liang was the third ruler of the state of Wei, whose capital was at Daliang, present-day Kaifeng, situated in the eastern part of China in the plains south of the Yellow River. The state of Wei was one of the seven major states called the Seven Warring States (Qin, Han, Wei, Zhao, Qi, Chu, and Yan), into which China was divided during the so-called Warring States period (475–221 BC) of Chinese history. The conversations King Hui had with Mencius are recorded in the *Mengzi* (Book of Master Meng), a collection of dialogues of Mencius with rulers of the period and one of the earliest Confucian texts. Book 1 of *Mengzi* opens with Mencius's first meetings with King Hui of Liang, one of which took place in King Hui's garden.

29 The *Guoyu* (Discourses of the States) is a collection of historical discourses and narratives from the Spring and Autumn period of pre-imperial Chinese history.

30 The state of Qin was one of the Seven Warring States. In the late third century BC, Qin conquered all the other states, unifying them under its rule and giving origin to the Qin dynasty (221–206 BC).

31 As suggested by Alison Hardie, Cibot might refer to the great Han dynasty poet and prose writer Yang Xiong (53 BC–18 AD). Alison Hardie, personal communication, March 5, 2014.

32 After conquering the other six warring states and unifying them under his rule, King Zheng of the state of Qin assumed the title of Qin Shi Huangdi, the Qin First Emperor (r. 221–210 BC). See also note 4.

33 Qin Shi Huangdi established his capital at Xianyang, northwest of the modern city of Xi'an, where he built an expansive park: Shanglin, the Supreme Forest. The park was mainly a wilderness preserve for imperial hunting, but it also had a symbolic value as a microcosm of the empire. In it, Shi Huangdi had reconstructed gardens and palaces of the countries he had conquered and he gathered there animals and plants offered as tribute from different parts of the empire. Keswick, *The Chinese Garden*, 44–45; Victoria M. Siu, *Gardens of a Chinese Emperor. Imperial Creations of the Qianlong Era, 1736–1796* (Bethlehem: Lehigh University Press, 2013), xxiii–xxiv.

34 Cibot is possibly referring to Zhang Liang (d. 186 BC), a noble of the state of Han, one of the states of the Warring States period, who planned an assassination

attempt on Qin Shi Huangdi. Zhang Liang played an important role in establishing the Han dynasty and was later to become a statesman under the founder and first emperor of the Han dynasty, Gaozu (r. 206–194 BC). Wai-Yee Li, "Early Qing to 1723," in Chang and Owen, *The Cambridge History of Chinese Literature*, vol. 1, 181.

35 Cibot refers to the Immortals of Daoism, semidivine beings who had attained immortality through Daoist practices; they were thought to live in mythical wooded mountainous islands beyond the eastern coasts of China.

36 After Qin Shiu Huangdi's death his son succeeded him with the name of Qin Er Shi, the Qin Second Emperor (r. 210–206 BC). His excesses provoked protests culminating in a rebellion, which brought about the collapse of the Qin empire.

37 Sixth emperor of the Han dynasty (206 BC–220 AD), Wudi reigned between 141 and 87 BC. The Han dynasty is divided into Western Han (206 BC–9 AD), with its capital at Chang'an (today's Xi'an), built along the southern bank of the river Wei, near the site of the former capital of the Qin, and the Eastern Han (25–220 AD), with its capital city at Luoyang, further east along the Yellow River. Wudi expanded the Shanglin park, inherited from the preceding emperor Shi Huangdi, and enriched it with plants and animals from distant lands, pavilions, temples, and an extensive artificial lake. Even though it remained mainly a hunting park, Shanglin became a symbolic representation of the empire itself, with wooded hills, rivers, and lakes. Rinaldi, *The Chinese Garden: Garden Types*, 15.

38 Cibot refers to the Sui dynasty (581–618).

39 A widespread use of water characterized garden design during the Sui dynasty, as exemplified by the Xiyuan, or West Garden, built near Luoyang, the capital city of the Sui empire. In that garden, a complex system of pools and serpentine channels, which ran into a central lake, created a navigable network that connected the various parts of the parks. This aesthetic interest in water in garden design reflected the significant advances imperial China had made in hydraulic engineering, epitomized by an impressive territorial achievement of the Sui dynasty: the Grand Canal. Rinaldi, *The Chinese Garden: Garden Types*, 17.

40 The aesthetic of a collection of landscapes was one of the main characteristics of Chinese garden design developed through time.

41 Yangdi (r. 604–617) was the second emperor of the Sui dynasty.

42 The Tang dynasty (618–907), which followed the Sui dynasty, was founded by the emperor Gaozu (r. 618–626).

43 The Song dynasty is divided chronologically into two periods: the Northern Song, with its capital at Bianliang (present-day Kaifeng) and the Southern Song (1127–79) with its capital at Lin'an (present-day Hangzhou). The Mongol's Yuan dynasty (1279–1368) was established by Kublai Khan, who built Dadu (The Great Capital) on the site of what is now Beijing.

44 Cibot refers to the tree peony (*Paeonia suffruticosa* Andr.). Its Chinese name is *mu dan*. Fèvre and Métailié, *Dictionnaire Ricci*, 330. The *mu dan* peony was first introduced to Europe from China in 1787, when Sir Joseph Banks planted it at the Royal Botanic Gardens at Kew. Jane Kilpatrick, *Gifts from the Gardens of China* (London: Frances Lincoln, 2007), 99.

45 Cibot is probably referring to the begonia (*Begonia evansiana* Andr.), whose Chinese name is *qiu hai tang*. Fèvre and Métailié, *Dictionnaire Ricci*, 370.

46 As Alison Hardie suggested, these names seem to be proper names of gardens. The Valley of Gold, or Golden Valley Garden, was the name of the garden that the wealthy Jin dynasty writer Shi Chong (249–300) had built northwest of Luoyang. Alison Hardie, personal communication, March 5, 2014.

47 This most likely is one of the first descriptions by a Western traveler of the dwarf shrubs and trees forced to grow in low pots or ceramic or stone trays: the socalled *pentsai* (tray plant or dwarf potted trees).

48 The Chinese Ming dynasty (1368–1644) replaced the Mongol dynasty of the Yuan.

49 The Qing dynasty (1644–1911) was founded in 1644 when the Manchus defeated the Ming empire.

50 I am very grateful to Alison Hardie for her suggestions for the translation for this specific paragraph.

51 Cibot seems to recognize the role of feng shui (geomancy) in the choice of site for a garden or park. According to the principles of feng shui, the sites considered especially fortunate were flat ones, open to the south, protected from unfavorable northern winds by hills or mountains and surrounded on the other sides by gentle elevations. If the chosen site did not present the intended topographical characteristics, even though it was considered propitious, it was possible to intervene, even significantly, in the place's conformation. Thus, following the principles of feng shui, artificial hills could be constructed in the northern part of the park to protect it against evil influences coming from the north.

52 Cibot probably refers here to Liu Zongyuan (773–819), Tang poet and scholar, known particularly for his essays on landscape. To his contemporaries he was known as Liu Liuzhou, as he was exiled to this town in southern China. I am grateful to Duncan Campbell for this information.

53 This part of the long quote by Liu Zongyuan included in Cibot's "Essai" was translated and used by Osvald Sirén in his book *Gardens of China*. See Osvald Sirén, *Gardens of China* (New York: Ronald Press, 1949), 136.

54 Allée covered by the foliage of trees trained to form a vault. My italics.

55 Clipped hedges of trees, my italics.

56 André Le Nôtre, the designer of Versailles. Cibot uses a reference to Le Nôtre, as the emblematic figure representing the French formal garden, to simbolically evokes the greater designers of gardens in China.

57 Cibot probably refers here to the prickly water lily (*Euryale ferox* Salisb.), called in Chinese *ji tou zi*. Fèvre and Métailié, *Dictionnaire Ricci*, 218.

58 With his mention of "a fine wit of the last century," Cibot is perhaps referring to the French diplomat and writer Saint-Simon (1675–1755), one of first detractors of Versailles. In 1715, in his *Mémoires*, published posthumously in 1788, Saint-Simon defined Versailles as "le plus triste et le plus ingrat de tous les lieux" (the saddest and most ungrateful of all places) and criticized the gardens of Versailles harshly because they were, he thought, "du plus mauvais goût" (of the most horrible taste) and where Louis XIV "se plut à tyranniser la nature, à la dompter

à force d'art et de trésors" (takes pleasure in tyrannizing nature, in taming it by means of art and riches). Louis de Rouvroy, duc de Saint-Simon, *Mémoires complets et authentiques du duc de Saint-Simon sur le siècle de Louis XIV*, vol. 1 (Paris: Buisson, 1789, second edition), 129–30.

59 With his allusion to "the ingenious author of an Essay on Architecture" Cibot refers to the distinguished architecture theorist Marc-Antoine Laugier. In 1753 Laugier, who had been a member of the Society of Jesus until 1756, published his influential *Essai sur l'Architecture*, which played an important role in neoclassical architecture theory. In it, Laugier had proposed as an antidote to the monotony of Versailles the simplicity of Chinese gardens and had invited Westerners to consider that "by ingeniously fusing Chinese conceptions with ours we would succeed in creating gardens to which nature with all its charm has returned again." Marc-Antoine Laugier, *An Essay on Architecture*, trans. Wolfgang and Anni Herrmann (Los Angeles: Hennessey and Ingalls, 1977), 139. In support of his idea to introduce Chinese design concepts into Western gardens, Cibot calls on the authority of Laugier.

CHAPTER 19

Pierre-Martial Cibot (1727–80)

Despite its title, Cibot's essay "Observations sur les plantes, les fleurs et les arbres de Chine qu'il est possible et utile de se procurer en France," published in 1786, is not really concerned with the introduction of Chinese plants into France.[1] Rather, it offers Cibot's miscellaneous commentaries on some of his main interests concerning China: gardens, botany, horticulture, and cultivation techniques. The following passages extracted from this essay are dedicated specifically to the Chinese garden.

In the first extract, Cibot recognizes the presence of artificial mountains as an ancient and persistent fundamental characteristic of the gardens of China. He offers a functional motive that evokes agricultural practice for raising wooded artificial hills in Chinese gardens, relating it to the fertility of the slopes and the better conditions of exposure they offer. The artificial hills that Western travelers had noted in Chinese gardens since the time of Marco Polo were therefore not only decorative elements, functional in the garden's composition, but had, at least according to Cibot, a utilitarian explanation.

In the second passage, taking into consideration the extensive use of aquatic plants in the imperial park of Yuanming yuan, Cibot shows that the gardens of China present the wide variety of nature in their enclosures. For a Western reader, the integration of aquatic vegetation into the design of a garden would have seemed quite bizarre. In eighteenth-century Western parks, water plants had no place and, in fact, were considered invasive and needed to be combated because they covered pools and obstructed canals. But in the gardens of the Chinese emperor, as Cibot shows, they had an ornamental use, and water lentils, water lilies, and horsetails filled ponds, lakes, and other water features. Cibot justifies the aesthetic sensibility for aquatic plants on the basis of the design philosophy behind Chinese gardens: the cunning imitation of nature. This imitation, however, occurred without prejudices: the gardens in China were not intended to reproduce, in an absolutely unpredictable composition, only the most pleasant and charming aspects of nature, but rather they also replicated "her caprices, her negligence, even her faults and forgetfulness" that may be manifested in a peculiar exuberance of vegetation. If the use of aquatic plants as ornamental elements was thought to be in contrast with the Western gardening tradition, according to Cibot, these plants may instead find a place in a garden inspired by the natural landscape, following the Chinese example.

*   *   *

From Pierre-Martial Cibot, "Observations sur les plantes, les fleurs et les arbres de Chine qu'il est possible et utile de se procurer en France," in *Mémoires . . . des Chinois*, vol. 11 (1786), translated by Bianca Maria Rinaldi

Those who have seen the plans and descriptions of the great pleasure gardens of China, will no doubt have been struck by the mounds and little chains of hills that fill them. Let the connoisseurs and lovers of gardens pronounce according to their taste and decide how much these mounds and chains of hills, distributed with understanding and wisdom, work together with the other parts of the Chinese system to imitate beautiful nature, and can or cannot have a good effect. We rest fully on their supremacy and their infallibility. All the universe, for all centuries, is at their feet. We limit ourselves to observing that these mounds and mountain chains were chosen by the Ancients, just as Nature had prepared them, then were imitated in the following ages, in conformity with this first choice. But why? Because they were believed to be more appropriate for the planting of trees in general, and more advantageous for fruit trees in particular. On the other hand, on this point as on all the others we have spoken of and will speak further, it is not a question, for us, of setting down rules or guarantees, nor even of approving, but simply of giving an account of what we find. This affirmation is specific; it would be wrong not to take notice of it, all the more because we are leaving aside all the explanations of Chinese physicians, and we are limiting ourselves to the matters under consideration.

For example, people have said about mounds and hills that planting trees and bushes there always works out better, other things being equal,

than in a flat countryside, because the upper and lower slopes, their different positions and expositions, make it possible to put together to one's
liking all the types and species one wishes; something we have seen prac-
ticed very happily in the gardens of the Emperor. But in order to not make
the Chinese say what they do not in fact say, we note that they except trees
which demand proximity to water or humid soils, like willows, poplars,
etc., and agree that those which want deep soils there definitely do not
reach the same size and the same height. But on the other hand, they affirm
that all fruit trees, without exception, are always incomparably better there
than elsewhere, because it is possible to procure the exposure each one
demands, and, what is no less important for the goodness and healthiness
of their fruits, a situation that assures each a free, easy, and continuous
circulation of air.

In the gardens, or if you wish, in the imperial park of *Yuen-ming-yuen*
[Yuanming yuan], in the ponds and the pools, the canals and the streams,
in short, in all the places where there are waters which fall, which remain
still, which tumble crashing onto rocks, winding and getting lost, bathing
the grass, etc., they gathered all the flowers and plants which prefer the
borders or the center, the surface or the bottom of the waters. It is idle to
note that the Chinese have inherited from their ancestors the sense that
nothing in nature is so beautiful as nature herself; she alone pleases them,
and they don't want to see anything else then her in the most sumptuous
and most magnificent gardens. In the West we know today that, because of
this national prejudice, or, if you wish, this delicate and enlightened
acquired taste, the Emperors themselves have sought only to imitate nature
even in the plans of their gardens. If, on the one side, they have spared
nothing to assemble these admirable scenes, these charming horizons, these
smiling views, these passages, these long prospects, these contrasts, and
these surprises that she has dispersed throughout immense countryside; on
the other, they have striven also to imitate her in this assemblage to the
point of copying her caprices, her negligence, even her faults and forgetfulness. Any place one has seen does not prepare one for what one is going to
see; and coming away from that, it is necessary to expect a new surprise:
but an agreeable surprise, a satisfying surprise, a surprise which enchants
all the more delightfully because the art is hidden, and lets one see nature
alone. Thus, however many water features there may be, however numerous the streams, neither a ruler nor a cord have made the borders straight;

no preference seems to have determined their place; and their banks, which they dominate, and by which in turn they are dominated, are sometimes low, sometimes high; here rocky, there sandy; threatening on one side, ready to give way on the other, and everywhere strangely tortuous and indented, just as in the countryside.

Now, to come to our point, and to what we are going to indicate that must serve as a preamble, Chinese taste studied nature with too much intelligence and sagacity not to observe that even the wildest shrubs, flowers, aquatic plants and herbs were the true adornment of the water; and that leaving it without this interesting decoration of beautiful nature would disclose a pettiness in art. Therefore, its sole care is that of placing all that one finds of this sort in the countryside in the gardens' waters with understanding, arranging it there with taste, making it appear to the greatest effect.

Duckweed has its place there as do water lilies, the gladiolus as the iris, the reed as the arrowhead, the horsetail as the water chestnut, watercress as the fennel; the moss, even the most common, was not forgotten.[2] Now, all this continues to have its place today: and to judge by the gardens of the Emperor, that we saw with leisure in all seasons, we would not hesitate at all to say that the arrangement is so well made, and harmonizes so naively with all the rest, that the eye is truly satisfied, and seeks no more. Our France is prodigiously fertile in aquatic plants of all species; why does she not profit more from the gifts nature has lavished on her? Why should this wise Chinese taste not take hold among us, and have us find in the water, as they do, adornment for our gardens, and an annual crop and without labor for our Country workers? Let even the most biased, who find so much enjoyment in viewing a *jardin de plantes*, consider the pleasure they will have to see gathered so harmoniously so many beautifully cultivated plants.

NOTES

1   Pierre-Martial Cibot, "Observations sur les plantes, les fleurs et les arbres de Chine qu'il est possible et utile de se procurer en France," *Mémoires . . . des Chinois*, vol. 11 (Paris: Nyon, 1786), 183–268.

2   With regard to the term *fenouil* in the original French version, translated here as "fennel," Cibot probably refers to the water dropwort.

CHAPTER 20

George Leonard Staunton (1737–1801)

[handwritten: English diplomat. travelogue]

The British embassy to China, led by Lord George Macartney in 1792–94, was not a diplomatic success. Despite the mission's meticulous preparation and the numerous gifts sent by King George III to the Chinese emperor (bearing witness to the latest English technological advances at the time), none of the requests made by the British for an expansion and facilitation of trade relations between the East India Company and China were accepted by the Qianlong emperor.[1] Nonetheless, the diplomatic mission was an important occasion for adding to the already extensive Western knowledge of the Chinese empire, particularly through the travel accounts compiled by various participants in the embassy and published in the years immediately following their return to England.[2]

The diplomat George Leonard Staunton, who served as secretary and provisional minister plenipotentiary for that embassy, was entrusted with the writing of the official account of the diplomatic mission, which was published in 1797 with the title *An Authentic Account of an Embassy from the King of Great Britain to the Emperor of China*.[3] His narrative was based on his own observations, as well as those of others participating in the embassy: John Barrow, who served as the embassy's comptroller; Lord Macartney; and Erasmus Grover, the expedition's naval commander. Staunton's accurate narration of the embassy's travel to and throughout China was illustrated by engravings representing diverse aspects of the Chinese country and culture: from instruments of navigation to deities and furnishings, to artifacts and naturalistic subjects. Another series of engravings, many of them prepared by the painter William Alexander, who took part in the embassy as the official artist, was collected in a folio volume published in 1796 as an introduction to Staunton's travelogue. It included maps showing the mission's travel itinerary and views of architecture, costumes and culture, as well as landscapes of Qing imperial China.[4]

Staunton's travelogue begins with an account of the voyage and the places traversed, following the usual, and complicated, route from Europe to China. The text then concentrates on China, mixing a narration of events occurring over the course of the diplomatic mission with information on various aspects relating to the country and its culture that were likely to arouse the curiosity of Western readers. His observations touch on myriad topics including medicine and natural history, science and technology, material culture, fireworks, printing and papermaking and, obviously, garden art, as exemplified in the descriptions of the imperial parks presented in the two selected texts that follow.

The first extract is a description of the imperial summer residence of Bishu shanzhuang, in Chengde, where an embassy delegation was received by the Qianlong emperor on September 14, 1793. The second excerpt contains a brief description of the gardens in the Imperial City in Beijing, followed by an account of Yuanming yuan that Staunton wrote quoting from the commentary of John Barrow. The latter text, however, differs from the much less favorable description that Barrow himself published later in *Travels in China* (1804).

The embassy's participants were not well acquainted with the Qing imperial parks, especially in comparison to the missionaries who served at the imperial court; they remained in northern China only for a few weeks and were dismissed in Beijing on October 9, 1793. Nonetheless, Staunton, Barrow, and Lord Macartney were the first British to see and describe the Qing pleasure grounds. Their interpretation of the Chinese gardens they visited was influenced by their acquaintance with the picturesque gardens of their own country. The "irregular clumps of trees" and "the picturesque in the landscape" that Staunton perceives—through Barrow's observations—in the parks of the Chinese emperor suggest an almost too English atmosphere, which was disturbed, he writes, only by the different pavilions scattered through the park. Evidently, Staunton considered their architectonic language and their excessively bright coloring inappropriate for an authentic picturesque park.

Staunton was an eclectic character; he was a physician and an attorney, as well as a cultivated diplomat who had friendly relations with some of the most influential personalities of the time, including Edmund Burke, whose theory of the sublime had, in the second half of the eighteenth century, encouraged landscape garden aesthetics to evolve in the direction of more romantic atmospheres. In the words of Staunton, Bishu shanzhuang seems a perfect synthesis of the two opposing aesthetic categories proposed by Burke: the sublime, expressed by the wildest and brutish aspects of nature, and the beautiful, represented instead by all that is smooth, soft, gentle, and cultivated. The imperial park of Chengde, in the eyes of the British diplomat, was a summation of these aesthetic ideals as it "seemed calculated to exhibit the pleasing variety and striking contrast of the ruggedness of wild, and the softness of cultivated nature."

In the parks of the Qianlong emperor, Staunton recognizes some elements and compositional mechanisms of the English landscape garden: the role of landscape paintings in the design of the park and the use of devices to influence the visitor's perception. Through illustrating the clever use of vegetation in the composition of scenic views in Yuanming yuan, as well as the careful placement of pavilions erected at vantage points from which to enjoy the scenes, Staunton—again through Barrow's writing—recognizes a pictorial sensibility in the design strategy behind Chinese gardens. He noted, however, an essential and bizarre difference between Chinese garden design and Chinese paintings. While in gardens the careful arrangement of the various elements and modulation of shadows seemed to suggest the use of the conventions of perspective, these conventions did not find similar application in paintings.

* * *

From George Leonard Staunton, *An Authentic Account of an Embassy from the King of Great Britain to the Emperor of China*, vol. 2 (1797)

The next object of civility immediately from the Emperor, was an invitation to his Excellency [Lord Macartney] and his suite to see the gardens or pleasure grounds of Zhe-hol [Jehol].[5] In proceeding towards them at the early hour in the morning, at which all transactions are begun at this punctual court, they met his Imperial Majesty, who stopped to receive the Embassador's salutations, and to tell him that "he was going to his devotions in the temple of Poo-ta-la [Potala]; that as they did not adore the same gods, he would not desire his Excellency to accompany him but that he had ordered his ministers to attend him through his gardens."[6]

Figure 11. James George Fittler, after William Alexander, *The Approach of the Emperor of China to his Tent in Tartary, to Receive the British Embassador*. In George Leonard Staunton, *An Authentic Account of an Embassy from the King of Great Britain to the Emperor of China*, vol. 3, pl. 25, April 12, 1796 (London: printed for G. Nicol, 1797). Beinecke Rare Book and Manuscript Library, Yale University.

The Embassador, who thought that the appointment of any courtier of rank, unoccupied with the affairs of state, to accompany him on the proposed excursion, would have been a sufficient testimony of the Emperor's attention, was surprised to find Ho-choong-taung [He Zhongtang, the Honorable He] himself waiting in a pavilion for him.[7] The great Vizier of the empire, he, whom the people almost considered as a second Emperor, was now ordered to give up some portion of his time from the calls and cares of government, to keep a stranger company in a mere tour of pleasure and curiosity.

The satisfaction which his Excellency derived from the a circumstance that might contribute to an intimacy favourable to the general object of his mission, was damped by the presence of the Thibet general, who accompanied the Colao, as if fearful of the Embassador's gaining any ground with him, or that any explanation relative to the Thibet war might take place between them. The general's brother, who had a considerable share in the administration, was also present, together with another chieftain of high quality.

These personages took the trouble of conducting his Excellency and his suite through the pleasure grounds of a vast enclosure, forming, however, only a part of those great gardens, the remainder being reserved for the use of the female part of the Imperial family, where those ministers had admission as little as the English. They rode through a verdant valley, in which several trees, particularly willows of an uncommonly large girth, were interspersed, and between which the grass was suffered to attain its most luxuriant height, with little interruption from cattle or the mower. Arriving at the shores of an extensive lake of an irregular form, they sailed upon it till the yachts, in which they had embarked, were interrupted by a bridge thrown over the lake in the narrowest part; and beyond which it seemed to lose itself in distance and obscurity. The surface of the water was partly covered with the *lien-wha* [*lian hua*], or species of the lily mentioned in the last chapter to be growing in Pekin [Beijing] and which, tho in a more northern situation, and at a cooler season of the year, still adorned the lake with its spreading leaves and fragrant flowers.[8]

The party stopped at a number of small palaces, near the water's edge, there being no one very considerable edifice. There were other buildings erected on the pinnacles of the highest hills, and some buried in the dark recesses of the deepest vallies. They differed in construction and ornament from each other, almost every one having something, in the plan of it, analogous to the situation and surrounding objects; but, within each, was generally a public hall, having in the midst a throne and a few side rooms: the whole furnished with works of art from Europe, and rare or curious productions of nature found in Tartary. Among the latter was an agate of extraordinary size and beauty, supported on a marble pedestal, and standing in one of the pavilions upon the lake. This agate, of which there is an engraving on the opposite page, is four feet in length, carved into a landscape, and bears a copy of verses cut into it, which were written by the Emperor. The best works of art by natives of the country were carvings in wood, descriptive of natural objects grouped together with taste, and executed with truth and delicacy. Some of the walls were covered with paintings, representing the pleasures of the chase in Tartary. In these the Emperor is always seen at full gallop, shooting wild beasts with arrows. These paintings cannot stand the test of European criticism. The trees, the birds, some part of the landscape, and even the animals, were drawn with accuracy; but they failed in the human figure, with which the spectator being better acquainted, can more easily perceive where the imitation of it is defective. The proportions, the perspective were not preserved; and the Chinese, tho they succeed in a correct, and sometimes lively delineation of individual objects, cannot properly be said, in the present state of their arts, to be equal to the design and composition of a picture. One European portrait of a woman, of indifferent workmanship, was seen hanging in one or the rooms. A well executed statue in marble, of a naked boy resting upon his knees and hands, was discovered in a bed-chamber; and the figures in stone of a few animals stood in a flower garden; beside monstrous and disgusting lions and tigers, in porcelaine, before several of the buildings. The decorations which most abounded, and seemed to be most admired by the conductors of the party, were those artificial figures of men and animals, imported from Europe, which, by means of internal springs and wheels, produce movements apparently spontaneous. When these machines appeared first in China, they were considered as almost supernatural, and fetched enormous prices.

In continuing their ride, the party found that the grounds included the utmost inequality of surface; some bearing the hardy oaks of northern hills, and others the tender plants of southern valleys. Where a wide plain happened to occur, massy rocks were heaped together to diversify the scene; and the whole seemed calculated to exhibit the pleasing variety and striking contrast of the ruggedness of wild, and the softness of cultivated, nature. The gardens were enlivened by the movements, as well as sounds, of different kinds of herbivorous animals, both quadrupeds and birds; but no menagerie of wild beasts was perceived. Some monstrous varieties of gold and silver fishes were seen playing in ponds of pellucid water, upon a bottom studded with pebbles of agate, jasper, and other precious stones.

Throughout these grounds, they met no gravel walks; no trees planted in belts, nor collected in clumps. Every thing seemed to be avoided which betrayed a regularity of design.[9] Nothing was observed to be directed, unless for very short distances, by straight lines, or to turn at right angles. Natural objects seemed scattered round by accident, in such a manner as to render their position pleasing; while many of the works of human labour, tho answering every purpose of convenience, were made to appear the produce of rustic hands, without the assistance of a tool.[10]

Some of the elegancies and beauties which are described as taking place in Chinese gardens, were not perceived by the present visitors; but the gardens of Yuen-min-yuen [Yuanming yuan] near Pekin, from whence those descriptions are chiefly taken, are supposed to be more complete than those of Zhe-hol; and it were presumptuous to assert, that what is omitted in the one, has been falsely attributed to the other.

These strangers had no chance of seeing any part, if such there be at Zhe-hol, of the town in miniature, which is supposed to be enclosed within the boundaries of the garden destined for the ladies of the palace, where the scenes of common life, and the transactions and confusion of the capital, are faithfully represented, according to the accounts of a missionary, who, in quality of artist, is said to have been employed in the decoration of such a place, in the female part of the gardens at Yuen-min-yuen. That account, however it has been doubted, is not improbable.[11] The ladies of the palace, shut out from the world, would, no doubt, be delighted by such a representation of what passes in it; and the Emperor could feel no reluctance in gratifying their curiosity, and, in some instances, his own. The Embassador, in a former mission to Russia, saw, at one of the Imperial palaces of Petersburg, the image of a town, with a number of workshops and warehouses, pretended tradesmen, and the usual business of life, represented in a very lively manner for the amusement of the court; tho it promised less entertainment there, where none of the ladies were debarred, like those of China, from the sight of what was really passing in the world. . . . The excursion through the gardens of Zhe-hol . . . lasted several hours.

Mr. Barrow was present while the same ceremonies were observed at Yuen-min-yuen; and he was informed that they likewise took place on that day in every part of the empire, the prostrators being every where attentive to turn their faces towards the capital.

On all the days of new and full moon, similar, incense is burnt, and offerings are made before the throne by the officers of the household, in the several palaces of the Emperor.

Those palaces are very numerous throughout the empire. That of Pekin forms the centre of the Tartar city. Tho that capital stands in the midst of a dusty plain, from whence the mountains of Tartary can be perceived only at a distance, yet the walls which environ the palace, offices, and gardens, include every variety of ground in miniature which the sportive hand of nature has created upon the surface of the globe. Mountains and vallies, lakes and rivers, rude precipices and gentle slopes, have been produced where nature did not intend them; but in such correct proportions, and with so much harmony, that, were it not for the general uniform appearance of the surrounding country, a spectator would entertain some doubt whether they were the real productions, or the successful imitations of nature. This world, in miniature, has been created at the command and for the pleasure of one man, but by the hard labour of many thousands.[12] . . .

In the neighbourhood of Pekin, the gardens and pleasure grounds of Yuen-min-yuen occupy a considerable tract of ground, of which the circuit was, according to the observation of Mr. Barrow, at least twelve miles. That gentleman, who saw more of it than any other person of the Embassy, thought it "a delightful place. The grand and agreeable parts of nature were separated, connected, or arranged in so judicious a manner, as to compose one whole, in which there was no inconsistency or unmeaning jumble of objects; but such an order and proportion as generally prevail in scenes entirely natural. No round or oval, square or oblong lawns, with the grass shorn off close to the roots, were to be found any where in those grounds. The Chinese are particularly expert in magnifying the real dimensions of a piece of land, by a proper disposition of the objects intended to embellish its surface; for this purpose, tall and luxuriant trees of the deepest green were planted in the fore ground, from whence the view was to be taken; whilst those in the distance gradually diminished in size and depth of colouring; and in general the ground was terminated by broken and irregular clumps of trees, whose foliage varied as well by the different species of trees in the group, as by the different times of the year in which they were in vigour; and oftentimes the vegetation was apparently old and stunted, making with difficulty its way through the cliffs of rocks, either originally found or designedly collected upon the spot. The effect of intricacy and concealment, seemed also to be well understood by the Chinese. At Yuen-min-yuen, a slight wall was made to convey the idea of a magnificent building, when seen at a certain distance through the branches of a thicket. Sheets of made water, instead of being surrounded by sloping banks, like the glacis of a fortification, were occasionally hemmed in by artificial rocks, seemingly indigenous to the soil.

"The only circumstance which militated against the picturesque in the landscape of the Chinese, was the formal shape and glaring colouring of their buildings. Their undulating roofs are, however, an exception to the first part of the charge; and their projection throws a softening shadow upon the colonnade which supports it. Some of those high towers, which Europeans call pagodas, are well adapted objects for vistas, and are accordingly, for the most part, placed on elevated situations.[13] Notwithstanding the just ideas which the Chinese conceive of ornamental gardening, and the taste with which they dispose of every object to the greatest advantage, they are not only totally ignorant of the principles of perspective, and of the gradations of light and shade, but are utterly insensible of their effect, as appeared from their own performances with the pencil. When, likewise, several portraits by the best European artists, intended as presents for the Emperor, were exposed to view, the mandarines observing the variety of tints occasioned by the light and shade, asked whether the originals had the right and left sides of the figure of different colours? They considered the shadow of the nose as a great imperfection in the picture; and some supposed it to have been placed there by accident. An Italian missionary at the court of Pekin, of the name of Castiglione, who was an excellent painter, received orders from the Emperor to paint for him several pictures; but it was intimated to him at the same time, to imitate the Chinese style of painting, and not that of Europe, which was considered as unnatural.[14] Accordingly, in the performances meant to decorate the palace, houses above houses are seen in regular gradation to the top of the picture; figures in the fore and back ground are all of the same size, setting, in fact, nature and the senses at defiance. He also painted a set of characters occupied in the different trades of China. The pencilling and colouring of these were incomparably well executed; but for want of the proper shadows, the whole was without effect. Yet they please the Chinese in preference to any specimen of the arts that could be brought from Europe."

NOTES

1   On the Macartney embassy, see Mungello, *The Great Encounter*, 94–99; Hevia, *Cherishing Men from Afar*; Aubrey Singer, *The Lion and the Dragon: The Story of the First British Embassy to the Court of the Emperor Qianlong in Peking, 1792–1794* (London: Barrie and Jenkins, 1992); Alain Peyrefitte, *The Immobile Empire* (New York: Random House: 2013, 1st ed. 1992).

2   Aeneas Anderson, Lord Macartney's valet, published *A Narrative of the British Embassy to China* (1795); in 1797, Johann Christian Hüttner, the German tutor of Sir George Leonard Staunton's son, George Thomas Staunton, who joined the embassy as Lord Macartney's page, published his own account of the embassy entitled *Nachricht von der Brittischen Gesandtschaftsreise durch China*; Samuel Holmes, a sergeant major in Macartney's guard, published his *Journal* (1798); John Barrow, the embassy's comptroller, published his own account, *Travels in China*, in 1804. See Chang, *Britain's Chinese Eye*, 43; and also Kitson, *Forging Romantic China*, 129.

3   George Staunton, *An Authentic Account of an Embassy from the King of Great Britain to the Emperor of China*, 2 vols. (London: G. Nicol, 1797). Also in 1797

the publisher Nicol produced an octavo edition in three volumes. A second English edition was published in 1798, a first American edition was published in 1799, and an abridged English version was published in 1797 and entitled *An Historical Account of an Embassy to the Emperor of China.* A French translation appeared in 1798 and had several editions. A German translation was published in 1798–99. A Dutch translation was issued in 1798–1801.

4 The Atlas volume contains forty-four plates. William Alexander later published two illustrated volumes depicting landscapes, architecture, boats, customs and trades, people, and scenes from everyday life: *The Costume of China* (1805) and *Picturesque Representations of the Dress and Manners of the Chinese* (1814). On Alexander see Frances Wood, "Closely Observed China: From William Alexander's Sketches to His Published Work," *British Library Journal* 24 (1998): 98–121.

5 The invitation to visit the imperial park came after a series of gifts sent to the ambassador and his retinue that included "several dishes from his own table . . . a goblet of warm Chinese wine . . . silks, porcelaine, and tea." Staunton, *An Authentic Account,* vol. 2, 237 and 238.

6 "Potala" refers to the Putuozongcheng miao, a Buddhist temple built by Qianlong between 1765 and 1771, which was modeled after the Tibetan Potala Palace in Lhasa. It was part of Eight Outer Temples built to the north and east of Bishu shanzhuang, outside the palace walls.

7 Staunton refers here to the Minister and Grand Councillor Henshen (1745–99). Wong, *A Paradise Lost,* 89.

8 Staunton refers to the lotus, whose botanical name is *Nelumbo nucifera* Gaertn. He had already observed this aquatic plant in the western part of the Imperial City in Beijing, covering the Three Seas, which Staunton described as a "lake of some acres in extent, now, in autumn, almost entirely overspread with the peltated [peltate] leaf of the *nymphæa nelumbo,* or *lien-wha* of the Chinese." Staunton, *An Authentic Account,* vol. 2, 122.

9 Johann Christian Hüttner, in his travelogue, synthetized his perception of the imperial park, writing that its composition "owes much to nature, and very little to art, with the exception of the bodies of water, the buildings, and the groves of trees. The northern part consists of mountains, which raise on some occasions on combined masses, on some others on steep parts, separated by ravines, and they culminated in a high peak which dominate the whole area. Towards West, the park ends with hills, which are easy to ascend." Johann Christian Hüttner, *Voyage à la Chine* (Paris: Fuchs, 1798), 77–78: "Le parc, qui doit beaucoup à la nature, et très-peu à l'art, à l'exception des pieces d'eau, des edifices et des plantations d'arbres. La partie du nord consiste en montagnes, qui s'élèvent tantôt en masses réunies, tantôt par parties escarpées, séparées par des précipices, et se terminent par une pointe élevée qui domine toute la contrée. Vers l'occident, le parc est terminé par des collines faciles à monter."

10 Staunton expresses the same concept of the apparently casual arrangement of the different elements that compose Chinese gardens, in describing one of the imperial travel palaces where the delegation stopped during their travel from Beijing to Chengde. The complex, Staunton wrote, "stood upon an irregular surface near

the base of a gentle hill, which, with a part of the vale below, was inclosed, and divided into a park and pleasure grounds, with a very pleasing effect. Trees were here thickly interspersed, but permitted a view through them of a stream running at a little distance. Beyond it, the rising hills were some of them planted, and some left naked. The different objects seemed in their natural state, and as if assembled here only by a fortunate chance." Staunton, *An Authentic Account*, vol. 2, 172.

11 Staunton shows his familiarity with descriptions of the imperial parks written by earlier travelers. Visiting the parks of the emperor, Staunton expects to find elements that he had already read about, such as the celebrated miniature city described by Attiret and recalled in Chambers's *Dissertation*. Even though he learned about this particular feature through "the accounts of a missionary" (evidently referring to Attiret's text), Staunton is not certain in which imperial complex—Yuanming yuan or Bishu shanzhuang—the miniature city was created. None of the members of Lord Macartney's embassy, who visited the suburban residences of the Qianlong emperor, had been able to see this specific part of the parks and, therefore, to confirm, or deny, the account of the Jesuit missionary. Despite the apparent difference between what the British delegation saw in the imperial parks and Attiret's famous description, Staunton, lacking a direct experience of the place, is cautious in expressing a judgment on the reliability of what Attiret wrote. He limits himself to the comment that "this account . . . however it has been doubted, is not improbable."

12 Like Benoist and Attiret before him, Staunton also notes the exclusive quality of the imperial parks.

13 John Francis Davis included this description of Yuanming yuan in his own account of his experience of China. John Francis Davis, *The Chinese: A General Description of the Empire of China and Its Inhabitants*, vol. 2 (London: Knight and Co., 1836), 254–55.

14 Staunton refers to the Jesuit Giuseppe Castiglione.

CHAPTER 21

André Everard van Braam Houckgeest
(1739–1801)

A ndré Everard van Braam Houckgeest was a Dutch-American diplomat and trader for the Dutch East India Company, who, together with Isaac Titsingh (1745–1812), led the last Dutch embassy to China in 1794–95, one year after the Macartney embassy.[1] The delegation, sent from the Company to congratulate the Qianlong emperor on the sixtieth anniversary of his rule, arrived in Beijing from Guangzhou in January 1795. They were received in the Forbidden City and later in the imperial park of Yuanming yuan, remaining in the capital for about forty days before undertaking the voyage back home. Van Braam kept a journal of that diplomatic mission and of the embassy's reception at court; the account contains also his observations about the country's geography and places he visited, as well as agriculture, culture, and social conditions. Written in Dutch, his travel diary was translated into French and published in Philadelphia in 1797–98 with the title *Voyage de l'ambassade de la Compagnie des Indes Orientales hollandaises vers l'empereur de la Chine, dans les années 1794 et 1795*.[2] The following extracts are taken from the English version of Van Braam's travelogue published in London in 1798 and entitled *An Authentic Account of the Embassy of the Dutch East-India Company, to the Court of the Emperor of China*.[3]

The first extract describes Van Braam's itinerary through part of the imperial parks of Yuanming yuan, where the embassy was received several times between January 31 and February 8, 1795, and Qingyi yuan (Garden of Clear Ripples), in the northwestern outskirts of Beijing.[4] Unlike other descriptions of imperial parks included in this anthology, Van Braam focuses mainly on the garden buildings and the variety of their architectural forms. However, in describing Qingyi yuan, he did not fail to notice the spatial articulation of the park.[5] He describes it as a sequence of visual discoveries that awake "extraordinary sensations" in the visitor's mind. The narration of his visit to the imperial park is centered on the way in which the perception of the garden's space was modulated by the control that the layout of the garden imposed on the visitor's movement and vision. Van Braam describes some of the methods and visual devices used to screen, direct, or expand vision in the garden, intensifying the sense of surprise and, at the same time, influencing the perception of the garden's real scale: such as a large sculptural rock that had been placed just behind a gate to occlude the view of the garden beyond it, increasing the viewer's sense of expectation; or such as unexpected and extensive views that opened into distant landscapes beyond the park's enclosure. The latter is the result of a specific compositional technique used in Chinese garden design called "borrowed scenery," a technique that Van Braam could not have been aware of but whose effects he described quite precisely.[6]

The second extract is the description of a traveling imperial complex of palaces and gardens near the city of Yangzhou. The short text shows Van Braam's fascination with the variety and studied irregularity of the garden's layout.

In both texts, Van Braam comments on the role of verbal and visual accounts in conveying his experience of the imperial parks and in contributing to an understanding of Chinese garden design. Like Attiret, Van Braam affirms that since there was nothing like Qingyi yuan in Europe, his description would need to be supported by a plan and "a dozen of the most interesting views of this magnificent summer palace." Visiting the imperial complex in Yangzhou, he is so overwhelmed by that "studied confusion" that even plans and drawings, he writes, would not be able to represent the spatial complexity of the park: "What plan can shew the order of that which is only perfect because destitute of all order?"

Van Braam's fascination with China was reflected in the suburban residence he had built around 1796 on the Delaware River in Philadelphia and which he named China Retreat. The main building was crowned by a little pagoda, on which wind chimes were hung. Chinese servants and the collection of objects, drawings, and porcelain that Van Braam had brought from China contributed to the evocation of an exotic atmosphere. Moreau de Saint-Méry, the editor who had published Van Braam's travelogue, visited China Retreat and wrote afterward with admiration that in Van Braam's mansion "it is impossible to avoid fancying ourselves in China, while surrounded by living Chinese and by representations of their manners, monuments, and arts."[7]

*   *   *

Figure 12. Benjamin Thomas Pouncy, after William Alexander, after Henry William Parish, *A View of Poo-Ta-La of Great Temple near Zhe-Hol in Tartary.* In George Leonard Staunton, *An Authentic Account of an Embassy from the King of Great Britain to the Emperor of China*, vol. 3, pl. 27, April 12, 1796 (London: printed for G. Nicol, 1797). Beinecke Rare Book and Manuscript Library, Yale University.

From André Everard van Braam Houckgeest, *An Authentic Account of the Embassy of the Dutch East-India Company, to the Court of the Emperor of China, in the Years 1794 and 1795*, vol. 2 (1798)

January 31, 1795

The Ambassador and I set off this morning at five o'clock in little carts, in order to repair to the Imperial residence. . . . After being an hour on the road, we were conducted through a back gate within the walls. We were then shewn into an apartment at no great distance to the south, there to wait for break of day. That moment being come, we proceeded by a winding road, lined with large trees, towards a great open space in a wood, where a large tent of the Tartar kind, in the form of a dome, had been pitched for the Emperor. A square yellow tent was erected in the front of the other, while six little bell-tents, which stood on the two sides, were destined for the Ministers and Grandees of the Court. . . . The Emperor being gone, every one rose and followed his example. We were then conducted towards a serpentine canal, there to wait for the arrival of the two principal Ministers, who were not long before they made their appearance. We advanced a few steps to meet them, and saluted them in the European manner.

The *Voo-tchong-tang* [He Zhongtang, the Honorable He] spoke to us;[8] with the greatest air of kindness, and gave orders for our being conducted to the place whither he was going himself. He set off upon a sled, and we followed him in another. After being drawn a considerable distance, we came to the front of a building which the Ministers entered. We also alighted and followed them, passing through several apartments which, according to the Chinese custom, constantly opened into each other. They were all decently furnished.

Upon coming to a little pool that was entirely thawed, the Ministers stopped to make us remark a number of gold fish of an extraordinary size; for the smallest was about fifteen inches long, and the rest a great deal larger. We were assured that these beautiful animals were exceedingly old.

Hence we were shewn into all the little apartments which constituted the Emperors' daily habitation. They are very numerous, of small dimensions, neatly furnished in the Chinese taste, and containing a few books and some very valuable curiosities. Three only of these apartments can boast of European time-pieces. Each room has a sofa for the Monarch, as also a couple of stools, but no such things as a chair.

After having examined this edifice, the Prime Minister ordered the *Naa-fan-tayen* to carry us to see some other buildings. We then took leave of that worthy Minister, in order to follow our conductor.

After a quarter of an hour's walk along a high road, we came to a vast and magnificent palace, in the front of which is a very extensive square.[9] On each side of this square is a spacious paved court, corresponding with one of the wings of the building. These wings seem intended as lodgings for the officers of the court, and the inferior Mandarins. Two pedestals of white marble stand in the middle of the court-yards, and support two very large bronze lions, which may be considered as well executed by the artist, because they accord with the idea that the Chinese form of that animal, which is entirely unknown in their country.

The first hall in the front of the building is very large, and hung with a great many lanterns, in the Chinese fashion. In the middle of it, as in the other halls I have described, is an estrade [platform] and an arm-chair, or

Imperial throne. After having crossed this hall, we found ourselves in an inner paved court, of a square form. The buildings on the north and west sides of this court afford as rich and as beautiful a view as the eastern façade we first came to; while on the south side there is nothing but a great gate leading into it, with offices for servants at each end.

Within this gate, which corresponds with the north front, stands, as it were to mask it, a large rock of one entire piece upon a number of stones that serve it as a base. The carriage of this rock must have occasioned immense trouble and labour, as well as the operation of placing it upon its base; for its bulk and weight constitute a prodigious mass. Every side of it is honoured with inscriptions in the Emperor's own hand, and in that of several other persons of the highest rank who have imitated the example of the Monarch. In several parts of it are also dwarf trees and flowers.

Within this court, at the middle of the north front, stand two little stags, and two cranes, all of bronze, and of indifferent execution. The north side of the building contains an Imperial audience chamber with a throne in the centre, and lanterns in every part. Our conductor pointed out to us the coach of which Lord Macartney made a present to the Emperor last year, standing against the wall of the left side of the throne. It is exquisitely painted, perfectly well varnished, and the whole of the carriage is covered with gilding. The harness and the rest of the equipage are in the body of the coach, which is covered with a linen cloth. I perceived on the opposite side of the hall a thing which made a remarkable contrast with this splendid vehicle, that is to say a Chinese wagon with four wheels of equal height, very clumsy, painted green all over, and in every respect resembling the wagons used in Holland for the purpose of carrying manure.

I confess this sight set my imagination to work. Was this wagon placed here with a view of opposing the idea of its utility to that of the superfluity of a carriage so sumptuous, at least according to the estimation of the Chinese? I was thus giving way to my conjectures, when I was told that the wagon is the very same that is made use of at the annual ceremony when the Emperor pays a solemn homage to agriculture in the Temple of the Earth. Behind this hall are several small apartments which the Emperor occupies when resident here.

After passing through those apartments we came to the third range of buildings or western edifice which has only a small hall in the centre. The remainder is composed of a great number of little confined and irregular rooms opening into one another, and forming all together a sort of labyrinth.[10]

When we had inspected the whole of them, the Mandarin ushered us into the favourite cabinet of the Emperor, which bears the name of Tien (Heaven). It is indeed the most agreeable place of those that have been shewn us; as well on account of its situation, as of the different views which it commands. Nothing can equal the prospect that the Emperor may enjoy when, sitting in his arm-chair, he turns his eyes to a large window consisting of a single pane of glass—a prospect of which the reader will himself be able to form an idea from the sequel of this description. This cabinet is in a part of the building situated upon an extensive lake which washes its wall.

This lake was the first object that attracted our attention. In the midst of it is an island of considerable magnitude, on which several buildings have been erected that are dependencies of this Imperial residence, and overshadowed by lofty trees. The island communicates with the adjacent continent by a noble bridge of seventeen arches, built of hewn stone, and standing on the eastern side. This bridge was the next thing that our eyes rested upon.[11]

Turning to the westward, the sight is gratified by the view of a lake smaller than the former, and only separated from it by a wide road. In the midst of it is a kind of citadel of a circular form, with a handsome edifice in its centre. These two lakes communicate by a channel cut through the road that divided them, while a stone bridge of considerable height, and of a single arch, supplies the defect in the communication by land which the channel occasions.

Still further to the westward, and at a great distance, the eye is arrested by two towers standing on the tops of lofty mountains.[12]

To the north-west stands a magnificent range of edifices belonging to temples, constructed at the foot, in the middle, and upon the summit of a mountain entirely formed by art, with fragments of natural rocks, which, independently of the expence of the buildings, must have cost immense sums, since this kind of stone is only to be found at a great distance from the place. This work seems to represent the enterprize of the giants who attempted to scale the Heavens: at least rocks heaped upon rocks recal that ancient fiction to the mind. The assemblage of the buildings and picturesque embellishments of the mountains afford a view of which the pen can give no adequate idea. It is not then without reason that this cabinet is the favourite apartment of the aged Monarch.

The inside of it is furnished with a library, and shelves on which are collected all the most valuable and scarce Chinese productions, consisting both of precious stones and antiques; and certainly they are highly deserving of the attention with which we examined them.

After having passed a considerable time in this building with real pleasure, we came to the south front, where we found a sled, which conveyed us towards the Temples that I have mentioned above.

They are five separate pagodas; two are at the foot of the mountain; one fronting the north, the other the south. Two others are situated near its middle and in the same position; and the fifth is upon its summit.

The lower temple fronting the south contains an idol, which is the image of sensuality. It is very large, and entirely gilt. It represents a person of enormous corpulence sitting upon a cushion, with an air expressive of satisfaction and gaiety. In this pagoda there are besides a great number of other idols, but of smaller dimensions and less importance.

In the south temple in the middle of the mountain, the principal idol is the figure of a woman, about sixty feet high, with six faces and a thousand arms, like that of the Temple of *Tay-fay-tin* at *Pe-king*, [Beijing] of which I made mention the day before yesterday.

This temple forms, as it were, a nave and two aisles, by means of two rows of supports or pillars standing lengthwise. All along both the walls and the pillars are imitations of rocks, with cavities containing idols and saints by hundreds, and composing altogether a spectacle of a very singular and striking kind.

From this part of the mountain to which we had ascended by at least a hundred and twenty steps, we climbed towards its summit by means of a path winding between rocks, and of forty eight more steps, the shortest of which were a foot in height. Hence we discovered *Pe-king* in the south-east, and in the intermediate ground could distinguish several habitations or establishments, which are so many dependencies of *Yuen-ming-yuen* [Yuanming yuan].[13]

The fifth temple is upon the summit of the mountain; its construction is in many respects similar to that of a tower, and in it we found three images in a sitting posture of enormous size, and entirely gilt. These are the principal idols of the temple. In one of the lower stories, and opposite these great images, are nine goddesses also sitting and gilt, but much smaller, while on each side are nine bronze statues of saints, all of colossal size, and very well executed.

The walls behind the great idols are covered from one end to the other by large panels, each of which contains several hundred figures of gods made of bronze, and placed in small niches. The outer walls of the temple are coated with varnished bricks, such as I have described in speaking of the Temple of *Houing-ou-tzu* in the Imperial palace of *Pe-king*, and having like those of that temple the figure of a *Fos* [Buddha] in *bas-relief* in the middle.

Having taken a sufficient view of this last temple, we descended the north side of the mountain by steps of rugged stones, and came to the temple mid-way up the mountain, and fronting the north. Its principal idol is gilt all over, and represents a goddess with a number of arms. The lower part of this temple, like the second which we visited, is divided into three portions; and on the walls and pillars are imitations of clouds, full of images of *Fos*, which produce upon the whole a pleasing effect.

From this temple we descended to the lower one fronting the north, in which is a colossal goddess about ninety feet high, with four faces and forty-four arms. On each side, but standing a little forwarder, are two other idols, at least forty-five feet high, and seeming to adore the goddess. In this temple are also two superb quadrangular pyramids standing upon marble pedestals, the sides of which are covered with *Fos* of bronze.

The inner wall is entirely coated with bricks, enriched with flowers in bas-relief of different colours, and all of them varnished. Against the wall stand columns, the shafts of which rising six feet above the base are coated with bronze.

The five temples contain besides vases for perfumes and other sacred utensils all of bronze and exquisitely wrought. There is not a single one among them that for beauty of subject and delicacy of workmanship may not be justly compared with those that are to be seen in the temples at *Pe-king*.

Each of these temples has also a fore-court and a portico, with some marble decorations in the interior of the court.

Upon the top of the rocks piled upon one another in the stupendous manner I have mentioned, are two square open pavilions of symmetrical construction, as well as two little houses in the shape of towers, and several other small apartments. Their roofs are embellished with varnished tiles, green, blue, and yellow; sometimes disposed in squares or compartments in which those various tints are combined, or else being of one and the same colour. Some of these little buildings are even coated on the outside with smooth square tiles so varnished that when the sun strikes upon them they reflect all the splendor of his beams.

But instead of rashly undertaking to express and describe with my weak pen all that my eyes admired; instead of endeavouring to communicate to my reader's mind, the many, the varied and the extraordinary sensations produced incessantly in mind by the sight of so many things, in which singularity, magnificence, boldness of design, and skill of execution were combined, it will be more simple and more natural to confess my incapability. The pencil of a great master is wanting to create in some sort anew so many accumulated wonders, and even then I will venture to say, without seeking to save my own credit, that the copy will never be equal to the original.

With what pleasure would I have sacrificed a sum of money to obtain a plan, and a dozen of the most interesting views of this magnificent summer palace. For to try to give by description an idea of Chinese architecture, particularly that of the Imperial residence, would be a fruitless endeavour, and almost a loss of time, the mode of construction in that country not having the smallest analogy with European architecture. I am indeed so much convinced that every description of that kind, unassisted by drawings, would not be understood, that I shall abandon the attempt.

On quitting the pagodas we were led along a very pleasant winding road, neatly paved with little pebbles, overshadowed by trees, passing sometimes over hills, and sometimes through vallies; such a road in short, as in summer, when every thing is green, must make a most delightful promenade.

After a few minutes walk we came to a group of small buildings inclosed within the walls of an Imperial palace which overlooks them, being as much superior to them in height as it exceeds them in size. They form a kind of village, in the midst of which runs a stream of very limpid water, skirted with small rocks on each side, and at this moment free from ice. These buildings are not inhabited at present, but during summer, when his Majesty makes *Yuen-ming-yuen* his residence, they serve as shops for tradesmen of all sorts, who come there to sell their goods, and compose something not unlike one of our fairs. It is possible that this place may then be very lively and amusing, and that the water that runs through it may at once furnish the means of cleanliness, and serve to keep it cool.[14]

Thence we were conducted towards another assemblage of buildings where the *Voo-tchong-tang* waited for us in one of the halls. . . . He received us with an affability which had all the characteristics of sincerity, and asked us our opinion of what we had seen. Our interpreter conveyed to him the expression of our pleasure, our satisfaction, and our well-grounded astonishment, and above all, our praise of his Majesty's little cabinet. The Prime Minister then told us that the Emperor, being exceedingly pleased with the persons selected for the Dutch Embassy, had wished to give us a proof of his favour and affection, by granting more to us than to any other foreigner, since the foot of an alien had never before trod in the private apartments of his Majesty, nor had any European eye ever perceived what we had been permitted to examine; that very few even of the natives of the country were fortunate enough to approach those places; and that we might thence judge so far the Monarch had carried his preference and predilection.[15] . . . On going hence we passed along a winding and stony road, by the side of which runs murmuring along a stream of the most pellucid water. After a few turns we came to a building near a back gate, where our carts were waiting for us. . . .

8th. [February, 1795] This morning at eleven o'clock the Ambassador and I set off for the country house of *Yuen-ming-yuen*. . . . The fireworks being over, his Imperial Majesty repaired to a habitation in another part of this delightful retreat, going in a sled over the ice. We followed him in a flat sled, passing under trees, along a noble serpentine canal. We alighted at a great distance from our point of departure, and proceeded on foot to an illuminated edifice, near which the Emperor was already seated. We were desired to sit down on cushions upon the ground.

Some players began an insipid piece of buffoonery, after some singers had chaunted verses, the subject of which seemed to me to be the praises of his Majesty, celebrated and honoured by all the nations of the earth; for I remarked that mention was made of the Dutch.

Having remained half an hour longer in this place, the Monarch retired. We were then reconducted to the canal, where we got into a sled, which conveyed us, by a circuitous route, to a gate, where we found our carts. There the *Naa-fan-tayen*, who had also accompanied us the whole of this evening, took leave of us. We stepped into our carriages to return to the city, and congratulated ourselves when we got back to our lodgings, at past nine o'clock, so tiresome and disagreeable had been the constant jolting of our vehicles.

The only recompense for the fatigue we suffered in this short journey was the sight we obtained of the above-mentioned noble canal, forming several meanders through a wood in uneven ground. Its banks are composed of rocks, which, being used instead of bricks or stones, have taken, under the hand of man, a form which they seem only to have received from that of nature. How great must be the pleasure of navigating, in the summer season, on this tranquil stream in a light yacht, under the pleasant shade of trees, which at this moment only exist to afflict the eye!

How happy were we to have seen this part of the Emperor's country seat, which to this day had remained unknown to us! Perhaps, indeed, we have not seen the twentieth part of the beauties contained in *Yuen-ming-yuen*; for I have been assured that its total circumference is little short of three hundred *li* (thirty leagues).[16]

13th [March 1795]

We went on shore at an early hour in the morning to visit the country house which I mentioned yesterday.[17] The Emperor not having inhabited it for these twelve years past, it is much neglected; but if his Majesty were to testify the smallest desire to return to it, a fortnight would suffice to put everything in order.

Even in its present state, this place is rendered worthy of attention by the variety of its edifices, by the diversity of the ground interspersed with rocks, by its pavilions, lakes, its bridges, etc. Every thing is disposed according to a system in which art seems to hide herself in the midst of the irregularities of nature; while the studied confusion of trees, fruit, flowers, and brambles compose a scene that seems due to chance alone. Already the birds enlivened the groves by their songs, and enriched the verdure with their plumage. Voluptuous summer, when thou hast spread thy charms over the country, what supreme delight must be tasted in this enchanting place.

No, it is not possible to give a faithful description of a Chinese villa. Every thing is intermingled, and seems on the point of being confounded; but the triumph of genius is to prevent the smallest disorder that might hurt the eye. Every instant a new combination affords a new variety, so much the more agreeable and striking, as it has been the less possible to foresee it; the spectator's surprise being constantly kept up, because every moment produces a new scene. Perhaps plans and drawings might give an exact idea of their composition; but what plan can shew the order of that which is only perfect because destitute of all order? What drawing can produce the effect of things which seem so discordant; and how is it possible to introduce into it that life which the different objects borrow from one another?—Our charming walk lasted one hour and a half.

NOTES

1   Isaac Titsingh, the chief of the Dutch East India Company trading post on the island of Dejima in Japan, was appointed first ambassador, while Van Braam was appointed second ambassador. On the Dutch embassy to China see Jan Julius Lodewijk Duyvendak, "The Last Dutch Embassy to the Chinese Court (1794–1795)," *T'oung Pao* 33 (1937): 1–137. See also Wong, *A Paradise Lost*, 88–90; Mungello, *The Great Encounter*, 157–59.

2   The journal was published in two volumes and dedicated to George Washington; the first appeared in 1797 and the second in 1798. A number of pirate editions appeared soon after, but they were all based only on the text of volume 1. In 1798, the first volume of the Philadelphia edition was published in Paris in two volumes; an English translation of the Paris edition appeared in London, in two volumes, in 1798, and a German version was published in Leipzig in 1798–99.

3   André Everard van Braam Houckgeest, *An Authentic Account of the Embassy of the Dutch East-India Company, to the Court of the Emperor of China, in the Years 1794 and 1795*, 2 vols. (London: R. Phillips, 1798).

4   On Van Braam's detailed narrative of the Dutch embassy and his descriptions of the imperial parks see Malone, *History of the Peking Summer Palaces*, 119–21, and 166–70.

5   The origins of Qingyi yuan date back to a small palace built in 1153 during the Jin dynasty (1115–1234), used by the sovereigns as a residence during their travels throughout the empire. The area has changed often through the centuries, with the most important transformations taking place under the Qianlong emperor, who in 1750 decided to expand the park in honor of his mother's sixtieth birthday. Work was not completed until 1764, however. The design of the vast park is centered on the harmonious composition of an elevated crest and a great lake, both artificial, and evokes the scenery of the West Lake of Hangzhou, in southern China. Qianlong heightened the existing hill and renamed Wanshou shan (Longevity Hill). The wooded hill occupies the northern part of the site; it is graced by temples, pavilions, and gardens linked by winding paths. At the foot of the hill, the large Kunming Lake opens toward the south. Qianlong expanded the lake and subdivided it into three distinct but connected parts, separated by wooded causeways; each of these parts featured an island. To honor his mother's seventieth birthday, Qianlong added new buildings and pavilions to the complex and named the park Qingyi yuan (Garden of Clear Ripples). The park was damaged first in 1860 by the Anglo-French troops in the Arrow War and again in 1900 by the troops of the Eight Nations Alliance during the Boxer Rebellion. On both occasions, it was rebuilt by the Empress Dowager Cixi (1835–1908), and it was after the first reconstruction that it took its present name, Yihe yuan, "Garden of the Preservation of Harmony." The park is now popularly known as Summer Palace. Valder, *Gardens in China*, 172–73. For the expansion of Qingyi yuan under

the Qianlong emperor see Malone, *History of the Peking Summer Palaces*, 109–19, and Siu, *Gardens of a Chinese Emperor*, 107–40.

6 "Borrowed scenery" consists of integrating elements of the landscape beyond the perimeter of the garden into the scenic view from the garden enjoyed by the visitor. The garden, visually linked to the outer landscape, seems to expand measurelessly. Rinaldi, *The Chinese Garden*, 64. For a recent discussion of the concept of the borrowed scenery see Wybe Kuitert, "Borrowing Scenery and the Landscape that Lends—The Final Chapter of *Yuanye*," *Journal of Landscape Architecture* 10, no. 2 (2015): 32–43.

7 Van Braam Houckgeest, *An Authentic Account*, vol. 1, xiii. On Van Braam's journey though China, his reception at the Qing court, and his Chinese collection see John Rogers Haddad, *The Romance of China: Excursions to China in U.S. Culture, 1776–1876* (New York: Columbia University Press, 2009), 2–17. See also Alfred Owen Alridge, *The Dragon and the Eagle: The Presence of China in the American Enlightenment* (Detroit: Wayn State University Press, 1993), 161–81.

8 Van Braam refers here to the Minister and Grand Councillor Henshen. Wong, *A Paradise Lost*, 89.

9 As Carroll Malone suggested, Van Braam refers here to the residential complex built at the foot of the Wanshou shan (Longevity Hill), in Qingyi yuan (Garden of Clear Ripples). Malone, *History of the Peking Summer Palaces*, 168.

10 The term "labyrinth" here is associated with the articulation of the buildings. See Ricci and Nieuhof's descriptions presented in this anthology for other ways in which "labyrinth" is used in relation to the Chinese garden.

11 Van Braam refers here to the Kunming Lake and to the South Lake Island, an artificial island raised on the southern part of the lake. The island is linked to the shore by the long Seventeen-Arch Bridge, sustained by a series of arches of varying sizes.

12 This is an example of the borrowed view.

13 The discovery of a view of the city of Beijing, which opens up from an elevated point reached by a difficult winding path, is another example of the compositional technique of the borrowed view.

14 What Van Braam refers to as Yuanming yuan included probably the other parks and gardens close to the imperial complex of Yuanming yuan. Van Braam had probably not realized that, after the first audience at Yuanming yuan, he had been taken to a different imperial park and is convinced he is visiting parts of Yuanming yuan, instead of the nearby Qingyi yuan. What he describes here is the so-called Suzhou Street, with its rows of low buildings, which once housed shops facing the canals and evoking the canals of the city of Suzhou and the intense commercial activity conducted along their quays. When the Qianlong emperor had them built, they made up a living microcosm imitating an urban trading quarter, the occasion of amusement for the imperial court. As Malone explains: "The Emperor built for the amusement of his mother a street of shops called Soochow [Suzhou] Street. It contained bazaars, business streets, *pailous* [monumental archway], side lanes, all in imitation of the towns south of the Yangtze which the old lady had enjoyed on her journey to the south with him. . . . This

Soochow Street was probably carrying out on a larger scale the scene which was sometimes presented by the eunuchs inside the palace at the Yuan Ming Yuan." The scene in Yuanming yuan was described by Attiret in his letter. See Malone, *History of the Peking Summer Palaces*, 112.

15 Van Braam only regretted that, during his tour of the imperial parks, he was not able to see the European Palaces designed by the Jesuits.

16 Van Braam repeated this statement in his travelogue. After a conversation with the French Jesuit Nicolas Raux, to whom he asked information on the European Palaces in Yuanming yuan, Van Braam wrote: "M. Roux [Raux] added, that the country house of Yuen-ming-yuen contains thirty-six distinct habitations within its walls, at some distance from one another; that each of them has its dependencies, and the necessary accommodations for the Emperor and his suite, and that the European edifices form one of thirty six dwellings or divisions. According to this account, of the authenticity of which I have not the smallest doubt, I have reason to believe that we have not seen the twentieth part of the beauties of this immense domain, to which no habitation of any Prince in Europe is comparable, and of which the cost must have amounted to a prodigious sum." Van Braam Houckgeest, *An Authentic Account*, vol. 2, 69–70.

17 Van Braam refers to a summer palace he calles Ong-uan [Wang yuan, Prince's Garden], probably one of the many gardens along the banks of the Shouxihu (Slender West Lake), in the northwest of Yangzhou, which were built during the reign of the Qianlong emperor. Che Bing Chiu, *Jardins de Chine, ou la quête du paradis* (Paris: Éditions de la Martinière, 2010), 76. I am grateful to Stephen H. Whiteman for bringing to my attention a list of imperial traveling palaces in Yangzhou and for suggesting a possible interpretation of the name "Ong-uan" that Van Braam used to refer to a complex of palaces and gardens in that area.

CHAPTER 22

John Barrow (1764–1848)

John Barrow joined the British embassy to the Qianlong emperor led by Lord Macartney in 1792–94 and published his own account of that expedition in 1804, entitled *Travels in China*.[1] Barrow's narrative was remarkably successful in England and was praised for the contribution it made to the British understanding of China. Essayist Robert Southey, in his review of *Travels in China* for the periodical *The Annual Review*, affirmed that Barrow's work "communicated more information concerning this extraordinary empire and its inhabitants, than could be collected from all our former travellers."[2]

In the very first pages of his work, Barrow presents himself as an objective and detached observer, in contrast with those who had been hitherto considered the great experts, the Jesuit missionaries, whose reports on China, he observes, "are by no means satisfactory" and, according to him, are filled with errors. Barrow aimed to offer a realistic portrayal of China and "to shew this extraordinary [Chinese] people in their proper colours, not as their own moral maxims would represent them, but as they really are," and "to divest the court of the tinsel and tawdry varnish" that he believed characterized Jesuit writings.[3] But Barrow's narrative is far from being free of prejudices. He presented a critical portrait of China and of Chinese culture, emphasizing the decadence and stagnation of the Qing empire as compared to progressive and dynamic Britain, thus contributing to the deterioration of the image of China in Europe.[4]

The descriptions of the Qing imperial parks included in the third chapter of Barrow's *Travels in China*, and presented here, consist of Barrow's comments on Yuanming yuan and Macartney's account of Bishu shanzhuang.[5] Barrow's critical view of China is reflected in his skeptical observations on Chinese garden design. The appreciation, however detached, that he shows for the imperial park he visited depends in part on his recognition of some analogies between the Chinese garden and the picturesque garden and their general compositional methods. For instance, in the spatial strategy behind the design of Yuanming yuan, which he visited in 1793, Barrow reads the relation between landscape painting and the arrangement of scenes in the garden, perceiving the role of carefully positioned plantings in the "composition of the picture," like Chambers and Staunton before him. Barrow's reading of the design of the Chinese imperial park is filtered through the English landscape garden tradition. In fact, he compares Yuanming yuan to Richmond Park in suburban London, with its landscape of grasslands, wooded hills, and a sinuous lake.

The majority of Barrow's account about Chinese gardens quotes Lord Macartney's travel journal. Barrow was not part of the group from the British embassy that traveled from Beijing to Chengde for an imperial audience with Qianlong at Bishu shanzhuang. He remained at Yuanming yuan. Therefore, he inserts into his narrative Macartney's long and enthusiastic description of the vast imperial park. Macartney appreciates its atmosphere of "rural delight," the aesthetic of contrast, variety, and surprises, and the studied arrangement of compositional elements as well as of a sequence of vantage points. His account follows the itinerary of the British delegation through Bishu shanzhuang that first lead them through the eastern part of the park, with its grassy lowlands and lakes, then through the woody and mountainous western section, and finally to a pavilion on the top of an elevated hill, from which the ambassador attempts to get an understanding of the park's overall layout, as on an "illuminated map."[6]

The text closes with Macartney's synthesis of the analogies and differences between Chinese gardens and English gardens. In his account of Bishu shanzhuang, the ambassador had acknowledged the Qing imperial park as "perfectly similar" to some of England's finest landscape gardens, associating its "picturesque beauty" and "gently undulated ground" to the park of Stowe, Woburn Farm, and Painshill Park, which were among the earliest parks in England designed in the landscape style.[7] He also associated the woodlands in the western part of Bishu shanzhuang to Lowther Hall in Westmoreland, and another section of it to the hilly landscape of the English countryside around the town of Luton, in Bedfordshire. In his concluding remarks, Macartney explains that, for him, the garden's natural appearance, its arrangement, the aesthetic strategy underlying its design, and the use of visual devices to manipulate the spectator's perception of the garden, all represent the similarities between the two garden traditions of countries so far away from one another. Their main difference, explains Macartney, lies in a contrasting approach to nature, which is "improved" in the English landscape gardens while it is "conquered" by the Chinese.[8] This difference derives, according to Macartney, from the sort of Chinese indifference to the unique characteristics of a site chosen to lay out a garden, a component that, on the contrary, was essential in determining the design of any English landscape garden and that Alexander Pope had called the "genius of the place." Another disparity in the two approaches to garden design lies, for Macartney, in the different emotional responses that contemplation of the gardens produce in the visitor. Despite the formal similitude between the Chinese garden and the picturesque garden, and despite the fact that the Chinese garden seems to include all of the features that belong to the aesthetic category of the sublime, Macartney claims that the gardens of China are not able to awaken strong sentiments due to their general cheerfulness, which, he writes, "lights up the face of the scene." For the British ambassador, the Chinese garden is too exuberant to be truly sublime.

*   *   *

From John Barrow, *Travels in China* (1804)

But before I quit these renowned gardens of Yuen-min-yuen [Yuanming yuan], it will naturally be expected I should say something on their subject. From all that I had heard and read of the grandeur and beauty of the scenery and the magnificence of palaces, I had certainly expected to meet with a style of gardening and laying out of grounds superior, or at least equal, to any thing in the same line in Europe; and, perhaps indeed, I might have been fully gratified in all my expectations provided no restraint had seen thrown upon our walks, which was far from being the case. All the little excursions I made were by stealth. Even in the short distance between the hall of audience and our lodgings, which might be about three hundred paces, we were continually watched. The idea of being stopped by an eunuch, or some of the inferior officers belonging to the court, was sufficient to put us on our guard against meeting with any such mortification; pride, in such circumstances, generally gets the better of the desire, however

Figure 13. Thomas Medland, after William Alexander, after Henry William Parish, *View in the Eastern Side of the Imperial Park at Gehol*, after p. 128. In John Barrow, *Travels in China* (London: T. Cadell and W. Davies, 1804). Hand-colored aquatint, Yale Center for British Art, Paul Mellon Collection.

strong, of gratifying curiosity. I sometimes, however, ventured to stroll from our lodging in the evening in order to take a stolen glance at these celebrated gardens.

The grounds of *Yuen-min-Yuen* are calculated to comprehend an extent of at least ten English miles in diameter, or about sixty thousand acres, a great part of which, however, is wastes and woodland. The general appearance of those parts near where we lodged, as to the natural surface of the country, broken into hill and dale, and diversified with wood and lawn, may be compared with Richmond park, to which, however, they add the very great advantage of abundance of canals, rivers, and large sheets of water, whose banks, although artificial, are neither trimmed, nor shorn, nor sloped, like the glacis of a fortification, but have been thrown up with immense labour in an irregular, and, as it were, fortuitous manner, so as to represent, the free hand of nature.[9] Bold rocky promontories are seen jutting into a lake, and vallies retiring, some choaked with wood, others in a state of high cultivation. In particular spots where pleasure-houses, or places of rest or retirement, were erected, the views appeared to have been studied. The trees were not only placed according to their magnitudes, but the tints of their foliage seemed also to have been considered in the composition of the picture, which some of the landscapes might be called with great propriety. But, if an opinion may be formed from those parts of them which I have seen, and I understood there is a great similarity throughout the whole, they fall very short of the fanciful and extravagant descriptions that Sir William Chambers has given of Chinese gardening.[10] Much, however, has been done, and nothing that I saw could be considered as an offence to nature.

Thirty different places of residence for the Emperor, with all the necessary appendages of building to each, for lodging the several officers of state, who are required to be present on court days and particular occasions, for the eunuchs, servants, and artificers, each composing a village of no inconsiderable magnitude, are said to be contained within the inclosure of these gardens. These assemblages of buildings, which they dignify with the name of palaces, are, however, of such a nature as to be more remarkable for their number than for their splendour or magnificence. A great proportion of the buildings consists in mean cottages. The very dwelling of the Emperor and the grand hall in which he gives audience, when divested of the gilding and the gaudy colours with which they are daubed, are little superior, and much less solid, than the barns of a substantial English farmer. Their apartments are as deficient in proportion, as their construction is void of every rule and principle which we are apt to consider as essential to architecture. The principal hall of audience at Yuen-min-yuen stood upon a platform of granite, raised about four feet above the level of the court. A row of large wooden columns surrounding the building supported the projecting roof; and a second row within the first, and corresponding with it (the interstices between the columns being filled up with brick-work to the height of about four feet) served for the walls of the room. The upper part of these walls was a kind of lattice-work, covered over with large sheets of oiled paper, and was capable of being thrown entirely open on public occasions. The wooden columns had no capitals, and the only architrave was the horizontal beam that supported the rafters of the roof. This, in direct contradiction to the established mode in European architecture, was the uppermost member of what might be called the entablature or frize [frieze], which was a broad skreen of wood, fastened between the upper part of the columns, painted with the most vivid colours of blue, red, and green, and interlarded with gilding; and the whole had net-work of wire stretched over it, to prevent its being defiled by swallows, and other birds frequenting human dwellings. The length of this room within was one hundred and ten feet, breadth forty-two, and height twenty feet: the ceiling painted with circles, squares, and polygons, whimsically disposed, and loaded with a great variety of colours. The floor was paved with grey marble flag stones laid chequer-wise. The throne, placed in a recess, was supported by rows of pillars painted red like those without. It consisted entirely of wood, not unlike mahogany, the carving of which was exquisitely fine. The only furniture was a pair of brass kettle drums, two large paintings, two pair of ancient blue porcelain vases, a few volumes of manuscripts, and a table at one end of the room on which was placed an old English chiming clock, made in the seventeenth century by one Clarke of Leadenhall-street, and which our old friend the eunuch had the impudence to tell us was the workmanship of a Chinese. A pair of circular fans made of the wing feathers of the Argus pheasant, and mounted on long polished ebony poles stood, one on each side of the throne, over which was written in four characters, "true, great, refulgent, splendor;" and under these, in a lozenge; the character of *Happiness.* In the different courts were several miserable attempts at sculpture, and some bronze figures, but all the objects were fanciful, distorted, and entirely out of nature. The only specimen of workmanship about the palace, that would bear a close examination, besides the carving of the throne, was a brick wall enclosing the flower garden, which, perhaps, in no respect is exceeded by any thing of the sort in England.

With regard to the architecture and gardening of the Chinese, it may be expected that I should give a more detailed description, or offer some opinion on those subjects. The little I have to say on the former will be reserved for another place;[11] and, with respect to the latter, I regret that I had not opportunity of seeing so much as I could have wished, and particularly the Emperor's great park at Gehol [Bishu shanzhuang], which, from the description of the Embassador, seemed to be almost unrivalled for its features of beauty, sublimity, and amenity. But my own deficiency will be amply filled up with an extract or two from the Journal of his Lordship, whose taste and skill in landscape gardening are so well known. I have indeed much to regret that I could not enrich the present work with more extracts from it, but as it makes a complete picture of itself the partial selection of detached parts might have been injurious to it, by conveying wrong impressions, when unconnected with the rest. I am, therefore, the more obliged (and gladly embrace this opportunity of expressing the obligations I feel) to his Lordship, for what little he has allowed me to transcribe.[12]

Speaking of the route from Pekin [Beijing] to Gehol [Jehol] in Tartary, Lord Macartney observes: "Our journey, upon the whole, has been very pleasant and, being divided into seven days, not at all fatiguing. At the end of every stage we have been lodged and entertained in the wings or houses adjoining to the Emperor's palaces. These palaces, which occur at short distances from each other on the road, have been built for his reception, on his annual visit to Tartary. They are constructed upon nearly the same plan and in the same taste.

"They front the south, and are usually situated on irregular ground near the basis of gentle hills which, together with their adjoining vallies, are enclosed by high walls and laid out in parks and pleasure grounds, with every possible attention to picturesque beauty. Whenever water can be brought into the view it is not neglected; the distant hills are planted, cultivated, or left naked, according to their accompaniments in the prospect. The wall is often concealed in a sunk fence, in order to give an idea of greater extent. A Chinese gardener is the painter of nature, and though totally ignorant of perspective, as a science, produces the happiest effects by the management, or rather pencilling, of distances, if I may use the expression, by relieving or keeping down the features of the scene, by contrasting trees of a bright with those of a dusky foliage, by bringing them forward, or throwing them back, according to their bulk and their figure, and by introducing buildings of different dimensions, either heightened by strong colouring, or softened by simplicity, and omissions of ornament.[13]

"The Emperor having been informed that, in the course of our travels in China we had shewn a strong desire of seeing every thing curious and interesting, was pleased to give directions to the first minister to shew us his park or garden at Gehol. It is called in Chinese *Van-shoo-yuen*, or Paradise of ten thousand (or innumerable) trees [Wanshu yuan, "Garden of Ten Thousand Trees"]. In order to have this gratification (which is considered as an instance of uncommon favour) we rose this morning at three o'clock and went to the palace where we waited, mixed with all the great officers of state, for three hours (such is the etiquette of the place) till the Emperor's appearance. At last he came forth, borne in the usual manner by sixteen persons on a high open palankeen [palanquin], attended by guards, music, standards, and umbrellas without number; and observing us, as we stood in the front line, graciously beckoned us to approach, having ordered his people to stop; he entered into conversation with us; and, with great affability of manner, told us that he was on his way to the pagoda, where he usually paid his morning devotions; that as we professed a different religion from his he would not ask us to accompany him, but that he had ordered his first minister and chief Colaos to conduct us through his garden, and to shew us whatever we were desirous of seeing there.

"Having expressed my sense of this mark of his condescension in the proper manner, and my increasing admiration of every thing I had yet observed at Gehol, I retired and, whilst he proceeded to his adorations at the pagoda, I accompanied the ministers and other great Colaos of the court to a pavilion prepared for us, from whence, after a short collation, we set out on horseback to view this wonderful garden. We rode about three miles through a very beautiful park kept in the highest order and much resembling the approach to Luton in Bedfordshire; the grounds gently undulated and chequered with various groupes of well contrasted trees in the offskip. As we moved onward an extensive lake appeared before us, the extremities of which seemed to lose themselves in distance and obscurity. Here was a large and magnificent yacht ready to receive us, and a number of smaller ones for the attendants, elegantly fitted up and adorned with numberless vanes, pendants, and streamers. The shores of the lake have all the varieties of shape, which the fancy of a painter can delineate, and are so indented with bays, or broken with projections, that almost every stroke of the oar brought a new and unexpected object to our view. Nor are islands wanting, but they are situated only where they should be, each in its proper place and having its proper character: one marked by a pagoda, or other building; one quite destitute of ornament; some smooth and level; some steep and uneven; and others frowning with wood, or smiling with culture. Where any things particularly interesting were to be seen we disembarked, from time to time, to visit them, and I dare say that, in the course of our voyage, we stopped at forty or fifty different palaces or pavilions. These are all furnished in the richest manner with pictures of the Emperor's huntings and progresses, with stupendous vases of jasper and agate; with the finest porcelain and Japan, and with every kind of European toys and *sing-songs;* with spheres, orreries, clocks, and musical automatons of such exquisite workmanship, and in such profusion, that *our* presents must shrink from the comparison, and *hide their diminished heads;* and yet

I am told, that the fine things we have seen are far exceeded by others of the same kind in the apartments of the ladies, and in the European repository at *Yuen-min-yuen.* In every one of the pavilions was a throne, or imperial state, and a *Eu-jou* [*ruyi*, a jade scepter], or symbol of peace and prosperity, placed at one side of it resembling that which the Emperor delivered to me yesterday for the king.

"It would be an endless task were I to attempt a detail of all the wonders of this charming place. There is no beauty of distribution, no feature, of amenity, no reach of fancy which embellishes our pleasure grounds in England, that is not to be found here. Had China been accessible to Mr. Browne or Mr. Hamilton, I should have sworn they had drawn their happiest ideas from the rich sources, which I have tasted this day; for in the course of a few hours I have enjoyed such vicissitudes of rural delight, as I did not conceive could be felt out of England, being at different moments enchanted by scenes perfectly similar to those I had known there, to the magnificence of Stowe, the softer beauties of Wooburn [*sic*], and the fairyland of Paine's Hill.

"One thing I was particularly struck with, I mean the happy choice of situation for ornamental buildings. From attention to this circumstance they have not the air of being crowded or disproportioned; they never intrude upon the eye; but wherever they appear always shew themselves to advantage, and aid, improve, and enliven the prospect.

"In many places the lake is overspread with the Nenuphar or lotus (nelumbium) resembling our broad leaved water lilly.[14] This is an accompaniment which, though the Chinese are passionately fond of, cultivating it in all their pieces of water, I confess I don't much admire. Artificial rocks and ponds with gold and silver fish are perhaps too often introduced, and the monstrous porcelain figures of lions and tygers, usually placed before the pavilions, are displeasing to an European eye; but these are trifles of no great moment; and I am astonished that now, after a six hours critical survey of these gardens, I can scarcely recollect any thing besides to find fault with.

"At our taking leave of the minister, he told us that we had only seen the eastern side of the gardens, but that the western side, which was the larger part still remained for him to shew us, and that he should have that pleasure another day.[15]

"Accordingly, on the day of the Emperor's anniversary festival, after the ceremony was ended, the first or great Colao *Ho-chun-tong,* the *Foo-leou,* the *Foo-leou*'s brother *Foo-chan-tong*, and *Song-ta-gin*, with the other great men who attended us two days since, in our visit to the eastern garden, now proposed to accompany us to the western, which forms a strong contrast with the other, and exhibits all the sublimer beauties of nature in as high a degree as the part which we saw before possesses the attractions of softness and amenity. It is one of the finest forest-scenes in the world; wild, woody, mountainous and rocky, abounding with stags and deer of different species, and most of the other beasts of the chace, not dangerous to man. "In many places immense woods, chiefly oaks, pines, and chesnuts, grow upon almost perpendicular steeps, and force their sturdy roots through every resistance of surface and of soil, where vegetation would seem almost impossible. These woods often clamber over the loftiest pinnacles of the stony hills, or gathering on the skirts of them, descend with a rapid sweep, and bury themselves in the deepest vallies. There, at proper distances, you find palaces, banquetting houses, and monasteries, (but without bonzes) adapted to the situation and peculiar circumstances of the place, sometimes with a rivulet on one hand, gently stealing through the glade, at other with a cataract tumbling from above, raging with foam, and rebounding with a thousand echoes from below, or silently engulphed in a gloomy pool, or yawning chasm.

"The roads by which we approached these romantic scenes are often hewn out of the living rock, and conducted round the hills in a kind of rugged stair case, and yet no accident occurred in our progress, not a false step disturbed the regularity of our cavalcade, though the horses are spirited and all of them unshod. From the great irregularity of the ground, and the various heights to which we ascended, we had opportunities of catching many magnificent points of view by detached glances, but after wandering for several hours (and yet never wearied with wandering) we at last reached a covered pavilion open on all sides, and situated on a summit so elevated as perfectly to command the whole surrounding country to a vast extent. The radius of the horizon, I should suppose to be at least twenty miles from the central spot where we stood; and certainly so rich, so various, so beautiful, so sublime a prospect my eyes had never beheld. I saw every thing before me as on an illuminated map, palaces, pagodas, towns, villages, farmhouses, plains, and vallies, watered by innumerable streams, hills waving with woods, and meadows covered with cattle of the most beautiful marks and colours. All seemed to be nearly at my feet, and that a step would convey me within reach of them. I observed here a vast number of what we call in England *sheet* cows, also sheet horses, many pyeballs [piebalds], dappled, mottled and spotted, the latter chiefly strawberry.

"From hence was pointed out to us by the minister a vast enclosure below, which, he said, was not more accessible to him than to us, being never entered but by the Emperor, his women, or his Eunuchs. It includes within its bounds, though on a smaller scale, most of the beauties which distinguish the eastern and the western gardens which we have already seen; but from every thing I can learn it falls very short of the fanciful descriptions which father Attiret and Sir William Chambers have intruded upon us as realities. That within these private retreats, various entertainments of the most novel and expensive nature are prepared and exhibited by the Eunuchs, who are very numerous (perhaps some thousands) to amuse the Emperor and his ladies, I have no doubt; but that they are carried to all the lengths of extravagance and improbability those gentlemen have mentioned, I very much question, as from every enquiry I have made (and I have not been sparing to make them) I have by no means sufficient reason to warrant me in acceding to, or confirming, the accounts which they have given us.

"If any place in England can be said in any respect to have similar features to the western park, which I have seen this day, it is Lowther Hall in Westmoreland, which (when I knew it many years ago) from the extent of prospect, the grand surrounding objects, the noble situation, the diversity of surface, the extensive woods, and command of water, I thought might be rendered by a man of sense, spirit, and taste the finest scene in the British dominions."[16]

After this descriptive and interesting detail of the beauties of the two sides of the imperial park or gardens at Gehol, his Lordship makes a few general observations on Chinese gardening, and the ornamental edifices that are usually employed to aid the effect, as well as contribute to use and convenience. He observes,

"Whether our style of gardening was really copied from the Chinese, or originated with ourselves, I leave for vanity to assert, and idleness to discuss. A discovery which is the result of good sense and reflexion may equally occur to the most distant nations, without either borrowing from the other. There is certainly a great analogy between our gardening and the Chinese, but our excellence seems to be rather in improving nature, theirs to conquer her, and yet produce the same effect. It is indifferent to a Chinese where he makes his garden, whether on a spot favoured, or abandoned, by the rural deities. If the latter, he invites them, or compels them to return. His point is to change every thing from what he found it, to explode the old fashion of the creation, and introduce novelty in every corner. If there be a waste, he adorns it with trees; if a dry desert, he waters it with a river, or floats it with a lake. If there be a smooth flat, he varies it with all possible conversions. He undulates the surface he raises it in hills, scoops it into vallies, and roughens it with rocks. He softens asperities, brings amenity into the wilderness, or animates the tameness of an expanse, by accompanying it with the majesty of a forest. Deceptions and eye-traps the Chinese are not unacquainted with, but they use them very sparingly. I observed no artificial ruins, caves, or hermitages. Though the sublime predominates in its proper station, you are insensibly led to contemplate it, not startled by its sudden intrusion, for in the plan cheerfulness is the principal feature, and lights up the face of the scene. To enliven it still more, the aid of architecture is invited; all the buildings are perfect of their kind, either elegantly simple, or highly decorated, according to the effect that is intended to arise, erected at suitable distances; and judiciously contrasted, never crowded together in confusion, nor affectedly confronted, and staring at each other without meaning. Proper edifices in proper places. The summer-house, the pavilion, the pagodas, have all their respective situations, which *they* distinguish and improve, but which any other structures would injure or deform. The only things disagreeable to my eye are the large porcelain figures of lions, tygers, etc. and the rough hewn steps, and huge masses of rock work, which they seem studious of introducing near many of their houses and palaces. Considering their general good taste in the other points, I was much surprised at this, and could only account for it, by the expence and the difficulty of bringing together such incongruities, for it is a common effect of enormous riches to push every thing they can procure to bombast and extravagance, which are the death of taste. In other countries, however, as well as in China, I have seen some of the most boasted feats, either outgrowing their beauty from a plethora of their owner's wealth, or becoming capricious and hypocondriacal by a quackish application of it. A few fine places, even in England, might be pointed out that are labouring under these disorders; not to mention some celebrated houses where, twined stair-cases, window-glass cupolas, and embroidered chimney-pieces, convey nothing to us but the whims and dreams of sickly fancy, without an atom of grandeur, taste, or propriety.[17]

"The architecture of the Chinese is of a peculiar style, totally unlike any other, irreducible to our rules, but perfectly consistent with its own. It has certain principles, from which it never deviates, and although, when examined according to ours, it sins against the ideas we have imbibed of distribution, composition, and proportion; yet, upon the whole, it often produces a most pleasing effect, as we sometimes see a person without a single good feature in his face have, nevertheless, a very agreeable countenance."[18]

NOTES

1   John Barrow, *Travels in China, Containing Descriptions, Observations, and Comparisons, Made and Collected in the Course of a Short Residence at the Imperial Palace of Yuen-min-yuen, and on a Subsequent Journey through the Country from Pekin to Canton* (London: T. Cadell and W. Davies, 1804). The second edition was published in London in 1806 and a first American edition was published in Philadelphia in 1805. A first German translation was printed in Weimar 1804 and two others were published 1805, one in Vienna and the other in Hamburg. A French translation was published in Paris in the same year. *Travels in China* was reprinted in 2011 by the Cambridge University Press as part of the series "Travel and Exploration in Asia."

2   Robert Southey, "Travels in China . . . by John Barrow," in *The Annual Review and History of Literature; for 1804*, edited by Arthur Aikin, vol. 3 (London: Longman, 1805), 69.

3   Barrow, *Travels*, 3. Reed and Demattè, *China on Paper*, 158.

4   On the influence Barrow's *Travels in China* had in Europe, see Siegfried Huigen, *Knowledge and Colonialism: Eighteenth-Century Travellers in South Africa* (Leiden: Brill, 2009), 149–51.

5   Chapter 3 of *Travels in China* is entitled "Journey Through the Capital to a Country Villa of the Emperor. Return to Pekin. The Imperial Palace and Gardens of Yuen-min-yuen, and the Parks of Gehol." On the differences between Barrow's and Macartney's perception of Chinese gardens see Wong, *A Paradise Lost*, 83–88; for a recent discussion see Chang, *Britain's Chinese Eye*, 46–54. See also Peyrefitte, *The Immobile Empire*, 232–40.

6   The visit to the eastern part of Bishu shanzhuang took place on September 15, 1793; two days later, on September 17, the delegation was taken across the western part of the park.

7   Stowe was designed by William Kent from the 1730s and by Lancelot "Capability" Brown from 1741; Woburn Farm was laid out by Philip Southcote beginning in 1735; Painshill Park was designed from 1738 by Charles Hamilton. As Chang states, Macartney, in his account of Bishu shanzhuang, confirmed "China as an imperium equal to Britain in its sophisticated manipulation of landscape to further the construction of pleasure parks." Chang, *Britain's Chinese Eye*, 51.

8   For a political reading of Macartney's comment see Chang, *Britain's Chinese Eye*, 52–53.

9   Richmond Park was a large royal hunting park with open grassy areas and woods, created in 1637 by King Charles I in the southeast of London. The park had only one lake, Pen Ponds, dug in 1746. It was divided in two parts by a causeway.

10   Barrow agrees with Macartney that other Western travelers' accounts of Chinese gardens are not reliable. They both consider William Chambers's descriptions— Macartney also mentions Jean-Denis Attiret—as exaggerated and not faithful to the reality that the British delegation had personally experienced. Aeneas Anderson, Lord Macartney's own valet during the embassy, also commented on the unreliability of earlier accounts of the imperial complexes. In his report about the mission, he writes of the complex in the Imperial City of Beijing: "Of the magnificent and splendid apartments this palace contains for private use or public service; of its gardens appropriated to pleasure, or for the sole production of fruits and flowers, of which report said so much, I am not authorized to say any thing, as my view of the whole was very confined; but, though I am ready to acknowledge that the palace had something imposing in its appearance, when compared with the diminutive buildings of the city that surround it, I could see nothing that disposed me to believe the extraordinary accounts which I had heard and read of the wonders of the Imperial residence in Peking." Aeneas Anderson, *A Narrative of the British Embassy to China in the Years 1792, 1793 and 1794* (London: J. Debrett, 1795), 173.

11   Chinese architecture is discussed in chapter 6 of Barrow's *Travels in China*.

12   In 1807, Barrow published a series of Lord Macartney's writings, including the travel journal Lord Macartney kept during his mission to the court of the Qianlong emperor. John Barrow, *Some Account of the Public Life, and a Selection from the Unpublished Writings, of the Earl of Macartney*, vol. 2 (London: T. Cadell and W. Davis, 1807), 163–517.

13   Also in Barrow, *Some Account*, vol. 2, 249–50.

14   In Macartney's journal published by Barrow in *Some Account* the lotus is not specified as "nelumbium" but as "Nymphaea." Barrow, *Some Account*, vol. 2, 265. The Linnaean binomial *Nelumbo nucifera* (Gaert.) is the recognized name for the lotus; former names under which this species has been classified include *Nelumbium speciosum* (Willd.) and *Nymphaea nelumbo*.

15   Also in Barrow, *Some Account*, vol. 2, 261–65.

16   Also in Barrow, *Some Account*, vol. 2, 273–76. John Claudius Loudon described the park and pleasure grounds of Lowther Hall in Westmoreland as "of great extent, and command a variety of prospects and scenery. . . . There is a terrace of closely mown turf: the grasses of the finest mountain kind. It is nearly a mile in length, and runs along the brink of a limestone cliff, which overlooks a great part of the park, irregularly scattered with forest trees of immense growth, and well stocked with deer." John Claudius Loudon, *Encyclopaedia of Gardening* (London: Longman, Rees, Orme, Brown, Green, and Longman, 1824), 1081.

17   Also in Barrow, *Some Account*, vol. 2, 494–96.

18   Barrow expresses negative judgments on Chinese architecture: "The whole of their architecture, indeed, is as unsightly as unsolid; without elegance or convenience of design, and without any settled proportion; mean in its appearance and clumsey in the workmanship. Their pagodas of five, seven, and nine rounds, or roofs, are the most striking objects; but though they appear to be the imitations or, perhaps, more properly speaking, the models of a similar kind of pyramids

found in India, they are neither so well designed, nor so well executed: they are, in fact, so very ill constructed that half of them, without any marks of antiquity, appear in ruins; of these useless and whimsical edifices His Majesty's garden at Kew exhibits a specimen, which is not inferior in any respect to the very best I have met with in China." For Barrow, the Western evocation of a Chinese building, such as the pagoda at Kew Gardens designed by William Chambers, surpasses its Chinese model. Barrow, *Travels in China*, 330.

CHAPTER 23

George Macartney (1737–1806)

In 1807, John Barrow published a series of writings by Lord George
Macartney in a two-volume work entitled *Some Account of the Public
Life, and a Selection from the Unpublished Writings, of the Earl of Macartney*,
which included the journal the ambassador kept over the course of the
diplomatic mission he led to the court of the Qianlong emperor in 1792–
94.[1] Even though many of Macartney's observations about the imperial
parks had already been included in Barrow's earlier publication, *Travels in
China* (1804), the following extract, taken from Macartney's journal, offers
some additional remarks about Yuanming yuan, where the ambassador had
been invited to discuss the most appropriate hall for displaying some of the
many gifts the embassy had brought from England for Qianlong.

The following text confirms that Macartney's attitude toward the gardens of China is one of general admiration. He comments briefly on the
park's layout, its variety, the multitude of different buildings and their positioning. Also, he highlights the intricacy in the garden space obtained
through the ingenious arrangement of diverse compositional elements that
disguise "the real design of communication." Though the ambassador was
cautious about making judgments regarding China's influence on the
English landscape garden—as exemplified by his comments that were
included in Barrow's *Travels in China*—Macartney does attest to the vogue
in England at the time for Chinese taste. However, he does find one feature
in Chinese gardens not suitable to British taste: the stairs made of massive
irregular boulders that lead to some of the garden buildings. Though
Macartney recognizes that these "stone stairs" imitate "the rude simplicity
of nature" and thus participate in the general design philosophy of the
Chinese garden, he considers them to be an expression of "a sickly and
declining taste, meant solely to display vanity and expence." This judgment
reflects the change in Western perception of China, which was seen, from

the late eighteenth century, as effeminate and irrational in comparison to the civilized and vigorous European West.

* * *

From John Barrow, *Some Account of the Public Life, and a Selection from the Unpublished Writings, of the Earl of Macartney*, vol. 2 (1807)

Chou-ta-gin came to take us to the emperor's palace of *Yuen-min-yuen* [Yuanming yuan] or the garden of gardens, (as the name imports), and to ask our opinion, of the fittest apartments to contain the globes, the clocks, the lustres, and the planetarium.[2] This place is truly an imperial residence; the park is said to be eighteen miles round, laid out in all the taste, variety, and magnificence which distinguish the rural scenery of Chinese gardening.

There is no one very extensive contiguous building, but several hundreds of pavilions scattered through the grounds, and all connected together by close arbors, by passages apparently cut through stupendous rocks, or by fairy-land galleries, emerging or receding in the perspective, and so contrived as to conceal the real design of communication, and yet contribute to the general purpose and effect intended to arise from the whole.[3] The various beauties of this spot, its lakes and rivers, together with its superb edifices, which I saw, (and yet I saw but a very small part,) so strongly impress my mind at this moment that I feel incapable of describing them. I shall therefore chiefly confine myself to the great hall, or presence chamber, of the emperor. It is a hundred and fifty feet long and sixty feet wide. There are windows on one side only, and opposite to them is the imperial throne of carved mahogany, the logs of which were brought from England, and elevated by a few steps from the floor. Over the chair of state is an inscription in Chinese characters.

Ching-Tha-Quan-Ming-Foo.

The translation of which signifies,

Verus, Magnus, Gloriosus, Splendidus, Felix.

On each side of the chair of state is a beautiful argus pheasant's tail spread out into a magnificent fan of great extent.

Figure 14. Frontispiece of George Leonard Staunton, *An Historical Account of the Embassy to the Emperor of China* (London: J. Stockdale, 1797). © Dumbarton Oaks Research Library and Collection, Rare Book Collection, Washington, D.C.

The floor is of chequered marble, grey and white, with neat mats laid upon it in different places to walk upon. At one end I observed a musical clock that played twelve old English tunes, the Black Joke, Lillibullero, and other airs of the Beggars' Opera. It was decorated in a wretched old taste with ornaments of crystal and coloured stones, but had been, I dare say, very much admired in its time. On the dial appeared, in large characters, *George Clarke, clock, and watch maker, in Leadenhall Street, London.*

This saloon we determined on for the reception of some of our most magnificent presents, which were to be distributed as follows: on one side of the throne was to be placed the terrestrial globe, on the other, the celestial; the lustres were to be hung from the ceiling, at equal distances from the middle of the room; at the north end the planetarium was to stand, at the south end Vulleamy's clocks, with the barometer and Derbyshire porcelain vases, and figures, and Frazer's orrery; an assemblage of such ingenuity, utility, and beauty, as is not to be seen collected together in any other apartments, I believe, of the whole world besides. Before I quit the palace of *Yuen-min-yuen,* I must observe a singularity in the Chinese taste, which has not yet reached us, and which, in truth, is by no means worthy of our copying. Although you ascend to the principal buildings by regular flights of smooth or chiselled stone stairs, yet there are several others, even pavilions of elegant architecture, to which the approach is by rugged steps of rock, seemingly rendered rough and difficult by art, in order to imitate the rude simplicity of nature. In such situations the impropriety is glaring, and argues a sickly and declining taste, meant solely to display vanity and expence. The cost of sending for such enormous masses from the mountains of Tartary must be very great, for in my whole route through the province of *Pecheli* [Beizhili], from the mouth of the *Pay-ho* [Baihe, White River] to the city of Pekin [Beijing], I did not see a single pebble big enough to make a scal [scale] of.[4]

NOTES

1   John Barrow, *Some Account of the Public Life, and a Selection from the Unpublished Writings, of the Earl of Macartney,* 2 vols. (London: T. Cadell and W. Davies, 1870).

2   Some of the many elaborate gifts Macartney took with him were in order to show Britain's progress in the sciences and the arts, as well as to excite Qianlong's curiosity. Hevia, *Cherishing Men from Afar,* 77–80. On the unfavorable judgment of the Chinese for the sophisticated selection of gifts, considered inferior to those

of other embassies, see Patrick J. N. Tuck, introduction to *Britain and the China Trade, 1635–1842*, ed. Patrick J. N. Tuck (London: Routledge, 2000), xix.

3 A similar comment on the spatial articulation of the imperial complex, and the relation between architecture and landscape, was given by the British Henry Brougham Loch (1827–1900), who participated in Lord Elgin's mission to China. Describing Yuanming yuan just before its destruction, Loch wrote: "The buildings in themselves possessed but little architectural beauty; they were nearly all isolated from each other, being connected by gardens, courts, and terraces. . . . The largest of these were connected by courtyards, passing through which were entered spacious reception rooms that opened into gardens of considerable extent, which lead down to a marble terrace stretching along the shores of a lake some three miles in length." Henry Brougham Loch, *Personal Narrative of Occurrences During Lord Elgin's Second Embassy to China in 1860* (London: Murray, 1869), 272.

4 Baihe (White River) is the former name of the Hai River (Haihe, Sea River) that flows through Beijing into the Bohai Sea. The province of Beizhili, Northern Zhili, was centered on Beijing, which approximately corresponds to the modern province of Hebei.

CHAPTER 24

Chrétien-Louis-Joseph de Guignes
(1759–1845)

S on of the celebrated French orientalist Joseph de Guignes, who introduced him to the study of oriental languages, Chrétien-Louis-Joseph de
Guignes was in Guangzhou as a functionary of the French government
from 1783 to 1796, when he moved first to Manila, in the Philippines, and
then to the island of Mauritius.[1] Upon his return to Paris in 1801, he
recorded his experience of China in a travel account entitled *Voyages à
Péking, Manille et l'Île de France* . . . (1808).[2] From the very first pages of
his book, de Guignes positions himself as a realistic narrator and impartial
observer of China and Chinese culture. His travel account had a documen-
tary intent, which was expressed in the choice of the subjects he addressed.
The first part of his book is dedicated to a summary of ancient Chinese
history; the second is a record, in diary form, of the journey across the
Chinese empire from Guangzhou to Beijing in 1794–95 with the Dutch
embassy to the Qianlong emperor, led by Isaac Titsingh and André Everard
van Braam Houckgeest, whom de Guignes accompanied as interpreter. The
third and most substantial section of *Voyages à Péking* is entitled "Observations sur les Chinois"; it consists of thematic chapters based on de Guignes's observations and addresses various aspects of Chinese culture and
society, including the system of government, language, religion, usages and
customs, and the arts. In the passage provided below, de Guignes sketches
out his understanding of Chinese gardens.[3]

The short essay presents irregularity, contrasts, and the imitation of
nature as essential characteristics of Chinese garden design; it also emphasizes the pervasive presence of water in its many forms in the gardens.
Though de Guignes was able to see gardens that were extremely different—
the private gardens of the hong merchants in Guangzhou on the southeastern coast, part of the vast Yuanming yuan and of the imperial park
in Beijing, as well as the garden of an imperial travelling palace in

Note in right margin: late?

Figure 15. William Henry Capone, after Thomas Allom, *House of a Chinese Merchant, near Canton*. In Thomas Allom, *China in a Series of Views*, vol. 1 (London: Peter Jackson, Late Fisher, Son, and Co., 1843), p. 95. © Dumbarton Oaks Research Library and Collection, Rare Book Collection, Washington, D.C.

Yangzhou—he seems not to notice any stylistic differences between them and instead emphasizes a certain uniformity in design. He concludes that the Chinese, in composing their gardens, are "constantly attached to their same ideas," regardless of the dimension of the sites, and he recognized a consistent design method beyond Chinese gardens, aimed "to gather and represent on a small scale all that is picturesque and interesting in a vast country." According to de Guignes, such a design strategy, particularly with regard to the numerous elements and varied objects it entails, should be applied only to large sites, since when it is used in smaller spaces, the result is a confused and dense layout.

In addition to a general sense of the picturesque that permeates the whole description, de Guignes also continually remarks on the air of neglect pervading the gardens he visited; a sign of the decline of the Qing empire.[4]

*   *   *

From Chrétien-Louis-Joseph de Guignes, *Voyages à Péking,*
Manille et l'Île de France, faits dans l'intervalle des années
1784 à 1801 (1808), translated by Bianca Maria Rinaldi

GARDENS

In the arrangement of their gardens, the Chinese look for a good exposure, healthy air, and above all distance from neighbors and the curious. Among a people who permit polygamy, and where consequently the condition of women is disagreeable, the first concern of a husband must be that of procuring them some distraction and of keeping them out of sight of strangers. The art of gardens, among the Chinese, consists in copying nature: imitating its beauties and rendering its irregularities; for them that is the epitome of genius. Instead of these symmetrically planted alleys, instead of these flat terrains one sees in the gardens of Europe, in the gardens of China one sees only winding paths, trees scattered and thrown haphazardly, wooded hills or barren ones, deep valleys and narrow passes, whose steep precipitous sides are sprinkled with rocks and offer for the eyes a few miserable shrubs. Extremely bizarre in the composition of their gardens, the Chinese take delight in putting together, in the same view, cultivated land and arid fields; above all, they strive to make the terrain uneven, and to cover it with artificial rocks; they cut caves out of the mountains; they place half-ruined pavilions on the peaks, and through these disorders they delineate an imaginary nature, with paths which follow oblique lines and always twist back onto themselves, thus extending the terrain, so to speak, and doubling the pleasure of the stroll.

Water, when it can be procured, after crashing down from a height of the hills, and having opened a channel through the rocks, as a general rule runs through the gardens in different directions, and then feeds a pond on which boats of an elegant shape give the women the amusement of fishing and the charm of a sweet freshness.

Rocks scattered as though by accident, and even advancing into the water, support the earth along the channels, giving them an irregular contour; here and there isolated trees and weeping willows cast a melancholy shadow on a terrain covered with sand and shells.

The broad leaves of the water lilies and their tulip-like flowers cover the surface of the ponds, while a thousand small fish of a brilliant color swim across it, and find shelter from the heat among the canes where they can withdraw.

Some little islands adorned with pavilions and triumphal arches occupy the middle of these pools; and bridges of a bizarre construction, built along the several channels, make possible easy passage everywhere.

Such is the taste of the Chinese; they seek nothing in their gardens other than to imitate nature and to gather and represent on a small scale all that is picturesque and interesting in a vast country.

Such gardens call for large sites; but the Chinese do not always have them, and their fault is that of being constantly attached to their same ideas, without considering the largeness or smallness of a site; the result is that their gardens often present an excessive multitude of objects, and are extremely confused.

One can easily become acquainted, through the plan of the garden of the house occupied by M. de Grammont (*no. 90*), in Quanton [Guangzhou], with the method which the Chinese follow in the arrangement of their gardens.[5] In this plan, buildings occupy a large part of the terrain: the paths are not wide, but they suffice for Chinese women who walk little, and who cannot bear the fatigue, and are often obliged to rest in the pavilions which are multiplied expressly so that they may stop there.[6] This house, situated in a suburb of Quanton, was well-maintained so long as it was in the hands of its Chinese owner; but now that it has been abandoned, a part is threatening to collapse; several pavilions have caved in and are ready to fall down, something resulting from the negligent way the Chinese arrange the supports that they employ to set the foundations of the houses built along the channels.

The hannist merchants [hong merchants] of Quanton have many gardens on the other side of the river, in Honan [Honam Island]; one of them is quite narrow and features only a pond crossed by an embankment with a few little paths partly lined by quite high bamboo, which hides the walls; another is much larger and can give an idea of the Chinese gardens.[7] The owner had a big pavilion built almost at the center of the site to lay the body of his father, and he surrounded it with a canal that then runs through the garden, and flows into a good-sized pond; the rest of the terrain is filled with pavilions, bridges, and is adorned with trees and flowers; the meandering paths are made of stones of different colors in different patterns; but in one place he was satisfied to place on the ground, at a distance of a foot from one another, some rocks two feet long and eight inches high, to keep from the humidity.

I hoped that, while I was in Peking [Beijing], I would be able to examine the gardens of the emperor, but I only saw a portion of them; in great part, they are occupied by a river whose banks are planted with trees shading several pavilions, which look very pretty from the outside, but which are shabby within. The view of the gardens of the emperor from the bridge is beautiful (*n.° 2*), and the landscape is truly magnificent. I would not speak of the gardens of Yuen-ming-yuen [Yuanming yuan], the one I traversed merits no attention, even though the spot where we were placed was destined for the festivities the emperor offers to his court and the ambassadors.

The sole occasion when I was able to judge the taste of the Chinese in the composition of gardens was when I visited the emperor's one, situated beyond the city of Yang-tcheou-fou [Yangzhou].

This garden is very spacious, but so packed with buildings, pavilions, passageways, bridges, and paths that its extent seems diminished by half. The buildings are in a deplorable state; water is not running in the channel any more, and the wooden bridge constructed over it, which is twisting in shape, was so dilapidated that it could not take my weight. The paths are winding and decorated with stones; the artificial rocks alone are well preserved. The trees are beautiful and have a fine effect; finally, this garden, which is occupied in good part by a large pond, is altogether extremely curious, but too confused and too crowded. In the past, the emperor visited it from time to time, but he no longer comes; everything thus suffers from his absence.[8]

The gardens we saw near Lake Sy-hou [Xihu, West Lake], at Hang-tcheou-fou [Hangzhou], must have been very beautiful when they were in a good state; but, as I said above, the works of the Chinese demand continual maintenance, and even if they are slightly neglected, they are destroyed before too long.

NOTES

1   Reed and Demattè, *China on Paper*, 160.

2   Chrétien-Louis-Joseph de Guignes, *Voyages à Peking, Manille et l'Île de France, faits dans l'intervalle des années 1784 à 1801*, 3 vols. and atlas (Paris: Imprimerie Impériale, 1808). The three volumes were accompanied by a folio volume containing about a hundred engravings after the drawings done by de Guignes himself; they represented buildings and other architectonic structures, including tombs and bridges, gardens, processions, and festivals. A German edition of de Guignes's account was published in Leipzig in 1810; a first Italian edition was published in Milan in 1829–30, and another Italian edition was published in Naples in 1832.

3   De Guignes, "Jardins," in *Voyages à Peking*, vol. 2, 189–94.

4   The condition of disrepair and abandonment of Chinese gardens during the nine-
     teenth century was often recorded by Western travelers. Albert Smith (1816–60),
     an English author who traveled to southern China in 1858, noted that the private
     garden of a wealthy merchant in Guangzhou was "all rotten and neglected, and
     tumbling to pieces." Such a desolate vision of a garden prompted him to add: "I
     really believe that the reason for the Chinese having kept Canton so jealously shut
     up for centuries was, that they were ashamed of it." Albert Smith, *To China and
     Back: Being a Diary kept, out and Home* (London: By the author, 1859), 42.

5   The French Jesuit Jean-Baptiste-Joseph de Grammont (1736–1812?) reached
     Beijing in 1768 and was admitted to the court of the Qianlong emperor as a
     mathematician and musician. In 1785, he got the emperor's authorization to
     reside in Guangzhou and returned to Beijing in 1790. Henri Cordier, "Les corre-
     spondants de Bertin, Secrétaire d'Etat au XVIIIᵉ siècle," *T'oung Pao* 14, no. 4
     (1913): 465.

6   The map de Guignes is speaking of shows a garden whose space is occupied
     almost completely by water in the form of two little lakes of serpentine shores,
     connected with each other by two canals. A large island divided the waters and
     featured three pavilions, one of them rising over the water below. De Guignes,
     "Plan d'un jardin chinois à Quanton," in *Voyages à Peking*, atlas, no. 90.

7   Located opposite the old walled city of Guangzhou across the Pearl River, the
     island of Honam had a rural atmosphere and boasted the presence of temples,
     suburban residences, and gardens. William C. Hunter (1812–91), an American
     resident merchant who lived in Guangzhou from 1829 to 1842, first as an
     employee then as partner of the American trading house Russell and Company,
     described the gardens of the residences of the hong merchants as follows: "Their
     private residences, of which we visited several, were on a vast scale, comprising
     curiously laid-out gardens, with grottoes and lakes, crossed by carved stone brid-
     ges, pathways neatly paved with small stones of various colours forming designs
     of birds, or fish, or flowers." William C. Hunter, *The "Fan Kwae" at Canton
     Before Treaty Days, 1825–1844, by an Old Resident* (London: Kegan Paul, Trench
     and Co., 1882), 40.

8   In a report on his visit to the garden of Yangzhou with the Dutch embassy, de
     Guignes wrote, "These gardens will give us a complete idea of the ways the Chi-
     nese create them. They have many pavilions, clumps of trees, rocks, bridges,
     ponds, shores, but few walks." De Guignes, *Voyages à Péking*, vol. 2, 37.

CHAPTER 25

Félix Renouard de Sainte-Croix
(1767–1840)

On his way back from the Philippines, where he had gone in 1804, the French cavalry officer Carloman Louis François Félix Renouard, marquis de Sainte-Croix, reached the southeastern coast of China in 1807, staying first in Macao and then in Guangzhou. Upon returning to France, he published the travelogue of his Southeast Asia journey in the form of a collection of letters with the title of *Voyage commercial et politique aux Indes Orientales, aux Iles Philippines, à la Chine* (1810).[1]

Renouard de Sainte-Croix's "Lettre LXXV" contains a description of the garden at the private residence of the hong merchant known to Western traders as Puankhequa II (1755–1820), which he had visited in Guangzhou during one of the famous banquets the merchant habitually organized to entertain foreign traders.[2] Commenting on the garden's various features and its "picturesque" character, Renouard de Sainte-Croix considers the Chinese attitude toward nature. He feels perplexed by the preference of the Chinese for representing nature as decrepit and worn out by time; he feels also intrigued when he recognizes the "dwarf trees" as an expression of the aesthetic value that nature's oldness acquires in Chinese gardens. His observations prompted him to conclude that the Chinese do "not love nature." Renouard de Sainte-Croix uses what he perceives as the Chinese predilection for some of nature's more dilapidated aspects in the garden as a metaphor for the immobility of the Chinese empire, as well as the decadence and stagnation of Chinese civilization.

* * *

From Félix Renouard de Sainte-Croix, *Voyage commercial et politique aux Indes Orientales, aux Iles Philippines, à la Chine*, vol. 3 (1810), translated by Bianca Maria Rinaldi

LETTER LXXV. *CHINESE DINNER, THE HOUSE AND GARDEN OF A HANNIST.*

Canton [Guangzhou], 1 December 1807.

The hannist *Pankeq**** [Puankhequa II] invited the Spanish and Dutch merchants, including me in the party, to a dinner he gave in his garden outside Canton, for the ambassadors of Siam, who had come, as was the custom, to congratulate the Emperor. It was therefore a Chinese dinner, and I owe you a description.

We arrived in his garden, which is on the other side of the river across from the Factories: he had sent his servants to bring us in, as soon as we got out of the sampans which brought us.[3]

The entrance to this garden is not brilliant; I was astonished that such a rich man, one of the dozen to whom the Emperor had given the privilege of becoming even richer, had nothing [at the garden's entrance] which announced a man of great importance: but I remembered that for the Chinese, everything is for the inside. They keep themselves from displaying luxury outside that would appear scandalous to the mandarins; these magistrates would do justice quickly by asking them for a great deal of money.

We penetrated into the interior of the garden, which featured numerous pools surrounded in part by galleries and very well-maintained chambers, arranged in good taste, very breezy and opening onto the water. You would be tempted to believe that this is the favorite element of the Chinese, so much do they love to multiply these pools and arrange rooms around so that you cannot look anywhere without glimpsing water. All these buildings consist of two stories, decorated with furniture in the taste of the country: in the first room we found *Pankeq**** and his cousin *Conséq**** [Consequa] who were entertaining the ambassadors, along with the mandarin who served as interpreter.[4] After the customary ceremonies and the *chin-chin* salutations we left them, and I went to stroll in the garden.

I found something deliciously picturesque, grottos, rocks, vases, waters, flower pots, all so bizarrely mixed up yet so agreeable to the eyes that all that would be necessary to make the spectacle perfect would be a European taste. I saw with pleasure these dwarf trees whose forms please the Chinese.[5] You would believe that these dwarf trees are perfectly ancient; I would imagine, so to speak, that for this extraordinary people, so different from all others, a little old man, who is quite decrepit and deprived of all that constituted the ornament of his youth, is the symbol of perfection. The

Chinese does not love nature, at least in his demand that art imitate it insofar as it is small, weak, and nearly decrepit. This people will never rejuvenate anything; it is condemned to remain what it was, what it is, and what it will be in a thousand centuries.

Among the shrubs, I would point out the *coeffa*, whose flower gives off so sweet an odor, and many others which I never saw in our gardens in Europe. This same people, which seems so attached to dwarf trees provided that they present the signs of old age, is nonetheless an idolater of flowers, the charming image of the springtime of life. There is no Chinese who does not have at least one pot of flowers, which he attends to and cares for methodically.

NOTES

1   Félix Renouard de Sainte-Croix, *Voyage commercial et politique aux Indes Orien-tales, aux Iles Philippines, à la Chine*, 3 vols. (Paris: Crapelet, 1810).

2   Félix Renouard de Sainte-Croix, "Lettre LXXV: Diner chinois, la maison et le jardin d'un haniste, Canton, 1 December 1807," in *Voyage commercial et politique*, vol. 3, 154–56. Puankhequa II succeeded his father, Puankhequa I, in 1788 as the first of the hong merchants of Guangzhou. Concerning the banquets organized by the hong merchants in honor of Western traders, see May-bo Ching, "Chopsticks or Cutlery? How Canton Hong Merchants Entertained For-eign Guests in the Eighteenth- and Nineteenth-Centuries," in *Narratives of Free Trade: The Commercial Cultures of Early US-China Relations*, ed. Kendall John-son (Hong Kong: Hong Kong University Press, 2012), 103; Fan, *British Natural-ists in Qing China*, 32.

3   Puankhequa II's residence was located on the island of Honam, or Henam, in front of Shemian Island. Located on the northern shore of the Pearl River, imme-diately outside Guangzhou's city walls, Shemian Island was the site of the Factor-ies, the trading posts of the foreign merchants, which functioned both as residences and as warehouses and commercial offices for the foreign traders; it was the only area of Guangzhou where Westerners could trade and were allowed to reside during the trading season. Jonathan A. Farris, "Thirteen Factories of Canton: An Architecture of Sino-Western Collaboration and Confrontation," in *Buildings and Landscapes* 14 (2007): 66–83. Sir Henry Ellis, who visited Puan-khequa's garden in 1817, considered it "interesting as a specimen of Chinese taste in laying out grounds; the great object is to produce as much variety within a small compass as possible, and to furnish pretexts for excursions or entertain-ment." Ellis, *Journal of the Proceedings*, 416. George Thomas Staunton (1781–1859), who as a child had accompanied his father, George Leonard Staunton, on Lord Macartney's embassy to China, and who had lived in Guangzhou in the employ of the East India Company, wrote in a note to John Claudius Loudon that Puankhequa's was "the best garden about Canton." John Claudius Loudon,

The Gardener's Magazine, vol. 11 (London: Longman, Rees, Orme, Brown, Green, and Longman, 1835), 111.

4   Consequa, a wealthy hong merchant, had a villa and a garden on the island of Honam. This garden was recorded by John Claudius Loudon as "one of the finest in Canton," on the basis of a view of the garden owned by George Leonard Staunton, depicting the garden around 1806, and published by Loudon. Loudon, *An Encyclopaedia of Gardening*, 1200. The illustration representing the garden of the merchant Consequa is on page 1201.

5   A few years later, the British plant hunter Robert Fortune, visiting the garden of the hong merchant Howqua in Guangzhou, observed "a multitude of dwarf trees, without which, no Chinese garden would be considered complete." Fortune, *A Residence Among the Chinese*, 215.

CHAPTER 26

Irish-born American merchant

Peter Dobell (1772–1852)

Peter Dobell, an Irish-born American merchant who became a Russian citizen, reached China in 1798. He lived there for seven years before moving on to Manila, where he served as Russian consul in the Philippines. The narrative of his experiences in China forms the second volume of Dobell's account of his Far East Asian travels, entitled *Travels in Kamtchatka and Siberia with a Narrative of a Residence in China* (1830), from which the following brief extract is taken.[1]

When describing the gardens of southern China, Dobell enthusiastically comments on the general layout and on the intricate garden pathways. His minor concluding remark about the gardens of China as being "enchanted places" anticipates later travel literature, in which the Chinese garden is sublimated into a stereotype of a generic oriental setting and blurred into the exoticism of the tale *One Thousand and One Nights*. In the following years, references to the *Arabian Nights* were used to evoke the splendor and excessive decoration of the emperor's private quarters within Yuanming yuan, particularly by those French officers and soldiers who took part in its destruction.[2] Antoine Julien Fauchery, who was engaged by the French government in 1860 to follow the French military expedition to China as a photographer and journalist, wrote that the magnificence of Yuanming yuan made one "forget all the fatigues and privations of the road, leaving only memories of the dazzle of gold, silver, and silk, such as only the experience of reading the Thousand and One Nights could provide."[3]

* * *

From Peter Dobell, *Travels in Kamtchatka and Siberia, with a Narrative of a Residence in China*, vol. 2 (1830)

The houses are, for the most part, only one story high, and those of the lower orders have a mean and miserable appearance, whilst those of the rich have numbers of fine, ornamented, and airy apartments, with spaces between them to admit the light as well as the air. These spaces are always in front and at the back, the light being seldom given at the sides; and the houses are surrounded by extensive and beautiful gardens, adorned with artificial lakes, rocks, cascades, buildings of various descriptions, walks, bridges, etc.

In the ornamenting and beautifying of gardens the Chinese excel all other nations. By means of a variety of winding walks, they make a small place appear twice as large as it really is. Innumerable flower pots, containing a great variety of beautiful *asters*, of which they are very fond, are sometimes arranged in a labyrinth, from which you cannot get out again without a guide. They seem to have a very extensive assortment of *asters*; one species is quite white, as large as a rose, with long pending leaves, and the Chinese use it in the season for salad, justly esteeming it a very great delicacy. When the *asters* are all in full bloom, the pots arranged handsomely near a piece of water, and the walks and alleys well lighted, at night, with variously coloured lamps, a Chinese garden has the appearance of one of those enchanted places we read of in the Arabian Tales.[4]

NOTES

1   Peter Dobell, *Travels in Kamtchatka and Siberia, with a Narrative of a Residence in China*, 2 vols. (London: H. Colburn and R. Bentley, 1830). The second volume, translated into Russian and expanded with an account of Dobell's travels in Southeast Asia and of his stay in the Philippines, was published in Saint Petersburg in 1833: Peter Dobell, *Puteshestvia i novieishia nabludenia ve Nitae Manille, i Indo-Kitaiskot arxipelage bivshago rossiiskago reneralnago konsula na Filippinskix ostrovax, kolleshsk* (St. Petersburg: N. Grecha, 1833). A French translation of this new work appeared in 1842 with the title *Sept années en Chine: Nouvelles observations sur cet empire, l'archipel indo-chinois, les Philippines et les Iles Sandwich* (Paris: Librairie d'Amyot, 1842).

2   See, for instance, Paul Varin [Charles Dupin], *Expédition de Chine* (Paris: Lévy Frères, 1862), 235–36; Charles de Mutrécy, *Journal de la campagne de Chine*, vol. 2 (Paris: Bourdilliatet, 1862), 26. Also shown by Greg M. Thomas, who discusses the observations on Yuanming yuan by Charles Dupin and Charles de Mutrécy: Thomas, "The Looting of Yuanming," 5–7.

3   Antoine Julien Fauchery, "Lettres de Chine," *Le Moniteur universel* 362, December 28 (1860): 1533. Quoted in and translated by Greg M. Thomas, "The Looting of Yuanming," 7.

4   The French translation of Dobell's work here explicitly mentions *One Thousand and One Nights*. In it, the Chinese garden becomes an ideal representation of the garden of Aladdin: "Rien ne réalise mieux les jardins enchantés d'Aladin que la vue d'un jardin chinois." (Nothing represents Aladdin's enchanted gardens better than the view of a Chinese garden.) Dobell, *Sept années en Chine*, 182.

CHAPTER 27

Plant hunter

James Main (c. 1765–1846)

A trained gardener from Scotland, James Main was sent to Guangzhou in 1792 by Gilbert Slater, the manager and owner of several ships of the East India Company, to gather plants native to China to be acclimatized in England in the gardens of Knotts Green, Slater's country residence near Leyton.

At the time of Main's journey to China, Europeans were already familiar with a large number of Chinese plants, thanks to the accounts by Jesuit missionaries as well as a few specimens collected by travelers. From the very beginning of their mission to China, Jesuits, who traveled through different provinces of the Chinese empire, had celebrated in their accounts the rich variety of the flora of the country and had sent increasingly detailed descriptions of Chinese plants to Europe. In the second half of the eighteenth century, French Jesuits in Beijing collected and sent back seeds and specimens, contributing to the introduction of plants from China into the gardens of France. The rigid restrictions imposed by the Chinese government to foreign trade limited the explorations of the country by other Western travelers, confining their botanical research to southeastern China. Since by the end of the eighteenth century, international trade with China was still confined to Guangzhou, Westerners were allowed to reside there only during the trading season, from October to March, and were then requested each year to retire to Macao.[1] Thus merchants, naturalists, and plant hunters collected plants and botanical specimens primarily from local markets, nurseries, and the private gardens of the hong merchants.[2]

Main remained in China until 1794, managing to acquire a considerable collection of plants.[3] His account of his botanical expeditions, entitled "Reminiscences of a Voyage to and from China in the Years 1792–3–4," from which the following extracts are taken, includes some remarks on Chinese gardens. It was not published until 1836, when it appeared in the

Horticultural Register, a monthly magazine started by Joseph Paxton.[4] However, John Claudius Loudon had previously helped disseminate Main's observations on Chinese garden design. After extensive alterations, Loudon published them in the *Gardener's Magazine* (1827) and later, in briefer form, in the revised edition of his *Encyclopaedia of Gardening* (1835), as important sources to illustrate "the present state of gardening in China."[5]

Main's comments on Chinese gardens were based on his visits to several private gardens in Guangzhou: those of the residences of the hong merchants Munqua and Shykinqua, and the little garden of a "china-ware manufacturer." His assessments about the gardens of China display opposing views that move from aversion to admiration, from prejudice to curiosity. On the one hand, Main considers the imitation of the grandeur of nature's forms and their miniaturization in gardens to be both ridiculous and grotesque, resulting in a sort of caricature of nature; he recognizes a veiled contrast between Western sophisticated approach to garden design, resulting in the conception of a "spacious landscape," and the "peculiar" taste of the Chinese, whose gardens offer examples of "puerile efforts of unnatural taste." On the other hand, Main also acknowledges the Chinese skills in producing such forms of miniaturization, as manifested in the "dwarfed trees." He provides information about the botanical species best suited for growing in pots, as well as details on cultivation techniques and the modeling of plants. He also adds a remark about how these potted plants were considered an object of curiosity, almost a botanical form of chinoiserie, by Westerners in Guangzhou.

The only feature of the garden that receives the gardener-collector's unconditional admiration, as the sole aspect of the whole composition that was truly notable, is the wide variety of ornamental plants it contained.[6] Main's description is indicative of the progressive change in Europeans' interest in the gardens of China from the late eighteenth century: after their curiosity about the aesthetic, the spatial composition, and design principles had begun to diminish, scientific inquiry prevailed, and Western travelers contemplated the Chinese garden as a botanical microcosm.

*   *   *

From [James Main], "Reminiscences of a Voyage to and from China in the Years 1792–3–4," in *The Horticultural Register* (1836)

Figure 16. Thomas Daniell and William Daniell, *Chinese Gentleman*. In Thomas Daniell and William Daniell, *A Picturesque Voyage to India, by the Way of China* (London: Printed for Longman, Hurst, Rees, and Orme, 1810), p. 57. Hand-colored aquatint. Yale Center for British Art, Paul Mellon Collection.

We were very much confined in our perambulations about Canton [Guangzhou], by the systematic jealousy of the Chinese authorities. We saw none of their nurseries; but, by special favour of some of the Security Merchants, we were, in company with themselves, allowed to visit some of their finest gardens;—that of *Monqua* [Munqua], in the southern suburb, and the large garden and palace of *Shykinqua*, on the north side of the river. The latter was almost a public resort for Europeans while we were there, as it was getting ready for the reception of Lord Macartney and suite, as his residence while at Canton.

The style of Chinese gardening, like all their other arts, is peculiar; they have no idea of spacious landscape; there is a littleness in all their designs; they have a desire for a small part of every of the grandest features of nature: lakes, where a mackarel would be puzzled to turn; rocks which a man may carry away under his arm; aged trees fifteen inches high; and thick forests of pines composed of equisetum. Of whatever extent the ground may be, it is all divided into little squares, parallelograms, or irregular areas of a few square yards or perches. These compartments are surrounded by low brick walls, having a flat coping, on which are placed flowering plants, in fine glazed porcelain pots. The paths are often composed of flat stones, not two of which are on the same level, if near together. A great deal of trellis-work are in the gardens, either appearing like the remains of former fences, or as coverings of naked walls. If a ditch or artificial hollow be in the garden, it must be crossed by a semi-circular arch of four or five feet span. Their little tanks of water are not considered beautiful until they are completely covered with ducks'-meat (*Lemna*);[7] in short, there are so many childish freaks which constitute the beauty of a Chinese garden, that it is astonishing so clever and civilised a people can be gratified with such puerile efforts of unnatural taste. As far, however, as their collections of flowering plants decorate a garden, the assemblage is enchanting. Their Magnolias, Bombaces, Azaleas, Camellias, Ixoras, Paeonias, etc., not to mention the great variety of herbaceous and aquatic plants natural to the country, are indeed magnificent; indeed one of the finest traits of the Chinese character is their fondness for flowers.

So much is the love of flowers predominant in China, that almost every window-sill and every bit of a court in front or yard behind the houses of the shopkeepers and tradesmen are filled with plants either in the ground or in pots of different shapes, sizes, and colours. Some of the finest specimens of the Chinese *magnolias* we met with in the back courts of some of the merchants' houses; and in such confined places there are what they call complete pleasure-gardens to be seen. We will describe only one of these, to serve as a sample of their taste.

In a back court belonging to *Sinchong*, the great china-ware manufacturer, we saw one of these gardens on a very small scale indeed. It occupied one corner of a paved yard, and consisted of a little irregular pool of water, in a nook of which grew a *Leinfaa* (*Nelumbium speciosum*),[8] and in another, a fine plant of the *Tow-cow*, (*Alpinia nutans*).[9] The pool was surrounded by rugged stones, and an arch of the same was carried over to represent the mouth of a rocky cave. Between, and in the cavities of the stones, plants of the black bamboo were stuck here and there, to hang over the water, and roots of asparagus, which, with their slender and regularly branched stems of different heights, represented groves of trees. Around, and on the shelves of the stones, dwarfed trees, in pots covered with fragments of rock, were placed, and partly covered with moss and lichen and pieces of algae brought from the sea shore, altogether forming a spectacle of the most grotesque character. Such things we saw in many other places; and we verily believe that if a Chinese had a field of ten acres to beautify in his own style, it would be covered with the same kind of little fanciful freaks repeated a thousand times over.

Of their dwarfed tree—We have already observed that the Chinese are remarkable for their taste in wishing to have even the most stupendous objects in nature in miniature: mountains, rocks, lakes, rivers, aged trees, must all be represented and modelled upon a scale of a few inches. The former are formed of natural fragments curiously and fantastically cemented together, leaving water-tight hollows and little channels to represent lakes and rivers. The dwarfed trees are, however, very curiously trained, requiring considerable skill, and a considerable period of time, to get the trees into the desired form.

The trees which they commonly choose to train as dwarfs are, their native juniper (*J. Chinensis*), the dwarf elm (*Ulmus pumila*), and the Indian fig (*F. Indica*). The means employed in dwarfing these plants are,—keeping them always in the same pot—allowing but little earth for them to grow in, the pot being filled with rugged stones, which jut out of the surface;—among these some of the roots are brought out, twisted together, and the points again buried in the soil: no more water is given that but barely keeps the plants alive. The bark of the stem and branches is torn and mangled in all manner of ways; sometimes a branch is slipped from the stem, but not entirely off, so as to hang downward, and kept in that position by wire. By wires, also, the tortuous direction of the shoots are given; and being repeatedly stopped, and the half of every leaf cut off, tends materially to check all vegetative inherent vigour, and in the time produces a *vegetable cripple*. When the native vigour is thus subdued, the plant becomes subject to moss, lichens, and every weather-stain so desirable on such an object, to give the idea of hoar antiquity to a plant only of ten or a dozen years' growth. Such dwarfed trees are considered valuable; and some of the merchants imagine that they cannot make a more acceptable present to a European friend, than one of those dwarfed trees!

Orange, shaddock, and some other fruit-trees are kept in pots for ornamenting their shops or parlours; and if they happen to be destitute of fruit, others are fixed to the branches, to deceive the spectator. Many flowering-plants are treated in this way, as has already been mentioned; it is a species of self-deception which appears delightful to the minds of a nation of men who are by no means wanting in either natural acuteness of sagacity.

NOTES

1   For this short account I drew upon Fan, *British Naturalists in Qing China*, 14–19; Peter Valder, *The Garden Plants of China* (Portland, Ore.: Timber Press, 1999), 63–69.

2   As shown by Fa-ti Fan, *British Naturalists in Qing China*, 26–35. Important sources on Western discoveries of Chinese plants include Emil Bretschneider, *Early European Researchers into the Flora of China* (Shanghai: American Presbyterian Mission Press, 1881); Emil Bretschneider, *History of European Botanical Discoveries in China* (London: Sampson Low, Martson and Co., 1898).

3   Kilpatrick, *Gifts from the Gardens of China*, 125–29.

4   [James Main], "Reminiscences of a Voyage to and from China in the Years 1792–3–4," in *The Horticultural Register*, ed. by James Main, vol. 5 (London: W. S. Orr and Co., 1836), 62–67, 97–103, 143–49, 171–80, 215–20. Begun by Paxton in 1831, *The Horticultural Register* had only five volumes. Paxton was the editor of the first four, with the fifth and last being edited by James Main.

5   "Observations on Chinese Scenery, Plants, and Gardening, made on a Visit to the City of Canton and its Environs, in the Years 1793 and 1794; being an Extract from the Journal of Mr. James sent thither by the late Gilbert Slater, Esq. of Layton, Essex, to collect the Double Camellias, &c. Communicated by Mr. Main," in *The Gardener's Magazine and Register of Rural & Domestic Improvement*, ed. John Claudius Loudon, vol. 2 (London: Longman, Rees, Orme, Brown, and Green, 1827), 135–40; see also Loudon, *An Encyclopaedia of Gardening*, 386–87. On page 386, Loudon explains that the description of the garden and palace of Shykinqua compiled "by Mr. Main from personal inspection, in the years 1793 and 1794 . . . is amplified, in order to convey a general idea of Chinese landscape gardening."

6   On Main's judgment of Chinese garden design see Kilpatrick, *Gifts from the Gardens of China*, 127–28.

7   *Lemna* is a genus of free-floating small aquatic plants known as duckweed or water lentils.

8   Main is referring to the lotus. *Nelumbum speciosum* is a synonym of the currently recognized name for lotus: *Nelumbo nucifera*.

9   *Alpinia nutans* is the botanical name of false cardamom, a plant in the family of the Zingiberaceae. Peter Valder notes, among the plants used in Chinese gardens, two other species of *Alpinia*: *Alpinia globosa*, brittle-fruited mountain ginger, and *Alpinia officinarum*, the Gaoliang ginger. Valder, *The Garden Plants of China*, 349–50.

CHAPTER 28

John Francis Davis (1795–1890)

The extract that follows is taken from *The Chinese: A General Description of the Empire of China and Its Inhabitants* (1836), in which British diplomat and sinologist John Francis Davis narrates the history of Sino-European relations. The work aspired to be an encyclopedic account of Qing China, rendered through its geography and history, the arts and sciences, usages, language, literature, religion, botany, agriculture, and commerce.[1] Davis had an extensive experience of China, having spent over twenty years there. He reached Guangzhou in 1813 to work at the East India Company's factory, residing first in Macao and Guangzhou and then in the British colony of Hong Kong, of which he became governor in 1844, until his departure in 1848. His knowledge of the country was not limited to its southeastern regions. For his proficiency in Chinese, in 1816 he accompanied as interpreter the British embassy to the Qing court in Beijing, led by Lord William Amherst, traveling throughout the empire.[2] Davis recounted China in many different literary works that vary from travel accounts to studies of Chinese literature, as well as translations of Chinese texts, offering an important contribution to the European perception of China in the nineteenth century.[3]

In the following text, Davis presents Chinese gardens as a sort of brutal aberration and compares the "affected imitation of nature" he perceives there to the deformation caused by foot binding. Applying to his reading of gardens what was to become a stereotypical image in the West—the bound foot as a sign of barbarity, deviation, and gender inequalities in China's cultural tradition—Davis's description foreshadows a late nineteenth-century topos used in European garden treatises to denigrate the Chinese approach to garden design as an exercise in excess, deviation, and folly, imposing on nature the same cruelty and torture that was inflicted on Chinese women to form their artificially small feet.[4] The only example of Chinese garden design Davis praised is one he never saw: the imperial park of Yuanming yuan.

In his narrative about China, Davis often refers to other writings by earlier Western travelers. Other than his own experience, his sources on Chinese gardens are the accounts given by two British travelers, William Chambers and John Barrow. While Davis stigmatized Chambers's accounts as a "work of imagination," he considered Barrow to be one of the authoritative reporters on Chinese garden design, to the extent that he includes in his own work a lengthy quotation from Barrow's description of Yuanming yuan, published by George Leonard Staunton in 1797.[5] Davis never visited the imperial complex. The Amherst embassy to the Jiaqing emperor (r. 1796–1820), which he joined, was dismissed soon after its arrival in Beijing; Lord Amherst was denied an imperial audience and none of the members of his diplomatic mission were able to see Yuanming yuan.[6] Considering a general description of China incomplete without a comment on the celebrated imperial park, Davis used the descriptions of other travelers to compensate for his lack of personal experience of Yuanming yuan.

* * *

From John Francis Davis, *The Chinese: A General Description of the Empire of China and Its Inhabitants,* vol. 1 (1836)

In describing the dwellings of the Chinese, we may observe that, in their ordinary plan, they bear a curious resemblance to the remains of the Roman habitations disinterred from the scoriae and ashes of Pompeii.[7] They consist usually of a ground-floor, divided into several apartments within the dead wall that fronts the street, and lit only by windows looking into the internal court-yard. The principal room, next to the entrance, serves to receive visitors as well as for eating; and within are the more private apartments, the door-ways of which are screened by pendent curtains of silk or cotton. Near Peking [Bejing], the embassies found most of the apartments furnished with a couch or bed-place of brickwork, having a furnace below to warm it during the winter. This was usually covered with a felt rug or mat which, with the assistance of the warmth, gave perpetual lodging to swarms of vermin, and rendered the bed-places quite unavailable to the English travellers. These flues, however, are very necessary during the severe winters, when the fires in the better houses are lit on the outside; but in poorer ones the furnace is within, and serves the double purpose of cooking and warmth, the whole family huddling round it.

All houses of consequence are entered by a triple gateway, consisting of one large folding-door on the centre, and of a smaller one on either side. These last serve for ordinary occasions, while the first is thrown open for the reception of distinguished guests. Large lanterns of cylindrical shape are hung at the sides, on which are inscribed the name and titles of the inhabitant of the mansion, so as to be read either by day, or at night when the lanterns are lit. Just within the gates is the covered court, where the sedan-chairs stand, surrounded by red varnished label-boards, having inscribed in gilt characters the full titles of any person of rank and consequence. . . .

The magnificence of Chinese mansions is estimated in some measure by the ground which they cover, and by the number and size of the courts and buildings. The real space is often eked out by winding and complicated passages or galleries, decorated with carving and trelliswork in very good taste. The walks are often paved with figured tiles. Large tanks or ponds, with the nelumbium, or sacred lotus, are essential to every country-house, and these pools are generally filled with quantities of the golden carp, and other fish. Masses of artificial rock either rise out of the water, or are strewn about the grounds, in an affected imitation of nature, and on these are often planted their stunted trees. Sir William Chambers's description of Chinese gardening is a mere prose work of imagination, without a shadow of foundation in reality. Their taste is indeed extremely defective and vicious on this particular point, and, as an improvement of nature, ranks much on a par with the cramping of their women's feet.[8] The only exception exists in the gardens, or rather parks, of the Emperor at Yuen-ming-yuen [Yuanming yuan], which Mr. Barrow describes as grand both in plan and extent; but for a subject to imitate these would be almost criminal, even if it were possible. . . .

About eight miles to the north-west of Peking are the gardens, or rather the park, of Yuen-ming-yuen, which Mr. Barrow (who spent his time between that place and Peking) estimates at an extent of twelve square miles. As the face of the country on this side of Peking begins to rise towards the Great Wall, the diversity of hill and dale has afforded some natural facilities for embellishment, which have been improved by art.

According to the description of the forementioned writer, the landscape is diversified with woodlands and lawns, among which are numerous canals, rivulets, and sheets of water, the banks of which have been thrown up in an apparently fortuitous manner in imitation of the free hand of nature. Some parts are cultivated, and others left purposely wild; and wherever pleasure-houses are erected. The views appear to have been studied. It is said that within the enclosure of these gardens there exist no less than thirty distinct places of residence for the Emperor and his numerous suite of ministers, eunuchs, and servants, each constituting a considerable village.

NOTES

1   John Francis Davis, *The Chinese: A General Description of the Empire of China and Its Inhabitants*, 2 vols. (London: Knight, 1836).

2   Davis recounted his experience of China with the diplomatic mission of Lord Amherst in *Sketches of China*, published in two volumes in 1834. For a recent discussion on Davis's *Sketches of China* see Tamara S. Wagner, "Sketching China and the Self-Portrait of a Post-Romantic Traveler: John Francis Davis's Rewriting of China in the 1840s," in *A Century of Travels in China: Critical Essays on Travel Writing from the 1840s to the 1940s*, ed. Douglas Kerr and Julia Kuehn (Hong Kong: Hong Kong University Press, 2007), 13–26.

3   On Davis's life and work and his writings about China, my sources were Wagner, "Sketching China," 13–26; and Kitson, *Forging Romantic China*, 106–25, which discusses the importance of Davis in British sinology and the role of his writings in the British perception of China.

4   Clunas, "Nature and Ideology in Western Descriptions of Chinese Gardens," 26–27. For a discussion on Western accounts of footbinding see Patricia Buckley Ebrey, "Gender and Sinology: Shifting Western Interpretation of Footbinding, 1300–1890," *Late Imperial China* 20/2 (1999): 1–34.

5   Comparing Barrows's account with Chambers's essay on the Chinese garden, Davis affirmed that, "in connexion with drawing and the imitative arts, we may observe that the Chinese style of ornamental gardening, and of laying out pleasure-grounds, has been very much overdrawn by Sir William Chambers, in an essay on that subject, which may be considered quite as a work of imagination in itself. Mr. Barrow, however, who resided for a considerable time at *Yuen-ming-yuen*, 'the garden of perpetual brightness,' which is an extensive pleasure-ground of the emperor, lying north-west of Peking, and greatly exceeding Richmond Park in extent, has given a favourable account of their taste in this department of the arts." Davis, *The Chinese*, vol. 2, 254. Barrow's description, omitted here, is on pages 254–55.

6   The disappointment of the members of Lord Amherst's embassy at having reached, after a long journey through China, the gates of Yuanming yuan without having been able to go through them, was expressed well by the naturalist Clarke

Abel, who in his account of Amherst's diplomatic mission, wrote: "All the descriptions which I had ever read of the paradisiacal delight of Chinese Gardens [Yuanming yuan] occurred to my imagination; but in imagination only was I allowed to enjoy them." Clarke Abel, *Narrative of a Journey in the Interior of China* (London: Longman, Hurst, Rees, Orme, and Brown, 1818), 103.

7　A similar remark is offered by William C. Hunter, who, commenting on the architecture of the private "residences of wealthy Chinese," writes that "the disposition of the rooms reminds one of those of Pompeii, being separated by open courts across which awnings could be drawn, and colonnades." William C. Hunter, *Bits of Old China* (London: Kegan Paul, Trench and Co., 1885), 79.

8　A few years later, the North American traveler Osmond Tiffany, Jr., offered a similar comment on Chinese attitude to nature. Describing the dwarf trees he saw in the *Fa tee* gardens (Huadi, Flower Gardens) in Guangzhou, Tiffany wrote: "The Chinese are so fond of the queer and fantastic as to carry their taste even into nature, and not contented with bringing plants and flowers to the highest state of perfection, they must torture them into singular shapes and dwarf them, as they do the feet of their women." Osmond Tiffany, Jr., *The Canton Chinese; or, The American's Sojourn in the Celestial Empire* (Boston: Munroe and Co., 1849), 161.

CHAPTER 29

Robert Fortune (1813–80)

[handwritten: Compare to Marco Polo...] *[handwritten: plant hunter]*

In the 1840s and 1850s, the Scottish horticulturalist Robert Fortune made several journeys to China, and other parts of Asia, to collect botanical specimens to transplant to Britain.[1] Among the plant hunters sent to China, Fortune was one of the most capable; his research had important repercussions not only on Britain's botanical knowledge but also on the economy of the British Empire. In the course of his explorations, Fortune was able to collect and export to Britain a great variety of plants already known in the West, as well as numerous botanical species that were still unknown. On behalf of the East India Company, Fortune boldly managed to introduce the tea plant from China, whose government prohibited its export, to British India and thus, made possible the creation of tea plantations there.[2] *[handwritten: Tea.]*

Fortune narrated his journeys in a series of lively travel writings that were quite successful. He admitted that they were not intended to be exhaustive texts "upon China." Instead, he meant them to offer the reader a quick glance at the country through his own observations on the places he had visited, events he had seen, people he had met, and the various ways in which he gathered plants.[3]

In the extract presented here, taken from the narrative of his first journey to China, *Three Years' Wanderings in the Northern Provinces of China* (1847), Fortune gives an account of his visit to a small garden at the urban residence of a Mandarin in the coastal city of Ningbo.[4] His description focuses on the devices used to distort the apparent dimension of the garden space: the winding of the paths, the careful arrangement of openings to permit only partial views of the garden, and the judicious placement of plants to conceal the walls enclosing the garden. Fortune's brief description provides evidence of the familiarity that Westerners had, at the time, with Chinese garden design. Indeed, for Fortune, it was not necessary to linger on the details of appearance and the function of the manufactured hills and

Figure 17. John Thomson, *China: A Manchu Bride in Her Wedding Clothes with Her Maid, Beijing*. Photograph, 1869. Wellcome Library, London.

the arrangements of rocks in the garden, which his Western readers knew were among its essential design features; it was enough to report that in the gardens of this specific part of China, artificial rockworks were of a particularly refined quality.

* * *

From Robert Fortune, *Three Years' Wanderings in the Northern Provinces of China* (1847)

Among the Mandarins' gardens in the city of Ning-po [Ningbo], there is one in particular which is generally visited by all strangers, and is much admired. It is situated near the lake in the centre of the city. The old man to whom it belongs has long retired from trade with an independent fortune, and he now enjoys his declining years in the peaceful pursuits of gardening, and is passionately fond of flowers. Both his house and garden are unique in their way, but they are most difficult to describe, and must be seen to be appreciated. In this part of the country the building of artificial rockwork is so well understood, that the resemblance to nature is perfect, and it forms a principal feature in every garden. This old gentleman has the different parts of his house joined together by rude-looking caverns, and what at first sight appears to be a subterraneous passage, leading from room to room, through which the visitor passes to the garden which lies behind the house. The small courts, of which a glimpse is caught in passing through, are fitted up with this rockwork; dwarf trees are planted here and there in various places, and creepers hang down naturally and gracefully until their ends touch the little ponds of water which are always placed in front of the rockwork.

The small places being passed, we are again led through passages like those already noticed, when the garden, with its dwarf trees, vases, rockwork, ornamental windows, and beautiful flowering shrubs, is suddenly opened to the view.

It must be understood, however, that all which I have now described is very limited in extent, but the most is made of it by windings and glimpses through rockwork and arches in the walls, as well as by hiding the boundary with a mass of shrubs and threes.

Here old Dr. Chang—I believe that was his name—was spending the evening of his days in peaceful retirement. . . . The old mandarin now led me round his house, and showed me all the curiosities which it contained, and of which he was a great collector. Old bronzes, carved woods, specimens of porcelain, and other articles of that kind, were arranged with great taste in several of the rooms. From the house we proceeded to the garden, but as it was winter, and the trees were leafless, I could form but little idea of the rarity or beauty of the plants which it contained. I took my leave, after drinking some more tea, promising to visit the old man again whenever I returned to Nig-po.

I visited also at the time several other mandarins who had gardens, and from all of them I received the greatest civility. Some small articles which I

brought out with me as presents were of the greatest use, not only in procuring me a civil reception, but also in enabling me to get plants or cuttings
of rare species which were only found in the gardens of the rich, and which,
of course, were not for sale.

NOTES

1   Fortune traveled to China the first time in 1843–45 for the Horticultural Society
    of London, to explore the areas around the newly established treaty ports. He
    returned to China in 1848–51 on behalf of the East India Company, with the
    specific aim of gathering tea plants, went a third time in 1853–56, and returned
    again in 1858–59, that time for the American government, which was interested
    in introducing the tea plant to the southern states. He stopped in China once
    again on his way to Japan in 1861.
2   My sources were Susan Schoenbauer Thurin, *Victorian Travelers and the Opening
    of China, 1842–1907* (Athens: Ohio University Press, 1999), 27–37; Chang, *Brit-
    ain's Chinese Eye*, 59; and Kilpatrick, *Gifts from the Gardens of China*, 217–51,
    which discusses the role of Robert Fortune as a plant collector and his trips to
    China. On British botanical explorations in China see Fan, *British Naturalists in
    Qing China*.
3   Robert Fortune, *Three Years' Wanderings in the Northern Provinces of China* (Lon-
    don: J. Murray, 1847); *A Journey to the Tea Countries of China* (London: J. Mur-
    ray, 1852); *Two Visits to the Tea Countries of China and the British Tea Plantations
    in the Himalaya* (London: J. Murray, 1853*A Residence Among the Chinese* (Lon-
    don: J. Murray, 1857); *Yedo and Peking: A Narrative of a Journey to the Capitals of
    Japan and China* (London: J. Murray, 1863). In the course of his travels, Fortune
    sent numerous reports that were published in the British horticulture periodical
    The Gardener's Chronicle, which gave great resonance to his botanical missions:
    Robert Fortune, "Leaves from My Chinese Notebook," *Gardener's Chronicle* 1
    (1853): 230–31; "Leaves from My Chinese Notebook," *Gardener's Chronicle* 10
    (1855): 502–3. On Fortune's travel writings and the perception of China they
    conveyed, see Chang, *Britain's Chinese Eye*, 56–68; see also Schoenbauer Thurin,
    Victorian Travelers, 37–53.
4   The extract reproduced here is also included in a later work of Fortune, *Two Visits
    to the Tea Countries of China*, vol. 1, 75–77.

CHAPTER 30

Osmond Tiffany, Jr. (1823–95)

The garden of the wealthy Qing official and merchant Pan Shicheng, known to the Westerners as Pontinqua, was one of the most frequented among the private gardens in Guangzhou that Western travelers were able to enter and visit during the mid-nineteenth century. Located in Lizhi wan (Lychee Bay), in the western part of Guangzhou, and called Haishan xianguan, it was often described in the narratives of their travels to China. Jules Itier (1802–77), who visited the garden in the 1840s, noted the general picturesque effect of the artificial mountains and the large bodies of water that dominated the overall composition.[1] The garden's connected pools, the canals, the islands, and the bridges connecting them produced a design that Laurence Oliphant (1829–88), private secretary to the Earl of Elgin, characterized in 1859 as "the principle of Venice applied to a single residence."[2] In a less poetic tone, the British missionary and Bishop of Victoria (Hong Kong) George Smith (1815–71) focused on the presence of rare animals and plants within the garden's precincts.[3] British lawyer George Wingrove Cooke (1814–65), special correspondent for the *Times* of London during the Second Opium War, who visited the garden in the same years as Oliphant, briskly described it as characterized by "sixty acres of fishponds, pavilions, bridges, and aviaries, with painted barges, pretty flowers, cool stone seats, and every preparation for summer indolence—the whole dominated by a white pagoda, whence you have a complete view."[4] According to Western travelers, Pontinqua's garden offered a "fairly accurate picture of Chinese gardening."[5] It was so renowned that the first guidebook to the most important Chinese and Japanese port cities, published in 1867 and intended for Western visitors and new residents, included it among the most remarkable spots to visit in Guangzhou.[6]

Osmond Tiffany, Jr., son of a Baltimore merchant, gives the most detailed account of a visit to Pontinqua's garden in the narrative of his journey to China, *The Canton Chinese; or, The American's Sojourn in the Celestial Empire* (1849), from which the following extract is taken.[7] Tiffany reached China in 1844 spending several months in Guangzhou and leaving at the beginning of 1845, just before the Chinese New Year. Though Guangzhou was the only city in China that he was able to visit and describe—with the exception of a short trip to the British colony of Hong Kong and Macao—his travelogue soon became an editorial success.

In Pontinqua's garden Tiffany notes the role of water as the central element of the layout, the many bridges as means of communication between the different parts of the green space, and he offers a description of the garden's main building, which "stood in the midst of the water." In the composition of the garden, Tiffany perceives a reflection of the landscape scenes depicted on the shining surfaces of Chinese porcelains and lacquerware, thus proposing them as "faithful" representations of the gardens of China.[8] Appreciating the elaborate and costly refinement of the garden and its ornaments, and noting the complexity of its space, augmented by winding bridges and by an intricate rockwork, Tiffany recognizes the role of the garden as an expression of its owner's social status and refined aesthetic taste.

* * *

From Osmond Tiffany, Jr., *The Canton Chinese; or, The American's Sojourn in the Celestial Empire* (1849)

In a short time we passed the meadows; the grounds on each side were protected by a neat fence, and on the left hand side we saw a flight of stone steps towards which our boat was directed.

This was the entrance to Pontinqua's property, and we were admitted to the garden through a perfectly circular portal. A little lodge stood on one side of the gate occupied by a servant, who bowed obsequiously as we entered.

A curious scene presented itself, the whole garden was irrigated and planted with the Nymphea Nelumbo, (sacred lotus), which grew as pond lilies do, and spread their broad leaves over the surface of the water.

In some seasons this plant is in bloom, and then the gardens look like one flower-bed, and present a beautiful appearance.

Figure 18. Unknown photographer, *Jardin de Pow-[x]ing-kua* (Pontinqua), Canton (now Guangzhou), China. Between 1862 and 1879. Albumen silver print. PH1982:0363:004. Collection Centre Canadien d'Architecture / Canadian Centre for Architecture, Montréal.

The house stood in the midst of the water, and was approached by bridges winding about in various directions, and guarded by balustrades as intricate and fantastic as the ivory carvings. There were bridges beginning every where, and ending in nothing at all; some with covers, some without, some high in the air, and some almost under water. Every thing was queer, different from any thing we had ever before seen, and perfectly Chinese.

We thus learned that the extraordinary representations on porcelain and lac ware were not fictitious creations, but faithful realities.

The bridge shaped like a truncated triangle on Chinese plates we actually saw, one large middle arch and two small ones.

The garden of Pontinqua's is a real curiosity, and he has gone to enormous expense in decorating it.

The house is of two stories; the lower, appropriated to guests, has a large suite of beautiful rooms filled with costly furniture and objects of virtu.

One room was used for visitors of ceremony; there was an enormous chair for the host, and two parallel lines of chairs on either side for his guests. The furniture was the native rosewood, richly carved, and the backs and seats were formed of elegant marbles, or the curious stained stones which represent animals and human figures, each one of which cost no inconsiderable sum.

The rooms were separated from each other by lattice work of the most intricate patterns, or fine silk gauze, or a sort of net-work formed of the fibres of the bamboo, and which is very costly. Another apartment on the outer side was entirely glass, and just opposite to this room, but across the water, at a distance of ten feet, was a covered stage for theatrical representations. Thus the inmates of the house could behold the show through the glass, and were protected in case of cold winds or rainy weather. Behind the stage were several shelves, on which were little clay figures, dressed appropriately, and representing personages and scenes in Chinese life.

There were in and about the house several stone tablets, which bore witness to the friendship which Pontinqua had formed with illustrious persons. There was also an aviary filled with rare birds. The second story was devoted to sleeping apartments, which were all placed, as it were, in the middle of the house, and a gallery surrounded them, lighted by the outer windows.

In this gallery were pictures, arms, several models of foreign ships, and an English steamboat.

Pontinqua's portrait was conspicuous; he was adorned with the peacock's feather, though his worship was drawn without shade or background.

In one part of the grounds was a paddock for deer, in another part an artificial hermitage, with a bench, a pair of sandals, and a staff.

The master had pierced through a mound on his estate for a labyrinth, and the whole place gave evidence that money had been squandered on it in limitless profusion.

It is said that on one occasion, his own marriage or his mother's birthday, that Pontinqua entertained his friends at his villa for three days, in so splendid and costly a manner, that his expenditures amounted to ten thousand dollars a day.

NOTES

1   Jules Alphonse Eugène Itier (1802–77), who in 1843 accompanied the French diplomat Théodose de Lagrené to China to conclude the Treaty of Whampoa

between France and China, made an extensive account of his journey and described Pontinqua's garden as "orné de monticules de terre et de rochers factices d'un effet fort pittoresque, au sommet desquels on parvient par de jolis sentiers tournants; une vaste pièce d'eau, couverte de nélumbium, entoure la maison et communique par plusieurs embranchements à d'autres grands bassins, sur lesquels s'étendent dans tous les sens des ponts légers à doubles arcades et d'élégantes galeries de bois couvertes et disposées en zig-zag, seules voies de communication entre les diverses parties de cette espèce de parc marécageux." (The park is decorated with mounds of earth and artificial rocks of a very picturesque effect, whose summit can be reached by beautiful winding paths; a large body of water, covered with *Nelumbium*, surrounds the house and communicates by means of several branches with other large ponds, on which light bridges with double arches and elegant wooden covered galleries arranged in zig-zag extend in every direction, [being] the only means of communication between the various parts of this rather marshy park.) Jules Itier, *Journal d'un voyage en Chine en 1843, 1845, 1846*, vol. 2 (Paris: Dauvin et Fontaine, 1848), 41.

2   Laurence Oliphant (1829–88), who travelled to China as private secretary to the Earl of Elgin in 1857–59, described the garden as composed "of several acres of water surrounded by a wall, with here and there islands and bridges, and pathways leading to them, paved and covered in with trelliswork, and overrun with creepers, and in the centre of all the mansion of the owner, built on piles in the water, with drawbridges communicating with the bedrooms, and canals instead of passages. It was the principle of Venice applied to a single residence." Laurence Oliphant, *Narrative of the Earl of Elgin's Mission to China and Japan in the Years 1857, '58, '59*, vol. 1 (Edinburgh: Blackwood and Sons 1859), 181.

3   George Smith, *A Narrative of an Exploratory Visit to Each of the Consular Cities of China* (New York: Harper and Brothers, 1857), 103–4: "On entering the gardens, we proceeded to inspect the various attractions, passing over a number of bridges, which intersect in different parts the continuation of small lakes, of which this retreat is principally formed. These were not calculated, in their present shallow, muddy state, to add any beauty to the scene; but later in the year, especially in the month of June, they are well filled with water, and abound with lotuses, forming a beautiful carpet-like expanse of vegetation. In different parts of the grounds were little summer-retreats. . . . Gold and silver pheasants, mandarin-ducks, storks, peacocks, some deer, and other animals of rarity or beauty, were placed in cages along the raised walks, which led around and across the lakes. Beautiful trees, shrubs, and parterres of flowers, added their portion of variety and interest; while, again, lofty platforms, surmounted the roofs of the numerous summer-houses, afforded a prospect into neighboring localities."

4   George Wingrove Cooke, *China: Being "The Times" Special Correspondence from China in the Years 1857–58* (London: Routledge, 1858), 370–71.

5   Auguste Haussmann, *Voyage en Chine, Cochinchine, Inde et Malaisie*, vol 1. (Paris: Dessesart, 1847), 264.

6   Nicholas Belfield Dennys, William Frederick Mayers, Charles King, *The Treaty Ports of China and Japan* (London: Trübner; and Hong Kong: Shortrede, 1867),

147. Though the garden was severely damaged during the Arrow War, it was still described as a large one that "is well worth visiting, and is always accessible to foreigners. It occupies several acres in extent, and combines all those attributes of labyrinthine paths winding over ponds hidden by the spreading leaves of the water-lily, fantastic rock-work, latticed pavilions, and shrubs grotesquely clipped into representations of animal shapes, which constitute the Chinese ideal of horticultural beauty."

7 Osmond Tiffany, Jr., *The Canton Chinese; or, The American's Sojourn in the Celestial Empire* (Boston: Munroe and Co., 1849).

8 Describing the same garden in a letter written from Hong Kong in 1865, the British diplomat Algernon Bertram Freeman-Mitford (1837–1916), who served in the British mission at Beijing between 1865 and 1866, offered the same comparison between the different scenes in the Chinese garden and those painted on patterned porcelain, commenting: "Terraces, summer-houses, stairs, draw-bridges, carp-ponds, rock-work and flowers are thrown together most fantastically, exactly like the gardens that the ladies and gentlemen on tea-cups and plates walk about in. The doors are cut out of the walls in quaint shapes, such as circles, jars, bottles, etc. As the rainy season has set in the garden was not looking its best, but it was very pretty nevertheless, although there was a little too much stagnant water about for our ideas. Lord Bacon in his essay on gardens says: 'For fountains they are a great beauty and refreshment; but pools mar all and make the garden unwholesome, and full of flies and frogs.' If this is true in England, how much more does it apply to the East. Such things as flower-beds are unknown here. The plants grow anyhow, without order or arrangement, but they are carefully tended, and indeed the whole place was beautifully kept, and there seemed to be a large staff of gardeners and carpenters, who play a conspicuous part in a Chinese garden." Algernon Bertram Freeman-Mitford, *The Attaché at Peking* (London: Macmillan, 1900), 30–31. For a recent discussion on Tiffany's description, see Haddad, "Imagined Journeys," 71–72.

CHAPTER 31

Henry Charles Sirr (1807–72)

The British lawyer and diplomat Henry Charles Sirr arrived in Hong Kong in 1844 to assume the post of vice-consul of the British colony. Soon after he moved to Ceylon, where he was appointed the "Queen's advocate for the Southern Circuit," Sirr narrated his short experience of China in *China and the Chinese* (1849), a book published in two volumes that covered, as its title stated, "Religion, Character, Customs, and Manufactures" of the Chinese, describing the main southeastern coastal cities, the so-called treaty ports. The book also provided information on the opium trade as well as on the commercial relations between England and China.[1]

In the first of the following excerpts, taken from his account of China, Sirr briefly describes the garden of the private residence of an opium-addicted mandarin near the city of Xiamen (Amoy), and focuses on the arrangements of ornamental plants, rocks, and water features. In the second extract, Sirr implies that all gardens of wealthy Chinese are comparable, suggesting that they present the same design, offer the same scenes, and are composed of the same elements, which are assembled not for any functional reason but solely to produce an aesthetic effect. Perceiving the Chinese gardens as immutable and monotonous compositions, Sirr compares them to the images on the mass-produced willow pattern plates.[2] A blue-and-white earthenware and porcelain design inspired by Chinese motifs, the willow pattern was created in England around 1790 and gained immediate popularity. Everyday objects printed with its typical design representing a fanciful Chinese landscape, with a willow tree surrounded by pavilions, a bridge, and a zigzagging fence, were widely available throughout the nineteenth century. Sirr used the well-known image of the willow pattern to mock Chinese gardens.[3] His description of a garden scene exhibits both amusement and a sense of Western superiority. Sirr considered the gardens

Figure 19. Anonymous, *Plaat, beschilderd met chinoiseriedecoratie*. Delft, ca. 1670–ca. 1690. Rijksmuseum, Amsterdam, BK-1971-117.

of China aesthetically ambiguous and imbued with a trite theatricality. Regarding garden design, the Chinese seem to him incapable of envisioning a real composition or any sort of harmony or balance; the result is comical, distorted, vulgar, and even repulsive, despite the fact that their gardens are comprised of a rare selection of beautiful plants and animals.

*   *   *

From Henry Charles Sirr, *China and the Chinese*, vol. 1 (1849)

The house of the principal mandarin is situated in the environs of the town on the side of a rocky hill; this officer is, or rather was, peculiarly civil to the English, inviting them to his house, but we regret to add this man was a confirmed *opium* smoker, and addicted to all the vices which disgrace pellucid ?

the devotees of this position. The garden is situated at the back of the house, and is tastefully laid out; magnificent old banyan trees overshadowing the walks, forming a most agreeable and refreshing shelter from the sun's burning rays, whilst gay-coloured flowers of various hues are arranged fantastically in beds, representing grotesque monsters; rugged masses of rock, over which creepers are trained, form cool grottos and retreats; whilst from beneath a grey time-worn rock at the hill's side, gushes forth a stream of delicious, sparkling, pellucid water; more precious than silver or gold, oil or wine, is a stream of pure water in an eastern clime, whereat the weary can slake their thirst, or bath their burning temples.

The houses of the higher classes, who reside in cities, are built within walled enclosures; whilst those who live in the suburbs or country, occupy the centre of their grounds, the gardens of which are laid out in a most grotesque manner. The abode of a mandarin is invariably a collection of buildings of various sizes, which are devoted to several purposes; such as offices for the servants, smoking-rooms, summer-houses, theatre, and the largest is the dwelling-place of the family: the roofs of all these buildings slope outwards and are supported by pillars, the gable ends of the roofs being ornamented with bells, and figures of bamboo and porcelain. . . .

The pleasure-grounds are laid out in the most extraordinary manner, and we know not how better to describe them, than by referring our reader to a common blue dinner plate, the pattern of which is termed by the fair portion of humanity, as being only fit for the kitchen, but which is technically called in the crockery shops "the willow pattern." Bridges are erected, apparently for the mere gratification of ascending on one side to descend on the other; artificial rocks are formed for the express purpose of placing a summer-house on the summit, to which there is no possible means of ascent, unless some beneficent fairy were to furnish the spectator with a pair of wings for the occasion. A lake of some extent serves as a reservoir for gold and silver fish, which multiply rapidly, and grow to a large size. When a lake cannot be formed, then small ponds are made in its stead, in which are placed *jets d'eau*, streams of water issuing from the mouths and persons of imaginary monsters. On the sheet of water, or lake, a small boat will be moored, and numerous aquatic birds will disport on the bosom of the stream, and dabble luxuriously in the miry banks; near which, diminutive grottos, overgrown with creepers, offer cool retreats to porcelain mandarins, gorged with the presumed excesses of the table; their clothing loosened, and pendent bellies, presenting a complete illustration of a Chinaman's ideas of masculine beauty, and luxurious ease.

Being exceedingly fond of birds, an aviary is always to be found in the grounds, frequently filled with rare and curious specimens, totally unknown to European ornithologists, and which, we fear, are likely to remain so, as the Chinese pay large sums for rare birds, and those who have them to sell will not dispose of them to a European, if the bird is a curious or rare specimen. The aviary is usually of gilt lattice-work, with a sloping roof, having bells and ornaments pendent from the corners; whilst artificial trees, and baths for the use of the feathered captives, are to be found within. A covered gallery usually sweeps around the lake and aviary, extending from one angle of the house to the other; and as the Chinese invariably follow in the footsteps of their ancestors, the description of one mandarin's house and grounds will suffice for all, as little or no variation is to be found either in their grounds or dwellings.

Distributed about the garden in pots and beds, are a variety of oaks, bamboos, and fruit trees, all either being dwarfed or distorted, as the wealthy indulge in this strange taste to a most extraordinary extent, having an extreme liking for all stunted productions of vegetation. The flower-beds are so arranged, and the flowers so disposed, as to produce various and grotesque patterns; and these *floral* pictures are most pleasing to our eye, from the novelty of the devices, brilliancy and variety of the colours.

We believe that we have elsewhere remarked upon the passion which the Chinese evince for the chrysanthemum, this flower being cultivated to an extent, in every garden, that would appear incredible to those who had not witnessed, the affectionate fondness which a Chinaman bears to this flower. Amongst the flower-beds, porcelain monsters, in ludicrous attitudes, attract the attention; occasionally the positions of these earthenware monstrosities, although natural, are offensive to delicacy.

We regret to be compelled to add, that to most residences, are attached subterranean apartments devoted to the opium pipe and gambling. A kitchen garden, for the culture of vegetables and pot-herbs, with an orchard well stocked with fruit trees, are always to be found appertaining to the residence of a wealthy Chinaman, as their passion for vegetables, herbs, and fruit, nearly equals their fondness for the chrysanthemum.

NOTES

1   Henry Charles Sirr, *China and the Chinese: Their Religion, Character, Customs, and Manufactures*, 2 vols. (London: Orr and Co., 1849).

2 On the comparison between the Chinese garden and images on porcelain that Western travelers made in their accounts see Haddad, "Imagined Journeys," 69–73. The American poet and writer Bayard Taylor (1825–78), who accompanied the expedition of Commodore Matthew Calbraith Perry to Japan in 1853, also made reference to the scenes depicted on the blue-and-white Liverpool porcelain in his ironic description of the "Tea Garden" he visited in Shanghai in the early 1850s. The garden, Taylor wrote, was dominated by a building "of two stories, with the peaked, curved, overhanging roofs, which we always associate with Chinese architecture. It is reached by bridges which cross the water in curious zigzag lines, so that you walk more than double the actual distance. On the opposite side are several similar buildings, surrounded by masses of artificial rock-work, but the only token of a garden is a pair of magnolia trees, clothed in the glory of their fragrant, snowy blossoms. Every body remembers the old-fashioned plates of blue Liverpool ware, with a representation of two Chinese houses, a willow tree, a bridge with three Chinamen walking over it, and two crows in the air. These plates give a very good representation of the Tea Garden, which is a fair sample of what is most picturesque in Chinese life." Bayard Taylor, *A Visit to India, China, and Japan in the Year 1853* (New York: Putnam, 1855), 330. Partially quoted in Haddad, "Imagined Journeys," 72. Describing the same garden in Shanghai that he visited in 1857, the British correspondent for the *Times*, George Wingrove Cooke, compared its appearance to the willow pattern plate: "It is an irregular figure . . . traversed in all directions by broad canals of stagnant water, all grown over with green, and crossed by zigzag wooden bridges, of the willow-pattern plate model. . . . Where water is not, there are lumps of artificial rockwork, and large pavilion-shaped tea rooms." George Wingrove Cooke, *China*, 223.

3 On the role of the willow pattern plate, and, more generally, of blue-and-white china in eighteenth-century British satire of China, see Chang, *Britain's Chinese Eye*, 71–97.

refs sometimes cross-compare to complementary or opposing sources..

Asters + chrysanthemums

Tea again

CHAPTER 32

Robert Fortune (1813–80)

In 1852, Fortune was engaged a second time by the East India Company to explore the tea districts of China and gather tea plant varieties for the plantations of British India.[1] Fortune reached China in 1853 and remained there until 1856. It was his third botanical expedition to the Celestial Empire. The two extracts that follow are taken from Fortune's account of that journey, entitled *A Residence Among the Chinese* (1857).[2]

In the first passage, Fortune describes the garden of an urban residence in the city of Cixi, near the treaty port of Ningbo. His attentive botanist's eye could not help but appreciate the garden through the selection of ornamental plants arranged there. Fortune had to admit his pleasure in contemplating the garden botanical scene, despite his "English prejudice" against China and Chinese culture and, by extension, Chinese garden design, of which he was very well aware.[3]

The second extract is the description of one of the gardens of the Wu family, whose most prominent member was Wu Bingjian (1769–1843), the most senior of the hong merchants in Guangzhou, known among Europeans as Howqua. The garden was probably a popular destination among Western travelers and local residents. Fortune's witty descriptions of the notices listing rules for visitor behavior, written in tones of "true Chinese politeness," and scattered through the garden testify to its accessibility. The account concludes with Fortune's comments on the different spatial organizations of Western and Chinese gardens. He invites his readers to forget the "fine lawns, broad walks, and extensive views"—images evoking the typical features of the English landscape garden—while envisioning Chinese gardens, whose space is fragmented in individual parts and a multitude of elements; where everything is "on a small scale" and the visitor's spatial perception is continually being deceived. Fortune, who never visited the vast imperial parks, presents the Chinese garden as an

| 270 |

Figure 20. Charles Thomas Dixon, after Thomas Allom, *The Fountain Court in Conseequa's House, Canton.* In Thomas Allom, *China in a Series of Views,* vol. 2 (London: Peter Jackson, Late Fisher, Son, and Co.,1843), p. 52. © Dumbarton Oaks Research Library and Collection, Rare Book Collection, Washington, D.C.

autonomous typology, distant from the then dominant aesthetic canons of Western garden design.

* * *

From Robert Fortune, *A Residence Among the Chinese* (1857)

THE HOUSE AND GARDEN OF A COLLECTOR
OF ANCIENT WORKS OF ART

I found him the owner and occupant of a large house in the centre of the city, and apparently a man of considerable wealth. He received me with the greatest cordiality, and led me in the usual way to the seat of honour at the end of the reception-hall. His house was furnished and ornamented with great taste. In front of the room in which I had been received was a little garden containing a number of choice plants in pots, such as azaleas, camellias, and dwarfed trees of various kinds. The ground was paved with sandstone and granite, and, while some of the pots were placed on the floor, others were standing on stone tables. Small borders fenced with the same kinds of stone were filled with soil, in which were growing creepers of various kinds which covered the walls. Here were the favoured *Glycine sinensis,* roses, jasmines, etc., which not only scrambled over the walls, but were led inward and formed arbours to afford shade from the rays of the noonday sun. In front of these were such things as Moutans,[4] *Nandina* (sacred bamboo of the Chinese), *Weigela rosea, Forsythia viridissima,* and *Spiraea Reevesiana.* In opposite corners stood two noble trees of *Olea fragrans,* the celebrated "Kwei-hwa," [*gui hua*][5] whose flowers are often used in scenting tea; while many parts of the little border were carpeted with the pretty little *Lycopodium coesium,* which I introduced to England some years ago. This pretty fairy-like scene was exposed to our view as we sat sipping our tea, and with all my English prejudice I could not but acknowledge that it was exceedingly enjoyable.

HOWQUA'S GARDEN

The foreign merchants in China as a class are upright and honourable men, and quite incapable of lending themselves to frauds of this description. Besides, every house of any standing has a "tea-taster" who has a perfect knowledge of his business, and who can not only tell true tea from false, but, in most instances, can tell the identical district in which the sample presented to him has been produced.

As it seems only a step or two from the well-known "Howqua's Mixture"[6] to the less known Howqua's Garden, I now ask the reader to visit that with me before we leave Canton [Guangzhou]. This garden is situated near the well-known Fa-tee nurseries, a few miles above the city of Canton, and is a place of favourite resort both for Chinese and foreigners who reside in the neighbourhood, or who visit this part of the Celestial Empire.[7] I determined on paying it a visit in company with Mr. M'Donald, who is well known in this part of the world as an excellent Chinese scholar, and to whom I am indebted for some translations of Chinese notices, which appeared very amusing to us at the time, and which, I dare say, will amuse my readers.

Having reached the door of the garden, we presented the card with which we were provided, and were immediately admitted. The view from the entrance is rather pleasing, and particularly striking to a stranger who sees it for the first time. Looking "right ahead," as sailors say, there is a long and narrow paved walk lined on each side with plants in pots. This view is broken, and apparently lengthened, by means of an octagon arch which is thrown across, and beyond that a kind of alcove covers the pathway. Running parallel with the walk, and on each side behind the plants, are low walls of ornamental brickwork, latticed so that the ponds or small lakes which are on each side can be seen. Altogether the octagon arch, the alcove, the pretty ornamental flower-pots, and the water on each side, has a striking effect, and is thoroughly Chinese.

The plants consist of good specimens of southern Chinese things, all well known in England, such, for example, as *Cymbidium sinense, Olea fragrans,* oranges, roses, camellias, magnolias, etc., and, of course, a multitude of dwarf trees, without which no Chinese garden would be considered complete.

In the alcove alluded to there are some nice stone seats, which look cool in a climate like that of southern China. The floor of this building is raised a few feet above the ground-level, so that the visitor gets a good view of the water and other objects of interest in the garden. That this is a favourite lounge and smoking-place with the Chinese, the following Chinese notice, which we found on one of the pillars, will testify:—"*A careful and earnest notice:* This garden earnestly requests that visitors will spit betle[8] outside the railing, and knock the ashes of pipes also outside." Several fine fruit-trees and others are growing near the walks, and afford shade from the rays of the sun. On one of these we read the following:—"Ramblers here *will be excused* plucking the fruit on this tree." How exceedingly polite!

Near the centre of the garden stands a substantial summer-house, or hall, named "the Hall of Fragrant Plants." The same notice to smokers and chewers of betle-nut is also put up here; and there is another and a longer one which I must not forget to quote. It is this:—"In this garden the plants are intended to delight the eyes of all visitors: a great deal has been expended in planting and in keeping in order, and the garden is now beginning to yield some return. Those who come here to saunter about are earnestly prayed not to pluck the fruit or flowers, in order that the beauty of the place may be preserved." And then follows a piece of true Chinese politeness—"We beg persons who understand this notice to excuse it!"

Passing through the Hall of Fragrant Plants we approached, between two
rows of Olea fragrans, a fine ornamental suite of rooms tastefully furnished
and decorated, in which visitors are received and entertained. An inscription informs us that this is called "the Fragrant Hall of the Woo-che tree."
Leaving this place by a narrow door, we observed the following notice—
"Saunterers here will be excused entering." This apparently leads to the
private apartments of the family. In this side of the garden there is some
fine artificial rockwork, which the Chinese know well how to construct,
and various summer-houses tastefully decorated, one of which is called the
"Library of Verdant Purity." Between this part of the garden and the
straight walk already noticed there is a small pond or lake for fish and
water-lilies. This is crossed by a zigzag wooden bridge of many arches,
which looked rather dilapidated. A very necessary notice was put up here
informing "saunterers to stop their steps in case of accident."

On the outskirts of the garden we observed the potting sheds, a nursery
for rearing young plants and seeds, and the kitchen garden. Here a natural
curiosity was pointed out by one of the Chinese, which, at first sight,
appeared singularly curious. Three trees were growing in a row, and at
about twenty or thirty feet from the ground the two outer ones had sent
out shoots, and fairly united themselves with the centre one. When I mention that the outer trees are the Chinese banyan (Ficus nitida), it will readily
be seen how the appearance they presented was produced. The long roots
sent down by this species had lovingly embraced the centre tree, and
appeared at first sight to have really grafted themselves upon it.

I am afraid I have given a very imperfect description of this curious
garden. Those who know what a Chinese garden is will understand me well
enough, but it is really difficult to give a stranger an idea of the Chinese
style which I have been endeavouring to describe. In order to understand
the Chinese style of gardening it is necessary to dispel from the mind all
ideas of fine lawns, broad walks, and extensive views; and to picture in their
stead everything on a small scale—that is, narrow paved walks, dwarf walls
in all directions, with lattice-work or ornamental openings in them, in
order to give views of the scenery beyond; halls, summer-houses, and
alcoves, ponds or small lakes with zigzag walks over them—in short, an
endeavour to make small things appear large, and large things small, and
everything Chinese. There are some of these ornaments, however, which I
think might be imitated with advantage in our own gardens. Some of the
doorways and openings in walls seemed extremely pretty. In particular I

may notice a wall about ten feet high, having a number of open compartments filled with porcelain rods made to imitate the stems of the bamboo. I shall now close this notice with the modest lines of the Chinese poet, which we found written in the "Library of Verdant Purity," and which seemed to be an effort to describe the nature of the garden:—

> *Some few stems of bamboo-plants*
> *A cottage growing round;*
> *A few flowers here—some old trees there,*
> *And a mow⁹ of garden ground.*

NOTES

1   The East India Company had engaged Fortune a first time in 1848–52 "for the purpose of obtaining the finest variety of the Tea-plant, as well as native manufacturers and implements, for the Government Tea plantations in the Himalayas," as Fortune himself affirmed. Robert Fortune, *A Journey to the Tea Countries of China* (London: J. Murray, 1852), v.

2   Robert Fortune, *A Residence Among the Chinese* (London: J. Murray, 1857). Fortune reported that the aim of his mission was that of "adding to the collections already formed, and particularly for procuring some first-rate black-tea makers for the experimental tea-farms in India." Fortune, *A Residence*, v.

3   In his writings Fortune often devalued the arrangement of Chinese gardens in comparison to British gardens. See, for instance, Fortune, *Journey to the Tea Countries*, 79.

4   Tree peony (*Paeonia suffruticosa* Andr.) whose Chinese name is *mu dan*. Fèvre and Métailié, *Dictionnaire Ricci*, 330.

5   In the Chinese materia medica, the name *gui hua* indicates the flowers of the sweet olive (*Osmanthus fragrans* Lour.). Fèvre and Métailié, *Dictionnaire Ricci*, 157 and 329.

6   Fortune refers to the tea sold in mid-nineteenth century Britain as "Howqua's mixture," its name deriving from the famous hong merchant Howqua.

7   For Fortune's description of the group of nurseries named Fa-tee, "Flowers Gardens," in the outskirts of Guangzhou, see Robert Fortune, *Three Years' Wanderings in the Northern Provinces of China* (London: J. Murray, 1847), 141–45. On the Fa-tee nurseries, see Hazel Le Rougetel, "The Fa Tee Nurseries of South China," *Garden History* 10, no. 1 (1982): 70–73.

8   Note by Fortune about his text: "Betle-Nut [betel nut] is much used by the southern Chinese."

9   Note by Fortune about his text: "A mow is about the sixth part of an acre."

CHAPTER 33

Charles Taylor (1819–97)

American Methodists established their missions in China in the 1840s. After the separation of the northern and southern branches of the Methodist Episcopal Church in 1844, the Reverend Charles Taylor was entrusted with the task of founding the mission of the Methodist Episcopal Church, South, in China in 1847. He left Boston in April 1848 and reached Hong Kong in August of the same year, remaining in southern China for five years. After returning to the United States, he recorded his experiences in an elaborate travelogue entitled *Five Years in China* (1860), in which his descriptions of the places he had visited are interspersed with his observations on Chinese culture and customs.[1]

Having arrived in China a few years after the opening of the treaty ports, Taylor enjoyed greater freedom of movement than his predecessors, and he visited several cities on the southeastern coast. He gave an extended account of the city of Suzhou, the lively atmosphere of its canals lined with shops and shoppers, and its temples. However, he did not have much to say about the numerous gardens dotting the city, which were to be described by Western travelers only in the century to follow. The only garden in Suzhou that Taylor commented on briefly was Shizi lin (Lion Grove), about which he wrote: "It is a garden, containing a few trees, a small temple, a pool crossed in several places by bridges, and huge piles of artificial rock-work, threaded in every possible direction by the most intricate and puzzling paths, which led you winding about among grottoes and caverns, and formed a perfect labyrinth."[2]

The sole detailed narration of a green space in Taylor's writing is that of one of the gardens belonging to the hong merchant Howqua, in Guangzhou. Taylor's account, presented in the following extract, is organized around the main compositional elements of a Chinese garden: rocks, water, architecture, and vegetation. Taylor dedicates particular attention to the

Figure 21. Unknown photographer, *Jardin de Lee-ming*, Canton (now Guangzhou), China. Between 1862 and 1879. Albumen silver print. PH1982:0363:006. Collection Centre Canadien d'Architecture / Canadian Centre for Architecture, Montréal.

many ornamental species and to the potted plants placed throughout the garden; he focuses on the water lilies covering the surface of ponds, on the peonies, and, particularly, on the curiously shaped dwarf trees, which the missionary sees as proof of the Chinese ability to force the growth of trees and shrubs for decorative purposes. Taylor's insistence on the botanical character of Chinese gardens reflects the shift in Western interest in the gardens of China, increasingly focused on their botanical quality rather than on their design, a shift that was anticipated by James Main.[3] His viewpoint is also indicative of the growing Western scientific research about China's natural history that occurred in the mid-nineteenth century and resulted in an escalation of expeditions by European and American naturalists to study the flora and fauna of the Far East.

* * *

From Charles Taylor, *Five Years in China* (1860)

One afternoon we accompanied some friends in a boat, to visit the gardens of Howqua, one of the old "Hong merchants," or Chinese merchant-princes, who had made an immense fortune in the tea-trade with foreigners. They are two or three miles up the river, on the bank on which they stand, surrounded by a high wall, having a massive gate-way, which you enter by a flight of stone steps leading from the water's edge. The prominent features of these, and all other Chinese ornamental gardens, besides their flowers and shrubbery, are rocks, bridges, pools, and pavilions or arbors. The rocks are piled up and cemented together with a kind of plaster, which becomes, in a little time, as hard as the rock itself.

Sometimes these piles of artificial rock-work are twenty feet high—not always solid masses, but oftener so built up as to form arches and crevices, caverns and grottoes, nooks and corners, of every shape that can be thought of—the more odd and strange, the more beautiful in native estimation. Then these rocks have paths winding about in all directions, inside and out, up flights of steps and down, often forming an intricate labyrinth. Another feature in these gardens consists in the artificial ponds or pools of water. They generally fill up so much of the space, that the rocks seem rather like islands rising out of them. Then these pools are crossed in various directions by bridges, some straight, and others running as zigzag as if they had been modelled after a streak of lightning. They are built of well-hewn stone, for the most part, and are from three to five feet high above the water, supported by stone posts or pillars, and provided with curiously-wrought balustrades. Sometimes they are built high enough to admit of a beautiful arch for a support. China abounds in these finely-arched bridges, crossing the numerous canals and rivers, throughout the whole country. Then there are arbors or summer-houses, of various fanciful shapes, from square to five, six, or eight sided, built out in the water, with merely a column at each corner, to support a curiously-constructed roof, which runs up in the centre to a point like a steeple. Often, too, these pavilions are built on the tops of the artificial rocky eminences. In private gardens, and in some public ones also, these little buildings have tables and benches, where friends and visitors resort to sit and smoke, drink tea, and chat. There are temples also, sad to say, with richly-carved and gilded wooden idols in them.

Many of the flowers and shrubs are very beautiful. They are placed about in different parts of the garden, in odd-looking, yet handsome and costly flower-pots, and on stands and tables in the summerhouses and temples. There are great numbers of tea-shops in the public gardens, where hundreds of people daily congregate, to drink tea; smoke, and talk. The great fondness of the Chinese for flowers is proverbial. They have numerous different kinds, and many of them are exceedingly beautiful and fragrant. Here are many varieties of roses, lilies, violets, hollyhocks, sweet-williams, pinks, tuberoses, verbenas, peonies, bachelor's buttons, heliotropes, hibiscus, honey-suckles, geraniums, myrtles, cape-jessamines, hydrangeas, artemisias, coxcombs, chrysanthemums, iris, azaleas, magnolias, lagerstrœmias, altheas, convolvulus, japonicas, and many others. The splendid white lotus or water-lily, is seen resting on the surface of the pools, with its leaves often as large as a parasol. Its root is a favorite article of food, being both palatable and nutritious. There is a magnificent variety of the peony, called the *mau-tan* [*mu dan*], unknown in America.

Besides flowers, there is a great variety of evergreen shrubbery, such as the box, the arbor-vitæ, the cypress, cedar, and the pine.[4] These are highly prized by the Chinese, and they force them to grow into many odd shapes by confining some of the branches with strings, and bending others, so as to make them grow in any direction they wish. Here are figures of birds and animals growing in this way. A deer with horns, or a long-necked crane, standing on one foot while the other is lifted up, and all growing fresh and green out of a flower-pot, is a very singular sight. You will sometimes see one of these miniature trees that has been trained to resemble a pagoda of several stories in height. These Celestials [the Chinese] have a strange passion for dwarfing and distorting all those varieties of shrubbery that will admit of the process.

NOTES

1   Charles Taylor, *Five Years in China, with Some Account of the Great Rebellion, and a Description of St. Helena* (New York: Derby and Jackson, 1860).

2   Taylor, *Five Years in China*, 268.

3   Later travelers describing Chinese gardens focused on their botanical character. In his account of the garden of the private residence of a hong merchant in Guangzhou, the American merchant William C. Hunter, who lived in Guangzhou in 1829–42 and later in Macao, emphasized the ornamental plants arranged there, as well as the presence of live animals in the garden: "Many fine old trees were scattered about, as were varieties of fruit and flowers, such as the mandarin and cooly orange, the lychee and others unknown in Europe, as the kumquat, wampee, lung-gan [longan], and the singular flat peach. Amongst the flowers

were the white, red, and variegated camellia, the chrysanthemum, mourning bell, aster chinensis, and carnation. Differently from the western world, flowers are here cultivated in pots, these being tastefully arranged on circular shelves of a pyramidal form. The gravel-paved walks, the rough stone grottoes surmounted by small pavilions, the granite bridges across small lakes or running waters, the deer, peacock, storks, and the mandarin duck with its beautiful plumage, formed additional attractions." Hunter, *Bits of Old China*, 79.

4   With "arbor-vitæ" Taylor refers to the evergreen coniferous tree known as Chinese arborvitae, or Oriental arborvitae, or Oriental thuja. Its binomial name is *Platycladus orientalis* (L.) Franco.

CHAPTER 34

Robert Swinhoe (1836–77)

The history of the imperial park of Yuanming yuan is tragically linked to the commercial disputes that brought Qing China into conflict with the West during the mid-nineteenth century. The rapacity of Western imperialism toward China entailed the progressive acquisition of commercial bases through the use of military force. Under the terms of the 1842 Treaty of Nanjing, at the end of the First Opium War (1839–42), China opened five cities on the southeastern coast to Western trade. Greater privileges and trading rights followed with the Treaty of Tianjin, concluded in 1858, during the Second Opium War (1856–60), a conflict provoked by the Western nations' more pressing requests for trading privileges.[1] The imperial court's unwillingness to ratify the treaty had a drastic consequence: on October 7–8, 1860, Yuanming yuan was sacked, and, on October 18–19, it was set on fire by a joint French-British military mission led by Lord Elgin, the British high commissioner and plenipotentiary in China, and the French ambassador, the Baron Jean-Baptiste-Louis Gros. The destruction of Yuanming yuan and the damaging of other neighboring imperial parks was part of the strategy to end China's reluctance to sign the trade agreements; it was also a reaction to the imprisonment and torture by Qing officials of a group of Western diplomats and soldiers, and the murder of some of them. The imperial court's response was immediate: with the Convention of Peking, signed in 1860, China consented to the ratification of the Treaty of Tianjin, as well as to further economic and territorial concessions.[2]

Numerous firsthand narratives of the military expedition and the destruction of Yuanming yuan were published at that time.[3] In his account of the Arrow War, entitled *Narrative of the North China Campaign of 1860* (1861), the British naturalist, diplomat, and traveler Robert Swinhoe, who served as staff interpreter to the British delegation during that military campaign, included a description of the imperial parks in suburban Beijing, detailing the looting and plundering that took place at Yuanming yuan during October 1860.[4] Swinhoe stayed in China from 1854 to 1875. During his long residence as a British consular officer, first in Formosa (Taiwan), then in the treaty ports of Amoy and Ningbo and later in Yantay, he conducted research about Chinese natural history and, particularly, on birds and mammals of Eastern China, exploring regions that had previously been unreachable by Western naturalists. He published widely on the topics of Chinese flora and fauna and was a correspondent of Charles Darwin, to whom he sent specimens and information.[5]

The two extracts presented here are taken from Swinhoe's narrative of the 1860 military campaign. The first passage is a description of Yuanming yuan. The account is organized as an itinerary through the park and the buildings and pavilions left empty by Xianfeng (r. 1850–61), the Qing dynasty ninth emperor, and his family, who had fled Beijing to withdraw to his imperial residence in Chengde. The narrative's tone is reminiscent of both the language and approach used by eighteenth-century travelers to describe the gardens of China.[6] Swinhoe emphasizes the picturesque quality of Yuanming yuan, implicitly suggesting affinities with the landscape parks in England.[7] He presents its variety and design as reminiscent of Chinese landscape paintings, which contribute to making the park aesthetically pleasing but also difficult to describe. Swinhoe also recognizes the semiotic structure of the imperial complex, which incorporated strategies of political, economic, and cultural representation—a variety of symbolic meanings that Lord Elgin was well aware of when he decided to destroy the imperial complex.[8]

In the second extract, Swinhoe offers a detailed account of his route from Yuanming yuan to the neighboring imperial parks before they were looted and severely damaged by the Western troops: Qingyi yuan (Garden of Clear Ripples), which Swinhoe calls "Wan-show-yuen" from the name of its main section, the impressive artificial mountain Wanshou shan (Longevity Hill); the complex of Jingming yuan (Garden of Tranquil Brightness), on Jade Spring Hill; and Xiangshan (Fragrant Hill) on the Western Hills.

The devastation of Yuanming yuan was a cynical political move to strike at one of the Chinese empire's most powerful symbols of cultural and political identity, and it was much discussed at the time.[9] The Chinese and also some Western intellectuals saw it as a barbaric act that drew

Figure 22. John Thomson, *The Bronze Temple, Yuen-Ming-Yuen (Old Imperial Summer Palace), at Wan-Show-Shan, Peking, Pechili Province, China.* Photograph, 1874. In John Thomson, *Illustrations of China and Its People*, vol. 9 (London: Low, Marston, Low and Searle, 1873–74), pl. 19, figure 48. Wellcome Library, London.

widespread condemnation, particularly in France. In a letter written in 1861, an indignant Victor Hugo fiercely condemned it as a criminal act of cultural vandalism.[10] Swinhoe, however, justified it as a necessary measure to punish China for the brutal treatment of the Western prisoners taken by Qing officials.

* * *

From Robert Swinhoe, *Narrative of the North China
Campaign of 1860* (1861)

A paved roadway leaves the Palace inside Pekin [Beijing], and emerging
at the Se-che [Xizhi] gate on the west side continues with a few windings
in the direction of a group of villages of different names collectively called
Hai-teen [Haidian]. The stone way runs through this group of ugly hovels
on to a broad road with the pavement through its centre. Stone garden
walls stand to the right and left as you advance, enclosing the grounds of
nobles and imperial connections. You advance, *suivant le pavé*, across a
stone bridge, take a sweep to the left, and the road brings you between two
large pieces of water in front of the grand entrance to the Palace of Yuen-
ming-yuen [Yuanming yuan]. . . .

On the centre of the pavement, and facing the gate, stood the grand
reception hall, a large Chinese building, well adorned exteriorly with paint
and gilding, and netted with iron wire under the fretted eaves to keep the
birds off. We entered its central door, and found ourselves on a smooth
marble floor, in front of the Emperor's ebony throne. The carvings on the
throne consisted of dragons in various attitudes, and was quite a work of
art; but the material, on closer examination, proved to be some inferior
wood painted to imitate ebony. The floor of the throne was carpeted with
a light red cloth, and three low series of steps led up to it, of which the
central series was the widest and intended for kow-towing on before the
Emperor. The left side of the room was covered with one extensive picture,
representing the grounds of the Summer Palace. Side-tables were covered
with books in yellow silk binding and articles of virtu. There was somehow
an air of reverence throughout this simple but neat hall, and we could well
imagine the awe that it was calculated to inspire on the chosen few who
were privileged to draw near on ceremonial days, and render their obeisance before the much-dreaded Brother of the Sun and Moon. . . .

Behind the grand hall was rockery, and in rear of that again a large pond,
so that a pebbled path leading over a bridge and taking a semicircular sweep
of half the water, had to be traversed before you visited the next hall. The
distance was about 500 yards. This hall was smaller, and not got up with
such care: yellow sedan chairs and one mountain chair stood close to the

throne; on the right and left were small rooms adjoining, with images of Bhuddha [sic]. Behind stood another reception hall, and in rear of that again a third; and on the left the Emperor's private rooms, beautifully got up, the tables spread with all manner of precious articles, many of which were English or French. The house was small, and consisted chiefly of one moderately sized room, with a large double-seated throne, covered with gaudily coloured cloth, and having red drapery in rear, which formed a curtain to a waiting recess. . . .

The *Moniteur* correspondent, myself, and the eunuch, continued our rambles through the palaces.[11] On the extreme left were the Empress's two rooms and several smaller ones for the sundry wives, but none of them in style at all approaching those of the Emperor's. Several baskets of fruit and sweetmeats lay on the Empress's table, showing that her departure was of no long date. On the right of the grand hall were houses after houses well stored with silks, curios, and luxuries of all kinds, such as birdsnests, tea, tobacco, dried fruits, &c. Then followed the houses of the retainers. Narrow painted galleries connected all the imperial rooms "in endless maze intricate, perplexed."

Behind the chief building came the summer park, the extent of wall surrounding the whole being about twelve miles. Pebbled paths led you through groves of magnificent trees, round lakes, into picturesque summer-houses, over fantastic bridges. As you wandered along herds of deer would amble away from before you, tossing their antlered heads. Here a solitary building would rise fairy-like from the centre of a lake, reflecting its image on the limpid blue liquid in which it seemed to float, and then a sloping path would carry you into the heart of a mysterious cavern artificially formed of rockery, and leading out on to a grotto in the bosom of another lake. The variety of the picturesque was endless, and charming in the extreme; indeed, all that is most lovely in Chinese scenery, where art contrives to cheat the rude attempts of nature into the bewitching, seemed all associated in these delightful grounds. The resources of the designer appear to have been unending, and no money spared to bring his work to perfection. All the tasteful landscapes so often viewed in the better class of Chinese paintings, and which we had hitherto looked upon as wrought out of the imagination of the artist, were here bodied forth in life. I will not, however, venture on too minute a description, as it would doubtless prove tedious to the reader. Such spots can be better imagined than described.

Just within the walls that encircled the grounds on the right and left were large handsome llama temples with yellow tiled roofs.

A paved road leading from the left wall of the Summer Park passes close under the wall of another enclosed park, named the Wan-show-yuen, or Birthday Garden [Wanshou shan, "Longevity Hill"]. This consisted of a pleasantly wooded hill, not many acres in extent, and covered with magnificent temples, comprising the shrines of the three recognized superstitions of China, viz., the Confucian, the Taouist [Daoist], and Bhuddhist, with a few yellow-tiled halls, dedicated to the Llamas of Thibet. The temples and minarets in this ground were in excellent repair, and many of them were fine specimens of art, got up with much taste, and decorated with colours of gaudy hue. Within these temples the celestial monarchs were wont to sacrifice and pay their homage to the multitudinous deities and sages that the different sects of Chinese religionists suppose to overrule the destinies of man, on the occasion of each birthday of the "Monarch of Endless Years," as the ruling majesty of China is designated. A view from the hill-top in this garden of its palatial temples and the country around was most perfect; you looked down on a series of quaintly picturesque buildings, grouped together with much taste; and beyond the wall, toward the south-west, a large lake, with a temple standing on its bosom, connected with the shore by a marble bridge of arches; the flat champaign stretched away south, speckled with groups of trees and villages; a tier of hills shut in the prospect on the right, and Pekin's turrets loomed in the distance.

Continuing along the paved road, destined alone for the Emperor's use, but now blocked up at intervals with sand and stone barriers to keep passenger carts from availing themselves of it, you pass through the village of Tsing-lung-cheaow, so called from the short stone bridge it leads out on, which crosses a stream that connects the artificial waters of the park with a branch of the Peiho [Baihe, White River]. The bridge past the pavement winds to the left, and finishes its graceful curve round the walls of the next garden—the Chin-ming-yuen, or Gold and Brilliant Garden [Jingming yuan, "Garden of Tranquil Brightness"]. In this are two hills enclosed by a wall, the southernmost hill being surmounted by a tall stone monument; ascended internally by a winding staircase, with loopholes in each story, admitting light on small groups of josses arranged in niches inside. This column was named the Ya-tsing Pagoda, and, from its height, could be seen at a great distance, thus affording an excellent landmark. Its destruction would, consequently, have been more noticeable, but the General was struck with its simple beauty, and spared it as a work of art. The northernmost hill was crowned with a one-spired llama temple, approached by tunnels bored through the living rock, whose sides within were carved into fantastic bas-relief images and representations of Bhuddha. The temple, however, was neglected, and in ruins. The grand entrance to these gardens was by the south side, where the road widened into an outer courtyard. There were several reception halls, with thrones, within its precincts, a small lake, with a bath-house, and handsomely painted punts, tasty little minarets, triumphal arches, and some fine temples; but the whole bore the stamp of neglect, and most of the rooms appeared to have been used merely as store rooms for the reception of cast-away finery and old documents. The visits of the Emperor hitherwards must have been few and far between. It seems to have been the custom with the Chinese throughout their parks only to keep those parts in order which the imperial eyes were likely to behold. Elsewhere, bridges and other works, which cost much labour to construct, were allowed to drop to decay; and the watercourses supplying artificial basins were left choked up with dirt, and what should be a handsome piece of water to be converted into a spring was covered with rushes and dank weeds. On the west of the garden hill stood a stately yellow-tiled llama temple, with magnificent images of a towering size. In the back rooms of this temple were discovered several large chests, containing quantities of valuable old books and pictures. From the hills of this garden we could see, about three miles off on the side of the tier of hills, another collection of magnificent houses embosomed in trees, and girt round by a serpentine wall, which ran up the face of the hills, took a circuit over their tops, and again descended to the plain. This was called the Heangshan [Xiangshan], or Fragrant Hills, and formed the fourth and last park of the Emperor.[12]

The stone way led to its gate, but several large and uniformly built villages, tenanted by the families of the Mantchoo [Manchu] soldiers who ranged under the eight banners of the imperial army, had to be passed along the hard, even, sandy road, before you arrived at its walls. Close to the villages was the Mantchoo parade-ground, a walled-in space of land, about two acres in extent, where the bannermen practised archery, and went through their military evolutions. The inhabitants of these barracks were much alarmed, thinking their turn might come next, and consequently showed every eagerness to conciliate us. Women and boys stood at the doors of their houses with teapots and cups, tempting the troops to refresh themselves, while others dealt round trays of cakes. The arrangement of these Heangshan pleasure grounds was even more complete than that of the three before visited. The flights of stone steps leading from palace to palace, with the rural summer-houses, shady bowers, delightful terraces, made the spot quite unique and of a perfect loveliness all its own. Herds of deer bounded up the rocks, and halting on a projecting point would gaze with fixed and curious stare at the intruders.

Large quantities of rare and costly enamels and bronzes were obtained here by many, with articles of value; but most of the precious things were so bulky and cumbersome, that they were obliged to be destroyed, because no one could carry them away.

The day was not sufficient to accomplish the work of demolition, so the troops had to bivouac out, and finish their work on the morrow. I was there on duty both days, and was enabled to take a cursory view of the different grounds of which I have endeavoured to give a short description above. But I confess I feel, what all must feel, how impossible it is to call to the mind's eye of the reader, by any display of words, what one glance of his own eye, however hastily snatched, would have conveyed to himself.

Before sunset of the 19th, every place had been fired, and the troops were marched back to camp. We were among the last to leave, and we passed the Summer Palace on our return; flames and smouldering ruins deterred our passage every way, and unhappily many of the peasants' houses adjoining the contagious fire had caught, and were fast being reduced to ashes. We passed the chief entrance to the Yuen-ming-yuen, and watched with mournful pleasure the dancing flames curling into grotesque festoons and wreaths, as they twined in their last embrace round the grand portal of the Palace, while the black column of smoke that rose straight up into the sky from the already roof-fallen reception-hall, formed a deep background to this living picture of active red flame that hissed and crackled as if glorying in the destruction it spread around. "Good for evil," is a hard moral for man to learn; but however much we regretted the cruel destruction of those stately buildings, we yet could not help feeling a secret gratification that the blow had fallen, and the murder of our hapless countrymen revenged on the cruel and perfidious author and instigator of the crime.[13]

NOTES

1   Supported by the French and Americans, the British asked for the opening of six
     more treaty ports along the coasts; the expansion of Western trading activities

toward the more inland areas of China along the Yangtze River, where four more treaty ports would be established; the free circulation of foreigners within China; permanent diplomatic legations in the capital Beijing; and the liberalization of the opium trade, profitable for the British and disastrous for the Chinese.

2   For this brief historical account, I have relied on Wong, *A Paradise Lost*, 133–60; Keay, *China*, 467–76. For a detailed discussion see Hevia, *English Lessons*, 74–118.

3   Among the various accounts of that military expedition, see Armand Lucy, *Souvenirs de voyage: Lettres intimes sur la campagne de Chine en 1860* (Marseille: Barile, 1861); Charles de Mutrécy, *Journal de la campagne de Chine* (Paris: Bourdilliat, 1861); Garnet Joseph Wolseley, *A Narrative of the War with China in 1860* (London: Longman, Green, Longman, and Roberts, 1862); Paul Varin [Charles Dupin], *Expédition de Chine* (Paris: Michel Lévy Frères, 1862); Henry Brougham Loch, *Personal Narrative of Occurrences During Lord Elgin's Second Embassy to China in 1860* (London: Murray, 1869); Charles-Guillame-Marie-Apollinaire-Antoine Cousin de Montauban, *L'expédition de Chine de 1860* (Paris: Plon, 1932). As Greg M. Thomas noted, "British witnesses dwelt particularly on the gardens. . . . French witnesses, in contrast, focused more on the palace's art and treasure." Thomas, "The Looting of Yuanming," 3–4. For a discussion on the differences between French and British accounts of the event see Hevia, *English Lessons*, 76–82. The accounts by Swinhoe and Wolseley presented in this anthology have been chosen because they contain the most comprehensive descriptions of the imperial parks.

4   Robert Swinhoe, *Narrative of the North China Campaign of 1860* (London: Smith, Elder and Co., 1861).

5   On Swinhoe see Philip B. Hall, "Robert Swinhoe (1836–1877), FRS, FZS, FRGS: A Victorian Naturalist in Treaty Port China," *The Geographical Journal* 153, no. 1 (1987): 37–47.

6   As shown in Thomas, "The Looting of Yuanming," 3, 14.

7   Lord Elgin confirms the similarities between Yuanming yuan and the English landscape garden writing that the Chinese imperial park, "is really a fine thing, like an English park." *Extracts from the Letters of James, Earl of Elgin to Mary Louisa, Countess of Elgin, 1847–1862* (Edinburgh: Constable, 1864), 220.

8   Summing up his motives, Lord Elgin was convinced that the destruction of Yuanming yuan "was an act calculated to produce a greater effect in China, and on the Emperor. . . . It was the Emperor's favourite residence, and its destruction could not fail to be a blow to his pride as well as to his feelings." As recalled in Swinhoe, *Narrative*, 328–29.

9   For recent discussion on the looting and devastation of Yuanming yuan and on the different positions between the British and the French command, see Erik Ringmar, "Liberal Barbarism and the Oriental Sublime: The European Destruction of the Emperor's Summer Palace," *Millennium: Journal of International Studies* 34, no. 3 (2006): 917–33; Thomas, "The Looting of Yuanming"; Erik Ringmar, *Liberal Barbarism: The European Destruction of the Palace of the Emperor of China* (New York: Palgrave Macmillan, 2013).

10 Victor Hugo, "L'expédition de Chine: Lettre au Capitaine Butler. Hauteville-House, 25 novembre 1861," in *Œuvres complètes de Victor Hugo: Actes et paroles pendant l'exile, 1852–70* (Paris: J. Hetzel, 1880), 267–70.

11 "The *Moniteur* correspondent" was Antoine Julien Fauchery, a photographer and journalist attached to the French troops.

12 A hunting reserve for the Kangxi emperor, the park of Fragrant Hill was expanded in 1747 by the Qianlong emperor, who added to the park an elaborate garden, which was given the name Jingyi yuan (Garden of Tranquil Pleasure). Zou, *A Jesuit Garden in Beijing*, 11. Valder, *Gardens in China*, 182–84.

13 Swinhoe refers to the event that gave way to the destruction of Yuanming yuan: the torture and murder by Qing officials of a group of French and British prisoners. For a justification of the decision to burn the imperial complex see Loch, *Personal Narrative*, 268–74.

CHAPTER 35

Garnet Joseph Wolseley (1833–1913)

Bnhsh. soldier (handwritten)

Field Marshal Garnet Joseph Wolseley took part in the Arrow War under Sir James Hope Grant, the general in charge of British troops in China. In his own account of that military campaign, entitled *A Narrative of the War with China in 1860* and published in 1862, he included a long description of the state of Yuanming yuan before it was set on fire, and of other imperial parks in the northwestern suburbs of Beijing; they are presented in the two extracts that follow.[1]

Wolseley provides an account of the very imperial complexes that Robert Swinhoe described on the same occasion. However, while Swinhoe's narrative was characterized by appreciation and admiration, Wolseley's description is permeated with the idea of the ontological difference between the West and the East, as well as with a sense of England's moral and aesthetic-cultural superiority over China. His colonialist and imperialist attitude suggests an intent to justify the destruction of the park under the guise of a presumed civilizing European intervention.

In the first extract, Wolseley describes Yuanming yuan. In Wolseley's eyes, the imperial park, renowned in Europe for over a century, is the mirror of China's inferiority. That country's irrationality and weakness, its decadence and degeneration, as opposed to the rational and reasoning culture of the West, are manifested in the idea of space in architecture and garden art. According to Wolseley, the Chinese are unable to conceive "any great work capable of inspiring those sensations of awe or admiration which strike every one when first gazing upon the magnificent creations of European architects." All their inventiveness is reduced to an excess of decoration and ornament, and a constant miniaturization, which makes the great imperial park appear "more the design of a child in front of her doll's house than the work of grown-up men." The famous Yuanming yuan, Wolseley concludes, is inevitably a disappointment for a Western visitor.[2]

This attitude of disdain for China and the Chinese garden, seen as a symbol, and even a cause, of the decadence of the Qing empire, becomes apparent in the concluding sentences of the second extract presented here.[3] The text contains Wolseley's account of the imperial complex of Qingyi yuan (Garden of Clear Ripples) and of Jingming yuan (Garden of Tranquil Brightness), both damaged by the Anglo-French troops. It also contains an outline of the surprising view of the suburban area of Haidian, northwest of Beijing, and the surrounding countryside, where the imperial parks were located.

While the complex of Yuanming yuan was never completely rebuilt after its destruction,[4] Jingming yuan was partially restored and Qingyi yuan was reconstituted by the Empress Dowager Cixi (1835–1908); she renamed it Yihe yuan, "Garden of the Preservation of Harmony." Cixi, who after the death of the Xianfeng emperor unofficially ruled China, decided to reconstruct the Qingyi yuan as a symbolic gesture to reaffirm the role of the Qing dynasty during its irremediable decline, accelerated by the political turmoil of the end of the nineteenth century.[5] Cixi made her political plan evident to Westerners in Beijing through a network of public relations aimed at the promotion of the Qing rulers through the exhibition of the imperial park. The empress dowager regularly invited the wives of foreign diplomats residing in Beijing to Yihe yuan; they painted enthusiastic descriptions of their experiences at the imperial park and of their reception by Cixi.[6] After the destruction of Yuanming yuan, it was Yihe yuan that nurtured Western imagination in the late eighteenth and early nineteenth century, conveying the image of a great Chinese imperial park.

*   *   *

From Garnet Joseph Wolseley, *A Narrative of the War with China in 1860* (1862)

The gateway [to Yuanming yuan] was at one end of a courtyard, enclosed upon three sides with ranges of guard-houses, handsomely ornamented outside with curious carving, and roofed with variegated tiling. The eaves were studded with small representations of birds and beasts. There was a well-arranged combination of red, white, green, blue, and gilding

Figure 23. Felice Beato, *View of the Lake at the Imperial Summer Palace (Yuan Ming Yuan), Beijing, China, After Its Destruction by the English and French Armies.* October 1860. Wellcome Library, London.

about them, which gave a great richness of effect, without in any way pall-ing upon the eye as heavy or gaudy. The gateway itself, like all those in the various public buildings of the country, was a curious combination of brick and woodwork, the former being used as sparingly as possible, with due regard to the stability of the building.

As in all the royal edifices scattered about in the neighbourhood of Hai-teen [Haidian], the end of every beam or rafter visible from the outside was richly carved and painted. The doors were of massive woodwork coloured red and picked out with gilding. The entrance was not intended for wheeled conveyances, the gate sills being some two or three feet above the adjoining pavement, with gently-sloping ramps of granite upon either side. They were roughed over just sufficiently to admit of horses passing over safely. Within the gate as you entered there was a guard-room to the right and left, in which the French sentries had taken the place of the Tartar household bri-gade. As we passed through, I saw some of the eunuchs belonging to the palace, who had been taken prisoners by our allies the evening before; some had been badly wounded, and all were handcuffed. They looked the person-ification of misery, expecting death momentarily, and knowing that if they escaped it at the hands of the barbarians they should meet with it from their own authorities for failing in their defence of the palace. The gateway opened into a long, narrow courtyard, paved, or rather flagged over with the utmost exactness. Upon the far side was a lofty building resembling in shape and construction the better class of joss-house, but having a well-to-do-in-the-world air about it, which none that I had hitherto seen in China possessed. Its carving, gilding, and painting was fresh and clean; its tiling was in perfect order, and looked quite new; its doors swung easily upon their hinges, and altogether it had none of that tumble-down look of dilapidation, which is so universal with all public buildings in the "flowery land," that it would almost appear as if such was a part and parcel of the original design. A neatly finished wire network was stretched along under the wood carvings of the roof eaves to prevent the birds from building nests or roosting there, by which means the elaborate tracery and painting was preserved, maintaining all the freshness of recent finish, although executed many years since. This was the Hall of Audience, at the upper end of which opposite the door, stood the Imperial throne, before which so many princes and ambassadors of haughty monarchs had humbly prostrated themselves, according to the slave-like obeisance customary at the Chinese court. Upon entering, the effect was good, without being grand or in any way realising the preconceived ideas one had formed of it. Everything upon which the eye could rest was pretty and well designed, each little object being a gem of its kind, but there was nothing imposing in the *tout ensemble.* Chinese architecture can never be so; to produce such an effect is seemingly never attempted by the architects of that country. Both in landscape gardening and building, the Chinaman loses sight of grand or imposing effects, in his endeavours to load everything with ornament; he forgets the fine in his search after the curious. In their thirst after decoration, and in their inherent love for minute embellishment, the artists and architects of China have failed to produce any great work capable of inspiring those sensations of awe or admiration which strike every one when first gazing upon the magnificent creations of European architects. The grotto at Cremorne is a very fair specimen of what is esteemed in China as the *acme* of all that is beautiful; and as there are in the gardens at that place, crowded into a very small space, diminutive representations of mountains and rustic scenery, so in the pleasure grounds of Yuen-ming-yuen [Yuanming yuan], and all other ornamental localities of the empire, there are seen, compressed into every little nook or corner, tiny canals, ponds, bridges, stunted trees and rockery, so that it resembles more the design of a child in front of her doll's house than the work of grown-up men.[7] Size, space, or grandeur, produce no sentiments of admiration in the Chinese mind, nor are there any ruins in the country that we know of which would lead us to think that the ancestors of the present generation differed from them in this matter. In this respect they are unlike all the other great nations of antiquity. The pyramids of Egypt, the colossal figures of Nineveh, the massive structures of Thebes and Memphis, and the huge stone portals of long-forgotten races in South America, testify to the importance attached by their builders to size and substantiality of material; whereas, in the very Audience Hall of Hienfung [the Xianfeng emperor], there was no further attempt at effect than what could be obtained from gilding and high-colouring, tastefully distributed throughout the puzzle-like wooden roofing or unimposing-looking pillars of the same perishable material. The floor of this grand hall was of highly-polished marble, each piece cut into the form of some mathematical figure, and all joined so closely, that the divisions between each were marked only by the very thinnest line. An immense painting covered the upper portion of the wall upon the left hand as we entered; it was a representation of the summer palaces and surrounding gardens done in isometrical projection, at which the Chinese are rather clever, considering the childish house-that-Jack-built-like attempts which they make at ordinary perspective in their landscape drawings.[8]

The Imperial throne was a beautiful piece of workmanship, made of rose-wood. It stood upon a platform, raised about eighteen inches above the other part of the hall, and was surrounded by an open-work balustrad-ing, richly carved in representation of roses and other flowers. Upon each side of the throne stood a high pole screen decorated with blue enamel and peacocks' feathers, upon which small rubies and emeralds were strung. Handsomely carved tables and sideboards were ranged along around the room, upon which were numbers of enamel vases, porcelain bowls, jars of crackled china and other curiosities for which the empire is famous. Several large, gilt French time-pieces were also in the hall. Piled up in one place were all the Imperial decrees published during the past year, and large quantities of the Chinese classics were arranged so as to be at hand, in case any immediate reference might be required to them. All these were beauti-fully printed, and many had autograph remarks upon the margin, made by the Emperor.

To leave the hall and get into the gardens, you passed out behind a screen at the back of the throne. You then found yourself in a labyrinth of neatly laid out walks, with high, grassy mounds bounding them upon either side, the tops of which were thickly studded with trees of all the various kinds to be found in the empire. Beneath their shade there were, at various intervals, some rustic-looking stone benches, or well arranged piles of rockery, from the interstices between the stones of which sprang lichens and ferns of various sorts. Quaint shrubs and dwarf trees, stunted after the most approved fashion of Chinese gardeners, grew upon all sides. Upon proceeding some short distance along these winding paths, crossing over rustic bridges, ascending and descending many rural-looking steps, the walk opened out upon a tolerably sized pond, on the further side of which were the private apartments of his Majesty, surrounded by the houses of his many wives, concubines, eunuchs, and servants. The suite of rooms from which Hien-fung had fled only some fourteen days before, were one and all a vast curiosity shop, combining, in addition to the finest specimens of native art and workmanship, the most curious ornaments of European manufacture. The French had placed a guard over those apartments, and none were at first admitted but their own officers, so that when we arrived most of the furniture, etc., still remained as it had been when Hien-fung had occupied them.

His small cap, decorated with the character of longevity embroidered upon it, lay upon his bed; his pipe and tobacco pouch was upon a small table close by. In all the adjoining rooms were immense wardrobes filled with silks, satins, and fur coats. Cloaks covered with the richest golden needlework, mandarine dresses, edged with ermine and sable and marked with representations of the five-clawed dragons, showing they were intended for royalty, were stored in presses. The cushions upon the chairs and sofas were covered with the finest yellow satin embroidered over with figures of dragons and flowers. Yellow is the Imperial colour, and none but those of royal birth are permitted to wear clothes made of it. Jade stone is of all precious articles the most highly prized in China, some of it fetching immense prices. For centuries past the finest pieces have been purchased by the emperors and stored up in Yuen-ming-yuen. The description most highly prized is of a bright green colour, and is called in Chinese the feh-tsui. It is never found in any quantity, and even small pieces of it are very rare. Jade of a pure white, when quite clear, is highly esteemed, and of it there were vast quantities, all exquisitely carved. In some rooms large chests were found filled with cups, vases, plates, etc., made of jade stone.

As you left these buildings and wandered through the maze of walks and winding paths, which led seemingly nowhere in particular, one soon became lost amidst the multiplicity of turnings, marble bridges, canals and fish-ponds met with everywhere, and literally covering the park. Upon some of these little sheets of water there were lilliputian junks armed with small brass cannon, with which a naval fight was sometimes represented for the amusement of his Majesty, who watched the show from a neighbouring tea-house.

Taking Yuen-ming-yuen all in all, it was a gem of its kind, and yet I do not suppose there was a single man who visited it without being disappointed. There was an absence of grandeur about it, for which no amount of careful gardening and pretty ornaments can compensate. . . . Upon the 18th October, the 1st division, under the command of Major-General Sir John Michel, marched from our camp near Pekin [Beijing] to Yuen-ming-yuen, and set fire to all the royal palaces which lay scattered about in that neighbourhood. Throughout the whole of that day and the day following a dense cloud of black and heavy smoke hung over those scenes of former magnificence.[9] . . . By the evening of the 19th October, the summer palaces had ceased to exist, and in their immediate vicinity, the very face of nature seemed changed: some blackened gables and piles of burnt timbers alone indicating where the royal palaces had stood. In many places the inflammable pine trees near the buildings had been consumed with them, leaving nothing but their charred trunks to mark the site. When we first entered the gardens they reminded one of those magic grounds described in fairy tales; we marched from them upon the 19th October, leaving them a dreary waste of ruined nothings. The burning of the palaces was an act of vengeance pre-eminently calculated to fulfill all the purposes which circumstances required.

Whilst the work of demolition was going on, we had ample opportunity of inspecting the country around the palaces and that lying between them and the hills, which, as offshoots from the high range of Thibet, abut upon the plains near Yuen-ming-yuen. A well-kept paved road extends from the principal palace to that known as the Golden Palace, a distance of about three miles. It passes for some distance along the bank of a dried-up canal, the sides of which were tastefully adorned with ornamental rockery, which forms such an essential feature in all Chinese landscape gardening.

Upon each side of the canal there were high embankments of earth covered with cedar and pine trees, and here and there some little grotto of stonework. After leaving Yuen-ming-yuen, and when proceeding to the

Golden Palace, our road at first wound through a series of small official residences standing within walled enclosures and small parks; and then, passing over several grotesquely-built stone bridges, it crossed a number of little canals, some completely dry, others filled only with stagnant water, and almost covered up with water lilies and rushes. The remains of what were once, no doubt, very pretty little cascades testify to the care taken in the embellishment of the place and to the poverty of the present government, which has allowed them to become what they are. Some fine joss-houses or temples lay scattered about, the rich colouring of which contrasted well with the dark green foliage of the cedars. At the distance of about a mile along this paved road stood one of the entrances to the Wanshow-yuen [Wanshou shan, "Longevity Hill"], a palace situated upon a hog's-back-like hill overlooking a fine lake. This hill was enclosed by a high park wall, the space within being tastefully laid out with gardens, shrubberies and plantations, having tea-houses scattered about,—some perched upon rocky knolls commanding good views of the surrounding country, others almost hidden by the dense foliage of the trees, with terraces and flights of steps leading down to the water's edge. Crowning the highest point of the hill was the only building, of all the palaces, constructed exclusively of stone, and consequently the only one upon which the general conflagration took but little effect.[10]

The view from this building was charming.[11] Stretching away from it in the direction of Pekin there was a most substantial and well-finished embankment faced all over with slabs of cut granite. It was built for the purpose of damming up the waters of the streams which poured down from the hills, so as to form the various lakes and artificial ponds, constituting such an important feature in the landscape there. By this means the water was always at a much higher level than the ground upon which Pekin stood, so that a good water supply was at all seasons thus provided for the citizens of that city. Jutting out from this dam into the lake, at about half a mile's distance from the Wan-show gardens, was a long bridge with seventeen arches of beautiful proportions, richly decorated with stone carvings and balustradings, and leading to a small island upon which stood a water-palace closely surrounded with trees, the picturesque gables and upturned roofs of which were faithfully reflected in the calm water beneath. Standing upon the dam at the end of the bridge was a wooden building supported upon pillars, with all the sides open, and seemingly intended merely as a resting-place in which the wearied wanderer might find shelter from the sun during a temporary halt. Close by there was the representation, in bronze, of a cow in a recumbent position, so truly lifelike, that all who saw it mistook it for a veritable animal until they had actually approached it.[12]

The edge of the lake beneath the Wan-show [Wanshou] palaces was laid out in terraces, one rising above the other, the lowest one washed by the water, and having a balustrading of small stone pillars extending along its entire length. Handsome flights of stairs led down from it to the lake, at some of which were boat-houses for the protection of the imperial barges.

Upon leaving the Wan-show-yuen the road passes under a low stone archway, beyond which for about the next half mile it is lined on both sides with shops. They end upon the bank of an insignificant little river, over which the road crosses by an old masonry bridge, the parapet walls of which were sadly ruinous, but exhibited traces of considerable beauty and elaborate carving. This stream is one of the many feeders of the lakes, into the largest of which it discharges itself close by the bridge. Upon its opposite bank is the village of Tsung-lung-cheaou, called after the bridge itself, through which the paved road passes, and debouching from which it winds round between some undulating ground upon the right, and the low inundated fields upon the left, which extend to the margin of a series of small lakes in that direction. For the distance of a mile beyond the bridge the road is closely lined upon the right hand with farmhouses and enclosures, the country further back still in that direction being thickly studded with small villages and groups of Tartar barracks, which are very numerous. The paved road ends at the gates of the Golden Palace, which lies at the foot of a small hill, detached from all the others, and which is included within the park walls surrounding the palace itself. Standing upon the highest point of this hill is a tall white pagoda, which forms the great landmark of the locality, and from whence the finest view is to be had of the many palaces and gardens of Hai-teen [Haidian], by which name the entire place is generally known. The pagoda resembles most others met with everywhere in the empire. It is ascended by a winding staircase, but has none of those projecting balconies common in such buildings generally. Looking out from it, the eye wanders over as fair and lovely a scene as can well be imagined. The thickly-wooded parks of the palaces are shown off to the best advantage by the intervening lakes and numerous ponds within them. The little islands, wooded to the water's edge, send out their tremulous, wavy reflections along the glass-like lakes; here and there the oddly-shaped spires and minarets of a summer-house peer above the variegated foliage, whilst the neglected temples from their half-ruinous condition add much to the scenic effect; and, lastly, may be seen buildings of all sizes, from joss-houses of the most stately proportions with their many courtyards and richly ornamented roofs, down to the tiniest of roadside sanctuaries, nestling here and there amidst clumps of trees, and resembling more closely a child's baby-house than an edifice intended for the worship of some idol.

Beyond the precincts of the royal grounds the country looked richly cultivated, dotted over with farmhouses and Tartar villages, the homes of the several banners by whom the military duties of the place were performed, and the guards furnished for his Majesty's protection during his residence at the Summer Palace.

These villages were mostly built with all the regularity of barracks. To the north was a range of hills, bold in outline, upon which plantations and patches of cultivation seemed to contest possession with stony slopes and rugged cliffs. The commanding points of these hills were crowned with imposing looking buildings of castellated style and essentially un-Chinese in appearance. Far off to the north-east was a conically shaped hill, with a fortified military post upon it. To the west were the palaces of Tsain-tai extending up the sides of the Sian mountains [Xishan, western mountains], which stretch away south from the principal range. Between those palaces and the Kin-ming-yuen [Jingming yuan, "Garden of Tranquil Brightness"] a well-built aqueduct extended, by means of which the gardens of the Golden Palace were supplied with water. The massive gate towers of Pekin, and its several pagodas and cupolas, with (in some places) a small extent of the walls themselves, bounded the view to the south-east, completing the panorama. Taken as a whole, that is, including all the palaces and adjoining gardens, Hai-teen was certainly well suited for the residence of a monarch ruling over such a great nation. Chinamen may well have reckoned it the alpha and omega of all that was lovely on earth, leaving nothing to be wished for according to their notions of what is beautiful and magnificent.

Generation after generation of emperors had added to its works of art and artificial beauty. From thence mighty kings have issued their commands to the widest empire ever yet ruled by any one man; but the very gorgeousness of the scene has been one great promoting cause of the luxury and effeminacy which have served to debase the late rulers of China, causing the descendants of fierce warriors to degenerate into mere enervated debauchees, alike incapable of wielding the sword themselves or commanding in the field those who could. After a childhood passed in the seclusion of such palaces, the greatest exercise allowed being a daily stroll amidst the luxurious gardens around, it is scarcely to be wondered at that the royal heir should grow up into an indolent, dreamy, and unpractical manhood. After being assured from earliest childhood that he was immeasurably superior to all other human beings, and but little removed from Deity itself, it is no strange matter that such a monarch should believe his absolute power to be as much a part of himself as his hands or feet, or, in fact, as indisputable as his very existence.

NOTES

1   Garnet Joseph Wolseley, *A Narrative of the War with China in 1860* (London: Longman, Green, Longman, and Roberts, 1862). The volume was dedicated to Sir James Hope Grant.

2   On Wolseley's perception of Yuanming yuan, see Hevia, *English Lessons*, 100–102.

3   Chang, *Britain's Chinese Eye*, 68–69.

4   In 1873–74, the Tongzhi emperor (1861–75) planned to reconstruct sections of Yuanming yuan. See Emily Mokros, "Reconstructing the Imperial Retreat: Politics, Communications, and the Yuanming Yuan Under the Tongzhi Emperor, 1873–4," *Late Imperial China* 33, no. 2 (2012): 76–118.

5   On the reconstructions of the imperial park by Cixi see, for instance, Bianca Maria Rinaldi, "Ein Manifest politischer Autorität: der Wiederaufbau der *Yihe-yuan*," in *Kunst, Garten, Kultur*, ed. Stefanie Hennecke and Gert Gröning (Berlin: Reimer Verlag, 2010), 181–96.

6   Descriptions of the visits to the imperial park of Yihe yuan, at the invitation of the Empress Dowager Cixi, were written, for example, by Sarah Pike Conger, the wife of the American minister to China, and Katherine A. Carl, an American artist who painted a portrait of Cixi that was to be exhibited at the St. Louis World's Fair in 1904. See Sarah Pike Conger, *Letters from China* (Chicago: McClurg and Co., 1909), 137–240; Katharine A. Carl, *With the Empress Dowager of China* (New York: Century Co., 1907), 149–55, 165–69, 300–01. On Cixi's interaction with Sarah Pike Conger see Grant Heyter-Menzies, *The Empress and Mrs. Conger: The Uncommon Friendship of Two Women and Two Worlds* (Hong Kong: Hong Kong University Press, 2001).

7   It is interesting to note that the itinerary through Yuanming yuan, due to the variety of situations it presented and the presence of rockeries, provokes Wolseley to compare it to Cremorne Gardens, one of London's pleasure gardens. Opened in 1832, Cremorne Gardens was located at the west end of the village of Chelsea on the river Thames. A place famous for its amusements, Cremorne Gardens offered multiple attractions and entertainments including, as Anne Koval shows, a "marionette theater, circus, diorama, shooting gallery, bowling saloon, hermit's cave, gypsy's grotto, a garden maze, a fireworks gallery, two large halls, a stereorama and a large Chinese dancing pagoda." Anne Koval, " 'Strange Beauty in the

Night': Whistler's Nocturnes of Cremorne Gardens," in *The Pleasure Garden, from Vauxhall to Coney Island*, ed. Jonathan Conlin (Philadelphia: University of Pennsylvania Press, 2013), 198. See also Franco Panzini, *Per i piaceri del popolo: L'evoluzione del giardino pubblico in Europa dalle origini al XX secolo* (Bologna: Zanichelli, 1993), 107.

8   Ignoring the fact that Chinese painting obeys rules radically different from those of Western perspectival representation, Wolseley makes a comparison with a popular British nursery rhyme, "This Is the House That Jack Built," to show that perspective in Chinese landscape painting is created by objects that do not follow the canonical geometric construction of the drawing.

9   John Michel was commander of the British troops in Hong Kong.

10   Wolseley is referring to the Hall of the Sea of Wisdom, a building commissioned by the Qianlong emperor at the highest point of Longevity Hill.

11   Robert Swinhoe, in the extract from his account of the Arrow War included in this anthology, offers a more detailed description of the view he admired from the top of Longevity Hill. Swinhoe, *Narrative of the North China Campaign*, 332–33.

12   Wolseley is referring to the Bronze Ox, which was placed on the southeastern shore of Kunming Lake by the Qianlong emperor in 1755.

see p. 112.

APPENDIX

William Chambers (1723–96)
A Dissertation on Oriental Gardening

William Chambers's *Dissertation on Oriental Gardening* (1772) is a very different text in comparison to the other Western travelers' accounts of the gardens in China included in this anthology.[1] Even though it derives from an elaboration of the arguments Chambers expressed in his first essay about the Chinese garden aesthetic, "Of the Art of Laying Out Gardens Among the Chinese" (1757), the *Dissertation* cannot really be considered a theoretical treatment of Chinese garden design principles. It is more the vision of a new picturesque garden that Chambers advocated, almost foreboding the dramatic changes that the industrial revolution would bring to the social structure in Britain. It is presented here as a notable example of how the Chinese garden was used in Europe in the theoretical formulation of the development of the picturesque garden style.

Written in outright contrast with the rural and "natural" landscapes designed by Lancelot "Capability" Brown, defined by Chambers as "common fields,"[2] the *Dissertation* proposed a new form of modern garden: an envisioned composition that was filtered using the Chinese garden. The garden style Chambers proposed was characterized by a continuous variety and multiplication of surprising settings and scenes, close to one another, redolent of exoticism, and capable of eliciting different emotional responses from the visitor.

More than helping to disseminate the Chinese aesthetic in garden design, with its utopic and almost messianic tone the *Dissertation* engendered a growing criticism in England of the gardens of China. The *Dissertation* was harshly criticized by British intellectuals for all of Chambers's deliberate exaggerations, the extravagant elements he introduced to define the three new categories of scenes—the pleasing, the terrible, and the surprising—and for its polemic against the dominant models for garden design in England, as well as the reference to the Chinese gardens it proposed. In response to it, Chambers's greatest rival, the poet William Mason, published a satirical and very successful pamphlet entitled *An Heroic Epistle to William Chambers* (1773). The hostile reactions to the *Dissertation* were purely political. They were mainly concerned with a defense of the landscape garden as the image of England's political liberty, as well as with the rejection of the Chinese garden, which began to be considered an "unnatural" garden style and seen as the reflection of a despotic political government.[3] To support his view of garden design, Chambers published a second edition of the *Dissertation* in 1773, accompanied by "An Explanatory Discourse," which he attributed to the Chinese sculptor Tan Chetqua.[4] In it, Chambers confirmed the reference to Chinese garden design as a strategy aimed at creating more varied effects in the landscape garden. Chambers, who dedicated his *Dissertation* to King George III and had worked for him in the royal park of Kew, was actually advocating a new national natural garden as the political image of England. The political vision Chambers supported and confirmed in his "Explanatory Discourse" was, however, different from that of his opponents: while "Mason's landscape is an image of Whig oligarchy, Chambers's appears as that of Tory monarchism."[5]

* * *

PREFACE

Amongst the decorative arts, there is none of which the influence is so extensive as that of Gardening. The productions of other arts have their separate classes of admirers, who alone relish or set any great value upon them; to the rest of the world they are indifferent, sometimes disgusting. A building affords no pleasure to the generality of men, but what results from the grandeur of the object, or the value of its materials: nor doth a picture affect them, but by its resemblance to life. A thousand other beauties, of a higher kind, are loft upon them; for in Architecture, in Painting, and indeed in most other arts, men must learn before they can admire: their pleasure keeps pace with their judgment; and it is only by knowing much, that they can be highly delighted.

But Gardening is of a different nature: its dominion is general; its effects upon the human mind certain and invariable; without any previous information, without being taught, all men are delighted with the gay luxuriant scenery of summer, and depressed at the dismal aspect of autumnal prospects; the charms of cultivation are equally sensible to the ignorant and the learned, and they are equally disgusted at the rudeness of neglected nature; lawns, woods, shrubberies, rivers and mountains, affect them both in the same manner; and every combination of these will excite similar sensations in the minds of both.

Nor are the productions of this Art less permanent than general in their effects. Pictures, statues, buildings, soon glut the sight, and grow indifferent to the spectator: but in gardens there is a continual state of fluctuation that leaves no room for satiety; the progress of vegetation the vicissitudes of seasons, the changes of the weather, the different directions of the sun, the passage of clouds, the agitation and sounds produced by winds, together with the accidental intervention of living or moving objects, vary the appearances so often, and so considerably, that it is almost impossible to be cloyed, even wit the same prospects.

Is it not singular then, that an Art with which a considerable part of our enjoyments is so universally connected, should have no regular professors in our quarter of the world? Upon the continent it is a collateral branch of the architect's employment, who, immersed in the study and avocations of his own profession, finds no leisure for other disquisitions; and, in this island, it is abandoned to kitchen gardeners, well skilled in the culture of sallads, but little acquainted with the principles of Ornamental Gardening. It cannot be expected that men uneducated, and doomed by their condition to waste the vigor of life in hard labour, should ever go far in so refined, so difficult a pursuit.

To this unaccountable want of regular masters may, in a great measure, be ascribed the scarcity of perfect gardens. There are indeed very few in our part of the globe wherein nature has been improved to the best advantage, or art employed with the soundest judgment. The gardens of Italy, France, Germany, Spain, and of all the other countries where the antient style still prevails, are in general mere cities of verdure; the walks are like streets conducted in strait lines, regularly diverging from different large open spaces, resembling public squares; and the hedges with which they are bordered, are raised, in imitation of walls, adorned with pilasters, niches, windows and doors, or cut into colonades, arcades and porticos; all the detached trees are shaped into obelisks, pyramids and vases; and all the recesses in the thickets bear the names and forms of theatres, amphitheatres, temples, banqueting halls, ball rooms, cabinets and saloons. The streets and squares are well manned with statues of marble or lead, ranged in regular lines, like soldiers at a procession; which, to make them more natural, are sometimes painted in proper colours, and finely gilt. The lakes and rivers are confined by quais of hewn stone, and taught to flow in geometrick order; and the cascades glide from the heights by many a succession of marble steps: not a twig is suffered to grow as nature directs; nor is a form admitted but what is scientific, and determinable by the line or compass.

In England, where this antient style is held in detestation, and where, in opposition to the rest of Europe, a new manner is universally adopted, in which no appearance of art is tolerated, our gardens differ very little from common fields, so closely is common nature copied in most of them; there is generally so little variety in the objects, such a poverty of imagination in the contrivance, and of art in the arrangement, that these compositions rather appear the offsprings of chance than design; and a stranger is often at a loss to know whether he be walking in a meadow, or in a pleasure ground, made and kept at a very considerable expence: he sees nothing to amuse him, nothing to excite his curiosity, nor any thing to keep up his attention. At his first entrance, he is treated with the sight of a large green field, scattered over with a few draggling trees, and verged with a confused border of little shrubs and flowers; upon farther inspection, he finds a little serpentine path, twining in regular esses amongst the shrubs of the border, upon which he is to go round, to look on one side at what he has already seen, the large green field; and on the other fide at the boundary, which is never more than a few yards from him, and always obtruding upon his sight: from time to time he perceives a little seat or temple stuck up against the wall; he rejoices at the discovery, sits down, rests his wearied limbs, and then reels on again, cursing the line of beauty, till spent with fatigue, half roasted by the sun, for there is never any shade, and tired for what of entertainment, he resolves to see no more: vain resolution! there is but one path; he must either drag on to the end, or return back by the tedious way he came.

Such is the favourite plan of all our smaller gardens: and our larger works are only a repetition of the small ones; more green fields, more shrubberies, more serpentine walks, and more seats; like the honest, batchelor's feast, which consisted in nothing but a multiplication of his own dinner; three legs of mutton and turneps, three roasted geese, and three buttered apple-pies.

It is I think obvious that neither the artful nor the simple style of Gardening here mentioned, is right: the one being too extravagant a deviation from nature; the other too scrupulous an adherence to her. One manner is absurd; the other insipid and vulgar: a judicious mixture of both would certainly be more perfect than either.

But how this union can be effected, is difficult to say. The men of art, and the friends of nature, are equally violent in defence of their favourite system; and, like all other partizans, loth to give up any thing, however unreasonable.

Such a coalition is therefore now not to be expected: whoever should be bold enough to attempt it, would probably incur the censure of both sides; without reforming either; and consequently prejudice himself, without doing service to the Art.

But though it might be impertinent as well as useless to start a new system of one's own; it cannot be improper, nor totally unserviceable, to publish that of others; especially of a people whose skill in Gardening has often been the subject of praise; and whose manner has been set up amongst us as the standard of imitation, without ever having been properly defined. It is a common saying, That from the worst things some good may be extracted; and even if what I have to relate should be inferior to what is already known, yet surely some useful hints may be collected from it.

I may therefore, without danger to myself, and it is hoped without offence to others, offer the following account of the Chinese manner of Gardening; which is collected from my own observations in China, from conversations with their Artists, and remarks transmitted to me at different times by travellers. A sketch of what I have now attempted to finish, was published some years ago; and the favourable reception granted to that little performance, induced me to collect materials for this.[6]

Whether the Chinese manner of Gardening be better or worse than those now in use amongst the Europeans, I will not determine: comparison is the surest as well as the easiest test to of truth; it is in every man's power to compare and to judge for himself.—Should the present publication contain any thing useful, my purpose will be fully answered; if not, it may perhaps afford some little entertainment, or serve at worst to kill an idle hour.

I must not enter upon my subject, without apologizing for the liberties here taken with our English Gardens: there are, indeed, several that do not come within the compass of my description; some of which were laid out by their owners, who are as eminently skilled in Gardening, as in many other branches of polite knowledge; the rest owe most of their excellence to nature, and are upon the whole, very little improved by the interposition of art; which, though it may have heightened some of their beauties, has totally robbed them of many others.

It would be tedious to enumerate all the errors of a false taste: but the havock it has made in our old plantations, must ever be remembered with indignation: the ax has often, in one day, laid waste the growth of several ages; and thousands of venerable plants, whole woods of them, have been swept away, to make room for a little grass, and a few American weeds. Our virtuosi have scarcely left an acre of shade, nor three trees growing in a line, from the Land's-end to the Tweed; and if their humour for devastation continues to rage much longer, there will not be a forest-tree left standing in the whole kingdom.

DISSERTATION

Amongst the Chinese, Gardening is held in much higher esteem, than it is in Europe; they rank a perfect work in that Art, with the great productions of the human understanding; and say, that its efficacy in moving the passions, yields to that of few other arts whatever.

Their Gardeners are not only Botanists, but also Painters and Philosophers, having a thorough knowledge of the human mind, and of the arts by which its strongest feelings are excited. It is not in China, as in Italy and France, where every petty Architect is a Gardener; neither is it as in another famous country, where peasants emerge from the melon grounds to commence professors; so Sganarelle, the faggot-maker, laid down his hatchet to turn physician. In China, Gardening is a distinct profession, requiring an extensive study; to the perfection of which few arrive. The Gardeners there, far from being either ignorant or illiterate, are men of high abilities, who join to good natural parts, most ornaments that study, travelling, and long experience can supply them with: it is in consideration of these accomplishments only that they are permitted to exercise their profession; for with the Chinese the taste of Ornamental Gardening is an object of legislative attention, it being supposed to have an influence upon the general culture, and consequently upon the beauty of the whole country. They observe, that mistakes committed in this Art, are too important to be tolerated, being much exposed to view, and in a great measure irreparable; as it often requires the space of a century, to redress the blunders of an hour.

The Chinese Gardeners take nature for their pattern; and their aim is to imitate all her beautiful irregularities. Their first consideration is the nature of the ground they are to work upon: whether it be flat or sloping; hilly or mountainous; small or of considerable extent; abounding with springs and rivers, or labouring under a scarcity of water; whether woody or bare, rough or even, barren or rich; and whether the transitions be sudden, and the character grand, wild or tremendous; or whether they be gradual, and the general bent placid, gloomy or chearful. To all which circumstances they carefully attend; choosing such dispositions as humour the ground, hide its defects, improve or set off its advantages, and can be executed with expedition, at a moderate expence.

They are also attentive to the wealth or indigence of the patron by whom they are employed; to his age, his infirmities, temper, amusements, connections, business and manner of living; as likewise to the season of the year in which the Garden is likely to be most frequented by him: suiting themselves in their composition to his circumstances, and providing for his wants and recreations. Their skill consists in struggling with the imperfections and defect of nature, and with every other impediment; and in producing, in spite of every obstacle, works that are uncommon, and perfect in their kind.

Though the Chinese artists have nature for their general model, yet are they not so attached to her as to exclude all appearance of art; on the contrary, they think it, on many occasions, necessary to make an ostentatious shew of their labour. Nature, say they, affords us but few materials to work with. Plants, ground and water, are her only productions: and though both the forms and arrangements of these may be varied to an incredible degree, yet have they but few striking varieties, the rest being of the nature of changes rung upon bells, which, though in reality different, still produce the same uniform kind of jingling; the variation being too minute to be easily perceived.

Art must therefore supply the scantiness of nature; and not only be employed to produce variety, but also novelty and effect: for the simple arrangements of nature are met with in every common field, to a certain degree of perfection; and are therefore too familiar to excite any strong sensations in the mind of the beholder, or to produce any uncommon degree of pleasure.

It is indeed true that novelty and variety may both be attained by transplanting the peculiarities of one country to another; by introducing rocks, cataracts, impending woods, and other parts of romantic situations, in flat places; by employing much water where it is rare; and cultivated plains, amidst the rude irregularities of mountains: but even this resource is easily exhausted, and can seldom be put in practice, without a very great expence.

The Chinese are therefore no enemies to strait lines; because they are, generally speaking, productive of grandeur, which often cannot be attained without them: nor have they any aversion to regular geometrical figures, which they say are beautiful in themselves, and, well suited to small compositions, where the luxuriant irregularities of nature would fill up and embarrass the parts they should adorn. They likewise think them properest [most proper] for flower gardens, and all other compositions, where much art is apparent in the culture; and where it should therefore not be, omitted in the form.

Their regular buildings they generally surround with artificial terrasses, slopes, and many flights of steps; the angles of which are adorned with groupes of sculpture and vases, intermixed with all sorts of artificial water-works, which, connecting with the architecture, serve to give it consequence, and add to the gaiety, splendor, and bustle of the scenery.

Round the main habitation, and near all their decorated structures, the grounds are laid out with great regularity, and kept with great care: no plants are admitted that intercept the view of the buildings; nor no lines but such as accompany the architecture properly, and contribute to the general good effect of the whole composition: for they hold it absurd to surround an elegant fabric with disorderly rude vegetation; saying, that it looks like a diamond set in lead; and always conveys the idea of an unfinished work. When the buildings are rustic, the scenery which surrounds them is wild; when they are grand, it is gloomy; when gay, it is luxuriant: in short, the Chinese are scrupulously nice in preserving the same character through every part of the composition; which is one great cause of that surprizing variety with which their works abound.

They are fond of introducing statues, busts, bas-reliefs, and every production of the chisel, as well in other parts of their Gardens, as round their buildings; observing, that they are not only ornamental, but that by commemorating past events, and celebrated personages, they awaken the mind to pleasing contemplation, hurrying our reflections up into the remotest ages of antiquity: and they never fail to scatter antient inscriptions, verses, and moral sentences, about their grounds; which are placed on large ruinated stones; and columns of marble, or engraved on trees and rocks;

such situations being always chosen for them, as correspond with the sense of the inscriptions; which thereby acquire additional force in themselves and likewise give a stronger expression to the scene.

They say that all these decorations are necessary, to characterize and distinguish the different scenes of their compositions; among which, without such assistance, there must unavoidably be a tiresome similarity.

And whenever it is objected to them, that many of these things are unnatural, and ought therefore not to be suffered, they say, that most improvements are unnatural, yet they are allowed to do improvements, and not only tolerated, but admired. Our vestments, say they, are, neither of leather, nor like our skins, but formed of rich: silks and embroidery; our houses and palaces bear no, resemblance to caverns in the rocks, which are the only, natural habitations; nor is our music either like thunder, or the whistling of the northern wind, the harmony of nature. Nature produces nothing either boiled, roasted or stewed, and yet we do not eat raw meat; nor doth she supply us with any other tools for all our purposes, but teeth and hands; yet we have saws, hammers, axes, and a thousand other implements: in short, there is scarcely any thing in which art is not apparent; and why should its appearance be excluded from Gardening only? Poets and painters soar above the pitch of nature, when, they would give energy to their compositions the same privilege, therefore, should be allowed to Gardeners: inanimate, simple nature, is too insipid for our purposes; much is expected from us; and therefore, we have occasion for every aid that either art or nature can furnish. The scenery of a garden should differ as much from common nature as an heroic poem doth from a prose relation; and Gardeners, like poets, should give a loose to their imagination, and even fly beyond the bounds of truth, whenever it is necessary to elevate, to embellish, to enliven, or to add novelty to their subject.

The usual method of distributing Gardens in China, is to contrive a great variety of scenes, to be seen from certain, points of view; at which are placed seats or buildings, adapted to the different purposes of mental or sensual enjoyments. The perfection of their Gardens consists in the number and diversity of these scenes; and in the artful combination of their parts; which they endeavour to dispose in such a manner, as not only separately to appear to the best advantage, but also to unite in forming an elegant and striking whole.

Where the ground is extensive, and many scenes can be introduced, they generally adapt each to one single point of view; but where it is confined, and affords no room for variety, they dispose their objects, so, that being viewed from different points, they produce different representations; and often such as bear no resemblance to each other. They likewise endeavour to place the separate scenes of their compositions in such directions as to unite, and be seen all together, from one or more particular points of view, whence the eye may be delighted with an extensive, rich and variegated prospect. They take all possible advantage of exterior objects; hiding carefully the boundaries of their own grounds; and endeavouring to make an apparent union between them and the distant woods, fields and rivers: and where towns, castles, towers, or any other considerable objects are in sight, they artfully contrive to have them seen from as many points, and in as many direction as possible. The same they do with regard to navigable rivers, high roads, foot-paths, hills, and all other moving objects, which animate and add variety to the landscape.[7]

Besides the usual European methods of concealing boundaries by ha-has, and sunk fences, they have others, still more effectual. On flats, where they have naturally no prospects of exterior objects, they enclose their plantations with artificial terrasses, in the form of walks, to which you ascend by insensible slopes: these they border on the inside with thickets of lofty trees and underwood; and on the outside, with low shrubberies; over which the passenger sees the whole scenery of the adjacent country, in appearance forming a continuation of the Garden, as its fence is carefully concealed amongst the shrubs that cover the outside declivity of the terrass.

And where the Garden happens to stand on higher ground than the adjacent country, they carry artificial rivers round the outskirts, under the opposite banks of which the boundaries are concealed, amongst trees and shrubs. Sometimes too they make use of strong wire fences, painted green, fastened to the trees and shrubs that border the plantations, and carried round in many irregular directions, which are scarcely seen till you come very near them: and wherever ha-has, or sunk fences are used, they always fill the trenches with briars, and other thorny plants, to strengthen the fence, and to conceal the walls, which otherwise would have an ugly appearance from without.

In their large Gardens they contrive different scenes, for the different times of the day; disposing at the points of view buildings, which from their use point out the proper hour for enjoying the view in its perfections. And in their small ones, where, as has been, observed, one arrangement produces many representations, they make use of the same artifice. They have beside, scenes for every season of the year: some for winter, generally exposed, to the southern sun, and composed of pines, firs, cedars, evergreen oaks, phillyreas, hollies, yews, and many other evergreens; being enriched with laurels of various sorts, laurestinus, arbutus, and other plants and vegetables that grow and flourish in cold weather: and to give variety and gaiety to these gloomy productions, they plant amongst, them, in regular forms, divided by walks, all the rare shrubs, flowers and trees of the torrid zone; which they cover, during the winter, with frames of glass; disposed in the forms of temples, and other elegant buildings. These they call conservatories; they are warmed by subterraneous fires, and afford a comfortable and agreeable retreat, when the weather is too cold to walk in the open air. All sorts of beautiful and melodious birds are let loose in them: and they keep there, in large porcelain cisterns, placed on artificial rocks, gold and silver fishes; with various kinds of aquatic plants and flower: they also raise in them strawberries, cherries, figs, grapes, apricots and peaches, which cover the wood-work of their glass frames, and serve for ornament as well as use.

Their scenes of spring likewise abound with evergreens, intermixed with lilacks of all sorts, laburnums, limes, larixes, double blossomed thorn, almond and peach-trees; with sweet-bryar, early roses, and honey-suckles. The ground, and verges of the thickets and shrubberies, are adorned with wild hyacinths, wall-flowers, daffodils, violets, primroses, polianthes's, crocus's, dailies, snowdrops, and various species of the iris; with such other flowers as appear in the months of March and April: and as these scenes are also scanty in their natural productions, they intersperse amongst their plantations, menageries for all sorts of tame and ferocious animals, and birds of prey; aviaries and groves, with proper contrivances for breeding domestic fowls; decorated dairies; and buildings for the exercises of wrestling, boxing; quail-fighting, and other games known in China. They also contrive in the woods large open recesses for military sports; as riding, vaulting, fencing, shooting with the bow, and running.

Their summer scenes compose the richest and most studied parts of their Gardens. They abound with lakes, rivers, and water-works of every contrivance; and with vessels of every construction, calculated for the uses of sailing, rowing, fishing, fowling, and fighting. The woods consists of oak, beech, Indian chesnut, elm, ash, plane, sycamore, maple, abele and several other species of the poplar; with many other trees, peculiar to China. The thickets are composed of every fair deciduous plant that grows in that climate, and every flower or shrub that flourishes during the summer months; all uniting to form the finest verdure, the most brilliant; harmonious colouring imaginable. The buildings are spacious, splendid and numerous; every scene being marked by one or more some of them contrived for banquets, balls, concerts, learned disputations, plays, rope-dancing, and feats of activity; others again for bathing, swimming, reading, sleeping, or meditation.

In the center of these summer plantations, there is generally a large tract of ground set aside for more secret and voluptuous enjoyments; which is laid out in a great number of close walks, colonades and passages, turned with many intricate windings, so as to confuse and lead the passenger astray; being sometimes divided by thickets of underwood, intermixed with straggling large trees; and at other times by higher plantations, or by clumps of rose-trees, and other lofty flowering shrubs. The whole is a wilderness of sweets, adorned with all sorts of fragrant and gaudy productions: gold and silver pheasants, pea-fowls, partridges, bantam hens, quails, and game of every kind, swarm in the woods; doves, nightingales, and a thousand melodious birds, perch upon the branches; deer, antelopes, spotted buffaloes, sheep, and Tartarean horses, frisk upon the plains: every walk leads to some delightful object; to groves of orange and myrtle; to rivulets, whose banks are clad with roses, woodbine and jessamine; to murmuring fountains, with statues of sleeping nymphs, and water-gods; to cabinets of verdure, with beds of aromatic herbs and flowers; to grottos cut in rocks, adorned with incrustations of coral shells, ores, gems and christalisations, refreshed with rills of sweet scented water, and cooled by fragrant, artificial breezes.

Amongst the thickets which divide the walks, are many secret recesses; in each of which there is an elegant pavilion, consisting of one state-apartment, with outhouses, and proper conveniences for eunuchs and women servants. These are inhabited, during the summer, by their fairest and most accomplished concubines; each of them, with her attendants, occupying a separate pavilion.

The principal apartment of these buildings, consists of one or more large saloons, two cabinet or dressing-rooms, a library, a couple of bed-chambers and waiting-rooms, a bath, and several private closets; all which are magnificently furnished, and provided with entertaining books, amorous paintings, musical instruments, implements for gaming, writing, drawing, painting and embroidering; with beds, couches, and chairs, of various constructions, for the uses of fitting and lying in different postures.

The saloons generally open to little enclosed courts, set round with beautiful flower-pots, of different forms, made of porcelain, marble or copper, filled with the rarest flowers of the season: at the end of the court there is generally an aviary; an artificial rock with a fountain and bason for gold fish; a cascade; an arbor of bamboo or vine interwoven with flowering shrubs; or some other elegant contrivance, of the like nature.

Besides these separate habitations, in which the ladies are privately visited by the patron, as often as he is disposed to see them, there are, in other larger recesses of the thickets, more splendid and spacious buildings, where the women all meet at certain hours of the day, either to eat at the public tables, to drink their tea, to converse, bathe, swim, work, romp or to play at the mora [morra, guess finger game], and other games known in China; or else to divert the patron with music, singing, lascivious posture-dancing, and acting plays or pantomines; at all which they generally are very expert.

Some of these structures are entirely open; the roof being supported on columns of rose-wood, or cedar, with bases of Corean [*sic*] jasper; or upon wooden pillars, made in imitation of bamboo, and plantane-trees [plantain], surrounded with garlands of fruit and flowers, artfully carved, being painted and varnished in proper colours. Other are enclosed; and consist sometimes only of one spacious hall, and sometimes of many different sized rooms, of various; forms; as triangles, squares, hexagons, octagons, circles, ovals, and irregular whimsical shapes; all of them elegantly finished with incrustations of marble, inlaid precious woods, ivory, silver, gold, and mother of pearl; with a profusion of antient porcelain, mirrors, carving, gilding, painting and lacquering of all colours.

The doors of entrance to these apartments, are circular and polygonal, as well as rectangular: and the windows by which they are lighted, are made in the shapes of fans, birds, animals, fishes, insects, leaves and flowers; being filled with painted glass, or different coloured gause [gauze], to tinge the light, and give a glow to the objects in the apartment.

All these buildings are furnished at a very great expence, not only with the necessary moveables, but with pictures, sculptures, embroideries, trinkets, and pieces of clock-work of great value, being some of them very large, composed of many ingenious movements, and enriched with ornaments of gold, intermixed with pearls, diamonds, rubies, emeralds, and other gems.

Besides the different structures already mentioned, they have some made in the form of Persian tents; others built of roots and pollards, put together with great taste; and others, called Miau [Miao] Ting, or Halls of the Moon, of a prodigious size; composed each of one single vaulted room, made in the shape of a hemisphere; the concave of which is artfully painted, in imitation of a nocturnal sky, and pierced with an infinite number of little windows, made to represent the moon and stars, being filled with tinged glass, that admits the light in the quantities necessary to spread over the whole interior fabric the pleasing gloom of a fine summer's night.

The pavements of these rooms are sometimes laid out in parterres of flowers; amongst which are placed many rural seats, made of fine formed branches, varnished red to represent coral: but oftenest their bottom is full of a clear running water, which falls in rills from the sides of a rock in the center; many little islands float upon its surface, and move around as the current directs; some of them covered with tables for the banquet; others with seats for musicians; and others with arbors, containing beds of repose, with sophas, seats, and other furniture, for various uses.

To these halls of the moon the Chinese princes retire, with their favourite women, whenever the heat and intense light of the summer's day becomes disagreeable to them; and here they feast, and give a loose to every sort of voluptuous pleasure.

No nation ever equalled the Chinese in the splendor and number of their garden structures. We are told by Father Attiret, that in one of the imperial gardens near Pekin [Beijing], called Yven Ming Yven [Yuanming yuan], there are, besides the palace, which is of itself a city, four hundred pavilions, all so different in their architecture, that each seems the production of a different country.[8] He mentions one of them, that cost upwards of two hundred thousand pounds, exclusive of the furniture; another, consisting of a hundred room: and says, that most of them are sufficiently capacious to lodge the greatest European lord, and his whole retinue. There is likewise, in the same garden, a fortified town, with its port, streets, public squares, temples, markets, shops, and tribunals of justice in short, with every thing that is at Pekin; only upon a smaller scale.

In this town the emperors of China, who are too much the slaves of their greatness to appear in public, and their women, who are excluded from it by custom, are frequently diverted with the hurry and bustle of the capital; which is there represented, several times in the year, by the eunuchs of the palace: same of them personating merchants, others artists, artificers, officers, soldiers, shop-keepers, porters, and even thieves and pickpockets. On the appointed day, each puts on the habit of his profession: the ships arrive at the port, the shops are opened, and the goods are offered to sale;

tea-houses, taverns, and inns, are ready for the reception of company; fruits, and all sorts of refreshments, are cried about the streets: the shop-keepers teize [tease] the passengers to purchase their merchandize; and every liberty is permitted: there is no distinction of persons; even the emperor is confounded in the crowd: quarrels happen—battles ensue—the watch seizes upon the combatants—they are conveyed before the judge, he examines the dispute and condemns the culprit, who is sometimes very severely bastinadoed, to divert his imperial majesty, and the ladies of his train.

Neither are sharpers forgot in these festivals; that noble profession is generally allotted to a good number of the most dextrous eunuchs, who, like the Spartan youths of old, are punished or applauded, according to the merit of their exploits.

The plantations of their autumnal scenes consist of many sorts of oak, beech, and other deciduous trees that are retentive of the leaf, and afford in their decline a rich variegated colouring; with which they blend some ever-greens, some fruit-trees, and the few shrubs and flowers which blossom late in the year; placing amongst them decayed trees, pollards, and dead stumps, of picturesque forms, overspread with moss and ivy.

The buildings, with which these scenes are decorated, are generally such as indicate decay, being intended as mementos to the passenger. Some are hermitages and alms-houses, where the faithful old servants of the family spend the remains of life in peace, amidst the tombs of their predecessors, who lie buried around them: others are ruins, of castles, palaces, temples, and deserted religious houses; or half buried triumphal arches and mausoleums, with mutilated inscriptions, that once commemorated the heroes of antient times; or they are sepulchers of their ancestors, catacombs and cemeteries for their favourite domestic animals; or whatever else may serve to indicate the debility, the disappointments, and the dissolution of humanity; which, by co-operating with the dreary aspect of autumnal nature, and the inclement temperature of the air, fill the mind with melancholy, and incline it to serious reflections.

Such is the common scenery of the Chinese Gardens, where the ground has no striking tendency to any particular character. But where it is more strongly marked, their artists never fail to improve upon its singularities; their aim is to excite a great variety of passions in the mind of the spectator; and the fertility of their imaginations, always upon the stretch in search of novelty, furnishes, them with a thousand artifices to accomplish that aim.

The scenes which I have hitherto described, are chiefly of the pleasing kind: but the Chinese Gardeners have many sorts, which they employ as circumstances vary; all which they range in three separate classes; and distinguish them by the appellations of the pleasing, the terrible, and the surprizing.

The first of these are composed of the gayest and most perfect productions of the vegetable world; intermixed with river, lakes, cascades, fountains, and water-works of all sorts: being combined and disposed in all the picturesque forms that art or nature can suggest. Buildings, sculptures, and paintings are added, to give splendor and variety to these compositions; and the rarest productions of the animal creation are collected, to enliven them: nothing is forgot that can either exhilerate the mind, gratify the senses, or give a spur to the imagination.

Their scenes of terror are composed of gloomy woods, deep vallies inaccessible to the sun, impending barren rocks, dark caverns, and impetuous cataracts rushing down the mountains from all parts. The trees are ill formed, forced out of their natural directions, and seemingly torn to pieces by the violence of tempests: some are thrown down, and intercept the course of the torrents; others look as if blasted and shattered by the power of lightening: the buildings are in ruins; or half consumed by fire, or swept away by the fury of the waters: nothing remaining entire but a few miserable huts dispersed in the mountains which serve at once to indicate the existence and wretchedness of the inhabitants. Bats, owls, vultures, and every bird of prey flutter in the groves; wolves, tigers and jackalls howl in the forests; half-famished animals wander upon the plains; gibbets, crosses, wheels; and the whole apparatus of torture, are seen from the roads; and in the most dismal recesses of the woods, where the ways are rugged and overgrown with weeds, and where every object bear the marks of depopulation, are temples dedicated to the king of vengeance, deep caverns in the rocks, and descents to subterraneous habitations, overgrown with brushwood and brambles; near which are placed pillars of stone, with pathetic descriptions of tragical events, and many horrid acts of cruelty, perpetrated there by outlaws and robbers of former times: and to add both to the horror and sublimity of these scenes, they sometimes conceal in cavities, on the summits of the highest mountains, founderies [foundries], lime-kilns, and glass-works; which send forth large volumes of flame, and continued columns of thick smoke, that give to these mountains the appearance of volcanoes.

3) Their surprizing, or supernatural scenes, are of the romantic kind, and abound in the marvelous; being calculated to excite in the minds of the spectators, quick successions of opposite and violent sensations. Sometimes the passenger is hurried by steep descending paths to subterraneous vaults, divided into apartments, where lamps, which yield a faint glimmering light, discover the pale images of antient kings and heroes, reclining on beds of state; their heads are crowned with garlands of stars, and in their hands are tablets of moral sentences: flutes, and soft harmonious organs, impelled by subterraneous waters, interrupt, at stated intervals, the silence of the place, and fill the air with solemn melody.

Sometimes the traveller, after having wandered in the dusk of the forest, finds himself on the edge of precipices, in the glare of day-light, with cataracts falling from the mountains around, and torrents raging in the depths beneath him; or at the foot of impending rocks, in gloomy vallies, overhung with woods, on the banks of dull moving rivers, whose shores are covered with sepulchral monuments, under the shade of willows, laurels, and other plants, sacred to Manchew, the genius of sorrow.

His way now lies through dark passages cut in the rocks, on the side of which are recesses, filled with colossal figures of dragons, infernal fiends, and other horrid forms, which hold in their monstrous talons, mysterious, cabalistical sentences, inscribed on tables of brass; with preparations that yield a constant flame; serving at once to guide and to astonish the passenger: from time to time he is suprized with repeated shocks of electrical impulse, with showers of artificial rain, or sudden violent gusts of wind, and instantaneous explosions of fire; the earth trembles under him, by the power of confined air; and his ears are successively struck with many different sounds, produced by the same means; some resembling the cries of men in torment; others the roaring of bulls, and howl of ferocious animals, with the yell of hounds, and the voices of hunters; others are like the mixed croaking of ravenous birds; and others imitate thunder, the raging of the sea, the explosion of cannon, the sound of trumpets, and all the noise of war.

His road then lies through lofty woods, where serpents and lizards of many beautiful sorts crawl upon the ground, and where innumerable monkies, cats and parrots, clamber upon the trees, and intimidate him as he passes; or through flowery thickets, where he is delighted with the singing of birds, the harmony of flutes, and all kinds of soft instrumental music: sometimes, in this romantic excursion, the passenger finds himself in extensive recesses, surrounded with arbors of jessamine, vine and roses, where beauteous Tartarean damsels, in loose transparent robes, that flutter in the air, present him with rich wines, mangostans, ananas, and fruits of Quangsi; crown him with garlands of flowers, and invite him to taste the sweets of retirement, on Persian carpets, and beds of camusath skin down.

These enchanted scenes always abound with water-works, so contrived as to produce many surprizing effects; and many splendid pieces of scenery. Air is likewise employed with, great success, on different occasions; not only for the purposes above-mentioned, but likewise to form artificial and complicated echoes: some repeating the motion of the feet; some the rustling of garments; and others the human voice, in many different tones: all which are calculated to embarrass, to surprize, or to terrify the passenger in his, progress.

All sorts of optical deceptions are also made use of; such as paintings on prepared surfaces, contrived to vary the representations as often as the spectator changes place: exhibiting, in one view, groupes of men; in another; combats of animals; in a third, rocks, cascades, trees and mountains; in a fourth, temples and colonades; and a variety of other pleasing subjects. They likewise contrive pavements and incrustations for the walls of their apartments, of Mosaic work, composed of many pieces of marble, seemingly thrown together without order or design; which, when seen from certain points of view, unite in forming lively and exact representations of men, animals, buildings and landscapes: and they frequently introduce pieces of architecture, and even whole prospects in perspective; which are formed by introducing temples, bridges, vessels, and other fixed objects, lessened as they are more distant from the points of view, by giving greyish tints to the distant parts of the composition; and by planting: there trees of a fainter colour, and smaller growth, than those that appear in the foreground: thus rendering considerable in appearance, what in reality is trifling.

The Chinese Artists introduce into these enchanted scenes all kinds of sensitive, and other extraordinary trees, plants and flowers. They keep in them a surprizing variety of monstrous birds, reptiles, and animals, which they import from distant countries, or obtain by crossing the breeds. These are tamed by art; and guarded by enormous dogs of Tibet, and African giants, in the habits of magicians.

They likewise have amongst the plantations, cabinets, in which are collected all the extraordinary productions of the animal, vegetable and mineral kingdoms; as well as paintings, sculptures, medals, antiquities, and ingenious inventions of the mechanic arts: which, are a fresh source of entertainment, when the weather is bad, or when the heat is too intense to admit of being in the open air.

The communications to the different scenes and other parts of the Chinese Gardens, are by walks, roads, bridleways, navigable rivers, lakes, arid canals; in all which their artists introduce as much variety as possible; not only in the forms and dimensions, but also in their decoration: avoiding, nevertheless, all the absurdities with which our antient European style of Gardening abounds.

"I am not ignorant," said one of their artists, "that your European planters, thinking Nature scanty in her arrangements, or being perhaps disgusted with the familiarity and commonness of natural objects, introduce artificial forms into their plantations, and cut their trees in the shapes of pyramids, flower-pots, men, fishes, and brute animals; and I have heard of colonades, and whole palaces, formed by plants, cut as precisely as if they had been built of stone. But this is purchasing variety at the expence of reason: such extravagancies ought never to be tolerated, excepting in enchanted scenes: and there but very seldom; for they must be as destitute of beauty, as they are of propriety; and if the planter be a traveller, and a man of observation, he can want no such helps to variety, as he will recollect a thousand, beautiful effects along the common roads of the countries through which he has passed, that may be introduced with much better success."

Their roads, walks and avenues, are either directed in a single straight line, twined in a crooked one, or carried zig-zag, by several straight lines, altering their course at certain points. They observe that there are few objects more strikingly great than a spacious road, planted on each side with lofty trees, and stretching in a direct line, beyond the reach of the eye; and that there are few things more variously entertaining, than a winding one, which opening gradually to the sight, discovers, at every step, a new arrangement; and although, in itself, it has not the power of raising violent emotions, yet, by bringing the passenger suddenly and unexpectedly to great or uncommon things, it occasions strong impressions of surprize and astonishment, which are more forcibly felt, as being more opposite to the tranquil pleasure enjoyed in the confined parts of the road: and, in small compositions, they find crooked directions exceedingly useful to the planter, who, by winding his walks, may give an idea of great extent, notwithstanding the narrowness of his limits.

They say that roads which are composed of repeated straight lines, altering their directions at certain points, have all the advantages both of crooked and straight ones, with other properties, peculiar to themselves. The variety and new arrangement of objects, say they, which present themselves at every change of direction, occupy the mind agreeably: their abrupt appearance occasions surprize; which, when the extent is vast, and the repetitions frequent, swells into astonishment and admiration: the incertitude of the mind where these repetitions will end, and its anxiety as the spectator approaches towards the periods, are likewise very strong impressions, preventing that state of languor into which the mind naturally sinks by dwelling long on the same objects.

The straight directions, particularly the zig-zag, are, on account of these effects, well adapted to avenues or high roads, which lead to towns, palaces, bridges, or triumphal arches; to castles or prisons, for the reception of criminals; to mausoleums; and all other works of which the intent is to inspire horror, veneration or astonishment. To humbler objects, the waving line is a more proper approach; the smallness of their parts rendering them unfit for a distant inspection: and as they are trifling in themselves, they please most when their appearance, is unexpected: and from the very point whence all their little beauties are seen in the highest lustre.

In disposing the walks of their Gardens, the Chinese artists are very attentive to lead them successively to all the principal buildings, fine prospects, and other interesting parts of the composition; that the passenger may be conducted, insensibly, as it were by accident, and without turning back, or seeming to go out of the way, to every object deserving notice.

Both their straight and winding walks are, in some places, kept at a considerable distance from each other, and separated by close planted thickets, to hide all exterior objects; as well to keep the passenger in suspense with regard to the extent, as to excite those gloomy sensations which naturally steal upon the mind, in wandering through the intricacies of a solitary forest. In other places the walks approach each other; and the thickets growing gradually less deep, and more thinly planted, the ear is struck with the voices of those who are in the adjacent walks, and the eye amused with a confused sight of their persons, between the stems and foliage of the trees. Insensibly again the plantations spread and darken, the objects disappear, and the voices die in confused murmurs; when unexpectedly the walks are turned into the same open spaces, and the different companies are agreeably surprized to meet where they may view each other, and satisfy their curiosity without impediment.

The Chinese Gardeners very seldom finish any of their walks *en cul de sac*; carefully avoiding all unpleasant disappointments: but if at any time the nature of the situation obliges them to it, they always terminate at some interesting object; which lessens the disappointment, and takes off the idea of a childish conceit.

Neither do they ever carry a walk round the extremities of a piece of ground, and leave the middle entirely open, as it is too often done amongst us: for though it might render the first glance striking and noble, they think the pleasure would be of short duration; and that the spectator would be but moderately entertained, by walking several miles, with the same objects continually obtruding upon his sight. If the ground they have to work upon be small, and that they choose to exhibit a grand scene, either from the principal habitation, or any other capital point, they do indeed leave a great part of the space open; but still care is taken to have a good depth of thicket, which frequently breaks considerably in upon the open space, and hides many parts of it from the spectator's eye.

These projections produce variety, by altering the apparent figure of the open space from every point of view; and by constantly hiding parts of it, they create a mystery which excites the traveller's curiosity: they likewise occasion, in many places, a great depth in the thicket, to make recesses for buildings, seats, and other objects, as well as for bold windings of the principal walks, and for several smaller paths to branch off from the principal ones; all which take off the idea of a boundary, and afford amusement to the passenger in his course: and as it is not easy to pursue all the turns of the different lateral paths, there is still something left to desire, and a field for the imagination to work upon.

In their crooked walks, they carefully avoid all sudden or unnatural windings, particularly the regular serpentine curves, of which our English Gardeners are so fond; observing, that these eternal, uniform, undulating lines, are, of all things, the most unnatural, the most affected, and most tiresome to pursue. Having nature in view, they seldom turn their walks, without some apparent excuse; either to avoid impediments, naturally existing, or raised by art, to improve the scenery. A mountain, a precipice, a deep valley, a marsh, a piece of rugged ground, a building, or some old venerable plant, afford a striking reason for turning aside; and if a river, the sea, a wide extended lake, or a terrace commanding rich prospects, present themselves, they hold it judicious to follow them in all their windings; so to protract the enjoyments which these noble objects procure: but on a plain, either open, or formed into groves and thickets, where no impediments oblige, nor no curiosity invites to follow a winding path, they think it absurd, saying, that the road must either have been made by art, or be worn by the constant passage of travellers; in either of which cases, it cannot be supposed that men would go by a crooked line, where they could arrive by a straight one. In general, they are very sparing of their twists, which are always easy, and so managed that never more than one curve is perceptible at the same time.

They likewise take care to avoid an exact parallelism in these walks, both with regard to the trees which border them, and the ground of which they are composed. The usual width given to the walk, is from eight to twenty or even thirty feet, according to the extent of the plantation; but the trees, on each side, are, in many places, more distant; large spaces being left open, and covered with grass and wild flowers, or with fern, broom, briars, and underwood.

The ground of the walk is either of turf or gravel; neither of them finishing exactly at its edges, but running some way into the thickets, groves or shrubberies, on each side; in order to imitate nature more closely, and to take off that disagreeable formality and stiffness, which a contrary practice occasions in our European plantations.

In their straight roads or walks, when the extent is vast, the Chinese artists observe an exact order and symmetry, saying, that in stupendous works, the appearance of art is by no means disgusting; that it conveys to posterity instances of the grandeur of their ancestors; and gives birth to many sublime and pleasing reflections. The imperial roads are astonishing works of this nature; they are composed of triple avenues, adorned with four rows of enormous trees; generally Indian chesnuts, spruce firs, mountain cedars, and others of formal shapes; or oaks, elms, tulips, and others of the largest growth, planted at proper regular distances; and extending in straight lines, and almost on a perfect level, two, three, even four hundred miles. The center avenues are from one hundred and fifty, to two hundred feet wide; and the lateral ones, are generally from forty to fifty feet; the spreading branches of the trees forming over them a natural umbrella, under which the travellers pass, at all times of the day, unmolested by the sun.

In some places these roads are carried, by lofty vaulted passages, through the rocks and mountains; in others, upon causeways and bridges, over lakes, torrents, and arms of the sea; and in others, they are supported, between the precipices, upon chains of iron, or upon pillars, and many tire [tier] of arcades, over villages, pagodas, and cities: in short, no difficulty has been attended to in their construction; but every obstacle has been conquered with amazing industry, and at an almost incredible expence.

Does this mean anything to Li or Haipng?

There are, in different parts of China, many works of the kinds just mentioned; but amongst the most considerable, are counted the Passage of King-tong [Jinghong?], the Bridges of Fo-cheu [Fuzhou] and Lo-yang [Luoyang], and the Cientao [zhangdao], in the province of Xensi [Shaanxi].

The first of these is a communication between two precipices, composed of twenty enormous chains of iron, each two hundred feet in length, which are covered with planks and earth, to form the road.[9]

The second is a bridge between Fo-cheu and the suburb Nan-ti [Nantai], consisting of one hundred arches, of a sufficient size for the passage of ships under full sail: it is built of large blocks of hewn stone, and enclosed with a magnificent marble balustrade, the pedestals of which support two hundred colossal lions, artfully cut in the same material.[10]

The bridge of Lo-yang is in the province of Fokien [Fujian], and is the largest and most surprizing work of the sort that yet has been heard of. It is composed of three hundred piers of black marble, joined to each other by vast blocks of the same material, forming the road, which is enclosed with a marble balustrade, whose pedestals are adorned with lions, and other works of sculpture. The whole length of the bridge is sixteen thousand two hundred feet, or upwards of three miles; its width is forty-two feet; and the blocks of which it is composed are each fifty-four feet long, and six feet diameter.[11]

The Cientao, or Way of Pillars, is a communication between many precipices; built to shorten the road to Pekin. It is near four miles long, of a considerable width and supported over the vallies upon arches and stone piers of a terrifying height.[12]

In the mountains, on each side of these imperial roads, are erected a great number of buildings, adorned with colossal statues, and other works of sculpture, which afford constant entertainment to the passengers. These are the monuments of their wise men, their saints, and, their warriors, erected at the expence of the state, and furnished with nervous inscriptions, in the Chinese language, giving an account of the lives and actions of those they commemorate: some of these buildings are distributed into many spacious courts and stately apartments, being little inferior to palaces, either in magnificence or extent.

Instead of roads, the center avenues are sometimes formed into navigable canals, from one hundred to one hundred and fifty feet wide, being sufficiently deep to admit galleys and other small vessels; with horse-ways on each side of the canals, for the convenience of towing them, either against the wind or the stream. On these the emperor, and Chinese manda-rines, are frequently conveyed, in large magnificent sampans or barges, divided into many splendid rooms; being sometimes attended by a consid-erable train of smaller vessels, of different constructions, adorned with dragons, streamers, lanterns of painted silk, and various other ornaments, the whole composing a very brilliant and entertaining show.

All the imperial forests, besides the high roads which pass through them, have many spacious avenues cut in the woods, spreading from different centers, like rays of stars, and terminating at idol temples, towers, castles, and all the interesting objects of the circumjacent country. The centers from which these avenues part, are of a circular or octagonal figure, with eight avenues; or of a semi-circular form, with only three branching from them. Their area is generally very considerable; and its middle is adorned with a triumphal arch, a pagoda, a magnificent fountain, or some other consider-able monument.

Where the extent is vast, each single avenue has besides, in its course, one or more open spaces, from which a number of smaller avenues again branch out, and terminate at many buildings, erected in the woods, for various purposes; all which, without any confusion, add to the variety and intricacy of these compositions; giving them an appearance of immensity not to be conceived, but by such as have seen them: and wherever a deep valley, a large river, or an arm of the sea, interrupt and break off the course of the avenues, the plantations are nevertheless continued on the opposite shore, in order to make them appear more considerable.

In straight roads, of smaller dimensions, the Chinese very artfully imitate the irregular workings of nature; for although the general direction be a straight line, yet they easily avoid all appearance of stiffness or formality, by planting some of the trees out of the common line; by inclining some of them out of an upright; or by employing different species of plants, and by placing them at irregular distances, with their stems sometimes bare, and at other times covered with honey-suckles and sweet-bryar, or surrounded with underwood. They likewise cut and dispose the branches of the trees in various manners; some being suffered to spread, to cover and shade the walks; whilst others are shortened, to admit the sun. The ground too is composed of rises and falls; and the banks on each side of the walk are, in some places, of a considerable height, forming hollow ways, which they often cover at the top with bushes and trunks of fallen trees: frequently too the course of the walk is interrupted by a large oak, or elm, or tulipifera,[13] placed in the middle; or by a screen of trees running quite across; which, when the part on one side of the screen is opened and illuminated by the sun, and the part on the other side, close and shaded, produces a pleasing contrast.

I have often seen, in China, *berceaus*,[14] and arbors, not of lattice-work, as France, but of bamboo, hazel, and elm, whose branches being interwoven at the top, formed an arch not at all displeasing to the eye, and exceedingly useful, during the heats of summer: and to render these cool retreats more agreeable, jessamine, scarlet beans, sweet-scented pease, granadillas of several sorts, nasturtiums, the convulvus major, and many other sorts of climbers, were planted round the outside, which, forcing their way through, enriched the sides and arches of the walks in a very beautiful manner.

I have likewise seen, in Chinese plantations, walks bordered with the cut yew and elm hedges, so common in most countries of Europe, which the Chinese artists sometimes admit of, for variety's sake; but they never have the stiff appearance of our European ones: the shears are used sparingly; towards the top the branches are suffered to spread unmolested; and even in the cut parts of them are seen large masses of other plants forcing their way through; such as the sycamore, the fig, the vine, and others, whose foliage and verdure are most opposite to those of the edge.

The dimensions both of their straight roads and walks, vary according to the purposes they are designed for; and, in some degree too, according to their length. Roads or avenues to considerable objects, are, as has been observed, generally composed of three parallel walks: that in the middle being from thirty to one hundred and fifty, or even two hundred feet wide; those on the sides, from fifteen to forty. In their Gardens, the principal straight walks are never narrower than twenty feet; and seldom broader than forty-five or fifty: and the smallest straight walks are never narrower than twenty feet; and seldom broader than forty-five or fifty: and the smallest straight walks twelve feet wide. Thirty to thirty-six feet is called a sufficient width for a length of two hundred yards; forty to fifty for one of four hundred; sixty for one of six hundred; and seventy for a length of eight hundred yards: and when the extent is more than this last dimension, they do not tie themselves up to any proportion, but encrease their width as much as they conveniently can; never, however, exceeding one hundred and fifty, to two hundred feet; which they think the utmost width that can be given, without rendering the avenue disproportionate to the trees that border it.

In the construction of roads and walks, the Chinese Gardeners are very expert, and very circumspect: they never situate them at the foot of mountains or rising grounds, without contriving drains to receive the waters descending from the heights, which are afterwards discharged by arched gulleys under the roads, into the plains below; forming, in the rainy season, a great number of little cascades, that increase the beauty of the scenery. The roads which are designed for carriages, they make as level as possible; they give them a solid bottom, and shape them so as to throw off the rainwaters expeditiously: they use, as much as possible, the nearest materials, to save expence; and are very judicious in employing different soils to form mixtures, which never become either hard or slippery; never loose in dry weather, nor deep in wet; not easily ground into powder; nor ever forming a rough flinty surface, difficult and painful for horses to move upon.

Their walks are either of grass, of gravel, or chippings of stone, covered with a, small quantity of coarse river-sand. The first sort, which are seldom used but in private Gardens, they being too liable to be spoiled in public walks, are made of the finest and cleanest turf that can be found on downs and commons; and they are kept in order, by frequent mowing, and rowling with large iron rowlers. The second sort are made of binding gravel, laid about six inches deep, upon the natural ground: if it be dry, or if swampy, upon brick rubbish, flint stones, or any other hard materials, easiest to be had: and these are also kept firm, and in great beauty, by frequent rowling. Those of stone are composed of gallets, laid about a foot thick, rammed to a firm consistence, and a regular surface; upon which is laid a sufficient quantity of river-sand, to fill up all the interstices: which done, the whole is moistened, and well rammed again.

Both in their roads and walks, they are very careful to contrive sink-stones, with proper drains and cess-pools for carrying off the waters, after violent rains: and to those that are upon descents, they never give more fall at the most than half an inch to every foot, to prevent their being damaged by the current of the waters.

As China, even in the northern provinces, is exceedingly hot during summer, much water is employed in their Gardens. In the small ones, where the situation admits, they frequently lay the greatest part of the ground under water, leaving only some islands and rocks; and in their large compositions, every valley has its brook or rivulet, winding round the feet of the hills, and discharging themselves into larger rivers and lakes. Their artists assert, that no Garden, particularly if it be extensive, can be perfect, without that element, distributed in many shapes; saying, that it is refreshing and grateful to the sense, in the seasons when rural scenes are most frequented; that it is a principal source of variety, from the diversity of forms and changes of which it is susceptible; and from the different manners in which it may be combined with other objects; that its impressions are numerous, and uncommonly forcible; and that, by various modifications, it enables the artist to strengthen the character of every composition: to encrease the tranquility of the quiet scene; to give gloom to the melancholy, gaiety to the pleasing, sublimity to the great, and horror to the terrible.

They observe, that the different aquatic sports of rowing, sailing, swimming, fishing, hunting and combating, are an inexhaustible fund of amusement; that the birds and fishes, inhabitants of the water, are highly entertaining, especially to naturalists; and that the boats and vessels which appear upon its bosom, sometimes furiously impelled by tempests, at others gently gliding over the smooth surface, form, by their combinations, a thousand momentary varied pictures, that animate and embellish every prospect. They compare a clear lake, in a calm sunny day, to a rich piece of painting, upon which the circumambient objects are represented in the highest perfection; and say, it is like an aperture in the world, through which you see another world, another sun, and other skies.

They also say, that the beauty of vegetable nature depends, in a great degree, upon an abundant supply of water; which, at the same time that it produces variety and contrast in the scenery, enriches the verdure of the lawns, and gives health and vigor to the plantations.

Their lakes are made as large as the ground will admit; some several miles in circumference: and they are so shaped, that from no single point of view all their terminations can be seen; so that the spectator is always kept in ignorance of their extent. They intersperse in them many islands; which serve to give intricacy to the form, to conceal the bounds, and to enrich the scenery. Some of these are very small, sufficient only to contain one or two weeping willows, birch, larch, laburnum, or some other pendant plants, whose branches hang over the water: but others are large, highly cultivated, and enriched with lawns, shrubberies, thickets, and buildings: or they are rugged, mountainous, and surrounded with rocks and shoals; being covered with fern, high grass, and some straggling large trees, planted in the vallies: amongst which are often seen stalking along the elephant, the rhinoceros, the dromedary, the ostrich, and the giant baboon.

There are other islands, raised to a considerable height, by a succession of terraces, communicating to each other by various flights of magnificent steps. At the angles of all these terraces, as well as upon the sides of the steps, are placed many brazen tripods, that smoke with incense; and upon the uppermost platform is generally erected a lofty tower for astronomical observations; an elegant temple, filled with idols; the colossal statue of a god, or some other considerable work; serving, at the same time, as an ornament to the Garden, and as an object to the whole country.

They also introduce in their lakes large artificial rocks, built of a particular fine coloured stone, found on the sea-coast of China, and designed with much taste. These are pierced with many openings, through which you discover distant prospects; and have in them caverns for the reception of crocodiles, enormous water-serpents, and other monsters; cages for rare aquatic birds; and grottos, with many shining apartments, adorned with, marine productions, and gems of various sorts. They plant upon them all kinds of grass, creepers and shrubs which thrive on rocks, such as moss, ground-ivy, fern, stone-crop, common house-leek, and various other sorts of the sedum, crane's-bill, dwarf box, rock roses and broom; with some trees rooted into the crevices: and they place on their summits, hermitages and idol temples, to which you ascend by many rugged, winding steps, cut in the rock.

On the borders of their lakes are seen extensive galleries, and many detached buildings, of different forms and dimensions, surrounded with plantations, sea-ports with fleets of vessels lying before them, forts with flags flying, and batteries of cannon; also, thickets of flowering shrubs, meadows covered with cattle, corn lands, cotton and sugar plantations, orchards of various fruit-trees, and rice grounds, which project into the lakes; leaving, in the midst of them, passages for boats: and, in some places, the borders consist of lofty woods, with creeks and rivers for the admission of vessels, whose banks are covered with high grass, reeds, and wild spreading trees, forming close gloomy arbors, under which the vessels pass. From these arbors are cut many vistoes [vistas] through the woods, to distant prospects of towns, bridges, temples, and various other objects, which successively strike the eye, and fill the mind with expectation; when suddenly a farther progress is rendered impracticable, by rocks, strong branches, and whole trees lying cross the channel; between which the river is seen still to continue, with many islands; whereon, and also in the water, appear the remains of antient structures, monumental inscriptions, and fragments of sculpture: which serve to give an edge to curiosity, and to render the disappointment more affecting.

Sometimes too, instead of being intercepted in your passage, the vessel, together with the whole river, are, by the impetuosity and particular direction of the current, hurried into dark caverns, overhung with woods; whence, after having been furiously impelled for some time, you are again discharged into day-light, upon lakes encompassed with high hanging woods, rich prospects on mountains, and stately temples, dedicated to Tien-ho, and the celestial spirits.

Upon their lakes, the Chinese frequently exhibit sea-fights, processions, and ship-races; also fire-works and illuminations: in the two last of which they are more splendid, and more expert than the Europeans. On some occasions too, not only the lakes and rivers, but all the pavilions, and every part of their Gardens, are illuminated by an incredible number of beautiful lanterns, of a thousand different shapes, intermixed with lampions, torches, fire-pots, and sky-rockets; than which a more magnificent sight cannot be seen. Even the Girandola, and illumination of St. Peter's of the Vatican, though far the most splendid exhibitions of that sort in Europe, are trifles, when compared to these of China.

Their rivers are seldom straight, but winding, and broken into many irregular points: sometimes they are narrow, noisy and rapid; at other times deep, broad and slow. Their banks are variegated, in imitation of nature: being, in some places, bare and gravelly; in others, covered with woods quite to the water's edge; now flat and adorned with flowers and shrubs; then steep, rocky, and forming deep winding caverns, where pigeons of the wood, and water-fowl build their nests; or rising into many little hills, covered with hanging groves; between which are valleys and glades watered by rivulets, and adorned with pleasure-houses, cottages, and rustic temples; with flocks of sheep and goats feeding about them. The terminations of rivers the Chinese artists hide either in woods, or behind hills and buildings; or they turn them under bridges, direct them into caverns, or lose them amongst rocks and shoals.

Both in their lakes and rivers are seen many kinds of reeds, and other aquatic plants and flowers; serving for ornament, as well as for covert to their birds. They erect upon them mills and other hydraulic machines, wherever the situation will permit. They introduce a great many splendid vessels, built after the manner of all nations; and keep in them all kinds of curious and beautiful water-fowl, collected from different countries.

Nor are they less various and magnificent in their bridges than in their other decorations. Some they build of wood; and compose them of rough planks, laid in a rustic manner upon large roots of trees: some are made of many trunks of trees, thrown rudely over the stream; and fenced with decayed branches, intertwined with the convulvulus, and climbers of different sorts: and some are composed of vast arches of carpentry, artfully and neatly framed together. They have also bridges of stone and marble, adorned with colonades, triumphal arches, towers, loggias, fishing pavilions, statues, bas-reliefs, brazen tripods, and porcelain vases. Some of them are upon a curve, or a serpentine plan; others branching out into various directions: some straight, and some at the conflux of rivers or canals, triangular, quadrilateral, and circular, as the situation requires; with pavilions at their angles, and basons of water in their centers, adorned with *Jets d'eau*, and fountains of many sorts.

Some of these are entire, and executed with the utmost neatness and taste; others seem in ruins; and others are left half finished, and surrounded with scaffolds, machines, and the whole apparatus of building.

It is natural for the reader to imagine, that all these bridges, with the pavilions, temples, palaces, and other structures, which have been occasionally described in the course of this work, and which are so abundantly scattered over the Chinese Gardens, should entirely divest them of a rural character, and give them rather the appearance of splendid cities, than scenes of cultivated vegetation. But such is the judgment with which the Chinese artists situate their structures, that they enrich and beautify particular prospects, without any detriment to the general aspect of the whole composition, in which Nature almost always appears predominant; for though their Gardens are full of buildings, and other works of art, yet there are many points from which none of them appear: and more than two or three at a time are seldom discovered; so artfully are they concealed in valleys, behind rocks and mountains, or amongst woods and thickets.

There are, however, for variety's sake, in most of the Chinese Gardens, particular places, consecrated to scenes of an extraneous nature; from whence all, or the greatest part of the buildings are collected into one view, rising above each other in amphitheatrical order, spreading out to a considerable extent; and, by their whimsical combinations, exhibiting the most magnificent confusion imaginable. Their artists knowing how powerfully contrast agitates the human mind, lose no opportunity of practicing sudden transitions, or of displaying strong oppositions, as well in the nature of the objects which enter into their compositions, as in their modifications. Thus they conduct you from limited prospects to extensive views; from places of horror to scenes of delight; from lakes and rivers to woods and lawns; and from the simplest arrangements of nature, to the most complicated productions of art. To dull and gloomy colours, they oppose such as are brilliant; and to light, they oppose darkness: rendering, by these means, their productions not only distinct in the parts, but also uncommonly striking in their total effect.

The cascades of the Chinese, which are always introduced, where the ground admits, and where the supply of water is sufficient, are sometimes regular, like those of Marli, Frescati [*sic*] and Tivoli; but more frequently they are rude, like the falls of Trolhetta and the Nile. In one place a whole river is precipitated from the summit of the mountain, into the vallies beneath; where it foams and whirls amongst the rocks, till it falls down other precipices, and buries itself in the gloom of impenetrable forests. In another place the waters burst out with violence from many parts, spouting a great number of cascades, in different directions; which, through various impediments, at last unite, and form one great expanse of water. Sometimes the view of the cascade is in a great measure intercepted by the branches which hang over it; sometimes its passage is obstructed by trees, and heaps of enormous stones, that seem to have been brought down by the fury of the torrent: and frequently rough wooden bridges are thrown from one rock to another, over the steepest parts of the cataract; narrow winding paths are carried along the edges of the precipices; and mills and huts are suspended over the waters; the seeming dangerous situation of which, adds to the horror of the scene.

As the Chinese are so very fond of water, their Gardeners endeavour to obtain it by art, wherever it is denied by Nature. For this purpose, they have many ingenious inventions to collect water; and many machines, of simple construction, which raise it to almost any level, at a trifling expence. They use the same method for overflowing vallies, that is practised in Europe; by raising heads of earth or masonry at their extremities: where the soil is too porous to hold water, they clay the bottom, in the same manner that we do to make it tight: and in order to prevent the inconveniences arising from stagnant waters, they always contrive a considerable discharge to procure motion, even where the supply is scanty; which is done by conveying the discharged water back, through subterraneous drains, into reservoirs; whence it is again raised into the lake or river, by means of pumps, and other machines, proper for that purpose. They always give a consider-able depth to their waters, at least five or six feet, to prevent the rising of scum, and the floating of weeds upon the surface; and they are always provided with swans, and such other birds as feed on weeds, to keep them under.

In overflowing their grounds, and also ill draining them, they take all possible care not to kill many of their old trees, either by over moistening their roots, or draining them too much; saying, that the loss of a fine old plant is irreparable; that it impairs the beauty of the adjacent plantations; and often likewise destroys the effect of the scenery, from many distant points of view: and in shaping their grounds, they are, for the same reason, equally cautious with regard to the old plantations; carefully observing never to bury the stems, nor to expose the roots of any trees which they mean to preserve.

In their plantations, the Chinese artists do not, as is the practice of some European Gardeners, plant indiscriminately every thing that comes in their way; nor do they ignorantly imagine that the whole perfection of planta-tions consists in the variety of the trees and shrubs of which they are com-posed: on the contrary, their practice is guided by many rules, founded on reason and long observation, from which they seldom or ever deviate.

"Many trees, shrubs and flowers," sayeth Li-Tsong, a Chinese author of great antiquity, "thrive best in low moist situations; many on hills and mountains: some require a rich soil; but others will grow on clay, in sand, or even upon rocks; and in the water: to some a sunny exposition is neces-sary; but for others, the shade is preferable. There are plants which thrive best in exposed situations; but, in general, shelter is requisite. The skilful Gardener, to whom study and experience have taught these qualities, care-fully attends to them in his operations; knowing that thereon depend the health and growth of his plants; and consequently the beauty of his plantations."

In China, as in Europe, the usual times of planting, are the autumn and the spring; same things answering best when planted in the first, and some in the last of these seasons. Their Gardeners avoid planting, whenever the grounds are so moist as to endanger the rotting of the roots; or when the frosts are so near as to pinch the plants, before they have recovered the shock of transplantation; or when the earth and air are too dry to afford nurture to them; or when the weather is so tempestuous as to shake or overturn them, whilst loose and unrooted in the ground.

They observe, that the perfection of trees for ornamental Gardening, consists in their size; in the beauty and variety of their forms; in the colour and smoothness of their bark; in the quantity, shape, and rich verdure of their foliage; in its early appearance in the spring, and long duration in the autumn; in the quickness of their growth; in their hardiness to endure the extremities of heat; cold, drought and moisture; in their making no litter, during the spring or summer, by the fall of the blossom; and in the strength of their branches, to resist, unhurt the violence of tempests.

They say, that the perfection of shrubs consists not only in most of the above mentioned particulars, but also in the beauty, durability, or long succession of their blossom; and in their fair appearance before the bloom, and after it is gone.

"We are sensible," say they, "that no plant is possessed of all good qualities; but choose such as have the fewest faults; and avoid all the exotics, that vegetate with difficulty in our climate; for though they may be rare, they cannot be beautiful, being always in a sickly state: have, if you please, hot-houses and cool-houses, for plants of every region, to satisfy the curiosity of botanists; but they are mere infirmaries: the plants which they contain, are valetudinarians, divested of beauty and vigor; which only exist by the power of medicine, and by dint of good nursing."

The excessive variety of which some European Gardeners are so fond in their plantations, the Chinese artists blame, observing, that a great diversity of colours, foliage, and direction of branches, must create confusion, and destroy all the masses upon which effect and grandeur depend: they observe too; that it is unnatural; for, as in Nature most plants sow their own seeds, whole forests are generally composed of the same sort of trees. They admit, however, of a moderate variety; but are by no means promiscuous in the choice of their plants; attending, with great care, to the colour, form, and foliage of each; and only mixing together such as harmonize and assemble agreeably.

They say that some trees are only proper for thickets; others only fit to be employed singly; and others equally adapted to both these situations. The mountain-cedar, the spruce and silver firs, and all others whose branches have an horizontal direction, they hold improper for thickets; because their branches indent into each other; and likewise cut disagreeably upon the plants which back them. They never mix these horizontal branched trees with the cypress, the oriental arbor vitae, or other upright ones; nor with the larix, the weeping willow, the birch, the laburnum, or others of a pendant nature;

saying, that the intersection of their branches forms a very unpicturesque kind of net-work: neither do they employ together the catalpha and the acacia, the yew and the willow, the plane and the sumach, nor any of such heterogeneous sorts; but on the contrary, they assemble in their large woods, the oak, the elm, the beech, the tulip, the sycamore, maple and plane, the Indian chesnut and western walnut, the arbeal, the lime, and all whose luxuriant foliages hide the direction of their branches; and growing in globular masses, assemble well together; forming, by the harmonious combination of their tints, one grand mass of rich verdure.

In their smaller plantations, they employ trees of a smaller growth, but of the same concordant sorts; bordering them with Persian lilacks, gelder-roses, seringas, coronillas or sennas of various sorts, flowering rasberries, yellow jessamine, hypericum or St. John's wort, the spiraea frutex, altheas, roses, and other flowering shrubs; intermixed with flowers and with the padus of various species, elder, mountain ash, acacia, double blossomed thorn, and many other sorts of flowering trees: and wherever the ground is bare, they cover it with white, blue, purple and variegated periwinkle, the convulvulus minor, dwarf stocks, violets, primroses, and different kinds of creeping flowers; and with strawberries, tutsen and ivy which climbs up and covers the stems of the trees.

In their shrubberies they follow, as much as possible, the same rules; observing farther, in some of them to plant all such shrubs as flourish at one time; and in others, such as succeed each other: of which different methods the first is much the most brilliant; but its duration is short; and the appearance of the shrubbery is generally shabby, as soon as the bloom is off: they therefore seldom use it, but for scenes that are to be enjoyed at certain periods; preferring the last, on other occasions, as being of long duration, and less unpleasing after the flowers are gone.

The Chinese Gardeners do not scatter their flowers indiscriminately about their borders, as is usual in some parts of Europe, but, dispose them with great circumspection; and, if I may be allowed the expression, paint their way very artfully along the skirts of the plantations: and in other places, where flowers are to be introduced. They reject all that are of a straggling growth, of harsh colours, and poor foliage; choosing only such as are of some duration, grow either large, or in clusters, are of beautiful forms, well leaved, and of tints that harmonize with the greens that surround them. They avoid all sudden transitions, both with regard to dimension and colour; rising gradually from the smallest flowers to hollioaks, pœonies, sun-flowers, carnation-poppies, and others of the boldest growth; and varying their tints, by easy gradations, from white, straw colour, purple and incarnate, to the deepest blues, and most brilliant crimsons and scarlets. They frequently blend several roots together, whose leaves and flowers unite, and compose only one rich harmonious mass; such as the white and purple candituff, larkspurs, and mallows of various colours, double poppies, loopins, primroses, pinks and carnations; with many others, whose forms and colours accord with each other: and the same method they use with flowering shrubs; blending white, red, and variegated roses together; purple and white lilacks; yellow and white jessamine; altheas of various sorts; and as many others, as they can with any propriety unite.—By these mixtures they encrease considerably the variety and beauty of their compositions.

In their large plantations, the flowers generally grow in the natural ground; but in their flower-gardens, and in all other parts that are highly kept, they are in pots, buried in the ground; which, as fast as the bloom goes off, are removed, and others are brought in their places; so that there is a constant succession, for almost every month in the year; and the flowers are never seen, but in the height of their beauty.

Among the most interesting parts of the Chinese plantations, are their open groves; for as the women spend much of their time there, care is taken to situate them as pleasantly as possible, and to adorn them with all kinds of natural beauties.

The ground on which they are planted, is commonly uneven, yet not rugged; either on a plain, raised into many gentle swellings; on the easy declivity of a mountain, commanding rich prospects; or in vales, surrounded with woods, and watered with springs and rivulets.

Those which are in an open exposure, are generally bordered with flowery meadows, extensive corn-fields, or large lakes; the Chinese artists observing, that the brilliancy and gaiety of these objects, form a pleasing contrast with the gloom of the grove: and when they are confined in thickets, or close planted woods, the plantation is so formed that, from every approach, some part of the grove is hid; which opening gradually to the eye of the passenger, satisfies his curiosity by degrees.

Some of these groves are composed of evergreens, chiefly of pyramidal forms, thinly planted over the surface, with flowering shrubs scattered amongst them: others are composed of lofty spreading trees, whose foliage affords a shady retreat during the heat of the day. The plants are never crowded together; sufficient room being left between them for sitting or walking upon the grass; which, by reason of its shady situation, retains a constant verdure; and, in the spring, is adorned with a great variety of early flowers, such as violets, crocus's, polianthus's and primroses; hyacinths, cowslips, snow-drops, daffodils and daisies. Some trees of the grove are suffered to branch out from the very bottom of the stem upwards; others, for the sake of variety, have their stems bare: but far the greater number are surrounded with rose-trees, sweet-briar, honeysuckles, scarlet beans, nasturtiums, everlasting and sweet-scented peas, double-blossomed briar, and other odoriferous shrubs, which beautify the barren parts of the plant, and perfume the air.

Sometimes too their open groves are composed of lemon, orange, citron, pompelmose [pamplemousse], and myrtle-trees; which, as the climate varies, either grow in the earth, or in buried tubs and pots, which are removed to green houses during the winter. They also have groves of all sorts of fine formed fruit-trees; which, when they blossom, and also when their fruit is ripe, are exceedingly beautiful: and to add to the luxuriance of these scenes, the Chinese artists plant vines of different coloured grapes near many of the trees, which climb up their stems, and, afterwards hang in festoons from one tree to another.

In all their open groves are kept young broods or pheasants, partridges, pea-fowls, turkies, and all kinds of handsome domestic birds, who flocks thither, at certain times of the day, to be fed: they also retain in them, by the same method, squirrels, small monkies, cokatoos, parrots, hog deer, spotted capritos [cabritos]; lambs, Guinea pigs, and many other little beautiful birds and animals.

The trees which the Chinese Gardeners use in their open groves, and also for detached trees, or groupes of two three, or four together, are the mountain cedar, the spruce silver and balm of Gilead firs, the larix, the smooth stemmed or Weymouth pine, the arbor vitae, and cypress; the weeping willow, the ash, the maple, western walnut, arbeal, tulip, acacia, oak, elm, and all others that grow in picturesque forms: and whenever they loose their natural shape, either by too quick vegetation or other accidents, they endeavour to reduce them to an agreeable form, by lopping off their exuberances; or by forcing them into other directions. The Indian, or horse-chesnut, the lime, and some others of a stiff, formal growth, they never use detached; but, find them, on account of their rich verdure, their blossom, and abundant foliage, very fit for thickets, woods and avenues.

They have particular plants for the dressed gay parts of the Garden; others in their wilds and scenes of horror; and others appropriated to monuments and ruins; or to accompany buildings of various sorts; according as their properties fit them for these different purposes.

In planting, they are nicely attentive to the natural size of their plants; placing such as are of humble growth in the front; and those that are higher, gradually inwards: that all may be exposed to view at the same time. They appropriate certain plants to low moist situations; and others to those that are dry and lofty; strictly attending therein to Nature: for though a willow, say they, may grow upon a mountain, or an oak in a bog, yet are not these by any means natural situations for either.

When the patron is rich, they consider nothing but perfection in their plantations: but when he is poor, they have also an eye to œconomy; introducing such plants, trees and buildings, into their design, as are not only beautiful, but also useful. Instead of lawns, they have meadows and fields, covered with sheep and other cattle; or lands planted with rice and cotton, or sowed with corn, turneps, beans, pease, hemp, and other things that produce flowers, and variegated pieces of colouring. The groves are composed of all useful kinds of fruit-trees; such as apple, pear, cherry, mulberry, plumb, apricot, fig, olive, filbert, and many others, peculiar to China.

The woods are full of timber-trees, useful for fuel and building; which also produce chesnuts, walnuts, acorns, and other profitable fruits and feeds: and both woods and groves abound with game of all sorts.

The shrubberies consist of rose, rasberry, bramble, currant, lavender, vine and goosberry bushes; with barberry, alder, peach, nectarine and almond trees. All the walks are narrow, and carried under the drip of the trees, and skirts of the plantation, that they may occupy no useful ground: and of the buildings, some are barns for grain or hay; some stables for horses and oxen; some dairies, with their cow-houses and calf-pens; some cottages for the husbandmen, with sheds for implements of husbandry; some are dove-houses; others menageries for breeding poultry; and others stoves and green-houses, for raising early or rare fruits, vegetables and flowers: all judiciously placed, and designed with taste, though in a rustic style.

The lakes and rivers, are well stored with fish and water-fowl: and all the vessels contrived for fishing, hunting, and other sports that are profitable as well as entertaining. In their borders they plant, instead of flowers, sweet herbs, celery, carrots, potatoes, strawberries, scarlet beans, nasturtiums, endive, cucumbers, melons, pineapples, and other handsome fruits and vegetables: and all the less sightly productions for the kitchen, are carefully hid behind espaliers of fruit-trees.—Thus, they say, that every farmer may have a Garden without expence; and that if all land-holders were men of taste, the world might be formed into one continued Garden, without difficulty.

Such is the substance of what I have hitherto collected relative to the Gardens of the Chinese. My endeavour, in the present Publication, has been to give the general outline of their style of Gardening, without entering into trifling particulars, and without enumerating many little rules of which their artists occasionally avail themselves; being persuaded that, to men of genius, such minute discriminations are always unnecessary, and often prejudicial, as they burden the memory, and clog the imagination with superfluous restrictions.

The dispositions and different artifices mentioned in the preceding pages, are those which are chiefly practised in China, and such as best characterize their style of Gardening. But the artists of that country are so inventive, and so various in their combinations, that no two of their compositions are ever alike: they never copy nor imitate each other; they do not even repeat their own productions; saying, that what has once been seen, operates feebly at a second inspection; and that whatever bears even a distant resemblance to a known object, seldom excites a new idea. The reader is therefore not to imagine that what has been related is all that exists; on the contrary, a considerable number of other examples might have been produced: but those that have been offered will probably be sufficient; more especially as most of them are like certain compositions in musick, which, though simple in themselves, suggest, to a fertile imagination, an endless succession of complicated variations.

To the generality of Europeans many of the foregoing descriptions may seem improbable; and the execution of what has been described, in some measure impracticable: but those who are better acquainted with the East, know that nothing is too great for Eastern magnificence to attempt; and there can be few impossibilities, where treasures are inexhaustible, where power is unlimited, and where munificence has no bounds.

Europeans artists must not hope to rival Oriental splendor; yet let them look up to the sun, and copy as much of its lustre as they can, circumstances will frequently obstruct them in their course, and they may often be prevented from soaring high: but their attention should constantly be fixed on great objects; and their productions always demonstrate, that they knew the road to perfection, had they been enabled to proceed on the journey.

Where twining serpentine walks, scattering shrubs, digging holes to raise mole-hills, and ringing never-ceasing changes on lawns, groves and thickets, is called Gardening, it matters little who are the Gardeners; whether a peasant or a Poussin; whether a child in sport, or a man for hire: the meanest may do the little there is to be done, and the best could reach no farther. But wherever a better style is adopted, and Gardens are to be natural, without resemblance to vulgar Nature; new without affectation, and extraordinary without extravagance; where the spectator is to be amused, where his attention is constantly to be kept up, his curiosity excited, and his mind agitated by a great variety of opposite passions; there Gardeners must be men of genius, experience and judgement; quick in perception, rich in expedients, fertile in imagination, and thoroughly versed in all the affections of the human mind.

NOTES

1   William Chambers, *A Dissertation on Oriental Gardening* (London: Griffin, 1772). A French version was published in the same year.

2   Chambers, preface to *A Dissertation*, v.

3   Stephen Bending, "A Natural Revolution? Garden Politics in Eighteenth-Century England," in *Refiguring Revolutions: Aesthetics and Politics from the English Revolution to the Romantic Revolution*, ed. Kevin Sharpe and Steven N. Zwicker (Berkeley: University of California Press, 1998), 250–57. For this brief discussion on Chambers's *Dissertation*, its contents, and its reception in England, I have drawn upon the following recent and comprehensive studies, in addition to the essay by Stephen Bending: Porter, *The Chinese Taste*, 37–54 and 122–29; Chang, *Britain's Chinese Eye*, 28–37; Kitson, *Forging Romantic China*, 184–88, and Wiebenson, *The Picturesque Garden in France*, 50–63. On Chambers's *Dissertation* and its reception in France see Barrier, Mosser, and Chiu, *Aux jardins de Cathay*, 38–45.

4   William Chambers, *A Dissertation on Oriental Gardening: To which is annexed an Explanatory Discourse by Tan Chet-qua* (London: Griffin, 1773).

5   As shown by Stephen Bending, "A Natural Revolution?" 256, from which this quote is taken.

6   Chambers refers here to his short essay entitled "Of the Art of Laying Out Gardens Among the Chinese," published in 1757.

7   Chambers refers to the technique of "borrowed scenery." For further details on borrowed scenery, see the description by André Everard van Braam Houckgeest included in this anthology.

8   Chambers refers to the letter written from Beijing in 1743 in which the French Jesuit Jean-Denis Attiret gave a description of the imperial park of Yuanming yuan and the miniature city built within its perimeter.

9 The *Entwurff einer historischen Architectur* by Johann Bernhard Fischer von Erlach, first published in 1721, was probably among Chambers's sources for his description of Chinese bridges. Volume 3 of Fischer von Erlach's work, in fact, included engravings of notable expamples of Chinese bridges. Plate 15 depicts a suspended bridge accompanied by a text in German and French that identified the structure as "L'un des merveilleux Ponts de Chaînes en Chine près de la Ville de Kingtung." Johann Bernhard Fischer von Erlach, *Entwurff einer historischen Architectur* (Vienna, 1721), vol. 3, pl. 15.

10 Chambers refers here to the bridge on the Min River that linked the city of Fuzhou with Nantai Island. His reference is again Fischer von Erlach's *Entwurff einer historischen Architectur*, which contains an engraving of this bridge entitled "Le grand pont Chinois entre la capitale Focheu et le Fauxbourg Nantai." See Fischer von Erlach, *Entwurff*, vol. 3, pl. 13.

11 Luoyang Bridge in the city of Quanzhou. It was represented in *Entwurff einer historischen Architectur* (1721) by Fisher von Erlach with an engraving titled "Le Pont de Loyang dans la Province Chinoise Fokien." See Fischer von Erlach, *Entwurff*, vol. 3, pl. 14.

12 An engraving representing the bridge, and titled "Cientao, où le chemin des piliers, dans la Province Chinois Xensi," was published in Fischer von Erlach's *Entwurff einer historischen Architectur* (1721). See Fischer von Erlach, *Entwurff*, vol. 3, pl. 14.

13 Chambers refers here to the *Liriodendron tulipifera* L., known as tulip tree.

14 A berceau is an arched trellis for climbing plants.

BIBLIOGRAPHY

PRIMARY SOURCES

Abel, Clarke. *Narrative of a Journey in the Interior of China.* London: Longman, Hurst, Rees, Orme, and Brown, 1818.

Alexander, William. *The Costume of China.* London: Miller, 1805.

———. *Picturesque Representations of the Dress and Manners of the Chinese.* London: Murray, 1814.

Amiot, Jean Joseph Marie. "Lettre du Pere Amyot, Missionnaire de la Compagnie de Jesus, au Pere Allart de la même Compagnie. Pékin le 20 Octobre 1752." In *Lettres édifiantes et curieuses, écrites des missions étrangères, par quelques Missionnaires de la Compagnie de Jésus*, vol. 28, 171–215. Paris: Guerin et De la Tour, 1758.

———. "A Description of the Solemnities Observed at *Pe-king* on the Emperor's Mother entering on the sixtieth year of her age, from the French of P. *Amyot*, Jesuit." Translated by Thomas Percy. In *Miscellaneous Pieces Relating to the Chinese*, edited by Thomas Percy, vol. 2, 209–48. London: Dodsley, 1762.

———. "Extrait d'une lettre du P. Amiot à M.*** du 28 septembre 1777: Observations sur un livre de M. P*** [Pauw] intitulé: Recherches philosophiques sur les Égyptiens et les Chinois." In *Mémoires concernant l'histoire, les sciences, les arts, les mœurs, les usages, &c. des Chinois: Par les Missionnaires de Pekin*, vol. 6, 275–346. Paris: Nyon, 1780.

[Amiot, Jean Joseph Marie, or Pierre-Martial Cibot, attributed]. "Remarques sur un ecrit de M. P** [Pauw], intitulé: Recherches sur les Egyptiens & les Chinois." In *Mémoires concernant l'histoire, les sciences, les arts, les mœurs, les usages, &c. des Chinois: par les Missionnaires de Pekin*, vol. 2, 365–574. Paris: Nyon, 1777.

Anderson, Aeneas. *A Narrative of the British Embassy to China in the Years 1792, 1793 and 1794.* London: J. Debrett, 1795.

Attiret, Jean-Denis. "Lettre du frère Attiret de la Compagnie de Jésus, peintre au service de l'empereur de Chine, à M. d'Assaut. A Pékin le Iᵉʳ novembre 1743." In *Lettres édifiantes et curieuses, écrites des missions étrangères, par quelques missionnaires de la Compagnie de Jésus*, vol. 27, 1–57. Paris: Guerin, 1749.

————. *A Particular Account of the Emperor of China's Garden near Pekin*. Translated by Sir Harry Beaumont [Joseph Spence]. London: Dodsley, 1752.

————. "A Description of the Emperor of China's Gardens and Pleasure-Houses near Pe-king." Translated by Thomas Percy. In *Miscellaneous Pieces Relating to the Chinese*, edited by Thomas Percy, vol. 2, 146–201. London: Dodsley, 1762.

Barrow, John. *Johann Barrow's Reise durch China von Peking nach Canton im Gefolge der Großbrittannischen Gesandtschaft in den Jahren 1793 und 1794*. Translated by Johann Christian Hüttner. Weimar: Verlag d. Landes-Industrie-Comptoirs, 1804.

————. *Travels in China, Containing Descriptions, Observations, and Comparisons, Made and Collected in the Course of a Short Residence at the Imperial Palace of Yuen-min-yuen, and on a Subsequent Journey through the Country from Pekin to Canton*. London: T. Cadell and W. Davies, 1804.

————. *Voyage en Chine*. 3 vols. Paris: Buisson, 1805.

————. *Some Account of the Public Life, and a Selection from the Unpublished Writings, of the Earl of Macartney*. 2 vols. London: T. Cadell and W. Davies, 1807.

Bell, John. *Travels from St. Petersburg in Russia to Diverse Parts of Asia*. 2 vols. Glasgow: Robert and Andrew Foulis, 1763.

Bennett, George. *Wanderings in New South Wales, Batavia, Pedir Coast, Singapore and China: Being the Journal of a Naturalist in those Countries, During 1832, 1833, and 1834*. 2 vols. London: Bentley, 1834.

Benoist, Michel. "Troisieme Lettre du P. Benoit. A Pékin, le 4. Nov. 1773." In *Lettres édifiantes et curieuses, écrites des missions étrangères par quelques missionnaires de la C.[Compagnie] de J.[Jesus]*, vol. 33, 150–209. Paris: Berton, 1776.

————. "Lettre du Père Benoist à Monsieur Papillon d'Auteroche. A Péking, le 16 novembre 1767." In *Lettres édifiantes et curieuses écrites des missions étrangères: Mémoires de la Chine*, vol. 23, 534–47. Paris: Merigot, 1781.

————. "Lettre du Père Benoit, missionnaire, à Monsieur Papillon d'Auteroche. A Péking, le 16 novembre 1767." In *Lettres édifiantes et curieuses écrites des missions étrangères: Mémoires de la Chine*, vol. 23, 427–37. Toulouse: Sens et Gaude, 1811.

————. "Lettre du père Benoist, missionnaire, à M. Papillon d'Auteroche. A Péking, le 16 novembre 1767." In *Lettres édifiantes et curieuses écrites des missions étrangères: Mémoires de la Chine*, vol. 13, 176–84. Lyon: Vernarel et Cabin, 1819.

————. "Lettre du Père Benoist a M. Papillon d'Auteroche. Sur les jardins, les palais, les occupations de l'empereur. Pékin le 16 novembre 1767." In *Lettres édifiantes et curieuses concernant l'Asie, l'Afrique et l'Amérique, avec quelques relations nouvelles des missions, et des notes géographiques et historiques*, vol. 4, 120–23. Paris: Panthéon littéraire, 1843.

Berncastle, Julius. *A Voyage to China*. 2 vols. London: Shoberl, 1850.

Blondel, Jacques-François. *Architecture française*. 4 vols. Paris: Jombert, 1752–56.

———. *Cours d'Architecture*. 6 vols. Paris: Desaint, 1771–77.

Bourgeois, François. "Lettre d'un missionnaire a M. l'Abbé G. [Gallois] contenant une relation de son voyage de Canton à Pé-king. Péking, le 15 Septembre 1768." In *Mémoires concernant l'histoire, les sciences, les arts, les mœurs, les usages, &c. des Chinois: par les Missionnaires de Pekin*, vol. 8, 291–300. Paris: Nyon, 1782.

Carl, Katharine A. *With the Empress Dowager of China*. New York: The Century Co., 1907.

Castell, Robert. *The Villas of the Ancients Illustrated*. London: By the author, 1728.

Chambers, William. *Design of Chinese Buildings, Furniture, Dresses, Machines and Utensils . . . to which is annexed a Description of their Temples, Houses, Gardens*. London: Published for the author, 1757.

———. *Desseins des edifices, meubles, habits, machines, et ustenciles des Chinois: Gravés sur les originaux dessinés à la Chine . . . Auxquels est ajoutée une description de leurs temples, de leurs maisons, de leurs jardins, &c.* London: J. Haberkorn, 1757.

———. "Of the Art of Laying Out Gardens Among the Chinese." In *Design of Chinese Buildings, Furniture, Dresses, Machines, and Utensils*. London: Published for the author, 1757.

———. "Of the Art of Laying Out Gardens Among the Chinese." In *Miscellaneous Pieces Relating to the Chinese*, edited by Thomas Percy, vol. 2, 125–44. London: Dodsley, 1762.

———. *A Dissertation on Oriental Gardening*. London: Griffin, Davies, Dodsley, Wilson and Nicol, Elmslet, Walter, 1772.

———. *Dissertation sur le jardinage de l'Orient*. London: Griffin, Davies, Dodsley, Wilson and Nicol, Elmslet, Walter, 1772.

———. *A Dissertation on Oriental Gardening: To Which is Annexed an Explanatory Discourse by Tan Chet-qua*. London: Griffin, 1773.

———. "Traité des édifices, meubles, habits, machines et ustensiles des Chinois. . . . Compris une description de leurs temples, maisons, jardins, etc." In Georges-Louis Le Rouge, *Détails de nouveaux jardins à la mode*, cahier 5. Paris: Chez le Sieur Le Rouge, 1776.

Churchill, Awnsham and John. *A Collection of Voyages and Travels, Some Now First Printed From Original Manuscripts, Others Now First Published in English*. 6. vols. London: J. Walthoe, T. Whotton, S. Birt, D. Browne, T. Osborn, J. Shuckburgh, H. Lintot, 1732.

Cibot, Pierre-Martial. "De Sée-Ma-Kouang: Le jardin de Sée-Ma-Kouang." In *Mémoires concernant l'histoire, les sciences, les arts, les mœurs, les usages, &c. des Chinois: par les Missionnaires de Pekin*, vol. 2, 645–50. Paris: Nyon, 1777.

———. "Le jardin de Sée-Ma-Kouang: Pöeme." In *Mémoires concernant l'histoire, les sciences, les arts, les mœurs, les usages, &c. des Chinois: par les Missionnaires de Pekin*, vol. 2, 643–44. Paris: Nyon, 1777.

————. "Essai sur les jardins de plaisance des Chinois." In *Mémoires concernant l'histoire, les sciences, les arts, les mœurs, les usages, &c. des Chinois: par les Missionnaires de Pekin*, vol. 8, 301–26. Paris: Nyon, 1782.

————. "Observations sur les plantes, les fleurs et les arbres de Chine qu'il est possible et utile de se procurer en France." In *Mémoires concernant l'histoire, les sciences, les arts, les mœurs, les usages, &c. des Chinois: par les Missionnaires de Pekin*, vol. 11, 183–268. Paris: Nyon, 1786.

Confucius sinarum philosophus; sive, Scientia sinensis latine exposita. Paris: Hortemels, 1687.

Conger, Sarah Pike. *Letters from China*. Chicago: McClurg and Co., 1909.

Cooke, George Wingrove. *China: Being "The Times" Special Correspondence from China in the Years 1857–58*. London: Routledge, 1858.

Cousin (de) Montauban, Charles-Guillame-Marie-Apollinaire-Antoine. *L'expédition de Chine de 1860*. Paris: Plon, 1932.

Darly, Matthew. *A New Book of Chinese Designs*. London: By the author, 1754.

Davis, John Francis. *The Chinese: A General Description of the Empire of China and Its Inhabitants*. 2 vols. London: Knight and Co., 1836.

————. *Sketches of China: Partly during an Inland Journey of four Months, between Peking, Nanking, and Canton; with Notices and Observations relative to the Present War*. 2 vols. London: Knight and Co., 1841.

De Pauw, Cornelis. *Recherches philosophiques sur les Égyptiens et les Chinois*. Amsterdam: Barth, Vlam & J. Murray, 1773.

————. *Recherches philosophiques sur les Égyptiens et les Chinois*. 2 vols. Berlin: G. J. Decker, 1773.

Delatour, Louis-François. *Essais sur l'architecture des Chinois, sur leurs jardins, leurs principes de médecine, et leurs mœurs et usages*. Paris: Clousier, 1803.

Dennys, Nicholas Belfield, William Frederick Mayers, and Charles King. *The Treaty Ports of China and Japan*. London: Trübner; Hong Kong: Shortrede, 1867.

Dobell, Peter. *Travels in Kamtchatka and Siberia with a Narrative of a Residence in China*. 2 vols. London: Colburn and Bentley, 1830.

————. *Puteshestvia i novieishia nabludenia ve Nitae Manille, i Indo-Kitaiskot arxipelage bivshago rossiiskago reneralnago konsula na Filippinskix ostrovax, kolleshsk.* Saint Petersburg: N. Grecha, 1833.

————. *Sept années en Chine: Nouvelles observations sur cet empire, l'archipel indo-chinois, les Philippines et les Iles Sandwich*. Paris: Librairie d'Amyot, 1842.

Du Halde, Jean-Baptiste. *Description géographique, historique, chronologique, politique et physique de l'empire de la Chine et de la Tartarie chinoise*. 4 vols. Paris: Le Mercier, 1735.

[Ekeberg, Carl Gustav]. *Précis historique de l'économie rurale des Chinois, présenté à l'Academie Royale des Sciences des Suéde, en 1754: Par M. Charles Gustave*

Eckeberg Capitain, publié par M. Linnaeus. Translated from Swedish by Dominique de Blackford. Milan: Reycends, 1771.

Elgin, James Bruce, Earl of. *Extracts from the Letters of James, Earl of Elgin to Mary Louisa, Countess of Elgin, 1847–1862.* Edinburgh: Constable, 1864.

Ellis, Henry. *Journal of the Proceedings of the Late Embassy to China.* London: J. Murray, 1817.

The Emperor of China's Palace at Pekin, and His Principal Gardens, as well in Tartary, as at Pekin, Gehol and the Adjacent Countries; with the Temples, Pleasure-Houses, Artificial Mountains, Rocks, Lakes, etc. as Disposed in Different Parts of Those Royal Gardens. London: Sayer, Overton, Bowles, and Bowles and Son, 1753.

Fauchery, Antoine Julien. "Lettres de Chine." *Le Moniteur universel* 362, December 28 (1860): 1533–34.

Fortune, Robert. *Three Years' Wanderings in the Northern Provinces of China.* London: J. Murray, 1847.

———. *A Journey to the Tea Countries of China.* London: J. Murray, 1852.

———. "Leaves from My Chinese Notebook." *Gardener's Chronicle* 1 (1853): 230–31.

———. *Two Visits to the Tea Countries of China and the British Tea Plantations in the Himalaya.* 2 vols. London: J. Murray, 1853.

———. "Leaves from My Chinese Notebook." *Gardener's Chronicle* 10 (1855): 502–3.

———. *A Residence Among the Chinese.* London: J. Murray, 1857.

———. *Yedo and Peking: A Narrative of a Journey to the Capitals of Japan and China.* London: J. Murray, 1863.

Freeman-Mitford, Algernon Bertram. *The Attaché at Peking.* London: Macmillan and Co., 1900.

Gerbillon, Jean-François. "Lettre du Père Gerbillon a Peking en l'année 1705. Maison de plaisance de l'Empereur de la Chine à quelques lieues de Pekin." In *Lettres édifiantes et curieuses, écrites des missions étrangères, par quelques Missionnaires de la Compagnie de Jésus,* vol. 10, 412–19. Paris: Le Clerc, 1732.

———. "Seconde voyage fait par ordre de l'Empereur de la Chine en Tartarie par les Peres Gerbillon et Pereira en l'année 1689." In Jean-Baptiste Du Halde, *Description . . . de la Chine,* vol. 4, 163–251. Paris: Le Mercier, 1735.

Green, John. *A New General Collection of Voyages and Travels: Consisting of the Most Esteemed Relations, which have been Hitherto Published in Any Language: Comprehending Everything Remarkable in its Kind, in Europe, Asia, Africa, and America.* 4 vols. London: for T. Astley, 1745–47.

Guignes, Chrétien-Louis-Joseph de. *Voyages à Peking, Manille et l'Île de France, faits dans l'intervalle des années 1784 à 1801.* 3 vols. and atlas. Paris: Imprimerie Impériale, 1808.

——. *Reisen nach Peking, Manila und Isle de France in den Jahren 1784 bis 1801.* Translated by K. L. M. Müller. 2 vols. Leipzig: Hinrichs, 1810.

——. *Viaggi a Pekino, a Manilla ed all'isola di Francia fatti negli anni 1794* [sic] *a 1801.* 4 vols. Milan: Sonzogno, 1829–30.

Halfpenny, William and John. *Chinese and Gothic Architecture Properly Ornamented.* London: Sayer, 1752.

Haussmann, Auguste. *Voyage en Chine, Cochinchine, Inde et Malaisie.* 2 vols. Paris: Dessesart, 1847.

Hirschfeld, Christian Cajus Lorenz. *Théorie de l'art des jardins.* 4 vols. Leipzig: M. G. Weidmann and Reich, 1779.

Hugo, Victor. "L'expédition de Chine: Lettre au Capitaine Butler. Hauteville-House, 25 novembre 1861." In *Œuvres complètes de Victor Hugo: Actes et paroles pendant l'exile, 1852–70,* 267–70. Paris: Hetzel, 1880.

Hunter, William C. *The "Fan Kwae" at Canton, Before Treaty Days 1825–1844, By an Old Resident.* London: Kegan Paul, Trench and Co., 1882.

——. *Bits of Old China.* London: Kegan Paul, Trench and Co., 1885.

Hüttner, Johann Christian. *Nachricht von der Brittischen Gesandtschaftsreise durch China und einen Theil der Tartarei.* Berlin: Voss, 1797.

——. *Voyage à la Chine par J. C. Hüttner.* Translated by T. F. Winckler. Paris: J. J. Fuchs, 1798.

Itier, Jules. *Journal d'un voyage en Chine en 1843, 1845, 1846.* 2 vols. Paris: Dauvin et Fontaine, 1848.

Kircher, Athanasius. *China monumentis . . . illustrata.* Amsterdam: van Waesberge and Weyerstraet, 1667.

Laugier, Marc-Antoine. *Essai sur l'architecture.* Paris: Duchesne, 1753.

——. *An Essay on Architecture.* Translated by Wolfgang and Anni Herrmann. Los Angeles: Hennessey and Ingalls, 1977.

Le Comte, Louis. *Nouveaux mémoires sur l'état présent de la Chine.* 2 vols. Paris: Anisson, 1696.

——. *Memoirs and Observations . . . Made in a Late Journey Through the Empire of China.* London: Benj. Tooke and Sam Buckley, 1697.

——. *Nouveaux mémoires sur l'état présent de la Chine. Troisième édition reveüe et corrigée sur la dernière de Paris.* Amsterdam: Desbordes et Schelte, 1698 (first edition 1696).

——. *Un jésuite à Pékin: Nouveaux mémoires sur l'état présent de la Chine, 1687–1692.* Text edited and annotated by Frédérique Touboul-Boyeure. Paris: Phébus, 1990.

——. *Beschryvinge Van het machtige Keyserryk China.* 's Gravenhage: Boucquet, 1698.

Loch, Henry Brougham. *Personal Narrative of Occurrences During Lord Elgin's Second Embassy to China in 1860.* London: Murray, 1869.

Loudon, John Claudius. *An Encyclopaedia of Gardening*. London: Longman, Rees, Orme, Brown, Green, and Longman, 1835.

———. *The Gardener's Magazine*, vol. 11. London: Longman, Rees, Orme, Brown, Green, and Longman, 1835.

Lucy, Armand. *Souvenirs de voyage: Lettres intimes sur la campagne de Chine en 1860*. Marseille: Barile, 1861.

Magalhães, Gabriel de. *A New History of China, Containing a Description of the Most Considerable Particulars of That Vast Empire*. London: Newborough, 1688.

———. *Nouvelle relation de la Chine*. Translated by Sr. B[ernou]. Paris: Barbin, 1688.

[Main, James]. "Observations on Chinese Scenery, Plants, and Gardening, made on a Visit to the City of Canton and its Environs, in the Years 1793 and 1794; being an Extract from the Journal of Mr. James sent thither by the late Gilbert Slater, Esq. of Layton, Essex, to collect the Double Camellias, &c. Communicated by Mr. Main." In *The Gardener's Magazine*, edited by John Claudius Loudon, vol. 2, 135–40. London: Longman, Rees, Orme, Brown, and Green, 1827.

Main, James. "Reminiscences of a Voyage to and from China in the Years 1792–3–4." In *The Horticultural Register*, edited by James Main, vol. 5, 62–67, 97–103, 143–49, 171–80, 215–20. London: W. S. Orr and Co., 1836.

Mandeville, John. *Mandeville's Travels*. Edited by Maurice Charles Seymour. London: Oxford University Press, 1968.

Marshall, William. *Planting and Rural Ornament*. 2 vols. London: Nicol, Robinson and Debrett, 1796 (first edition 1785).

Martini, Martino. *Novus atlas sinensis*. Amsterdam: Blaeu, 1655.

Mayer, Brantz. "China and the Chinese." *Southern Quarterly Review* 12, no. 23 (July 1847): 1–51.

Mutrécy, Charles de. *Journal de la campagne de Chine, 1859–1860–1861*. 2 vols. Paris: Bourdilliat, 1861.

Nieuhof, Johannes. *Het gezantschap der Neërlandtsche Oost-Indische Compagnie, ann den grooten Tartarischen Cham*. Amsterdam: Jacob Van Meurs, 1665.

———. *L'ambassade de la Compagnie orientale des Provinces Unies vers l'empereur de la Chine, ou grand cam de Tartarie, faite par les Srs. Pierre de Goyer, & Jacob de Keyser. Mis en Français par Jean le Carpentier*. Leiden: Jacob Van Meurs, 1665.

———. *Die Gesandschaft der Ost-Indischen Gesellschaft in den Niederlanden an den Tartarischen Cham und nunmehr auch Sinischen Keiser. Ber. durch . . . Peter de Gojer u. Jacob Keiser mit 150 Kupferstükken*. Amsterdam: Jacob Van Meurs, 1666.

———. *Legatio batavica ad magnum Tartari;ae chamum Sungteium, modernum Sinæ imperatorem. Historiarum narratione. Latinitate donatam* Georgium Hornium [Georg Horn]. Amsterdam: Jacob Van Meurs, 1668.

————. *An Embassy from the East-India Company of the United Provinces, to the Great Tartar Cham, Emperor of China* . . . . Translated by John Ogilby. London: Macock, 1669.

————. *An Embassy from the East-India Company of the United Provinces, to the Grand Tartar Cham, emperor of China.* Translated by John Ogilby. London: By the author, 1673.

Odorico, da Pordenone. *The Travels of Friar Odoric.* Translated by Henry Yule. Grand Rapids, Mich.: W. B. Eerdmans, 2002.

Oliphant, Laurence. *Narrative of the Earl of Elgin's Mission to China and Japan in the Years 1857, '58, '59.* 2 vols. Edinburgh: Blackwood and Sons, 1859.

Osbeck, Pehr, and Olof Torén. *Dagbok öfwer en ostindisk resa åren 1750, 1751, 1752. med anmärkningar uti naturkunnigheten, främmande folkslags språk, seder, hushållning m.m.* Stockholm: Lor. Ludv. Grefing, 1757.

[Osbeck, Pehr, and Olof Torén.] *A Voyage to China and the East Indies, by Peter Osbeck: Together with A Voyage to Suratte, by Olof Toreen and an Account of the Chinese Husbandry, by Captain Charles Gustavus Eckeberg.* Translated from the German by John Reinhold Foster. 2 vols. London: B. White, 1771.

Osbeck, Pehr, Olof Torén, and C. G. Ekeberg. *Reise nach Ostindien und China, nebst O. Toreens Reise nach Suratte, und C. G. Ekebergs Nachricht von der Landwirthschaft der Chineser.* Translated by J. G. Georgi. Rostock: Koppe, 1765.

Over, Charles. *Ornamental Architecture in the Gothic, Chinese and Modern Taste.* London: Sayer, 1758.

Poivre, Pierre. *Voyages d'un philosophe ou observations sur les moeurs & les arts des peuples de l'Afrique, de l'Asie et de l'Amérique.* Yverdon: de Félice, 1768.

————. *Travels of a Philosopher: or, Observations on the Manners and Arts of Various Nations in Africa and Asia.* Glasgow: Urie, 1770.

Polo, Marco. *The Book of Ser Marco Polo, the Venetian, Concerning the Kingdoms and Marvels of the East.* Translated and edited by Henry Yule. 2 vols. London: John Murray, 1871.

Quatremère de Quincy, Antoine-Chrysostome. "Chinois jardins." In *Encyclopédie méthodique. Architecture*, vol. 1, 644–53. Paris: Panckoucke, 1788.

Quincy, Josiah. *The Journals of Major Samuel Shaw, the First American Consul at Canton.* Boston: W. Crosby and H. P. Nichols, 1847.

Renouard de Sainte-Croix, Félix. *Voyage commercial et politique aux Indes Orientales, aux Iles Philippines, à la Chine.* 3 vols. Paris: Crapelet, 1810.

Ripa, Matteo. *Storia della fondazione della Congregazione e del Collegio de' Cinesi sotto il titolo della Sacra Famiglia di G.C. scritta dallo stesso fondatore Matteo Ripa e de' viaggi da lui fatti.* 3 vols. Naples: Manfredi, 1832.

————. *Memoirs of Father Ripa, During Thirteen Years' Residence at the Court of Peking.* Selected and translated from the Italian by Fortunato Prandi. London: J. Murray, 1844.

————. *Giornale (1705–1724)*. Introduzione, testo critico e note di Michele Fatica. Collana "Matteo Ripa" 14. 2 vols. Naples: Istituto Universitario Orientale, 1991–96.

Saint-Simon, Louis de Rouvroy, duc de. *Mémoires complets et authentiques du duc de Saint-Simon sur le siècle de Louis XIV.* 3 vols. Paris: Buisson, 1789 (first edition 1788).

Semedo Álvaro. *Imperio de la China i cultura evangelica en èl por los religios de la Compañia de Iesus.* Madrid: Sanchez, 1642.

————. *Relatione della grande monarchia della Cina del P. Alvaro Semedo.* Rome: Scheus, 1643.

————. *Histoire universelle du grand royaume de la Chine, composée en Italien par le P. Alvarez Semedo Portugais, de la Compagnie de Jésus, et traduite en notre langue par Louis Coulon P., divisée en deux parties.* Paris: S. Cramoisy et G. Cramoisy, 1645.

————. *The History of That Great and Renowned Monarchy of China.* London: E. Tyler, 1655.

Sirr, Henry Charles. *China and the Chinese: Their Religion, Character, Customs, and Manufactures: The Evils Arising from the Opium Trade: with a Glance at Our Religious, Moral, Political and Commercial Intercourse with the Country.* 2 vols. London: Orr and Co., 1849.

Smith, Albert. *To China and Back: Being a Diary kept, out and Home.* London: By the author, 1859.

Smith, George. *A Narrative of an Exploratory Visit to Each of the Consular Cities of China, and to the Islands of Hong Kong and Chusan, in Behalf of the Church Missionary Society in the Years 1844, 1845, 1846.* New York: Harper and Brothers, 1857.

Southey, Robert. "Travels in China . . . by John Barrow." In *The Annual Review, and History of Literature; for 1804*, edited by Arthur Aikin, vol. 3, 69–83. London: Longman, 1805.

Staunton, George Leonard. *An Authentic Account of an Embassy from the King of Great Britain to the Emperor of China.* 2 vols. London: G. Nicol, 1797.

————. *Voyage dans l'intérieur de la Chine et en Tartarie fait dans les années 1792, 1793 et 1794 par lord Macartney.* Translated by J. Castéra. 4 vols. Paris: Buisson, 1798.

————. *Reis van lord Macartneij, naar China.* Amsterdam: Allart, 1798–1801.

Swinhoe, Robert. *Narrative of the North China Campaign of 1860.* London: Smith, Elder and Co., 1861.

Switzer, Stephen. *Iconographia rustica.* 3 vols. London: Browne, Barker, King, Mears, Gosling, 1718.

Taylor, Bayard. *A Visit to India, China, and Japan in the Year 1853.* New York: Putnam, 1859.

Taylor, Charles. *Five Years in China, with Some Account of the Great Rebellion, and a Description of St. Helena.* New York: Derby and Jackson, 1860.

Temple, William. *Miscellanea, the Second Part. In Four Essays.* 4th ed. London: Simpson, 1696.Tiffany, Osmond, Jr. *The Canton Chinese; or, The American's Sojourn in the Celestial Empire.* Boston: Munroe and Co., 1849.

Thévenot, Melchisédec. *Relations de divers Voyages curieux, qui n'ont point esté publiées. Et qu'on a traduit ou tiré des Originaux des Voyageurs François, Espagnols, Allemands, Portugais, Anglois, Hollandois, Persans, Arabes & autres Orientaux.* 2 vols. Paris: Moette, 1663–96.

The Travels of Several Learned Missioners of the Society of Jesus into Divers Parts of the Archipelago, India, China, and America. London: Printed for R. Gosling, 1714.

Trigault, Nicolas. *De Christiana expeditione apud Sinas suscepta a Societate Jesu, ex P. Matthaei Riccii eiusdem Societatis commentariis Libri V.* Augsburg: Mangius, 1615.

———. *Histoire de l'expedition chrestienne au royaume de la Chine entreprise par les PP. de la compagnie de Jesus.* Lyon: Cardon, 1616.

———. *Historia von Einführung der christlichen Religion in das große Königreich China durch die Societet Jesu.* Augsburg: Hierat von Cöllen, 1617.

———. *Istoria de la China i cristiana empresa hecha en ella.* Seville: Ramos Veiarano, 1621.

Van Braam Houckgeest, André Everard. *Voyage de l'ambassade de la Compagnie des Indes Orientales hollandaises vers l'empereur de la Chine, dans les années 1794 et 1795.* 2 vols. Philadelphia: Moreau de Saint-Méry, 1797–98.

———. *An Authentic Account of the Embassy of the Dutch East-India Company, to the Court of the Emperor of China, in the Years 1794 and 1795.* 2 vols. London: R. Phillips, 1798.

———. *Voyage de l'ambassade de la Compagnie des Indes Orientales hollandaises vers l'empereur de la Chine, dans les années 1794 et 1795.* 2 vols. Pairs: Garnery, 1798.

———. *Reise der Gesandtschaft der Holländisch-Ostindischen Gesellschaft an den Kaiser von China, in den Jahren 1794 und 1795.* 2 vols. Leipzig: Heinsius, 1798–99.

Varin, Paul [Charles Dupin]. *Expédition de Chine.* Paris: Lévy Frères, 1862.

Walpole, Horace. "On Modern Gardening." In *Anecdotes of Painting in England,* vol. 4, 117–51. Strawberry Hill: Kirgate, 1771.

Ware, Isaac. *The Four Books of Andrea Palladio's Architecture.* London: Ware, 1738.

———. *A Complete Body of Architecture.* London: Osborne and Shipton, 1756.

Watelet, Claude-Henri. *Essai sur les jardins.* Paris: Prault, 1774.

———. *Essay on Gardens: A Chapter of the French Picturesque.* Edited and translated by Samuel Danon. Philadelphia: University of Pennsylvania Press, 2003.

Whately, Thomas. *Observations on Modern Gardening.* London: Exshaw, 1770.

———. *L'art de former les jardins modernes, ou l'art des jardins anglois.* Translated by François de Paul Latapie. Paris: Jombert, 1771.

Wolseley, Garnet Joseph. *A Narrative of the War with China in 1860.* London: Longman, Green, Longman, and Roberts, 1862.

SECONDARY SOURCES

Akbari, Suzanne Conklin, and Amilcare Iannucci, eds. *Marco Polo and the Encounter of East and West.* Toronto: University of Toronto Press, 2008.

Alridge, Alfred Owen. *The Dragon and the Eagle: The Presence of China in the American Enlightenment.* Detroit: Wayn State University Press, 1993.

Appleton, William W. *A Cycle of Cathay: The Chinese Vogue in England During the Seventeenth and Eighteenth Centuries.* New York: Columbia University Press, 1951.

Backer de, Augustin et Alois. *Bibliothèque des écrivains de la Compagnie de Jésus.* Liege: Grandmont-Donders, 1856.

Bald, Robert C. "Sir William Chambers and the Chinese Garden." *Journal of the History of Ideas* 2, no. 3 (1950): 287–320.

Baltrušaitis, Jurgis. "Land of Illusion: China and the 18th Century Garden." *Landscape* 11, no. 2 (1961–62): 5–11.

———. "Gardens and Lands of Illusion." In *Aberrations: An Essay on the Legend of Forms.* 138–81. Cambridge, Mass.: MIT Press, 1989.

Barmé, Geremie R. *The Forbidden City.* Cambridge, Mass.: Harvard University Press, 2008.

Barrier, Janine, Monique Mosser, and Che Bing Chiu, eds. *Aux jardins de Cathay: L'imaginaire anglo-chinois en Occident. William Chambers.* Besançon: Éditions de l'Imprimeur, 2004.

Batchelor, Robert Kinnaird, Jr. "The European Aristocratic Imaginary and the Eastern Paradise: Europe, Islam and China, 1100–1780." Ph.D. diss., University of California, 1999.

Belevitch-Stanevitch, H. *Le goût chinois en France au temps de Louis XIV.* Geneva: Slatkine Reprints, 1970.

Bending, Stephen. "A Natural Revolution? Garden Politics in Eighteenth-Century England." In *Refiguring Revolutions: Aesthetics and Politics from the English Revolution to the Romantic Revolution,* edited by Kevin Sharpe and Steven N. Zwicker, 241–66. Berkeley: University of California Press, 1998.

Berger, Patricia. *Empire of Emptiness: Buddhist Art and Political Authority in Qing China.* Honolulu: University of Hawaii Press, 2003.

Bernard-Maitre, Henri. "Catalogue des objets envoyés de Chine par les missionnaires de 1765 à 1786." *Bulletin de l'Université l'Aurore* 3, no. 9 (1948): 135–39.

Birrell, Anne, trans. *The Classic of Mountains and Seas.* London: Penguin, 1999.

Blussé, Leonard, and R. Falkenburg. *Johan Nieuhofs beelden van een Chinareis, 1655–1657.* Middelburg: Stichting VOC Publicaties, 1987.

Bretschneider, Emil. *Early European Researchers into the Flora of China.* Shanghai: American Presbyterian Mission Press, 1881.

———. *History of European Botanical Discoveries in China.* London: Sampson Low, Martson and Co., 1898.

Chang, Elizabeth Hope. *Britain's Chinese Eye: Literature, Empire, and Aesthetics in Nineteenth-Century Britain.* Stanford, Calif.: Stanford University Press, 2010.

Chang, Kang-i Sun, and Stephen Owen, eds. *The Cambridge History of Chinese Literature,* vol. 1, *To 1375.* Cambridge: Cambridge University Press, 2010.

Cheng, Liyao. *Imperial Gardens.* Vienna: Springer, 1998.

Ching, Julia, and Willard G. Oxtoby, eds. *Discovering China: European Interpretations in the Enlightenment.* Rochester, N.Y.: University of Rochester Press, 1992.

Ching, May-bo. "Chopsticks or Cutlery? How Canton Hong Merchants Entertained Foreign Guests in the Eighteenth and Nineteenth Centuries." In *Narratives of Free Trade: The Commercial Cultures of Early U.S.-China Relations,* edited by Kendall Johnson, 99–116. Hong Kong: Hong Kong University Press, 2012.

Chiu, Che Bing. *Yuan ming yuan: Le jardin de la clarté parfaite.* Besançon: Les Éditions de l'Imprimeur, 2000.

———. *Jardins de Chine, ou la quête du paradis.* Paris: Éditions de la Martinière, 2010.

Clarke, J. J. *Oriental Enlightenment: The Encounter Between Asian and Western Thought.* London: Routledge, 1997.

Clunas, Craig. "Nature and Ideology in Western Descriptions of Chinese Gardens." In *Nature and Ideology: Natural Garden Design in the Twentieth Century,* edited by Joachim Wolschke-Bulmahn, 21–33. Washington, D.C.: Dumbarton Oaks Research Library and Collection, 1997.

Conner, Patrick. "China and the Landscape Garden: Reports, Engravings and Misconceptions." *Art History* 2, no. 4 (1979): 430–40.

———. *Oriental Architecture in the West.* London: Thames and Hudson, 1979.

Cordier, Henri. "Les correspondants de Bertin, Secrétaire d'Etat au XVIIIᵉ siècle." *T'oung Pao* 14, no. 4 (1913): 465–72.

Davin, Emmanuel. "Un éminent sinologue toulonnais du XVIIIᵉ siècle, le R. P. Amiot, S.J. (1718–1793)." *Bulletin de l'Association Guillaume Budé* 1, no. 3 (1961): 380–95.

Decker, Paul. *Chinese Architecture, Civil and Ornamental.* London: By the author, 1759.

Dehergne, Joseph. "Une grande collection: Mémoires concernant les Chinois (1776–1814)." *Bulletin de l'Ecole Française d'Extrême-Orient* 72 (1983): 267–98.

Droguet, Vincent. "Les Palais Européens de l'empereur Qianlong et leurs sources italiennes." *Histoire de l'Art* 25–26 (May 1994): 15–28.

Duyvendak, Jan Julius Lodewijk. "The Last Dutch Embassy to the Chinese Court (1794–1795)." *T'oung Pao* 33 (1937): 1–137.

Ebrey, Patricia Buckley. "Gender and Sinology: Shifting Western Interpretation of Footbinding, 1300–1890." *Late Imperial China* 20, no. 2 (1999): 1–34.

Erdberg, Eleanor von. *Chinese Influence on European Garden Structures*. Cambridge, Mass.: Harvard University Press, 1936.

Fairbank, John King. *Trade and Diplomacy on the China Coast: The Opening of the Treaty Ports, 1842–1854*. Cambridge, Mass.: Harvard University Press, 1953.

Fan, Fa-ti. *British Naturalists in Qing China: Science, Empire and Cultural Encounter*. Cambridge, Mass.: Harvard University Press, 2004.

Farris, Jonathan A. "Thirteen Factories of Canton: An Architecture of Sino-Western Collaboration and Confrontation." *Buildings and Landscapes* 14 (2007): 66–83.

Fèvre, Francine, and Georges Métailié. *Dictionnaire Ricci des plantes de Chine*. Paris: Cerf, 2005.

Forêt, Philippe. *Mapping Chengde: The Qing Landscape Enterprise*. Honolulu: University of Hawaii Press, 2000.

Gaunt, Simon. *Marco Polo's "Le Devisement du Monde": Narrative Voice, Language and Diversity*. Cambridge: Brewer, 2013.

Ge, Liangyan. "On the Eighteenth-Century Misreading of the Chinese Garden." *Comparative Civilizations Review* 27 (1992): 106–26.

Genest, Gilles. "Les Palais Européens du Yuanmingyuan: Essai sur la végétation dans les jardins." *Arts Asiatiques* 49 (1994): 82–90.

Goodman, Jennifer Robin. *Chivalry and Exploration, 1298–1630*. Woodbridge: Boydell Press, 1998.

Gournay, Antoine. "Jardins chinois en France à la fin du XVIIIᵉ siècle." *Bulletin de l'Ecole Française d'Extrême-Orient* 78 (1991): 259–73.

Gray, Basil. "Lord Burlington and Father Ripa's Chinese Engravings." *British Museum Quarterly* 22, no. 1–2 (1960): 40–43.

Guy, Basil. *The French Image of China Before and After Voltaire*. Studies on Voltaire and the Eighteenth Century 21. Geneva: Institut et Musée Voltaire, 1963.

Haddad, John Rogers. "Imagined Journeys to Distant Cathay: Constructing China with Ceramics, 1780–1920." *Winterthur Portfolio* 41, no. 1 (Spring 2007): 53–80.

———. *The Romance of China: Excursions to China in U.S. Culture, 1776–1876*. New York: Columbia University Press, 2009.

Hall, Philip B. "Robert Swinhoe (1836–1877), FRS, FZS, FRGS: A Victorian Naturalist in Treaty Port China." *The Geographical Journal* 153, no. 1 (1987): 37–47.

Harris, Eileen. "Burke and Chambers on the Sublime and the Beautiful." In *Essays in the History of Architecture Presented to Rudolf Wittkower*, edited by Douglas Fraser, Howard Hibbard, and Milton J. Lewine, 207–13. London: Phaidon, 1967.

————. "Design of Chinese Buildings and the Dissertation on Oriental Gardening." In *Sir William Chambers, Knight of the Polar Star*, edited by John Harris, 144–62. University Park: Pennsylvania State University Press, 1970.

Heyter-Menzies, Grant. *The Empress and Mrs. Conger: The Uncommon Friendship of Two Women and Two Worlds*. Hong Kong: Hong Kong University Press, 2001.

Hevia, James L. *Cherishing Men from Afar: Qing Guest Ritual and the Macartney Embassy of 1793*. Durham, N.C.: Duke University Press, 1995.

————. *English Lessons: The Pedagogy of Imperialism in Nineteenth-Century China*. Durham, N.C.: Duke University Press, 2003.

Hostetler, Laura. "Mapping Dutch Travels to and Translations of China: Jan Nieuhof's Account of the First East India Company Embassy, 1655–57." *Horizons* 1, no. 2 (2010): 147–73.

Hsia, Adrian. *Chinesia: The European Construction of China in the Literature of the 17th and 18th Centuries*. Tübingen: Max Niemeyer, 1998.

Huigen, Siegfried. *Knowledge and Colonialism: Eighteenth-Century Travellers in South Africa*. Leiden: Brill, 2009.

Hunt, John Dixon. *Gardens and the Picturesque: Studies in the History of Landscape Architecture*. Cambridge, Mass.: MIT Press, 1992.

————. *The Picturesque Garden in Europe*. London: Thames and Hudson, 2002.

————. *The Afterlife of Gardens*. Philadelphia: University of Pennsylvania Press, 2004.

————. *A World of Gardens*. London: Reaktion, 2012.

Hunt, John Dixon, and Peter Willis, eds. *The Genius of the Place: The English Landscape Garden, 1620–1820*. Cambridge, Mass.: MIT Press, 1988.

Jacob, Michael, "On Mountains: Scalable and Unscalable." In *Landform Building: Architecture's New Terrain*, edited by Stan Allen and Marc McQuade, 136–64. Baden: Lars Müller, 2011.

Jacobson, Dawn. *Chinoiserie*. London: Phaidon, 1993.

Jacques, David. "On the Supposed Chineseness of the English Landscape Garden." *Garden History* 18, no. 2 (1990): 181–87.

Jami, Catherine. *The Emperor's New Mathematics: Western Learning and Imperial Authority During the Kangxi Reign (1661–1722)*. New York: Oxford University Press, 2012.

Jardins en France, 1760–1820: Pays d'illusion, terre d'expériences. Paris: Caisse Nationale des Monuments Historiques et des Sites, 1977.

Jarry, Madeleine. *Chinoiseries: Le rayonnement du goût chinois sur les arts décoratifs des XVIIᵉ et XVIIIᵉ siècles*. Fribourg: Office du Livre, 1981.

Kallieris, Christina. *Inventis addere: Chinesische Gartenkunst und englische Landschaftsgärten: Die Auswirkungen von Utopien und Reisebeschreibungen auf gardentheoretische Schriften Englands im 18. Jahrhundert*. Worms-am-Rhein, Wernersche Verlagsgesellschaft, 2012.

Keay, John. *China: A History*. London: Harper, 2008.

Keightley, David N. "The Shang: China's First Historical Dynasty." In *The Cambridge History of Ancient China: From the Origins of Civilization to 221 B.C.*, edited by Michael Loewe and Edward L. Shaughnessy, 232–91. Cambridge: Cambridge University Press, 1999.

Keswick, Maggie. *The Chinese Garden: History, Art and Architecture*. London: Frances Lincoln, 2003 (first edition 1978).

Kohn, Linda, ed. *Daoism Handbook*. Leiden: Brill, 2000.

Kilpatrick, Jane. *Gifts from the Gardens of China*. London: Frances Lincoln, 2007.

Kitson, Peter J. *Forging Romantic China: Sino-British Cultural Exchange, 1760–1840*. Cambridge: Cambridge University Press, 2013.

Koppelkamm, Stefan. *The Imaginary Orient: Exotic Buildings of the 18th and 19th Centuries in Europe*. Fellbach: Menges, 2014.

Koval, Anne. "'Strange Beauty in the Night': Whistler's Nocturnes of Cremorne Gardens." In *The Pleasure Garden, from Vauxhall to Coney Island*, edited by Jonathan Conlin, 195–216. Philadelphia: University of Pennsylvania Press, 2013.

Kuitert, Wybe. "Georg Meister: A Seventeenth Century Gardener and His Reports on Oriental Garden Art." *Japan Review*, no. 2 (1991): 125–43.

———. "Borrowing Scenery and the Landscape that Lends—The Final Chapter of *Yuanye*." *Journal of Landscape Architecture* 10, no. 2 (2015): 32–43.

Lach, Donald F., and Edwin J. Van Kley. *Asia in the Making of Europe*, vol. 3, *A Century of Advance*. Chicago: University of Chicago Press, 1998.

Larner, John. *Marco Polo and the Discovery of the World*. New Haven, Conn.: Yale University Press, 1999.

Le Ménahèze, Sophie. *L'invention du jardin romantique en France, 1761–1808*. Neuilly-sur-Seine: Éditions Spiralinthe, 2001.

Le Rougetel, Hazel. "The Fa Tee Nurseries of South China." *Garden History* 10, no. 1 (1982): 70–73.

Lee, Thomas H. C., ed. *China and Europe: Images and Influences in Sixteenth to Eighteenth Century*. Hong Kong: Chinese University Press, 1991.

Lin, Shuen-fu. "A Good Place Need Not Be a Nowhere: The Garden and Utopian Thought in the Six Dynasties." In *Chinese Aesthetics: The Ordering of Literature, the Arts, and the Universe in the Six Dynasties*, edited by Zongqi Cai, 123–68. Honolulu: University of Hawaii Press: 2004.

Liu, Cary Y. "Archive of Power: The Qing Dynasty Imperial Garden-Palace at Rehe." *Meishushi yanjiu jikan* 28 (2010): 43–66.

Liu, Yu. "The Inspiration for a Different Eden: Chinese Gardening Ideas in England in the Early Modern Period." *Comparative Civilizations Review* 53 (2005): 86–106.

———. *Seeds of a Different Eden: Chinese Gardening Ideas and a New English Aesthetic Ideal*. Columbia: University of South Carolina Press, 2008.

———. "Transplanting a Different Gardening Style into England: Matteo Ripa and His Visit to London in 1724." *Diogenes* 55, no. 2 (2008): 83–96.

Loehr, George. "L'artiste Jean-Denis Attiret et l'influence exercée par sa description des jardins impériaux." In *La mission française de Pékin aus XVIIe et XVIIIe siècles: Actes du Colloque international de Sinologie, Chantilly 20–22 sept. 1974*, 69–83. Paris: Les Belles Lettres, 1976.

Loewe, Michael, and Edward L. Shaughnessy, eds. *The Cambridge History of Ancient China: From the Origins of Civilization to 221 B.C.* Cambridge: Cambridge University Press, 1999.

Lovejoy, Arthur O. "The Chinese Origin of a Romanticism." In *Essays in the History of Ideas*, 99–135. Baltimore, Md.: John Hopkins University Press, 1948.

Mackerras, Colin. *Western Images of China.* Oxford: Oxford University Press, 1989.

Malone, Carroll Brown. *History of the Peking Summer Palaces Under the Ch'ing Dynasty.* Urbana: University of Illinois, 1934.

Mokros, Emily. "Reconstructing the Imperial Retreat: Politics, Communications, and the Yuanming Yuan Under the Tongzhi Emperor, 1873–4." *Late Imperial China* 33, no. 2 (2012): 76–118.

Mungello, David E. *Curious Land: Jesuit Accommodation and the Origins of Sinology.* Honolulu: University of Hawaii Press, 1989.

———. "Confucianism in the Enlightenment: Antagonism and Collaboration Between the Jesuits and the Philosophes." In *China and Europe: Images and Influences in Sixteenth to Eighteenth Centuries*, edited by Thomas H. C. Lee, 99–128. Hong Kong: Chinese University Press, 1991.

———, ed. *The Chinese Rites Controversy: Its History and Meaning.* Nettetal: Steyler, 1994.

———. *The Great Encounter of China and the West, 1500–1800.* Lanham, Md.: Rowman and Littlefield, 2013 (first edition 1999).

Panzini, Franco. *Per i piaceri del popolo: L'evoluzione del giardino pubblico in Europa dalle origini al XX secolo.* Bologna: Zanichelli, 1993.

———. *Progettare la natura: Architettura del paesaggio e dei giardini dalle origini all'epoca contemporanea.* Bologna: Zanichelli, 2005.

Peyrefitte, Alain. *The Immobile Empire.* New York: Randon House: 2013 (first edition 1992).

Pfister, Louis. *Notices biographiques et bibliographiques sur les Jésuites de l'ancienne mission de Chine 1552–1773.* 2 vols. Shanghai: Imprimerie de la Mission Catholique, 1932–34.

Pinot, Virgile, ed. *Documents inédits relatifs à la connaissance de la Chine en France de 1685 à 1740.* Geneva: Slatkine Reprints, 1971 (first editon Paris: Geuthner, 1932).

Pirazzoli-t'Serstevens, Michèle. "Les Palais Européens, histoire et légendes." In *Le Yuanmingyuan: Jeux d'eau et palais européens du XVIII siècle à la cour de Chine,* edited by Michèle Pirazzoli-t'Serstevens, 6–10. Paris: Éditions Recherche sur les Civilisations, 1987.

Porter, David. "Writing China: Legitimacy and Representation, 1606–1773." *Comparative Literature Studies* 33, no. 1 (1996): 98–122.

———. *Ideographia: The Chinese Cipher in Early Modern Europe*. Stanford, Calif.: Stanford University Press, 2001.

———. "Monstrous Beauty: Eighteenth-Century Fashion in Aesthetics of the Chinese Taste." *Eighteenth-Century Studies* 35, no. 3 (2002): 395–411.

———. "Beyond the Bounds of Truth: Cultural Translation and William Chambers's Chinese Garden," *Mosaic* 37, no. 2 (2004): 41–58.

———. *The Chinese Taste in Eighteenth-Century England*. Cambridge: Cambridge University Press, 2010.

Psaki, F. Regina. "The Book's Two Fathers: Marco Polo, Rustichello da Pisa, and *Le Devisement du Monde.*" *Mediaevalia* 32 (2011): 69–97.

Quaintance, Richard. "Toward Distinguishing Among Theme Park Publics: William Chambers's Landscape Theory vs. His Kew Practice." In *Theme Park Landscapes: Antecedents and Variations*, edited by Terence Young and Robert Riley, 25–47. Washington, D.C.: Dumbarton Oaks Research Library and Collection, 2002.

Reed, Marcia. "A Perfume Is Best from Afar: Publishing China in Europe." In *China on Paper: European and Chinese Works from the Late Sixteenth to the Early Nineteenth Century*, edited by Marcia Reed and Paola Demattè, 9–27. Los Angeles: Getty Research Institute, 2007.

Reed, Marcia, and Paola Demattè, eds. *China on Paper: European and Chinese Works from the Late Sixteenth to the Early Nineteenth Century*. Los Angeles: Getty Research Institute, 2007.

Ricci, Matteo. *China in the Sixteenth Century: The Journals of Matthew Ricci, 1583–1610*. Translated by Louis J. Gallagher. New York: Random House, 1953.

———. *Della entrata della Compagnia di Giesù e Cristianità nella Cina*. Edited by Maddalena Del Gatto. Macerata: Quodlibet, 2001.

Rinaldi, Bianca Maria. "Borrowing from China: The Society of Jesus and the Ideal of Naturalness in XVII and XVIII Century European Gardens." *Die Gartenkunst* 17, no. 2 (2005): 319–37.

———. *The "Chinese Garden in Good Taste": Jesuits and Europe's Knowledge of Chinese Flora and Art of the Garden in the 17th and 18th Centuries*. Munich: Meidenbauer 2006.

———. "Ein Manifest politischer Autorität: Der Wiederaufbau der *Yiheyuan.*" In *Kunst, Garten, Kultur*, edited by Stefanie Hennecke and Gert Gröning, 181–96. Berlin: Reimer, 2010.

———. *The Chinese Garden: Garden Types for Contemporary Landscape Architecture*. Basel: Birkhäuser, 2011.

———. "Die Reise nach China: Die chinesischen Gärten in den Beschreibungen westlicher Reisender." In *Reisen in Parks und Gärten: Umrisse einer Rezeptions- und Imaginationsgeschichte*, edited by Hubertus Fischer, Siegrid Thielking, and Joachim Wolschke-Bulmahn, 291–308. Munich: Meidenbauer, 2012.

Ringmar, Erik. "Liberal Barbarism and the Oriental Sublime: The European Destruction of the Emperor's Summer Palace." *Millennium: Journal of International Studies* 34, no. 3 (2006): 917–33.

———. "Malice in Wonderland: Dreams of the Orient and Destruction of the Palace of the Emperor of China." *Journal of World History* 22, no. 2 (2011): 273–97.

———. *Liberal Barbarism: The European Destruction of the Palace of the Emperor of China.* New York: Palgrave Macmillan, 2013.

Royet, Véronique, ed. *Georges Louis Le Rouge: Jardins anglo-chinois.* Inventaire du fonds français, graveurs du XVIIIᵉ siècle, vol. 15. Paris: Bibliothèque nationale de France, 2004.

Singer, Aubrey. *The Lion and the Dragon: The Story of the First British Embassy to the Court of the Emperor Qianlong in Peking, 1792–1794.* London: Barrie and Jenkins, 1992.

Sirén, Osvald. *Gardens of China.* New York: Ronald Press, 1949.

———. *China and the Gardens of Europe of the Eighteenth Century.* New York: Ronald Press, 1950.

Siu, Victoria M. "China and Europe Intertwined: A New View of the European Sector of the Chang Chun Yuan." *Studies in the History of Gardens and Designed Landscapes* 19, no. 3–4 (1999): 376–93.

———. *Gardens of a Chinese Emperor. Imperial Creations of the Qianlong Era, 1736–1796.* Bethlehem: Lehigh University Press, 2013.

Spence, Jonathan D. *The Chan's Great Continent: China in Western Minds.* New York: W. W. Norton, 1998.

Stålmarck, Torkel. *Ostindiefararen Carl Gustav Ekeberg, 1716–1784.* Göteborg: Kungl. Vetenskaps- och vitterhets-samhället, 2012.

Steinhardt, Nancy Shatzman. *Chinese Imperial City Planning.* Honolulu: University of Hawaii Press, 1990.

Strassberg, Richard E., ed. and trans. *A Chinese Bestiary: Strange Creatures from the Guideways Through Mountains and Seas.* Berkeley: University of California Press, 2003.

———. "War and Peace: Four Intercultural Landscapes." In *China on Paper: European and Chinese Works from the Late Sixteenth to the Early Nineteenth Century*, edited by Marcia Reed and Paola Demattè, 89–138. Los Angeles: Getty Research Institute, 2007.

Sun, Jing. "The Illusion of Verisimilitude: Johan Nieuhof's Images of China." Ph.D. diss., Leiden University, 2013.

Svensson, Thommy, and Elisabeth Lind. "Early Indonesian Studies in Sweden: The Linnaen Tradition and the Emergence of Ethnography Before 1900." *Archipel* 33 (1987): 57–78.

Thomas, Greg M. "The Looting of Yuanming and the Translation of Chinese Art in Europe." *Nineteenth-Century Art Worldwide: A Journal of Nineteenth-Century Visual Culture* 7, no. 2 (Autumn 2008). http://www.19thc-artworld wide.org/index.php/autumn08/93-the-looting-of-yuanming-and-the-transla tion-of-chinese-art-in-europe.

———. "Yuanming Yuan/Versailles: Intercultural Interactions Between Chinese and European Palace Cultures." *Art History* 32 (2009): 115–43.

Thomaz de Bossiere, Yves de, Mme. *Jean-François Gerbillon, S.J. (1654–1707): Un des cinq mathématiciens envoyés en Chine par Louis XIV.* Leuven: Ferdinand Verbiest Fondation, 1994.

Thurin, Susan Schoenbauer. *Victorian Travelers and the Opening of China, 1842–1907.* Athens: Ohio University Press, 1999.

Tuck, Patrick J. N., ed. *Britain and the China Trade, 1635–1842.* London: Routledge, 2000.

Ulrichs, Friederike. *Johan Nieuhofs Blick auf China (1655–1657): Die Kupferstiche in seinem Chinabuch und ihre Wirkung auf den Verleger Jacob van Meurs.* Wiesbaden: Harrassowitz, 2003.

Valder, Peter. *The Garden Plants of China.* Portland, Ore.: Timber Press, 1999.

———. *Gardens in China.* Portland, Ore.: Timber Press, 2002.

Van Dyke, Paul A. *The Canton Trade: Life and Enterprise on the China Coast, 1700–1845.* Hong Kong: Hong Kong University Press, 2005.

Vogel, Gerd-Helge. "Wunderland Cathay: Chinoise Architekturen in Europa; Teil 1." *Die Gartenkunst* 1 (2004): 125–72.

———. "Wunderland Cathay: Chinoise Architekturen in Europa; Teil 2." *Die Gartenkunst* 2 (2004): 339–82.

Wagner, Tamara S. "Sketching China and the Self-Portrait of a Post-Romantic Traveler: John Francis Davis's Rewriting of China in the 1840s." In *A Century of Travels in China: Critical Essays on Travel Writing from the 1840s to the 1940s,* edited by Douglas Kerr and Julia Kuehn, 13–26. Hong Kong: Hong Kong University Press, 2007.

Watelet, Claude-Henry. *Essay on Gardens: A Chapter in the French Picturesque.* Edited and translated by Samuel Danon. Philadelphia: University of Pennsylvania Press, 2003.

Whiteman, Stephen H. "Creating the Kangxi Landscape: Bishu Shanzhuang and the Mediation of Qing Imperial Identity." Ph.D. diss., Stanford University, 2011.

———. "From Upper Camp to Mountain Estate: Recovering Historical Narratives in Qing Imperial Landscapes." *Studies in the History of Gardens and Designed Landscapes* 33, no. 4 (2013): 249–79.

Wiebenson, Dora. *The Picturesque Garden in France*. Princeton, N.J.: Princeton University Press, 1978.

Wilkinson, Endymion. *Chinese History: A Manual*. Rev. ed. Cambridge, Mass.: Harvard University Asia Center for the Harvard-Yenching Institute, 2000.

Wills, John E. Jr. *Embassies and Illusions: Dutch and Portuguese Envoys to K'ang-hsi, 1666–1687*. Cambridge, Mass.: Council on East Asian Studies, Harvard University 1984.

Wittkower, Rudolph. *Palladio and English Palladianism*. London: Thames and Hudson, 1974.

Wong, Young-tsu. *A Paradise Lost: The Imperial Garden Yuanming Yuan*. Honolulu: University of Hawaii Press, 2001.

Wood, Frances. "Closely Observed China: From William Alexander's Sketches to His Published Work." *British Library Journal* 24 (1998): 98–121.

———."Imperial Architecture of the Qing: Palaces and Retreats." In *China, the Three Emperors, 1662–1795*, edited by Evelyn S. Rawsky and Jessica Rawson, 54–62. London: Royal Academy of Arts, 2005.

Zantop, Susanne. *Colonial Fantasies: Conquest, Family and Nation in Precolonial Germany, 1170–1870*. Durham, N.C.: Duke University Press, 1997.

Zoli, Sergio. "L'immagine dell'Oriente nella cultura italiana da Marco Polo al Settecento." In *Il paesaggio*, edited by Cesare de Seta, 47–123. Vol. 5 of *Storia d'Italia: annali*, edited by Ruggiero Romano and Corrado Vivanti. Turin: Einaudi, 1982.

Zou, Hui. *A Jesuit Garden in Beijing and Early Modern Chinese Culture*. West Lafayette, Ind.: Purdue University Press, 2011.

INDEX

*Page numbers in **bold** refer to illustrations*

ACKNOWLEDGMENTS

This book has been a long journey and it is a pleasure to express my gratitude here to the numerous people and institutions that have contributed significantly to it.

My interest in the Western reception of the gardens of China developed in 2002 at the Center for Garden Art and Landscape Architecture (CGL) at Leibniz University Hanover, when I was researching seventeenth- and eighteenth-century Jesuits' descriptions of Chinese plants and gardens. Therefore, I would like to thank, first and foremost, the CGL, which accepted me as a research fellow at that time, and Joachim Wolschke-Bulmahn for the constant support and encouragement he provided over the years.

Dumbarton Oaks Research Library and Collection in Washington, D.C., generously offered me a fellowship in 2012–13 to develop this study. I was fortunate to be able to conduct research in such a stimulating environment and to meet wonderful and generous scholars there. I am particularly grateful to John Beardsley, Director of Garden and Landscape Studies, Anatole Tchickine, Jane Padelford, and the other Fellows in Garden and Landscape Studies Mirka Beneš, Christine Ruane, and Maggie Cao for the inspiring discussions. Robert Osterhaut, Floris Bernard, and Beatrice Daskas also provided valuable advice. I also wish to extend my gratitude to the librarians and all the other members of the staff at Dumbarton Oaks for their kind assistance during my stay.

Many scholars, colleagues, and friends provided precious comments, advice, information, and resources at various stages. I am much indebted to Alison Hardie for her valuable comments on my annotations to Chapter 18 and for the many important suggestions she offered. Stephen H. Whiteman generously shared with me his knowledge on Qing imperial parks and advised on matters of Chinese language offering a rich exchange of ideas. I am also most grateful to Duncan Campbell, Emily T. Cooperman, D. Fairchild Ruggles, Marcia Reed, Josepha Richards, Richard Strassberg, Lucia Tongiorgi Tomasi, and Claudia von Collani.

Very special thanks go to Anita Hussey, who copyedited a final draft of the manuscript, and, particularly, to Barringer Fifield who carefully revised all the translations from French, Italian, and Latin providing invaluable assistance.

The Research Library at the Getty Research Institute in Los Angeles, the Rare Book Collection at Dumbarton Oaks, Washington, D.C., the Bibliothèque Nationale de France in Paris, and the Biblioteca Comunale "Mozzi-Borgetti" in Macerata allowed me to make extensive use of their collections and I am most thankful for this. I also gratefully acknowledge the following libraries and institutions for providing the illustrations and for giving permission to reproduce them, or for making them freely available through their online catalogues: the Biblioteca Comunale "Mozzi-Borgetti" in Macerata, the Wellcome Library in London, the Rijksmuseum in Amsterdam, the Rare Book Collection at Dumbarton Oaks in Washington, D.C., the Canadian Centre for Architecture in Montréal, the Yale Center for British Art, and the Beinecke Rare Book and Manuscript Library at Yale University.

I am extremely grateful to John Dixon Hunt, series editor, for his enthusiasm and support of the project from the very beginning. The thoughtful comments he provided on the manuscript's various drafts and, particularly, on the introduction, have significantly improved this book's contents and structure.

At the University of Pennsylvania Press, I wish to express my gratitude to Jerry Singerman for his professional assistance through the different phases of this book's production, Noreen O'Connor-Abel who chaperoned the manuscript to publication with the greatest care and attention to details, Hannah Blake, and the entire wonderful production team. I am also grateful to two anonymous readers for their comments on the manuscript.

Finally, I wish to thank Franco Panzini, mentor and friend, not only for his careful and critical reading of the manuscript's versions, but for having been the first to inspire me to study the gardens of China. I have been extraordinarily privileged to receive his continuous support, encouragement, and intellectual stimulation through the years. For all these reasons, it is to him that I dedicate this book.